JUST NEIGHBORS?

JUST NEIGHBORS?

Research on African American
and Latino Relations in the
United States

Edward Telles, Mark Q. Sawyer,
and Gaspar Rivera-Salgado,
editors

Russell Sage Foundation • New York

The Russell Sage Foundation

Library of Congress Cataloging-in-Publication Data

Just neighbors? : research on African American and Latino relations in the US / Edward
Telles, Mark Q. Sawyer and Gaspar Rivera-Salgado, editors.
    p. cm.
Includes bibliographical references and index.
  ISBN 978-0-87154-828-3 (alk. paper)
  1. African Americans-Relations with Hispanic Americans.   2. African Americans-
Social conditions.   3. Hispanic Americans-Social conditions.   4. Social conflict-
United States.   5. United States-Race relations.   6. United States-Ethnic rela-
tions.   I. Telles,EdwardEric,1956–   II. Sawyer,MarkQ.,1972–   III. Rivera-Salgado,
Gaspar.
  E185.615.J87 2011
  305.800973—dc23   2011016971

Text design by Suzanne Nichols.

RUSSELL SAGE FOUNDATION
112 East 64th Street, New York, New York 10065
10 9 8 7 6 5 4 3 2 1

Contents

Contributors

EDWARD TELLES is professor of sociology at Princeton University and vice president of the American Sociological Association.

MARK Q. SAWYER is associate professor of African American studies and political science at the University of California, Los Angeles, and is also director of the Center for the Study of Race, Ethnicity, and Politics.

GASPAR RIVERA-SALGADO is project director at the UCLA Center for Labor Research and Education, where he teaches classes on immigration issues and work, labor, and social justice in the United States.

JAMES D. BACHMEIER is post-doctoral research associate in the Population Research Institute at Pennsylvania State University.

MATT A. BARRETO is associate professor of political science at the University of Washington.

FRANK D. BEAN is Chancellor's Professor of Sociology in the School of Social Sciences and director of the Center for Research on Immigration, Population, and Public Policy at the University of California, Irvine.

SUSAN K. BROWN is associate professor of sociology at the University of California, Irvine.

JESSICA JOHNSON CAREW is graduate fellow in political science at the Center for the Study of Race, Ethnicity, and Gender in the Social Sciences at Duke University.

NIAMBI M. CARTER is assistant professor of political science at Purdue University.

REGINA M. FREER is professor of politics at Occidental College.

MICHAEL JONES-CORREA is professor of government at Cornell University.

GERALD F. LACKEY is National Institutes of Health Predoctoral Fellow in sociology at the University of North Carolina, Chapel Hill.

CLAUDIA SANDOVAL LOPEZ is Ph.D. candidate in political science at the University of Chicago.

MONIQUE L. LYLE is assistant professor of political science at Vanderbilt University.

CID MARTINEZ is assistant professor of sociology at California State University, Sacramento.

PAULA D. McCLAIN is professor of political science and public policy at Duke University. She is also codirector of the Center for the Study of Race, Ethnicity, and Gender in the Social Sciences at Duke University.

MONICA McDERMOTT is associate professor of sociology at the University of Illinois, Urbana-Champaign.

TATCHO MINDIOLA JR. is associate professor of sociology and director of Mexican American studies at the University of Houston.

JASON L. MORIN is Ph.D. candidate in political science at the University of New Mexico.

TATISHE M. NTETA is assistant professor of political science at the University of Massachusetts, Amherst.

SHAYLA C. NUNNALLY is associate professor of political science and African American studies at the University of Connecticut.

EFRÉN O. PÉREZ is assistant professor of political science at Vanderbilt University and affiliate of its Research on Individuals, Politics, and Society (RIPS) experimental lab.

VICTOR M. RIOS is assistant professor of sociology at the University of California, Santa Barbara.

NESTOR RODRIGUEZ is professor of sociology at the University of Texas at Austin.

GABRIEL R. SANCHEZ is assistant professor of political science at the University of New Mexico.

CANDIS WATTS SMITH is postdoctoral fellow in political science at Texas A&M University.

ROSAURA TAFOYA-ESTRADA is assistant professor of sociology at Boise State University.

JAMES DIEGO VIGIL is professor in the Department of Criminology, Law, and Society at the University of California, Irvine.

KEVIN WALLSTEN is assistant professor of political science at the University of California, Berkeley.

EUGENE WALTON JR. is graduate fellow in political science at the Center for the Study of Race, Ethnicity, and Gender in the Social Sciences at Duke University.

SYLVIA ZAMORA is Ph.D. candidate in sociology at the University of California, Los Angeles.

Introduction

Edward Telles, Gaspar Rivera-Salgado,
Mark Q. Sawyer, and Sylvia Zamora

The dominant paradigm of American race relations has changed dramatically in the last two decades, as the prevailing white-black binary model is being challenged by recent large-scale immigration, mostly from Latin America. The size of the Latino[1] or Hispanic population has now surpassed that of the African American population and it will probably be double the size of the black population by 2050. Latinos now make up about 15 percent of the American population (and Mexicans in turn make up the largest majority of Latinos) and are projected to increase to 25 percent by 2050. In comparison, African Americans make up 13 percent of the U.S. population today, a proportion expected to remain stable to 2050. Moreover, immigration from various African and West Indian nations is making the African American population more heterogeneous—an issue we turn to later in this introduction. In a few short years, black-Latino relations have emerged as central to understanding the evolving racial dynamics in the United States, and they are likely to become increasingly important as interactions between the groups increase.

Traditionally, social scientists have examined black-white relations. When ethnic and race relations are examined between groups other than blacks and whites, the focus has tended to be on relations of these other groups with whites. As the dominant group, whites have always been the reference group for comparisons with respect to disadvantage, segregation, and assimilation. The study of relations between whites and non-European immigrant groups and their descendants, though, has clearly been secondary to understanding the relation between blacks and whites. With their history of mass slavery in the United States, decades of official segregation and exclusion, persistent economic disadvantage and social exclusion in American society, and population size, African Americans have become the predominant Other in American social science. Other groups have been either demographically small, regionally concentrated, or thought to have assimilated. However, with the tremendous growth of the Latino and Asian populations and their dispersion through the country, social scientists have recently begun to examine relations between whites and either Latinos or Asians. Studies of relations among nonwhite groups, such as between African Americans and Latinos, are relatively few despite the dynamic ways that they are shaping U.S. society in the twenty-first century.[2]

With this book, we address the shortfall by bringing together important and rigorous social science research in the emerging field of African American and Latino relations. We are fairly certain that this area of research is likely to grow rapidly, especially as the Latino population grows and becomes increasingly U.S. born, and to the extent that both Latinos and African Americans remain disadvantaged relative to whites. This volume provides a collection of studies by leading scholars that may serve as models or points of departure for future work. We have sought to engage research that focuses on different levels of analysis (national, regional, local, and community), uses different methodologies (such as quantitative and qualitative), and examines public opinion as well as different types of social interactions (such as labor market, community group, gangs, and youth). Rather than a mere collection of disparate chapters, this work addresses important sociological questions and theoretical frameworks that can help guide the development of the field. We begin this introductory chapter by outlining the relevant demographic, social, and political changes in recent decades, then seek to provide elements of a developing paradigm of black-Latino relations, and finally describe the chapters that make up this volume.

Among the issues we seek to address in this collection is whether the traditional theoretical lenses of interethnic relations, particularly that of conflict and cooperation, are adequate for understanding Latino-black relations. We question whether close interaction between blacks and Latinos fosters understanding, contempt, or something else altogether, or whether other models better explain the nature of these relations. In general, we have sought to promote a dialogue among the authors so that the chapters address common themes as well as seeming contradictions among them. In each chapter, authors are explicit about which segment of the heterogeneous black and Latino populations they describe, as we find that patterns of interaction, often cooperation on the basis of common or complementary identities, depend on internal differences between the groups along dimensions such as class, color, nationality, legal status, gender, and age. Overall, the chapters in this volume show the complexity of black-Latino relations and how they depend on such demographic factors as well as the nature of local communities, institutions, and political responses by the individuals involved. Conflict is far from inevitable, and any particular outcome depends largely on the (in)actions of communities and their leaders. An important lesson from this volume is thus that leadership matters and policymakers can make a difference by encouraging and supporting coalitional activities between blacks and Latinos.

LATINO POPULATION GROWTH AND RACIALIZATION

Since 1965, when the United States instituted major changes in immigration policy, immigration from throughout Latin America (and Asia) has resulted in the diversification and a quadrupling of the Latino population across the country.[3] The historical origins, reasons for immigration, and places of settlement among the diverse Latin American national groups are often quite distinct. Mexicans have long been by far the largest group and have the longest record of immigration. Since 1848, when the United States annexed Mexican land (what is now the Southwest region of the United States), Mexicans have continuously migrated into the United States, with immigration peaking during the 1910s and 1920s and then again after the 1970s. Immigration from Mexico, which shares a 2,000-mile border with the United States, has been characterized in recent years as largely unauthorized. Puerto Ricans, who are U.S. citizens by birth, have been migrating to the U.S. mainland (and mostly New York) in large numbers since the 1940s. Cubans have settled largely in Miami and southern Florida since the 1960s, mostly as refugees escaping Fidel Castro's socialist regime. Since 1965, large numbers of Dominicans have settled in the Northeast, Salvadorans and Guatemalans have largely settled in Los Angeles, Houston, and Washington, D.C., and several other nationalities have arrived in smaller but significant numbers (Durand, Telles, and Flashman 2006).

Immigrants currently make up about 45 percent of all Latinos, up from about 30 percent in the 1970s. Although the number of later-generation Latinos is considerable, most Latinos are either immigrants or children living with immigrant parents. Furthermore, most of the Latino immigrant population today have arrived since 1990 and are unauthorized. According to the latest estimates, unauthorized immigrants number about 11 million,[4] of whom 6.2 million are from Mexico and 2.5 million from other Latin American countries (Passel and Cohn 2011). These immigrants are denied basic public services, subject to constant harassment and deportation by police and immigration authorities, and relegated to the lowest jobs and status available in U.S. society. Their exclusion is official and fairly complete, unlike that any other group in the United States currently faces. From the perspective of conservative media outlets and the supporters of anti-immigrant policies, this exclusion is justified. Although the conservative media also present African Americans in a negative context, the basic rights of blacks in the United States are rarely questioned.[5]

In terms of perceptions, Latino immigrants often arrive in the United States with defined notions about African Americans that are shaped by the Latino national background and personal experience, which in turn shapes the nature of Latino-black interactions. Racial attitudes and stereotypes about blacks are in fact often shaped in immigrants' home societies by images on television and other media or by personal experiences, particularly in the case of countries with large African-descendant populations, such as the Dominican Republic, Colombia, or Brazil. In addition, how Latino immigrants racially perceive themselves and African Americans is also shaped and transformed by their own distinct racialized experiences in the United States, including their interactions with African Americans, which are also transmitted back to the home society by immigrants. In other words, the social meaning of race and identity may begin in the country of origin but is constantly contested and reformulated within the larger Latino community.

The geographic spread of the Latino population has made black-Latino relations relevant and increasingly important throughout most of the United States. Latinos traditionally concentrated in only a few regions until the 1990s. Latinos, especially Mexican Americans, have lived predominantly in the Southwest and Chicago, Puerto Ricans in New York and Chicago, and Cubans in southern Florida. As a result, the points of contact between African Americans and Latinos were generally limited to several southwestern cities as well as Chicago, New York, and Miami. Among rural areas and small towns there was little overlap in most of the twentieth century except in places like central Texas (Foley 1997), where the South and Southwest meet. However, as traditional destinations for Latin American immigrants have become saturated and as employers in nontraditional regions actively recruit these workers, Latinos have begun migrating in large numbers to new destinations since the 1990s (Zúñiga and Hernández-León 2005; Light 2006; Durand, Telles, and Flashman 2006). Today, Latinos have multiplied their numbers in new destinations, including southern cities (and some rural areas), which have long had exclusively black and white populations. Moreover, the Latino population in traditional places of settlement, such as Los Angeles and Houston, continues to grow tremendously, often significantly surpassing the size of the black population.

Although it is clear that Latino immigrants, especially the undocumented, are racialized and excluded in various ways, a nagging question remains about whether they will eventually assimilate the way the descendants of European immigrants did. Central and southern Europeans, who arrived between 1880 and 1920, were economically disadvantaged and treated as ethnic others, but that status, which we term *racialized*, was transcended within one or two generations after immigration (Gordon 1964; Alba and Nee 2003). The success of their descendants in becoming part of the mainstream is hailed in the American narrative, which is, largely because of this, generally optimistic about immigrants. Empirical evidence thus far shows that the children of Latino immigrants improve their status compared with their immigrant parents, though a gap remains when their socioeconomic status is compared with non-Hispanic whites (Kasinitz et al. 2008; Itzigsohn 2009; Telles and Ortiz 2008).

Unlike European Americans, Latinos may be racialized into the third and fourth generations post-immigration. Edward Telles and Vilma Ortiz (2008) find mobility for the Mexican immigrant second generation compared with their immigrant parents but, unlike European Americans, stalled mobility for the third and fourth generation. In contrast to European Americans, their rates of imprisonment, gang activity, and educational dropout are high despite high acculturation. Moreover, the majority of these later-generation Mexican Americans experience racial discrimination, believe that they are racially stereotyped, or do not identify as white, all of which further suggest an experience of racialization (Telles and Ortiz 2008). We understand racialization as a concept that cannot be reduced to the African American experience but instead refers to a more comparative cross-societal notion that includes various forms of exclusion and categorization, including those experienced by Latinos and Asians in the United States (Kim 1999; Almaguer 1994; Mendieta 2000), African descendants in Latin America (Telles 2004; Sawyer 2006), and a variety of peoples in western Europe (Hine, Keaton, and Small 2009; Winant 2001).

Whether Latinos have been racialized and whether they are developing a group identity is based in part on the concept of a shared experience of racism in the United States, which may be important to understanding the possibility of Latino and African American coalitions. The chapters in this book demonstrate that Latinos are often seen as a group apart from other groups, whether or not the authors refer to them as a racial or racialized group. Although it may be neither a necessary nor a sufficient condition for coalition formation, some sense of shared fate, or belief that African Americans and Latinos occupy a similar status as groups who suffer from discrimination or exclusion, might be important for developing a shared identity despite antagonisms between the two groups. If Latinos generally come to occupy persistently low-status positions and politically cohere, it is likely that they as a racial-ethnic group and their relations with other groups will continue to be of social scientific interest. Black and Latino relations will grow in importance only to the extent that the Latino population grows, Latinos continue to geographically overlap with blacks, and both groups remain disadvantaged relative to whites, creating the potential for similar political interests. On the other hand, the possibility remains of high levels of assimilation and acculturation for some Latinos, as significant rates of intermarriage suggest, which raises the question of whether race or ethnicity is consequential for those individuals and whether it makes sense to treat that segment of the population as part of the general Latino population.

AFRICAN AMERICANS AND
BLACK IMMIGRANTS

African Americans have long been the nation's largest minority group and perhaps the most disadvantaged. More than any other group, blacks are residentially segregated and overrepresented in America's prisons and unemployment lines (Massey and Denton 1993; Brown et al. 2003). Although often sympathetic to the social exclusion of Latinos, many blacks worry that immigrant workers will displace them in the labor market. Like earlier waves of European immigrants (and their children) who leapfrogged over African Americans into higher-status positions and eventually joined the mainstream, concerns have been raised about whether Latino (and to some extent Asian) immigrants will advance at the expense of blacks. This concern has been heightened in the context of deindustrialization, where many factories closed shop and relocated abroad, taking with them thousands of stable jobs previously held by African Americans (Wilson 1979, 2010). The new political economy has resulted in growing systemic inequality and job insecurity even for those who still hold relatively stable jobs. This feeling can be heightened when African Americans feel that another group may be competing with them for jobs and reaping the social services and other rewards that they fought so hard to gain during the civil rights movement. Such negative feelings are heightened when they question the legitimacy of Latino immigrants to live and work in the United States.

Outside the labor market, African Americans who are trapped in poor and segregated neighborhoods tend to feel pessimistic about how race and racism have affected their life chances, which might further their negative attitudes and sense of perceived threat from Latinos (Gay 2006). Less-skilled African Americans are especially more likely to perceive a greater sense of threat from Latino immigrants than highly skilled blacks are (Gay 2006; chapter 8, this volume), a problem that Claudine Gay (2006) believes can best be alleviated not by restricting immigration but by creating jobs and increasing educational and vocational opportunities for young African Americans.

Today's mass immigration has also added many new blacks to the population, many of whom share similar concerns with Latinos about immigration issues (Alex-Assensoh and Hanks 2009). This wave includes immigrants from Africa and the British-, French-, and Spanish-speaking Caribbean. Although these immigrants often seek to distance themselves from the highly stigmatized and native African Americans by (among other things) not identifying as African American or black, they are often considered as such by the rest of American society and official statistics (Waters 1999; Itzigsohn 2009). Their children, however, whose ties to their parents' language and culture have generally weakened, are more likely to identify and be perceived as African American.

Many Dominicans, Puerto Ricans, Panamanians, and other Latinos are also considered black, and thus the black-Latino distinctions we make in this book are actually sometimes fluid. About 20 percent of Latin Americans are African descendants, given that fifteen times as many enslaved Africans were brought to Latin America as to the United States (Eltis 2010; Andrews 2007). Also, only about 3 percent of Latinos-Hispanics in the United States identify as black in the U.S. census (Logan 2003). This suggests that African Latinos are less likely than others to immigrate to the United States or that they do not identify as black in the United States. This is partly due to the predominance of Mexicans among all Latinos, whereas Mexicans of African descent constitute a very small part of Mexico's national population.[6] Also, although many African-descendant immigrants from Latin America might be perceived as black, they may in fact eschew such an identity, resulting in an underestimation of the Latino population that could also be considered as African American (Landale and Oropeza 2002; Candelario 2007; Itzigsohn 2009). This does not undermine the fact that, regardless of the complexity of identities, minorities are becoming a larger share of the American population and increasingly coming into contact with one another in neighborhood, workplace, and leisure settings in many big cities and some rural areas.

BECOMING NEIGHBORS

Together, African Americans and Latinos are numerical majorities in most of America's largest cities and in many smaller cities as well. They now constitute the majority in seven of the ten largest cities in the United States—New York, Los Angeles, Chicago, Houston, Philadelphia, San Antonio, and Dallas—and more than one-third of the population in the remaining three—Phoenix, San Diego, and San Jose. Separately, though, blacks are not a majority in any and Latinos are a majority in only one, San Antonio (U.S. Census Bureau 2010). These figures show that the largest cities are now majority minority, a result of the recent growth of the Latino population, along with white flight out of central cities and the persistent residential isolation of many black Americans in the nation's largest cities.

African Americans and Latinos are increasingly likely to be neighbors in many metropolitan areas. Table I.1 shows segregation indexes over the last thirty years for the seven metropolitan areas with a majority-minority central city, as indicated in the previous paragraph. The first four columns show dissimilarity indexes between blacks and Latinos (Hispanics according to the Census Bureau) using the 1980, 1990, and 2000 censuses and the American Community Survey in the years leading up to 2010. Specifically, dissimilarity indexes show the extent to which the Latino and African American populations in each metropolitan area are geographically distributed with respect to each other. Thus, the dissimilarity index is independent of the relative size of the groups being compared. An index of 100 means that they are completely segregated from one another, that is, live in separate census tracts, whereas an index of 0 means that they are evenly distributed in the city, that is, live in equal proportions in all census tracts.

In all of these metropolitan areas, the trend has been toward increasing residential integration of blacks and Latinos, and the pattern is strongest in the four Southwest metropolitan areas: Los Angeles, Houston, San Antonio, and Dallas. Using a rule of thumb that dissimilarity indexes above 60 are high and 30 to 60 are moderate (Massey and Denton 1993), black-Latino segregation has dropped from high levels to the moderate range since 1980 in these southwestern metropolitan areas. By contrast, New York City has had only moderate levels of black-Latino segregation since 1980, though with a slight drop in the period, and in Chicago, black-Latino segregation has remained high throughout, though it has dropped considerably in recent years. In Philadelphia, where the Latino population is much smaller (but growing) than the African American population, there has also been a drop from high to moderate.

The exposure indexes in the last four columns of table I.1 show, for 1980 and 2010, the actual chances that blacks and Latinos are neighbors. Specifically, these indexes model the percentage of African Americans who live in an average Latino person's census tract in a particular metropolitan area (columns 4 and 5) or vice versa (columns 6 and 7). Thus the distinct exposure indexes for the two groups reflect the fact that the neighborhood experiences with members of the other group may differ from those of either Latinos or African Americans. Unlike the dissimilarity index, exposure indexes are not symmetrical and are affected by the relative size of the groups.

The indexes in columns 4 and 5 reveal that Latino exposure to blacks was fairly stable in these metropolitan areas, rising slightly in

Table I.1 Segregation in Major Metropolitan Areas

	Black-Hispanic Dissimilarity Index				Hispanic Exposure to Blacks		Black Exposure to Hispanic	
	1980	1990	2000	2010	1980	2010	1980	2010
New York	60	57	54	56	21	18	16	23
Los Angeles	72	59	54	55	8	8	19	43
Chicago	85	81	78	72	9	10	4	12
Houston	67	57	51	43	12	16	10	33
Philadelphia	66	64	57	57	27	25	4	8
San Antonio	65	57	52	45	5	6	32	49
Dallas	68	54	50	44	12	15	7	27

Source: Authors' compilation based on data from the American Communities Project (Logan 2010).

New York and Philadelphia and dipping slightly in Houston and Dallas. In contrast, the exposure of blacks to Latinos increased much more in all of these metropolitan areas, most surely as a result of rapidly growing Latino immigration. Today, at least one-third of the neighbors of the typical African American are Latino in San Antonio, Los Angeles, and Houston. In San Antonio, about half (49 percent) of the neighbors of the average African American resident are now Latino, though about a third (32 percent) were in 1980, where Latinos have far outnumbered African Americans. The percentages in black exposure to Latinos more than doubled in Los Angeles and Houston as well as in Chicago, Philadelphia, and Dallas. Thus African Americans have seen a dramatic change in their residential experiences since 1980, when they were relatively isolated from any group, to the present, when segregation has declined but largely in the way of having many more Latino neighbors. However, from the perspective of the Latino population, changes in residential contact with African Americans have been smaller.

Language and cultural barriers, along with persisting racial stereotypes and prejudices, continue to serve as challenges to black and Latino relations at the neighborhood level. Today, however, young blacks and Latinos are increasingly being raised in the same neighborhoods and coming into more contact with each other, particularly in school settings. Interracial contact also increases for those who go on to college and eventually enter diverse work settings. The psychological literature suggests that increased contact should lead to fewer stereotypes about each other (Allport 1954; Fiske 2000). In several chapters of this book, we examine the result of this growing neighborhood interaction between African Americans and Latinos. However, these relations are filtered through the practice of politics at state, local, and national levels.

POLITICS

Relations between African Americans and Latinos are largely mediated by politics. American politics, and local politics in particular, have been largely about race and ethnicity. Whereas blacks have been a long-term and central fixture of urban politics, their traditional rivals (outside a few traditional Latino cities) have been whites, often as ethnics early on (Dahl 1961), and later as part of an ethnically undifferentiated white population—except perhaps Jews. African

Americans have had great success in building political power in big cities with large African American populations, electing mayors and local legislators. They have also been quite successful at the congressional level. Recently, African Americans have built coalitions with Latinos to win at the statewide level, as in Deval Patrick's election as governor of Massachusetts and Barack Obama's election to the U.S. Senate. Although black political power is still on the rise, the relative size of the African American population is slowly decreasing, and black politicians depend increasingly on Latino voters to get elected.[7] Electoral support for Obama has been unprecedented among Latino voters in key states such as Florida, New Mexico, Colorado, and Nevada. Fully two-thirds of Latinos voted for Obama, and an astounding 85 percent of those under age thirty did, which bodes well for the future of black-Latino political relations.[8] Also, Latinos themselves are an emerging political power in important parts of the country, as symbolized by the election of Antonio Villaraigosa as mayor of Los Angeles in 2004 and of three Latinos as mayor of San Antonio, beginning with Henry Cisneros in 1981. However, political power for either group has not significantly diminished their economic and social disparities.

Black-Latino relations have also been notable at the grassroots level. Social movement actors and radical organizations have on occasion allied in their struggle for change. Groups like the Black Panther Party for Self Defense, the Puerto Rican Young Lords, and the Brown Berets worked together and were simultaneously inspired both ideologically and tactically by one another (Pulido 2006). This was also the case with the less radical Martin Luther King Jr. and the mainstream civil rights movement and the solidarity with groups like the United Farm Workers, led by Cesar Chavez. However, neither these coalitions nor the social movements that created them were sustained engagements. As a result, we have mixed patterns of conflict and cooperation between communities across time, space, and political ideology (Sawyer 2005). That many of the same actors in the 1980s worked on campaigns to end apartheid in South Africa and halt U.S. support for the repressive Salvadoran government and the Contras in Nicaragua demonstrates that—though not explicitly stated—leftist social movements dealing with black and Latino issues have on occasion found common cause. However, even the mainstream political coalitions between blacks and Latinos that led to the election of black mayors in Chicago and New York involved some strains, including the inability to translate them into sustainable effective coalitions that would consistently carry mayoral elections.

Following reports of racial tension between African American and Latino residents in Los Angeles, community activists in places like Los Angeles have again sought to form interethnic coalitions, such as the Latino and African American Leadership Alliance and the Community Coalition. The reported tension seemed to be fueled in a new way by the explosion of a mostly Latino-driven immigrant rights movement that raised concerns among African Americans about the growing Latino population and its growing political organization. At a national level, black and Latino activists have recently come together to form the Black-Latino Summit, which seeks to support black and Latino political leaders who have formed black-Latino alliances on issues around criminal justice, education, housing, and immigration reform and to develop an agenda to shape investment and leadership priorities for the current administration.[9] These efforts, however, do not mean that tensions do not exist between the two communities.

COMMONALITY AND TENSIONS

A common conceptualization of black-Latino relations has been as either conflict or cooperation, despite the fact, as many of the chapters in this volume show, that black and Latino relations rarely are either clearly conflicted or clearly cooperative. Nicolás Vaca (2004) provocatively argues that African Americans and Latinos are at odds with each other, particularly with regards to employment and controlling other valuable resources. He goes as far as to say that blacks and Latinos face a zero-sum situation, in which gains for one group signal losses for the other. He asserts, for example, that African Americans have fiercely defended their overrepresentation among Los Angeles County employees to the detriment of Latinos (Vaca 2004). However, based on the chapters in this book and on other systematic social science research, zero-sum scenarios do not seem typical of black-Latino relations (for a review, see Sawyer 2005). In another well-known book, Earl Ofari Hutchinson emphasizes the continuing growth of the Latino population, and its eventual rise as the nation's largest minority, as presenting a challenge to black Americans in the way of education, politics, immigration issues, and political coalitions (2007). He identifies "black fears" and negative black and Latino stereotypes as driving the black and Latino conflict and, most important, calls for a much-needed conversation between the two groups.

The labor market has arguably been the predominant focus of black-Latino relations, but most of the literature shows very little, if any, displacement (for a review, see Smith and Edmonston 1998). The perceptions of displacement may themselves affect the social relations, however. Surely, the massive entry of low-skilled immigrants into new labor markets involves disruptions in the labor market that may seem like displacements. But the issue is complex and far from a zero-sum situation, because growing immigration does not mean automatic displacement of natives. The dynamics of black and Latino job market shifts in labor markets can be seen in their changing occupational concentration, in which the relative growth of one group and thus the decrease of the other is sometimes perceived as displacement. For example, Telles and Sylvia Zamora (2008) found that, from 1990 to 2005, building and grounds cleaning and maintenance occupations in many metropolitan areas shifted from a largely African American to a largely Latino immigrant workforce. However, labor market analyses have mostly concluded that the employment and earnings levels of African Americans were not affected by these shifts partly because African Americans steadily increased their representation in protective service and in health-care support occupations during the same period (Telles and Zamora 2008). Immigrants are also consumers and thus they create jobs; they use health, educational, and other municipal services staffed by native workers; and they often provide low-cost labor, which keeps entire industries from fleeing to overseas locations, thus providing employment at other levels as well. In addition, their low-cost labor reduces production and consumer prices, thus improving American standards of living (Smith and Edmonston 1998).

Rather than making conclusive statements about the nature of black-Latino conflict, more careful researchers have sought to identify and understand the factors that lead to certain outcomes, including conflict or cooperation (Mindiola, Niemann, and Rodriguez 2003; Betancur and Gills 2000; McClain 1993; Gay 2006). One notable example is Tatcho Mindiola, Yolanda Flores Niemann, and Nestor Rodriguez's (2003) study of Houston, which examines the role of stereotypes in shaping interethnic relations between blacks and Latinos. They found that stereotypes largely shape intergroup relations between blacks and Latinos and that, in general, African Americans had more positive views of Latinos than vice versa (see Oliver and Wong 2003; McClain et al. 2006; Kaufmann 2003; Gay 2006; Vaca 2004). Moreover, intergroup perceptions were more positive among males of both groups than among females, and among Latinos, the foreign born had less favorable views of African Americans than the U.S. born did.

Neither African Americans nor Latinos are homogenous groups that can be lumped together when discussing relations between them. Differences include important national, immigrant-generational, class, age, and other characteristics. The chapters in this volume are careful to distinguish segments of the African American and Latino populations, such as those based on income, education level, region of settlement, age, sexuality, immigration status, and racial-ethnic identity, that shape the outcome of group relations, often providing a sense of commonality between them. For example, chapter 9 shows the importance of age and popular culture as an important point of commonality, particularly for youth. Chapter 8 finds differences by class in how African Americans view Latinos.

Blacks and Latinos are also more likely to form coalitions when both groups share common interests around specific issues, such as education and economic issues. Sylvia Zamora's chapter in this volume highlights how similar concerns over educational disparities in Los Angeles public high schools and lack of healthy food options bring black and Latino residents of a community together. Rather than conceiving them as either black or Latino issues, community leaders emphasize the commonality that blacks and Latinos share as poor and working-class residents of South Los Angeles. This sense of linked fate has led to the emergence of a powerful grassroots black and Latino coalition. However, at the national level, rarely are black-Latino coalitions sustained.

Jonn J. Betancur and Douglas C. Gills's volume on the opportunities and struggles of blacks and Latinos focuses on the challenges in creating such coalitions, and calls for both groups to "confront their differences and to search for common ground toward the solution of many of the problems that they confront together in cities" (2000, 12). In the genre of social action research, the authors also search for solutions by examining the pitfalls of previous coalitional efforts to develop new strategies for action. Addressing several themes leading to contention between blacks and Latinos at the grassroots level, such as class differences, racism, the uneven economic and social development of each group in cities, and the political manipulation by institutional elites, the authors found that blacks and Latinos were likely to form coalitions when both groups shared interests around specific issues, although so far these coalitions have rarely been sustained. At the same time, this volume seeks to test critical theories of social interaction that have been the bedrock of the study of intergroup relations and perhaps generate new insights from studying relations among minority groups, with an eye toward understanding that neither population is monolithic.

TOWARD A NEW FRAMEWORK OF INTERMINORITY GROUP RELATIONS

We call for a fresh approach to understanding relations between African Americans and Latinos, which have become important because of the demographic revolution that has occurred in the largest urban centers of the country. It has become increasingly important to conceptualize the relations between racial and ethnic minority groups in the United States in a way that is distinct from conceptualizations of intergroup relations between the dominant (white) group and a non-white subordinate group. Both Latinos and African Americans are economically disadvantaged with respect to whites and have little control of major political and material resources, except perhaps in some large cities, where resources are incidentally dwindling. Relying on the conventional social science approach to race relations is inadequate for addressing black and Latino relations in the twenty-first century.

The intellectual history of race relations in the United States has been dominated by a binary hierarchical model of race relations between whites and blacks. The central axis of this analysis has been the socioeconomic dimension of oppression and subordination of the African American population by the white dominant group. This conventional approach to the study of race relations runs the gamut of theoretical positions, from the liberal approach to racism and racial injustice in the United States, best represented by Daniel Patrick Moynihan (1965) and Gunnar Myrdal and Sissela Bok (2005), to the radical analysis developed by racial formation and critical studies of race (Omi and Winant 1994). Attempts to theorize about the immigrant experience and intergroup relations have resulted in models of assimilation, incorporation, or exclusion, which are limited in their ability to explain current trends in minority-minority relations.

The undeniable existence of unequal power relations permeating the black-white divide was key to the development of a racist ideology that justified social and economic policies of exclusion that have led to the systematic oppression of African Americans nationwide. Racism is not an individual act stemming from prejudicial views but a powerful and historic tool of oppression over subordinate nonwhite groups (Omi and Winant 1994; Sidanius and Pratto 2001; Fredrickson 2003). Hegemonic racial ideologies of white superiority, however, are often uncontested and taken for granted by nonwhite groups. Rather than being white, or at the top of the racial hierarchy, the implicit positioning of any particular group becomes proximity to the top in relation to another other group. This includes not only social, physical, or geographic proximity to whiteness but also other claims to value or legitimacy, such as citizenship (Murguia and Forman 2003). Thus manifestations of racism and racial prejudice can also operate within and among communities of color. The same stereotypes of blacks and Latinos often held by whites are also often shared by blacks and Latinos about each other.

These stereotypes and the discriminatory behaviors that stem from them are important for understanding dimensions of racial prejudice and intergroup relations. Issues of racial hierarchy are similarly important in black and Latino relations. Latinos often hold negative and prejudicial views of blacks, sometimes filtered by greater interaction with blacks and, in some cases, by a shared similar socioeconomic status. Consequently, minority groups can face accusations of being racist in a way that parallels white-on-black racism. Along these lines, some African Americans may perceive Latinos as having the advantage of being able to pass as white, or nearer to white, or as immigrant outsiders with a weaker claim to American citizenship and the civil rights policies that blacks have historically struggled for.

Stereotypes, discrimination, and ideas of racial hierarchy provide elements that help understanding of or map relations between subordinate groups; but finer-grain theoretical and conceptual tools are needed to characterize these relations, where some features resemble those between dominant and subordinate groups but other key features are missing in some substantial way. However, the manifestation of such social elements among blacks and Latinos falls short of producing systemic racism in which racial ideologies are matched with a series of institutional and individual acts that turn ideologies of hierarchy into a social, political, and economic reality. These ideologies help enable those acts and, ex post facto, justify the outcomes themselves.

We therefore have to begin to examine the interaction between African Americans and Latinos for what they are and not continue to try to use the framework of black-white relations as a theoretical guide.[10] Blacks and Latinos often interact in a context largely shaped by decisions they have little control of. Failing institutions such as schools provide an important context in which black-Latino interactions take place, but the context itself cannot be understood through relations between the two groups. That context, though, potentially creates a common sense of struggle for better schools and against a white-dominated system.

We believe that a paradigm for understanding black-Latino relations requires a solid empirical base and that this volume helps build it. We are probably still far from a clear understanding of these important relations but have learned from this volume, for example, that black and Latino relations can be understood as falling along a continuum of interaction types, from tension filled to intentional coexistence to avoidance. These interactions also vary by class, age, immigration generation, and various other demographic factors, as well as by economic contexts, and can also be shaped by politics, institutional development, and community organizing. Also, as various chapters make clear, active leadership makes a difference for developing successful cooperative relations between blacks and Latinos and thus public policy should encourage such efforts.

Several findings from these chapters may provide important elements to be considered in this new paradigm. For example, chapter 3 suggests that Latinos actually view coethnics as a greater source of competition than Africa Americans. Chapter 4 demonstrates that political awareness and cues from political leaders affect commonalities between blacks and Latinos more than the individual-level determinants often raised in existing studies, such as racial identity or contact with the other group. Chapter 9 indicates that having a strong sense of pride in, and linked fate with, one's own racial-ethnic group does not impede the development of support for coalitions. Chapter 10 finds that black-Latino coalitions depend on the ability of community leaders to frame issues in ways that appeal to both African Americans and Latinos. Chapter 12 discovers that avoidance, rather than conflict or cooperation, is the dominant outcome in black-Latino social relations in marginalized urban communities, and chapter 11 makes it clear that the high-profile conflicts in the media between black and Latino youth in Los Angeles cannot be reduced to racial antagonisms. These are just some of the important contributions in this volume.

BACKGROUND

Our interest in this volume was motivated by several concerns: that Latino-black relations were becoming increasingly important in the Los Angeles area for demographic reasons; that several cases, as reported by the media, were highly conflictive; that little attention has been paid to interracial organizing; that these communities were unaware of the other's history and culture, including the presence of blacks in Latin America, including Mexico; and that an exchange with scholars might help on both sides. With support from the Ford Foundation, the UCLA Institute for Research on Labor and Employment Fund, and the University of California's Institute for Research on Labor and Employment, we held a two-day conference on the state of black-Latino relations at the UCLA Labor Center in April of 2008. We brought together leading scholars with community, labor, and youth activists with experiences in black-Latino community organizing. We sought to spark a conversation on these issues and develop a roadmap for collaborative and productive organizing. That conference proved a success in that the presentations were rich and enthusiastically received by an audience of fifty to a hundred people at any one time over the two days. Many of the scholarly presentations ended up as chapters in this volume, which we believe made the initial conference an academic success. These papers were informed and strengthened by the dialogue with the community activists and would later be discussed and fine-tuned at a second UCLA conference held a year later and through subsequent email discussions.

Previous research on the subject is best exemplified in the book *Prismatic Metropolis*, which systematically shows attitudes among the four major racial-ethnic groups in the Los Angeles area (Bobo et al. 2000). Raphael Sonenshein's *Politics in Black and White: Race and Power in Los Angeles* shows how political alliances among blacks, Latinos, Jews, Asians, and others were formed to elect Tom Bradley as

mayor of Los Angeles and later James Hahn and then Antonio Villaraigosa (Sonenshein 1993). Sonenshein argues that such political
coalitions could exist alongside racial tensions like stereotyping, violent incidents, and resource battles that typically render those coalitions potentially fragile. However, much of the educated public's understanding of the topic had been shaped by journalistic and anecdotal
accounts, which were often especially provocative and alarmist but
not based on strong empirical evidence. These included accounts
that blamed either Latinos or African Americans for conflictual and
even violent relations or for the problems of the other group (Miles
1992; Hayes-Bautista 2004; Newsweek 2007; Vaca 2004).

In contrast, the chapters in this volume represent systematic cutting-edge research in an increasingly important area for which few
sources of information are available. Many chapters contemplate both
behavioral and attitudinal aspects of black-Latino relations at the national and regional levels, and they deal with politics and policy, as
well as coalition-building efforts. Like the focus of our conference,
many chapters are California based. Much to our lament, important
areas of research under the more general rubric of black-Latino relations were covered at the conference but could not be included here,
mostly because of space limitations.

THE CHAPTERS

We have organized the book by levels of analysis on racial cooperation and competition—beginning with a macro-view (on the labor
market and national politics), followed by a meso-view (on studies of
cities), and ending with a micro-view (mostly on ethnographic studies of Los Angeles)—involving a well-established black-Latino coalition and interactions among youth and gangs. A theme of conflict
versus cooperation underlies all the chapters. More specific themes
group chapters together into parts.

We focus on social aspects of black-Latino relations beside the labor market but feature one important review and analysis. In chapter
1, Frank Bean, James Bachmeier, Susan Brown, and Rosaura Tafoya-
Estrada present a distillation of major work in this field. Such research on the labor market impacts of immigration often involve
seemingly esoteric debates about how best to statistically model this
impact and the assumptions that should underlie the econometric
models used. Bean and his colleagues instead present time series and

cross-sectional data from 1980 to 2006 in this accessible synthesis of cutting-edge research. They find, as does the bulk of this literature, that immigration—whether in general or Mexican immigration in particular—has little or no impact on the employment or earnings of African Americans. We believe that at least an elementary understanding of the labor market impact literature, offered here in a succinct form, is fundamental for understanding other dimensions of black and Latino interactions.

In part II, "Politics," three chapters deal broadly with commonality and competition between Latinos and African Americans. Traditionally, scholars have argued that if groups perceive themselves to have certain commonalities they are more likely to form bonds, whereas if they perceive themselves to be in competition they are less likely to do so. The authors of chapters 2 through 4 use the Latino National Survey (LNS), which was designed partly with this issue in mind. Specifically, the LNS is a representative telephone survey of 8,634 Latino residents in sixteen states, and broadly seeks to understand the nature of Latino political and social life in America (Fraga et al. 2006). The survey sampled adult Latinos with surveys conducted in the preferred language of the respondent—English, Spanish, or both. The LNS is especially valuable because of its large sample size, which allows scholars to reliably distinguish Latinos by four generational groups and by various national origin groups, especially Mexican, Cuban, Puerto Rican, Dominican, and Salvadoran.

In chapter 2, Michael Jones-Correa examines geographic differences, which are further explored in the remaining chapters. Specifically, he focuses on what makes these new destinations different from traditional Latino settlement areas, especially in regard to relations with African Americans. He finds that Latinos evaluate relations with African Americans and whites in new destination sites as being as good as, and perhaps better than, those relations in traditional areas of settlement. Perceptions of commonality with African Americans and whites are greater for Latinos in more integrated areas and for those who share social networks with them. However, Latinos who are more integrated and who share networks with blacks and whites also perceive greater competition in education, the labor market, and politics.

Jones-Correa also finds that the same factors that drive closeness also raise perceptions of competition. For example, integration and acculturation drive feelings of closeness with blacks. The converse, however, is also true: interaction between African Americans and Latinos also promotes perceptions of competition. This raises a concern in part answered in chapter 3, which suggests that the variable of competition with blacks in the LNS may be telling a different story. Those likely to perceive competition with blacks are more likely to perceive competition with other Latinos as well. In chapter 3, Jason Morin, Gabriel Sanchez, and Matt Barreto develop what they call a relative measure of intergroup competition for studying African American and Latino relations and examine Latino perceptions of competition with blacks relative to perceptions of competition with other groups, including other Latinos.

Chapters 2 and 3 allow us to see this not as a paradox, because Latinos who feel connected with blacks may see them more like their in-group than a hostile out-group. Closeness therefore does not breed contempt, and even perceptions of competition need not be poisonous to interactions between the two groups. These chapters show that enterprising political elites can positively affect opinions and that even things we thought might be troubling, like perceptions of competition, are perhaps not as much a concern as once thought. In fact, perceptions of competition are often a product of feeling closer and more integrated.

This is mirrored in chapter 4, in which Kevin Wallsten and Tatishe Nteta find that messages by political elites help drive a sense of commonality. The authors suggest that we assess the impact that cues provided by Latino or African American political elites, or elite messages, have on perceptions of commonality between African Americans and Latinos. They find that politically aware Latinos, regardless of ideological leanings, are more likely to form opinions on commonality with African Americans: liberal Latinos saw more in common, whereas conservatives saw less. Wallsten and Nteta suggest the importance of moving beyond individual-level determinants of Latino perceptions of commonality toward "bringing politics back in" to an analysis of how the Latino and African American public forms opinions on the nature of intergroup relations.

The remaining eight chapters of the volume use a variety of sources, including local surveys, ethnographic, interview, and archival data. Six chapters are about the Southwest—one about Houston, four about Los Angeles, and one comparing Oakland and Los Angeles. Two chapters address the South. The Southwest has a longer history of black and Latino relations than other regions of the United

States, given that African Americans and Latinos, particularly Mexican Americans, have long shared the same or proximate neighborhoods and low economic status throughout the region. South Los Angeles,[11] the site in five of these chapters, is notable for its history as well as the fairly quick demographic change since the 1960s from an almost entirely African American district to one with shared Latinos and African American neighborhoods. Houston is one of the most diverse cities in the United States, and contact between African Americans and Latinos is substantial. The final three of these chapters are about new Latino immigrant destinations in the South and Midwest, where Latinos have rapidly become a significant presence.[12]

Part III examines social science surveys of the two urban areas. In chapter 5, Rodriguez and Mindiola use the 1996 and 2008 Houston area survey to examine trends in Houston regarding how intergroup attitudes have changed among African Americans and Latinos (mostly Mexican Americans) over time. They also explore black-Latino comparisons of attitudes regarding new social issues that have emerged since the 1996 study. They are particularly interested in issues concerning immigrants, who make up a large sector of the resident Latino population, including education for undocumented migrant children, the construction of a border fence, and policies for Spanish-speaking children in schools. They find that African Americans have complex views on immigration and simultaneously support restrictionist policies along with policies that would help aid and develop Latino communities, including a pathway to citizenship. They believe that black attitudes are driven by a complex mix of their own interests, group relations, and a sense of historical fairness that includes a sense of solidarity with the Latino community in Houston. They also believe that a common political destiny in the Texas Democratic Party helps forge coalitions and cooperation between the groups.

In chapter 6, using data from the 2007 Los Angeles County survey, Mark Sawyer examines the state of relations between blacks and Latinos in Los Angeles, a city that epitomizes the opportunities and challenges facing Latinos and African Americans sharing geographic space. Sawyer finds that blacks and Latinos are open to working together, but that these relations are hampered by stereotyping by both groups and black attitudes about immigration. However, he stresses, there are openings for intergroup coalitions because, unlike classic group conflict theory, these stereotypes do not necessarily structure the political beliefs of blacks and Latinos or their willingness to cooperate. Sawyer discovers that racial identity for Latinos is a far more complex issue than a causal observer may think because it is not bounded by the prevalent binary model of black-white race relations. Furthermore, Sawyer finds, African Americans in Los Angeles are more concerned with education, unemployment, and discrimination than immigration. These two findings, Sawyer maintains, open the possibility for productive coalition work based on a "political commonality" between Latinos and African Americans. Taken together, the chapters by Sawyer, Wallsten and Nteta, and Rodriguez and Mindiola point to the potential positive role that elites and organizations can play in advancing shared group interests and notions of common fate. These chapters each note significant problems with stereotypes and other dominant messages that must be overcome with strategic coalitional efforts.

The two chapters in part IV, "New Relations in New Destinations," focus on the South, which has experienced the largest growth in Latino population over the last two decades. Latinos in the South, unlike those in the Southwest, are almost entirely immigrants or their young children. They also include secondary migrants who have been deflected from traditional destinations such as Los Angeles (Light 2006), as well as those who have been directly recruited from Mexico by employers seeking cheap labor. These immigrants have increasingly extended their social networks and ventured into destinations where few Latinos had gone before, often bringing their entire families with them. As a result, the visibility and permanence of Latinos has increased most dramatically, raising concerns about their impact on local labor markets, schools, hospitals, and other institutions, pointing to perceived economic threat as a primary factor shaping black-Latino relations in new destinations. These two chapters show that relations tend to be highly contextualized, especially by region and class. Given the newness of the Latino population, residents still seem to be in the process of making up their minds about how to react. Whereas the diverse composition of the Latino population in the Southwest, as argued in part II of this volume, has led Latino and black political elites to seek alliances to strengthen their political standing, no Latino political elite has yet emerged in the South to shape discourse toward this population.

In chapter 7, Paula McClain and her colleagues raise important questions about how native-born black and white Americans are reacting to the rapid emergence of the Latino population as well as how these new immigrants perceive their new black and white neighbors. By comparing residents in three locations—Durham, Memphis, and Little Rock—using the 2003 Durham Survey of Intergroup Relations and the 2007 Three City Survey of Intergroup Relations, McClain and her colleagues find that city contexts often make a difference. Whereas whites do not perceive an economic threat from Latino immigration but sometimes feel politically threatened by Latinos, blacks in all three cities feel that they have the most to lose—politically and economically—from rising Latino immigration. Chapter 7 shows us that the South is not homogenous and that black, Latino, and white intergroup relations may vary based on the particular setting, where racial compositions, histories regarding black-white relations, extent of anti-immigration organizing, and types of elected officials each varies significantly.

In chapter 8, Monica McDermott examines the impact of the new Latino immigration on the everyday lives of the native-born population in Greenville, South Carolina, particularly among blacks and whites of varied class backgrounds. She conducts interviews and ethnographic research in and around Greenville over an extended period, working primarily as a traveling sales vendor and living in a racially diverse neighborhood. She finds a general practice of black avoidance of and underlying hostility toward Latinos but highlights the salience of social class in varying patterns of reception. She also finds a nonmonotonic class pattern among black attitudes, the lower middle class being the most positive and the working and the upper middle classes largely negative. McDermott's findings suggest that the black lower middle class could be an important source of support for black-Latino coalitions, particularly in lower-income communities.

Each chapter presented in this volume has major implications for coalition building; the two chapters of part V focus on it. These chapters are concerned with the circumstances and conditions that increase the likelihood that blacks and Latinos will cooperate rather than engage in conflict. In chapter 9, relying on semi-structured interviews and the 2005 University of Chicago Black Youth Project Survey, Regina Freer and Claudia Sandoval Lopez analyze the relationship between racial and ethnic self-identity and willingness to form coalitions across racial boundaries. Contrary to claims that racial pride should be deemphasized in coalition-building efforts, they find that youth with a strong sense of racial identity are more willing to engage in interracial coalitions than those without. They demonstrate the need to go beyond measuring openness to the idea of collaboration to examining actual coalition behavior in order to theorize the elements that lead to their success. By explaining the role of racial identity in coalition building among black and Latino youth, the authors present a useful pedagogical tool for activists on the ground.

In chapter 10, Sylvia Zamora focuses on community activists aiming to build a black and Latino coalition in South Los Angeles. She draws on participant observations and interviews among coalition staff and members and finds that organizational leaders create a sense of commonality across racial-ethnic lines by deploying an injustice frame rooted in racial, economic, and regional inequality. She finds that in areas where blacks and Latinos hold a similarly disadvantaged social and economic status, community leaders are able to deploy "injustice" frames that emphasize a collective sense of we-ness that can be contrasted to more affluent white communities. Constructing black and Latino commonality based on social and economic injustice that is neighborhood and class based, rather than merely race based, has proven crucial to coalition building among working-class blacks and Latinos in Los Angeles. Taken together, these two chapters provide rich data that can be useful for developing a broader strategy for black-Latino coalitional work in large urban centers across the United States.

Part VI, the final section, focuses on street culture in Los Angeles and Oakland, California. In chapter 11, James Diego Vigil examines South Los Angeles from the perspective of gangs, over a period of eighty years or so. In recent years, the media has gone as far as invoking the specter of ethnic cleansing, based largely on the declarations of a leading police official about a growing black-Latino conflict. Using his personal history and long-standing research on gangs in Los Angeles, Vigil provides an insider account, supported by police records and ethnographic evidence. He shows changing relations among blacks and Latinos with respect to gangs and their neighborhoods, as the result of dramatic demographic changes in the distressed neighborhoods in which they reside. Despite some intergroup friction, he finds that gang conflicts between blacks and Latinos, in the few cases they occur, are rarely race based but instead generally involve other sources, despite media hype to the contrary. A few cases, however, suggest that racial polarization could grow to the extent that often hostile black-Latino relations in prison can be promoted on the street and as gang conflict becomes increasingly lethal.

In chapter 12, Cid Martinez and Victor Rios further examine relations between black and Latino gang members in the inner city, by comparing ethnographic observations from South Los Angeles and East Oakland, California. They find that avoidance, rather than conflict or cooperation, is the dominant outcome in marginalized urban communities, particularly among youth. Even under ideal conditions, Martinez and Rios find very few cases of cooperation or conflict. Like Vigil, Martinez and Rios argue that conflict is rare and not reducible to race. Rather, neighborhood dynamics, particularly informal neighborhood practices, and a host of other factors shape interracial relations. It is often the convergence of two or more factors that can inhibit gang activity and growth, such as territorial control and affiliation and control of the illicit underground economy and neighborhood, where conflict is likely. Martinez and Rios go on to note the importance of gangs to understanding black-Latino relations in the ghetto and how the tactic of avoidance both acknowledges each other's presence and acts to maintain nonviolent social relations and order in a potentially dangerous environment.

We hope that the chapters in this book shed light on this increasingly important area and suggest pathways for further conceptual and empirical development. We expect that the chapters offer a greater understanding of the paradox posed by the seemingly contradictory relations between blacks and Latinos as well as provide guides for future political action. Analytically, they suggest a possible beginning for how we approach the analysis of minority-on-minority social behaviors. It cannot be taken for granted that as two racialized minority groups, blacks and Latinos will perceive each other as natural allies, as some have predicted, nor necessarily as natural adversaries, as others suggest. Rather, these relations are complex and they can be mediated by the efforts of leaders, among other factors.

The chapters in this volume provide rich data documenting the variety of factors that lead to various outcomes, highlighting the idea that black-Latino relations are context specific and vary over time, space, class, and gender. As two subordinated groups come head to head in large urban centers (and rural areas) of the nation, new possibilities open up, but these opportunities can only be seized when and if the two groups discard the reflexive negative way they view each other. Politically, we believe that African Americans and Latinos must shed the mainstream view and develop a new way to see themselves, and others in the process.

NOTES

1. Though it may seem insignificant for some, we acknowledge our preference for the term *Latino* rather than *Hispanic*. We use Latino in most cases but also Hispanic when referring to that population as counted in the U.S. census. Although most Latinos or Hispanics prefer to identify with their country of origin, both pan-ethnic terms have become common in recent decades as the population has become more diverse and Spanish-language media, civil rights organizations, and the U.S. Census Bureau have found utility in using a designator that aggregates many national groups (Mora 2009). Our preference for Latino is mostly a conceptual one that we think is fundamental for dealing with issues of relations with African Americans. Our objection to Hispanic is largely based in the idea of hispanicity (hispanidad) as reflecting a European-based national identity rather than an indigenous, black, or mixed identity. This is clear for the Dominican Republic, where elites built a national ideology of hispanicity to distance Dominicans from neighboring Haiti and from blackness in general (Candelario 2007), and in the American Southwest, where Mexican American leaders emphasized their whiteness and sought acceptance as white by virtue of their hispanicity, despite their treatment as nonwhite (Foley 1997; Almaguer 1994).
2. A spate of works appeared on Asian and black relations after the Los Angeles riots and a series of incidents in major U.S. cities, but material on blacks and Latinos is more rare.
3. The Latino population increased from 9.6 million in 1970 (4.7 percent of the population) to 45.5 million by July 1, 2007 (15.1 percent of the population). The Census Bureau projects a count of 102.6 million Latinos in the United States in 2050, approximately 24.4 percent of the population (U.S. Census Bureau 2010), though Emilio Parrado (2011) considers that projection too high because of the overestimation of birth rates.
4. This number is down from the 12 million just before the 2009 economic downturn (see Passel and Cohn 2011).
5. The recent historical context is important in light of the massive anti-immigrant media campaign between 2005 and 2007, when there was a media firestorm of protest against George W. Bush's immigration reform initiative. Glenn Beck and Lou Dobbs greatly increased their audience,

the number of newspaper stories about illegal immigration nearly tripled, and hate crimes against Latinos increased substantially (Kabili 2010). This massive media coverage had an impact on the attitudes of Americans toward Latino immigrants and even all Latinos (see chapter 1, this volume).

6. Based on self-identity data from the Latin American Public Opinion Project, fewer than 2 percent of the Mexican population identify as black or mulatto. This compares with about 50 percent of the population of Latin America's largest country—Brazil, from which there has been much less immigration (Telles 2004). Certainly many enslaved Africans were brought to Mexico (officially, 200,000), but slavery ended early there, and their descendants were largely absorbed by the much larger indigenous population (Aguirre Beltran 1946). Moreover, Mexico's national ideology tends to ignore that population in favor of its indigenous and Spanish-origin populations.

7. In many cases, they represent districts that have substantial numbers of Latinos, many of whom are unable to vote due to their noncitizen status. Thus, although black political power may have reached its height in the 1980s, there has been a recent resurgence of black elected officials due to growing voting coalitions in some big cities between African Americans and Latinos.

8. Julia Preston, "In Big Shift, Latino Vote Was Heavily for Obama," *New York Times*, November 6, 2008.

9. Available at: http://www.policylink.org/site/c.lkIXLbMNJrE/b.5136695/k.6346/The_National_Black_Latino_Summit_Solidarity_for_America8217s_Future.htm (accessed May 11, 2011).

10. We do, though, find some use in the emerging literature about Asian, white, and black relations, but even here Latinos are distinct (Chang 2000; Min 1996; Yoon 1997; Kim 2008). Latinos are similar to Asians in that their societal valorization is that of between whites and blacks (though probably less than Asians) but, as immigrants or perceived immigrants, they are also largely excluded from the American body politic, unlike whites and, arguably, blacks (Kim 1999). On the other hand, Latinos in general tend to come to the United States without the same kind of cultural or human capital as some Asian migrants and thus occupy a very different niche in local political economies.

11. Previously referred to as South Central Los Angeles.

12. Clearly, New York and Chicago have had large numbers of Latinos for many decades, along with African Americans. The Miami case is still more distinct, with large numbers of Latinos particularly within the last five decades, since the beginnings of immigration from Cuba. Unfortunately, we cannot cover the wide geographic scope of this phenomenon in a single volume.

REFERENCES

Aguirre Beltrán, Gonzalo. 1946. *La Población Negra de México*. México: Fuente Cultural.

Alba, Richard, and Victor Nee. 2003. *Remaking the American Mainstream: Assimilation and Contemporary Immigration*. Cambridge, Mass.: Harvard University Press.

Alex-Assensoh, Yvette, and Lawrence Hanks. 2009. *Black and Multiracial Politics in America*. New York: New York University Press.

Allport, Gordon. 1954. *The Nature of Prejudice*. Cambridge, Mass.: Perseus.

Almaguer, Tomas. 1994. *Racial Fault Lines: The Historical Origins of White Supremacy in California*. Berkeley: University of California Press.

Andrews, George Reid. 2007. *Afro Latin America: 1800–2000*. Chapel Hill: University of North Carolina Press.

Betancur, John J., and Douglas C. Gills, eds. 2000. *The Collaborative City: Opportunities and Struggles for Blacks and Latinos in U.S. Cities*. New York and London: Garland Publishing.

Bobo, Lawrence D., Melvin L. Oliver, James H. Johnson, and Abel Valenzuela, eds. 2000. *Prismatic Metropolis*. New York: Russell Sage Foundation.

Brown, Michael K., Martin Carnoy, Elliott Currie, Troy Duster, David B. Oppenheimer, Marjorie M. Shultz, and David Wellman. 2003. *Whitewashing Race: The Myth of a Color-Blind Society*. Berkeley: University of California Press.

Candelario, Ginetta. 2007. *Black Behind the Ears: Dominican Racial Identity from Museums to Beauty Shops*. Durham, N.C.: Duke University Press.

Chang, Robert. 2000. *Disoriented: Asian Americans, Law, and the Nation-State*. New York: New York University Press.

Dahl, Robert A. 1961. *Who Governs? Democracy and Power in an American City*. New Haven, Conn.: Yale University Press.

Durand, Jorge, Edward Telles, and Jennifer Flashman. 2006. "The Demographic Foundations of the Latino Population." In *Hispanics and the Future of America*, edited by Marta Tienda and Faith Mitchell. Washington, D.C.: National Academies Press.

Eltis, Stanley (grant holder). 2010. *Trans-Atlantic Slave Trade Database*. Available at: http://www.slavevoyages.org/tast/index.faces (accessed May 12, 2011).

Fiske, Susan. 2000. "Interdependence and the Reduction of Prejudice." In *Reducing Prejudice and Discrimination*, edited by Stuart Oskamp. Mahwah, N.J.: Lawrence Erlbaum.

Foley, Douglas. 1997. *The White Scourge: Mexicans, Blacks, and Poor Whites in Texas Cotton Culture*. Berkeley: University of California Press.

Fraga, Luis R., John A. Garcia, Rodney Hero, Michael Jones-Correa, Valerie Martinez-Ebers, and Gary M. Segura. 2006. *Latino National Survey*

(LNS), 2006 [Computer file]. 2006. ICPSR20862-v4. Ann Arbor, Mich.: Inter-university Consortium for Political and Social Research [distributor]. Available at http://dx.doi.org/10.3886/ICPSR20862 (accessed May 12, 2011).

Fredrickson, George. 2003. *Racism: A Short History*. Princeton, N.J.: Princeton University Press.

Gay, Claudine. 2006. "Seeing Difference: The Effect of Economic Disparity on Black Attitudes Toward Latinos." *American Journal of Political Science* 50(4): 982–97.

Gordon, Milton Myron. 1964. *Assimilation in American Life: The Role of Race, Religion, and National Origins*. New York: Oxford University Press.

Hayes-Bautista, David. 2004. *La Nueva California: Latinos in the Golden State*. Berkeley: University of California Press.

Hine, Darlene C., Tricia D. Keaton, and Stephen Small. 2009. *Black Europe and the African Diaspora*. Chicago: University of Illinois Press.

Hutchinson, Earl Ofari. 2007. *The Latino Challenge to Black America: Towards a Conversation between African Americans and Hispanics*. Chicago, Ill.: Middle Passage Press.

Itzigsohn, José. 2009. *Encountering American Faultlines: Race, Class, and Dominican Incorporation in Providence*. New York: Russell Sage Foundation.

Kabili, Ben. 2010. "CNN, Latinos, and Brand Values." Blog post. Available at: http://alwayson.goingon.com/2010/CNN-Latinos-and-brand-values (accessed July 25, 2011).

Kasinitz, Philip, John Mollenkopf, Mary C. Waters, and Jennifer Holdaway. 2008. *Inheriting the City: The Children of Immigrants Come of Age*. New York: Russell Sage Foundation.

Kaufmann, Karen M. 2003. "Cracks in the Rainbow: Group Commonality as a Basis for Latino and African-American Political Coalitions." *Political Research Quarterly* 56(2):199–210.

Kim, Claire Jean. 1999. "The Racial Triangulation of Asian Americans." *Politics and Society* 27(1): 105–38.

Kim, Nadia Y. 2008. *Imperial Citizens: Koreans and Race from Seoul to LA*. Palo Alto, Cali.: Stanford University Press.

Landale, Nancy, and Ralph Oropeza. 2002. "White, Black, or Puerto Rican? Racial Self-Identification among Mainland and Island Puerto Ricans" *Social Forces* 81: 231–54.

Light, Ivan. 2006. *Deflecting Immigration: Networks, Markets, and Regulation in Los Angeles*. New York: Russell Sage Foundation.

Logan, John. 2003. "How Race Counts for Hispanic Americans." Paper for American Communities Project, Initiative in Spatial Structures and Processes, Brown University. Available at: http://mumford.albany.edu/census/BlackLatinoReport/BlackLatino01.htm (accessed May 12, 2011).

————. 2010. *American Communities Project* [database]. Produced jointly by the Initiative in Spatial Structures in the Social Sciences, Brown University, and the Lewis Mumford Center, University at Albany. Available at: http://www.s4.brown.edu/cen2000/data.html (accessed May 12, 2011).

Massey, Douglas S., and Nancy A. Denton.1993. *American Apartheid: Segregation and the Making of the Underclass.* Cambridge, Mass.: Harvard University Press.

McClain, Paula D. 1993. "The Changing Dynamics of Urban Politics: Black and Hispanic Municipal Employment—Is there Competition?" *Journal of Politics* 55(May): 399–414.

McClain, Paula D., Niambi M. Carter, Victoria M. DeFrancesco Soto, Monique L. Lyle, Jeffrey D. Grynaviski, Shayla C. Nunnally, Thomas J. Scotto, J. Alan Kendrick, Gerald F. Lackey, and Kendra Davenport Cotton. 2006. "Racial Distancing in a Southern City: Latino Immigrants' Views of Black Americans." *Journal of Politics* 68(3): 571–84.

Miles, Jack. 1992. "Blacks vs. Browns." *Atlantic Monthly*, October 1992, pp. 41–68.

Min, Pyong Gap. 1996. *Caught in the Middle: Korean Communities in New York and Los Angeles.* Berkeley: University of California Press.

Mindiola, Tatcho, Jr., Yolanda Flores Niemann, and Nestor Rodriguez. 2003. *Black-Brown Relations and Stereotypes.* Austin: University of Texas Press.

Moynihan, Daniel Patrick. 1965. *The Negro Family: The Case for National Action.* Washington: U.S. Department of Labor, Office of Policy and Planning Research.

Murguia, Edward, and Tyrone Forman. 2003. "Shades of Whiteness: The Mexican American Experience in Relation to Anglos and Blacks." In *White Out: The Continuing Significance of Racism,* edited by Ashley W. Doane and Eduardo Bonilla-Silva. New York: Routledge.

Myrdal, Gunnar, and Sissela Bok. 2005. *An American Dilemma: The Negro Problem and Modern Democracy,* vols. 1 and 2. New York: Transaction Publishers.

Newsweek. 2007. "Racial Cleansing in Los Angeles." October 23, 2007.

Oliver, Eric J., and Janelle Wong. 2003. "Intergroup Prejudice in Multiethnic Settings." *American Journal of Political Science* 47(4): 567–82.

Omi, Michael, and Howard Winant. 1994. *Racial Formation in the United States: From the 1960s to the 1990s.* 2nd ed. New York: Routledge.

Parrado, Emilio A. 2011 "How High Is Hispanic Fertility? Immigration and Tempo Considerations." *Demography* 48: 1059–80.

Passel, Jeffrey, and D'Vera Cohn. 2011. *Unauthorized Immigrant Population: National and State Trends, 2010.* Washington, D.C.: Pew Hispanic Center.

Pulido, Laura. 2006. *Black, Brown, Yellow, and Left: Radical Activism in Los Angeles.* Berkeley: University of California Press.

Sawyer, Mark. 2005. "Racial Politics in Multi-Ethnic America: Black and

Latino Identities and Coalitions." In *Neither Enemies nor Friends: Latinos, Blacks, Afro-Latinos*, edited by Anani Dzidzienyo and Suzanne Oboler. New York: Palgrave Press.

———. 2006. *Politics in Post-Revolutionary Cuba.* Cambridge: Cambridge University Press.

Sidanius, Jim, and Felicia Pratto. 2001. *Social Dominance: An Intergroup Theory of Social Hierarchy and Oppression.* Cambridge: Cambridge University Press.

Smith, James P., and Barry Edmonston. 1998. *The Immigration Debate: Studies on the Economic, Demographic, and Fiscal Effects of Immigration.* Washington, D.C.: National Academies Press.

Sonenshein, Raphael J. 1993. *Politics in Black and White: Race and Power in Los Angeles.* Princeton, N.J.: Princeton University Press.

Telles, Edward. 2004. *Race in Another America: The Significance of Skin Color in Brazil.* Princeton, N.J.: Princeton University.

Telles, Edward, and Vilma Ortiz. 2008. *Generations of Exclusion: Mexican Americans, Assimilation, and Race.* New York: Russell Sage Foundation.

Telles, Edward, and Sylvia Zamora. 2008. "African American and Latino Immigrant Occupational Concentration." Unpublished report. Ford Foundation, New York.

U.S. Bureau of the Census. 2010. "Hispanic Population of the United States." Available at: http://www.census.gov/population/www/socdemo/hispanic/hispanic_pop_presentation.html (accessed March 26, 2010).

Vaca, Nicolás. 2004. *The Presumed Alliance: The Unspoken Conflict between Latinos and Blacks and What It Means for America.* New York: HarperCollins.

Waters, Mary C. 1999. *Black Identities: West Indian American Dreams and American Realities.* New York: Russell Sage Foundation.

Wilson, William Julius. 1979. *The Declining Significance of Race: Blacks and Changing American Institutions.* Chicago: University of Chicago Press.

———. 2010. *More than Just Race: Being Black and Poor in the Inner City.* New York: W. W. Norton.

Winant, Howard. 2001. *The World Is a Ghetto: Race and Democracy Since World War II.* New York: Basic Books.

Yoon, In-Jin. 1997. *On My Own: Korean Businesses and Race Relations in America.* Chicago: University of Chicago Press.

Zúñiga, Víctor, and Rubén Hernández-León, eds. 2005. *New Destinations: Mexican Immigration in the United States.* New York: Russell Sage Foundation.

PART I

Labor Markets

CHAPTER 1

Immigration and Labor Market Dynamics

Frank D. Bean, James D. Bachmeier, Susan K. Brown, and Rosaura Tafoya-Estrada

By several indications, anti-immigrant sentiment—long an under-current in American social history—most recently resurfaced in the mid-2000s. One indicator was adamant opposition to further im-migration on the part of an increasingly vociferous minority, any-where from one-fifth to one-quarter of those polled in public opinion surveys (Jacoby 2006). A second was Congress's voting down bipar-tisan immigrant-friendly proposals for immigration reform in 2007. A third was the emergence in 2008 of several candidates for high-level federal and state offices who sought to ride the crest of negative attitudes toward newcomers to political victory (Brown, Bean, and Bachmeier 2009). Although such candidates made immigration re-striction the centerpiece of their campaigns, none succeeded at the polls. Even though only a minority of the electorate strongly opposed immigration, broader public opinion was nonetheless diffusely skep-tical, particularly toward unauthorized migrants and proposals for legalization. In this chapter, we note that unfavorable perceptions of immigrants often manifest themselves in claims that newcomers, in-cluding the unauthorized, undermine employment and earnings among native workers, especially less-educated African Americans. But, as we shall see, the evidence for such claims, which has never been strong, remains dubious (Somerville and Sumption 2009; Card and Lewis 2007).

To be sure, recent U.S. immigration controversies arise over more than labor market issues. Two examples are allegations that immi-grants exhibit higher crime rates than natives (Feere and Vaughan 2008) and assertions that many immigrants, particularly Latinos, neither learn English very quickly nor want to assimilate (Hunting-ton 2004). Again, research suggests the contrary (see, for example, Rumbaut, Massey, and Bean 2006; Sampson 2009). Still other analysts have noted that relatively poor immigrants increase state and local costs for hospitals, education, and criminal justice facilities, even as immigrants contribute greatly to federal tax coffers (Bean and Stevens 2003; Smith and Edmonston 1997). Such concerns about immigration aside, recent popular support for restricting immigration nonetheless tends to emphasize labor market questions, as has almost always been the case (Bean and Stevens 2003; Zolberg 2006). That contradictions persist between the findings of policy-relevant research and public rhetoric about immigration's effects points to the importance of continually reexamining immigration's labor market implications for ethnoracial minority groups, if for no other reason than to ascertain whether their fundamental patterns have recently changed.

This chapter undertakes such a review and evaluation, focusing especially on Latino-black dynamics. By this, we mean the labor market implications of immigration, much of which is Latino, for both blacks and Latinos, particularly those of Mexican origin. Among Latinos, Mexicans are by far the majority of both legal and unauthorized immigrants to the country (Brown, Bean, and Bachmeier 2009). One reason for the recent change in labor market dynamics is that Mexican migration has become a national rather than a regional phenomenon. For example, between 1900 and 1990, only about one in ten Mexican-born persons living in the United States lived outside the five traditional destination states of Arizona, California, Illinois (mostly Chicago), New Mexico, and Texas (Leach and Bean 2008). By 2007, about one in three did—more than triple in less than two decades (U.S. Bureau of the Census 2007). More important, Mexicans have migrated not just to a few new destinations but to almost all parts of the country, albeit to varying degrees (Zúñiga and Hernández-León 2005). Many of these destinations have had little or no experience with immigration, let alone with Mexicans speaking mostly Spanish and seemingly embracing different cultural outlooks (Hirschman and Massey 2008). Perhaps the arrival of foreign-born Mexicans in such places has generated adverse labor market consequences for natives, including native blacks, with less education. It is thus important to revisit the question of the labor market implications of immigration for the native born, especially ethnoracial minorities. In particular, we focus on the effects of recent Mexican immigration (because it is so large), not only for native born African Americans but also for the Mexican immigrants already here.

HISTORICAL AND CULTURAL BACKGROUND

Immigration and race sometimes seem to represent features of the American experience that are very nearly opposites, at least as they have been characterized in the postwar period (Bean and Bell-Rose 1999). Few phenomena have so captured the American imagination as immigration, at least in its mythologized form (Handlin 1973), and none has so contradicted American ideals as race (Cose 1992). Slavery and the failure of Reconstruction after the Civil War have long plagued race relations in the United States (Berlin 2003; Du Bois 1935), and slavery's negative legacy has never disappeared (Bean and Lee 2009; Fields 1990). On the other hand, immigration metaphors invoke the Promised Land, the American Dream, and the Golden Door epitomized in the Emma Lazarus poem at the Statue of Liberty (see, for example, Borjas 1999; Reimers 1985; Waldinger 1996).

During the 1960s, the juxtaposition of immigration and race issues began painfully to reveal their contradictions. The geostrategic exigencies of the Cold War, as well as the not easily ignored claims for equal opportunity from post–World War II black veterans, contributed in 1964 and 1965 to two landmark pieces of legislation—the Civil Rights Act, making discrimination against blacks illegal, and the Hart-Celler Act, abolishing national origin quotas as bases for immigrant admissions (Bean and Bell-Rose 1999; Reimers 1992). Many scholars thought the Civil Rights Act would quickly lead to full incorporation of blacks into American society (Glazer 1997), whereas others generally expected Hart-Celler not to generate much in the way of new immigration but instead to simply eliminate the source of the country's international embarrassment over its discriminatory admissions policies (Brown, Bachmeier, and Bean 2009). At the time, each act was thought to offer the prospect of improving the economic status of racial-ethnic groups in the United States.

Neither, however, turned out as anticipated. African Americans did not quickly become economically incorporated, and the country drew in millions of new nonwhite and often poor immigrants, especially Mexicans (Bean and Stevens 2003). As postwar economic prosperity created new job opportunities and expanding cities brought people from different backgrounds increasingly into contact with one another (Fischer and Hout 2006), religious and ethnic group intermarriage flourished (Pagnini and Morgan 1990; Lee and Bean 2010).

The politics of racial identity gained new—if controversial—traction, leading to heightened awareness that tangible benefits could accrue to those with official minority status (Skrentny 2002). Partly in response to affirmative action and strong economic productivity through the 1960s (Freeman 2007), some economic progress occurred, though the hope of quickly achieving parity between racial-ethnic minority groups and whites proved more difficult than optimistic observers initially foresaw. Just as popular ideas about the historical experience of immigrants raised hopes for black success as a result of the passage of civil rights legislation in Congress during the 1960s (Massey and Sampson 2009), the slow progress that actually resulted in bridging the divide between black and white may have hastened the emergence of pessimistic assessments about the benefits of Mexican immigration for America in the late twentieth century (Huntington 2004). Rightly or wrongly, the African American experience appears to have contributed to the disillusionment of many Americans with targeted interest-group policies for other nonwhite groups (Fuchs 1995, 1997; Suro 1998). It is against this historical backdrop that we revisit the question of how contemporary immigration—including Mexican—affects blacks, Latinos, and Mexican immigrants already in the country.

RECENT TRENDS IN IMMIGRATION AND RACIAL-ETHNIC DIVERSITY

The expectation that immigrants might adversely influence natives in general and blacks in particular derives from the substantial increases in immigration over the past forty years. As often noted, the changing volume and composition of immigration during this period has converted the United States from a largely biracial society with a sizeable white majority and a small black minority (together with a very small Native American minority of less than 1 percent) into a multiracial and multiethnic society of numerous racial and ethnic groups (Lee and Bean 2004). Moreover, these trends have not subsided. In 2000, nearly one-third of the U.S. population designated itself as black, Latino, or Asian. By 2007, this fraction was almost two-fifths. The speed with which the Latino and Asian groups have grown has meant that the proportion of African Americans in the racial and ethnic minority population has declined. By 1990, blacks were no longer a majority of the minority-group (racial-ethnic) population, numbering only 48 percent of the total. By 2008, this number had fallen even further, to 40 percent (U.S. Bureau of the Census 2008).

How much difference immigration per se has made to changing the racial and ethnic composition of the U.S. population and to its overall growth during the twentieth century can be ascertained by examining its contribution since 1900 to population growth for each of the major racial-ethnic groups (as distinct from the amount of growth that resulted from any excess of births over deaths among the pre-1900 immigrants and native-born members of each of the groups). Barry Edmonston and Jeffrey Passel (1994) found that post-1900 immigration has accounted for about 30 percent of the growth of the total U.S. population since the beginning of the twentieth century. But immigration's contribution to the rise of some of the various major racial and ethnic subgroups has been much greater, accounting for nearly all of the growth among Latinos and Asians (85.7 percent and 97.3 percent, respectively), but virtually none of the overall twentieth-century growth among blacks. Since 1980, growing black immigration from Africa and the Caribbean has begun to change this trend slightly and explains almost a quarter of the recent population growth among blacks (Djamba and Bean 1999). Even with this uptick, however, the large volume of immigration of other groups during the last third of the century contributed to a decline in the relative size of the black population as a component of the overall non-European-origin minority population of the United States.

This change came about in part because the Hart-Celler Act of 1965, passed after a four-decade hiatus in immigration, modified the social logic of immigrant admissions by abolishing national-origin quotas. This led both to increases in legal immigration and to shifts toward largely non-European entrants (Bean and Stevens 2003). As a result, by 2008, 39 million foreign-born persons were living in the United States, outnumbering the country's 35 million native-born African Americans (U.S. Bureau of the Census 2008). To be sure, a few of these foreign born were students or visitors, but the vast majority were immigrants. If we were to include children of the foreign born in the total, the figure would be more than 68 million, more than twice the number of native blacks. Moreover, about two-thirds of the newcomers arriving since 1965 have come from Asian, African, or Latino countries (Office of Immigration Statistics 2007). Thus, about 42 million first- or second-generation nonwhites, if we classify Latinos as nonwhite, now live in the United States (U.S. Census Bureau

2008). Immigration trends since 1965 have therefore not only generated a recent nonwhite minority larger than the native black minority; the numbers of immigrants and their children have increased much faster than the black population.

TRENDS IN LABOR MARKET OUTCOMES: EVIDENCE OF INTERGROUP COMPETITION?

These trends in immigration and composition of the U.S. population compel close examination of those in labor market outcomes for native-born blacks and Latinos, and for the Mexican born, since 1970, the year of the first decennial census after passage of the Civil Rights Act of 1964, Hart-Celler in 1965, and the Voting Rights Act of 1965.[1] In seeking to gauge empirically the implications of immigration for various native groups, we can follow any of three comparative strategies. One is to compare any two groups of interest to ascertain whether they exhibit divergent time trends with respect to key labor market outcomes (for example, Reischauer 1989). A second is to compare places with respect to how much those areas with more immigration diverge from those with less immigration (Bean, Telles, and Lowell 1987; Bean, Lowell, and Taylor 1988). A third is to ascertain at a national level the extent to which different categories of workers (for example, grouped by industry, occupation, or skill categories) with relatively more immigrants differ from those with fewer immigrants (Borjas and Katz 2007; Peri 2010). Such comparisons may generate insights about the effects of immigration on natives' labor market outcomes.

We start with the first of these. In addressing the question of whether racial-ethnic groups, especially Mexicans, differ in their labor market outcomes, we focus primarily on labor force participation rather than on unemployment and earnings, for two reasons. One is that being employed constitutes the sine qua non of the Mexican labor-migrant experience (Van Hook and Bean 2009). The second is that not being in the workforce—because of incarceration, the availability of preferable alternatives, or lack of opportunity—appears increasingly characteristic of the black male experience since the early 1970s (Western and Wildemann 2009; Bean and Bell-Rose 1999). In other words, among black males, job seekers are not only less able to find work, but also less likely to seek employment in the first place, no doubt in part because of discouragement (Holzer 2009). Hence, for either Mexicans or blacks, to focus only on job seeking or earnings would miss much of the story concerning their labor market experiences over the past forty years.

The dramatic increases in the absolute and relative numbers of immigrants suggest that examining even crude trends in employment may be instructive. If new immigrants were taking jobs away from native blacks, we would expect to see more adverse trends in employment for native blacks than for whites, and that this pattern would hold among men and women. The reason is that labor market competition should be greatest among more similar workers. Because blacks at the beginning of the 1970s were in general less well educated than whites, and because so many of the new immigrants (for example, Mexicans) also had such low levels of schooling, the highest degree of competition (adverse employment trends) would be expected to occur between Mexicans and blacks, regardless of gender.

When we consider employment trends by group and gender over this time frame, however, it is immediately apparent that, regardless of racial-ethnic group, the trends are dramatically different for men and women (figures 1.1 and 1.2). Employment trends since 1970 for native black, native Latino, foreign-born Latino, and white men are all similar, and show a pattern of gradual but steady decline, with the single exception of an increase for foreign-born Latinos from 2000 to 2007. Among the groups of women, employment not only rises but, relative to the male decline, does so quite sharply. But scarcely any evidence of more adverse black outcomes (as represented by either more substantial black male decline or less pronounced black female increase) occurs, except for black men during the 1970s, when relatively little immigration occurred overall and Mexican immigration was concentrated in the Southwest, where few blacks lived. A conclusion of minimal impacts on blacks is reinforced by more detailed annual data since the early 1990s, when a major economic recession had just ended. From 1993 through 2000, black employment (expressed as the percentage of working-age males holding a job) actually increased, despite substantial immigration during this time (figure 1.3). Hence, in broad outline, black male employment does not appear to have moved downward in concert with rising immigration. To be sure, it is substantially lower than that of other groups, but this difference stems from other factors, especially the loss of manufacturing jobs in the wake of economic restructuring and deindustrialization during the 1970s (Berg and Kalleberg 2001).

Figure 1.1 U.S. Employment, Men Age Twenty-Five to Sixty-Four, 1970 to 2006

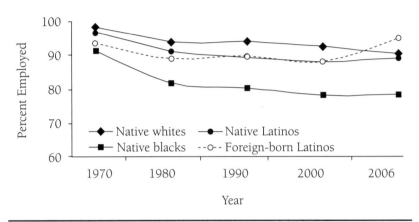

Source: Authors' compilation based on data from IPUMS, 1970 1-percent state sample; 1980 to 2000 5-percent samples; and 2005 to 2007 American Community Surveys (Ruggles et al. 2009).
Note: Instructions for obtaining and using these data sources, and all others cited at the bottom of subsequent figures and tables in this chapter, are included in Ruggles et al. (2009).

These trends, however, do not examine Mexicans specifically. When we look at the Mexican born separately, we see, perhaps not surprisingly given that the majority of Latinos are Mexican, that the trend in employment for Mexican-born males and females of working age is generally similar to that for all Latinos (figure 1.4). Relative employment for males declines slightly from a very high level (over 90 percent) between 1970 and 2000, and then increases through 2006. The pattern of unusually high male employment among Mexican immigrants is also evident when we scrutinize more detailed annual data since 1993 (figure 1.5). Among Mexican-born women, employment levels hold steady over time, but far below the levels of whites and blacks (figure 1.6). Although some might see this as reflecting the influence of Mexican cultural values emphasizing familism and discouragement of women from working, we think an adequate interpretation also involves another factor: that it is difficult to gauge employment levels for Mexican immigrant women from aggregate official statistics. Even though the Mexican labor migration experience involves and reinforces a strong work ethic among both males and females (Van Hook and Bean 2009), the literature on work among Mexican-born women presents considerable evidence that of-

Figure 1.2 U.S. Employment, Women Age Twenty-Five to Sixty-Four, 1970 to 2006

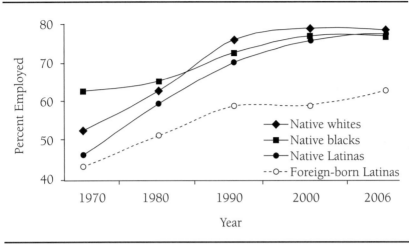

Source: Authors' compilation based on data from IPUMS, 1970 1-percent state sample; 1980 to 2000 5-percent samples; and 2005 to 2007 American Community Surveys (Ruggles et al. 2009).

ficial surveys from which national employment and labor force statistics are calculated underestimate their employment. The reason is that Mexican immigrant women in particular are disproportionately employed in the cash and informal economy, in such jobs as street vendors, child-care workers, domestics, and piece-rate workers—

Figure 1.3 U.S. Employment, Men Age Twenty-Five to Sixty-Four, 1993 to 2007

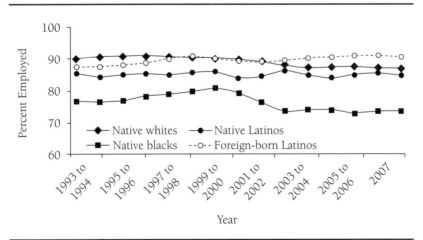

Source: Authors' compilation based on data from Current Population Survey, Annual March Demographic Supplement, 1994 to 2008 (Ruggles et al. 2009).

Figure 1.4 U.S. Employment, Mexican Born Age Twenty-Five to Sixty-Four, 1970 to 2006

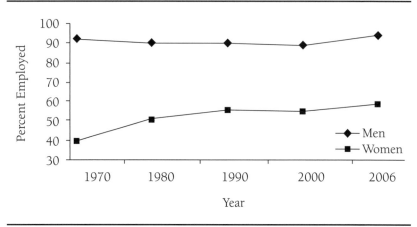

Source: Authors' compilation based on data from IPUMS, 1970 1-percent state sample; 1980 to 2000 5-percent samples; and 2005 to 2007 American Community Surveys (Ruggles et al. 2009).

jobs that often involve working at unconventional sites (Melville 1988; Ojeda de la Peña 2007; Ruiz 1998; Segura 2007; Tafoya-Estrada 2004). In general, Mexican immigrant women undoubtedly work at considerably higher rates than statistics from the census and other official national-level government surveys indicate.

Figure 1.5 U.S. Employment, Men Age Twenty-Five to Sixty-Four, 1993 to 2007

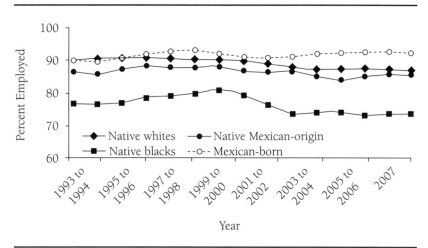

Source: Authors' compilation based on data from Current Population Survey, Annual March Demographic Supplement, 1994 to 2008 (Ruggles et al. 2009).

Figure 1.6 U.S. Employment, Women Age Twenty-Five to Sixty-Four, 1993 to 2007

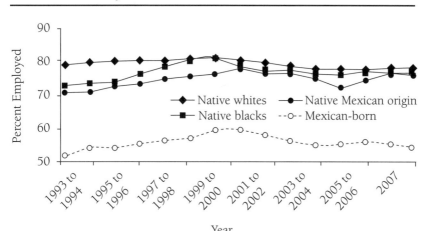

Source: Authors' compilation based on data from Current Population Survey, Annual March Demographic Supplement, 1994 to 2008 (Ruggles et al. 2009).

When we turn our attention to other labor market outcomes (that is, unemployment and earnings), further insight about the picture of racial-ethnic labor market dynamics emerges. In the case of unemployment, or the percentage of the workforce without a job and actively seeking work, figure 1.7 reveals the influence of the very strong labor market in the latter half of the 1990s deriving from the high-tech boom. Unemployment rates for all groups of men—native white, black, and Mexican-origin men, as well as Mexican born—declined. After 2000, however, the unemployment rates increased for whites and blacks but not for Mexican-born men, reflecting their heavy participation in the enormous jump in construction work during the 2000s. Thus, since 2000, the unemployment trend for black and Mexican immigrant men has diverged. However, this same divergence characterized Mexican immigrants and native white males, who mostly would not be expected to compete with less well educated immigrants. Thus it is unlikely that the divergent trends for Mexican immigrants and blacks over this period derive from competition in the labor market.

In the case of earnings (figure 1.8), further nuance is suggested. The average annual earnings of Mexican immigrant males show a slight but steady decline since 1970, even when construction was booming and the earnings of native groups were increasing. This de-

Figure 1.7 U.S. Unemployment, Men Age Twenty-Five to
Sixty-Four, 1970 to 2006

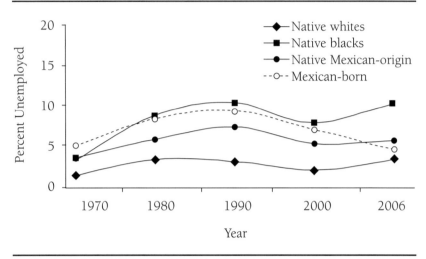

Source: Authors' compilation based on data from IPUMS, 1970 1-percent state sample; 1980 to 2000 5-percent samples; and 2005 to 2007 American Community Surveys (Ruggles et al. 2009).

cline implies that newly arriving Mexican immigrants compete in the labor market with their previously arrived counterparts. Such a finding has consistently emerged in the research on the labor market impacts of immigration (Card 2005; Ottaviano and Peri 2008). But, in general, broad trends in employment do not provide much indication that Mexican immigration, male or female, bears much relationship to the work prospects of blacks, even though this is not the case for earlier Mexican immigrants.

One reason that blacks and Mexican immigrants do not seem to affect each other appreciably is that the two groups tend to live in different parts of the country. This has been the case historically (Foley 1997) and was emphasized in the comprehensive National Research Council examination of immigration's economic and demographic effects on the country (Smith and Edmonston 1997). It has also been suggested that this situation might have changed as a result of shifting patterns of Sunbelt and Mexican migration in the 1980s (Bean and Bell-Rose 1999). To examine this idea here with current data, we look at the largest labor markets in the country between 1980 and 2006 (table 1.1). We calculate correlations between per-

Figure 1.8 U.S. Median Earnings, Men Age Twenty-Five to Sixty-Four, 1970 to 2006

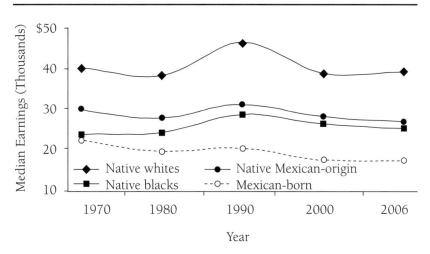

Source: Authors' compilation based on data from IPUMS, 1970 1-percent state sample; 1980 to 2000 5-percent samples; and 2005 to 2007 American Community Surveys (Ruggles et al. 2009).

centage black in these metropolitan areas and various percentage foreign-born measures: percentage total, Latino, or Mexican foreign born. The calculations are weighted for size of metropolitan area, which means that they reflect the degree to which individuals in those labor markets face relatively fewer or larger numbers of a potentially competing group in their labor market. Regardless of the measure of foreign born used, however, the results show that blacks and immigrants, especially Mexican immigrants, tend to live in different local labor markets, and that this tendency has strengthened over time. This trend holds even if we exclude labor markets in the deep South, where one might think such a tendency toward living apart would be most pronounced.

The pattern of geographic separation has withstood the recent enormous spread of the Mexican-born population to new destination states and labor markets. Indeed, one could conclude that such tendencies perhaps result to some extent from such movement, the exact estimation of which remains for future research. Interestingly, the change seems recently also to have been characteristic of smaller rather than larger labor markets. That is, the tendency for blacks and

Table 1.1 Correlations with U.S.-Born Blacks of Working Age in Metro Areas (Weighted by Total MSA Population)[a]

	All 175 Metros				153 Non-Deep-South Metros[b]			
	1980	1990	2000	2006	1980	1990	2000	2006
Percent Foreign Born	-0.091	-0.196	-0.288	-0.321	0.028	-0.096	-0.205	-0.242
Percent Foreign Born, Latino	-0.109	-0.212	-0.288	-0.318	-0.037	-0.149	-0.238	-0.273
Percent Mexican Born	-0.231	-0.295	-0.330	-0.350	-0.191	-0.264	-0.310	-0.336

Source: Authors' compilation based on data from IPUMS, 1980 to 2000 5-percent samples; and 2005 to 2007 American Community Surveys (Ruggles et al. 2009).
[a] Working age is defined as eighteen to fifty-five.
[b] Deep South metros are those located in Alabama, Georgia, Louisiana, Mississippi, North Carolina, and South Carolina.

Mexicans to not live in the same places is now about equally a property of large and small labor markets, whereas formerly it was much less true in smaller labor markets. For example, in the twenty-five smallest labor markets in 1980, the correlation was only –0.13, whereas in 2006 it was –0.36, almost identical to that for large labor markets, –0.37 (see table 1.2). To clarify the overall pattern of separation in detail, we show in table 1.3 the percentages of these groups for the country's ten largest labor markets: blacks and Mexicans are present in opposite degrees in the various cities, perhaps reflecting regional differences in economic and restructuring and geographic migration. For example, the four metropolitan areas with the largest relative black populations (nearly 20 percent or higher)—Atlanta, Washington, Detroit, and Philadelphia—range from only 1.1 percent to 7.7 percent foreign-born Latino.

The other two comparative research approaches mentioned earlier for detecting labor market impacts of immigrants on other groups involve comparing geographic areas or work categories. The results of the many such studies have been recently summarized and assessed by researchers at the Migration Policy Institute in the United States and the Equality and Human Rights Commission in Britain (Somerville and Sumption 2009). The main problem with research comparing areas, such as cities, is that it cannot readily resolve the so-called endogeneity problem. That is, were an increase in labor supply (as from immigration) to generate competition that lowered other groups' labor market outcomes, evidence of this competition could be masked by the additional tendency for labor to move to places or job categories that provide better labor market outcomes. Such movements would mean that any greater supply observed in such places or categories would not be exogenous and would obscure any negative competition effects. As a result, the net labor market impacts would tend to be small, except among the most unskilled workers in jobs not requiring language skills, which could help explain the fact that new Mexican immigrants appear to compete with previously arriving immigrants.

This conclusion is buttressed by the results of the latest studies of this type, including the recent work of David Card and Ethan Lewis (2007), Gianmarco Ottaviano and Giovanni Peri (2008), and Giovanni Peri (2010), who find additional new evidence that low-skilled immigration exerts only small adverse effects on the labor market outcomes of other low-skilled groups, except in the case of other low-skilled earlier-arriving immigrants. Peri finds that over the

Table 1.2 Characteristics of Working-Age[a] Population in U.S. Metropolitan Areas

	1980	1990	2000	2006
25 largest MSAs				
A. Mean percent U.S. black	12.4	12.3	11.5	11.9
B. Mean percent foreign-born	9.6	13.9	20.7	22.4
C. Mean percent foreign-born, Latino	3.7	6.3	10.0	11.5
D. Mean percent Mexican-born	1.5	3.1	5.6	6.7
Correlations[b]				
A with B	−0.148	−0.306	−0.372	−0.377
A with C	−0.149	−0.297	−0.331	−0.350
A with D	−0.261	−0.377	−0.367	−0.368
25 smallest MSAs[c]				
A. Mean percent U.S. black	8.1	10.9	8.8	8.3
B. Mean percent foreign-born	4.2	4.9	7.5	9.7
C. Mean percent foreign-born, Latino	0.9	2.0	4.3	6.1
D. Mean percent Mexican-born	0.6	1.6	3.6	5.4
Correlations[b]				
A with B	−0.289	−0.296	−0.311	−0.374
A with C	−0.104	−0.247	−0.288	−0.372
A with D	−0.131	−0.266	−0.304	−0.363

Source: Authors' compilation based on data from IPUMS, 1980 to 2000 5-percent samples; and 2005 to 2007 American Community Surveys (Ruggles et al. 2009).
[a] Working age is defined as ages eighteen to fifty-five.
[b] Weighted by total MSA population in a given year.
[c] Of the largest 175 MSAs overall in a given year.

long run, immigration increases natives' employment, although market adjustments, especially during economic downturns, may take several years to play out, often resulting in the observation of short-run negative effects (2010). Overall, the general conclusion, from econometric research following either an area- or work-category approach, is that even the recent high levels of unskilled migration to the United States, most of which has originated in Mexico, do not appear to threaten substantially the labor market outcomes of other

Table 1.3 Characteristics of Populations in U.S. Metropolitan Areas, 2000

		Percentage in Total Population				Percentage in Working-Age Population[a]			
	Total Population	U.S.-Born Black	Foreign-Born	Foreign-Born, Latino	Mexican-Born	U.S.-Born Black	Foreign-Born	Foreign-Born, Latino	Mexican-Born
Atlanta	3,987,990	27.9	10.5	4.2	2.9	27.1	13.8	5.8	4.0
Washington, D.C.	4,733,359	23.8	17.4	5.6	0.7	22.4	22.4	7.7	1.0
Detroit	4,430,477	22.4	7.5	0.8	0.6	21.9	8.6	1.1	0.8
Philadelphia	5,082,137	18.7	7.0	0.9	0.3	18.2	8.6	1.2	0.4
Chicago	8,804,453	18.4	16.5	7.7	6.5	17.2	21.6	11.0	9.4
Houston	4,413,414	16.2	19.7	13.0	9.4	15.8	26.8	18.1	13.1
New York	17,244,066	13.3	27.5	8.9	1.1	11.7	34.8	12.2	1.7
Dallas–Forth Worth	5,043,876	13.3	15.5	10.3	8.5	12.8	21.1	14.2	11.8
San Francisco–Oakland	4,645,830	9.2	26.3	8.3	5.3	8.8	32.2	11.1	7.2
Los Angeles–Long Beach	12,368,516	7.2	34.9	20.4	14.5	6.8	46.2	28.6	20.3

Source: Authors' compilation based on data from IPUMS, 2000 5-percent samples (Ruggles et al. 2009).
[a] Working age is defined as eighteen to fifty-five.

unskilled groups, with the important exception of earlier-arriving unskilled immigrants.[2]

CONCLUSIONS

With respect to Mexican immigrants and native blacks, how might we explain such results? One strong possibility is that these two alternative sources of labor are imperfect substitutes in the labor market. That is, unskilled workers, who are often immigrants from Mexico, generally do not end up doing work similar to what unskilled blacks or unskilled whites do. Although this imperfect substitution may minimize cross-group differences in labor market impacts, it may also reflect new sources of stratification in the labor market involving race-ethnicity and nativity. Such structural segmentation, though associated with smaller relative group differences or group changes in labor market outcomes across time, place, or job category, nonetheless occurs in conjunction with immigration and may help account for different outcomes across groups. Thus, blacks exhibit worse employment outcomes than Mexicans but better earnings, at least for those employed (Bean and Bell-Rose 1999). This pattern apparently does not result from immigration, but may be attributable to segmentation.

Immigration may also contribute to the emergence of a more complex racial-ethnic stratification. The presence of so many Mexican immigrants, many unauthorized and often unfamiliar with English, adds another dimension beyond race-ethnicity. That is, to the degree that such immigrants are channeled into certain sectors of employment, labor market segmentation may be increasing by nativity even more than it is by race-ethnicity. Undoubtedly these two kinds of segmentation overlap, but the diversity introduced by Mexican immigration multiplies the possible dimensions for segmentation. It is not clear yet how to conceptualize these structural arrangements. Some of them may have positive implications for African American employment, such as ethnic enclaves and patterns of residential autonomy, whereas others seem to operate in harmful ways, such as concentrations of ethnic- and immigrant-specific network hiring (see Bean and Bell-Rose 1999). An important challenge for future research is to conceptualize these new structural arrangements and to develop theories about their change and persistence. This is critical given recent research suggesting that the migration of Mexicans to new destinations in the South may result in new opportunities for white employers to discriminate against blacks by hiring Mexican workers (Marrow 2011; Lopez-Sanders 2011; Piatt 1997). Of course, whether this has a wider negative labor market implication for blacks depends on the degree to which such displaced African Americans find comparable employment elsewhere (Hamermesh and Bean 1998).

Further theory and research also need to focus on how the increased diversity deriving from immigration ultimately affects racial-ethnic identity in the United States. David Reimers (1998) attributes much of the U.S. turn against immigration in the early 1990s—Proposition 187 in California, for example—to concerns that American identity is becoming fragmented and less Europe-oriented, even though this turn coincided with an economic recession. In writing about the implications of Latino immigration for the United States, Roberto Suro notes that "identity has once again become a problem for the United States, and as before, the crisis or reinvention will create a new identity that embraces the nation's new constituents. The presence of so many Latinos ensures that matters of race and language, of poverty and opportunity, of immigration policy and nationality will be central issues in the process" (1998, 321). One possible outcome of the process of identity reformation may be that racial-ethnic status will simply become less relevant as a basis for workplace and occupational stratification as well as other forms of social organization in the United States (Alba and Nee 2003). Increasing rates of racial-ethnic intermarriage and multiracial reporting in the United States over the past two decades are examples of trends consistent with this possibility (Lee and Bean 2010).

Alternatively, fault lines may emerge within Latino groups, especially among those of Mexican origin. That Mexican immigrant workers appear both increasingly necessary to the country's economy, at least during nonrecessionary times, even as they drive down employment possibilities and earnings among other Mexican immigrants suggests that many parts of the country may actually be receiving more unskilled migrants than their labor markets need (Bean et al. 2010). When economic downturns come, the fiscal costs of migration still have to be paid at the state and local level, even though the taxes immigrants pay accrue disproportionately at the federal level. That is, the costs of education, criminal justice, and health care for immigrants, including unauthorized immigrants, do not diminish with hard economic times at the state and local level even though local labor demand for such workers may decline. This imbalance may fuel resentment among natives, even among members of the same immigrant group who arrived earlier. Hence, although low-skilled immigrant workers may play increasingly important and necessary roles in the U.S. labor market that are largely complementary to the roles played by natives, including those of native blacks and Mexican Americans, when more immigrants arrive than are needed in hard economic times, such a surplus may foster resentment against immigrants for several reasons, not the least of which is their contribution to fiscal imbalances and the resulting upward pressure on taxes. Under such circumstances, public perceptions of immigrants can easily become more negative, even though the overall economic effects of immigration are positive and the labor market consequences for natives very small.

NOTES

1. As a practical matter, it is impossible to gauge the effect of black immigrants on native blacks on a national basis using cities as the unit of analysis because only two or three cities have received enough black immigrants to constitute an appreciable influence on the labor market.
2. *Unskilled* generally refers to workers whose education ended with high school completion or less.

REFERENCES

Alba, Richard, and Victor Nee. 2003. *Remaking the American Mainstream: Assimilation and Contemporary Immigration.* Cambridge, Mass.: Harvard University Press.

Bean, Frank D., and Stephanie Bell-Rose. 1999. *Immigration and Opportunity: Race, Ethnicity, and Employment in the United States.* New York: Russell Sage Foundation.

Bean, Frank D., Susan K. Brown, James Bachmeier, and Christopher Smith. 2010. "Are Unskilled Immigrants Necessary in the United States?" Presentation at Center for Comparative Immigration Studies conference. University of California, San Diego (September 12, 2010).

Bean, Frank D., and Jennifer Lee. 2009. "Plus Ça Change. . . ?: Multiraciality and the Dynamics of Race Relations in the United States." *Journal of Social Issues* 65(1): 205–19.

Bean, Frank D., B. Lindsay Lowell, and Lowell J. Taylor. 1988. "Undocumented Mexican Immigrants and the Earnings of Other Workers in the United States." *Demography* 25(1): 35–52.

Bean, Frank D., and Gillian Stevens. 2003. *America's Newcomers and the Dynamics of Diversity.* New York: Russell Sage Foundation.

Bean, Frank D., Edward E. Telles, and B. Lindsay Lowell. 1987. "Undocumented Migration to the United States: Perceptions and Evidence." *Population and Development Review* 13(4): 671–90.

Berg, Ivar, and Arne Kalleberg. 2001. *Sourcebook on Labor Markets: Evolving Structures and Processes*. New York: Plenum Press.

Berlin, Ira. 2003. *Generations of Captivity: A History of African-American Slaves*. Cambridge, Mass.: Harvard University Press.

Borjas, George J. 1999. *Heaven's Door: Immigration Policy and the American Economy*. Princeton, N.J.: Princeton University Press.

Borjas, George J., and Lawrence F. Katz. 2007. "The Evolution of the Mexican-Born Workforce in the United States." In *Mexican Immigration to the United States*, edited by George J. Borjas. Chicago: University of Chicago Press / Cambridge, Mass.: National Bureau of Economic Research.

Brown, Susan K., James Bachmeier, and Frank D. Bean. 2009. "Trends in U.S. Immigration." In *Nations of Immigrants: Australia and the USA Compared*, edited by John Higley and John Nieuwenhuysen. Northampton, Mass.: Edward Elgar.

Brown, Susan K., Frank D. Bean, and James Bachmeier. 2009. "Aging Societies and the Changing Logic of Immigration." *Generations* 32(4): 11–17.

Card, David. 2005. "Is the New Immigration Really So Bad?" *Economic Journal* 115: F300–23.

Card, David, and Ethan G. Lewis. 2007. "The Diffusion of Mexican Immigrants During the 1990s: Explanations and Impacts." In *Mexican Immigration to the United States*, edited by George J. Borjas. Chicago: University of Chicago Press / Cambridge, Mass.: National Bureau of Economic Research.

Cose, Ellis. 1992. *Nation of Strangers: Prejudice, Politics, and the Populating America*. New York: HarperCollins.

Djamba, Yanyi, and Frank D. Bean. 1999. "Black and White African Women in America: Demographic Profile and Socio-Economic Assimilation." *African Population Studies* 14(1): 25–33.

Du Bois, W. E. B. 1935. *Black Reconstruction in America*. New York: Harcourt, Brace.

Edmonston, Barry, and Jeffrey S. Passel. 1994. *Immigration and Ethnicity: The Integration of America's Newest Arrivals*. Washington, D.C.: Urban Institute Press.

Feere, Jon, and Jessica Vaughan. 2008. "Taking Back the Streets: ICE and Local Law Enforcement Target Immigrant Gangs." Washington, D.C.: Center for Immigration Studies.

Fields, Barbara J. 1990. "Slavery, Race, and Ideology in the United States of America." *New Left Review* 181(May–June): 95–118.

Fischer, Claude S., and Michael Hout. 2006. *Century of Difference: How America Changed in the Last One Hundred Years*. New York: Russell Sage Foundation.

Foley, Neil. 1997. *The White Scourge: Mexicans, Blacks, and Poor Whites in Texas Cotton Culture*. Berkeley: University of California Press.

Freeman, Richard B. 2007. *America Works: Critical Thoughts on the Exceptional U.S. Labor Market*. New York: Russell Sage Foundation.

Fuchs, Lawrence H. 1995. "A Negative Impact of Affirmative Action: Including Immigrants in Such Programs Flies in the Face of Civil Rights." *Washington Post National Weekly Edition*, February 25–26, 1995.

———. 1997. "The Changing Meaning of Civil Rights, 1954–1994." In *Civil Rights and Social Wrongs: Black-White Relations Since World War II*, edited by John Higham. University Park: Pennsylvania State University Press.

Glazer, Nathan. 1997. *We Are All Multiculturalists Now*. Cambridge, Mass.: Harvard University Press.

Hamermesh, Dan, and Frank D. Bean, eds. 1998. *Help or Hindrance? The Economic Implications of Immigration for African Americans*. New York: Russell Sage Foundation.

Handlin, Oscar. 1973. *The Uprooted: The Epic Story of the Great Migrations That Made the American People*, 2d ed. Boston, Mass.: Little, Brown.

Hirschman, Charles, and Douglas S. Massey. 2008. "Places and Peoples: The New American Mosaic." In *New Faces in New Places: The Changing Geography of American Immigration*, edited by Douglas S. Massey. New York: Russell Sage Foundation.

Holzer, Harry J. 2009. "The Labor Market and Young Black Men: Updating Moynihan's Perspective." *Annals of the AAPSS* 621(January): 47–69.

Huntington, Samuel P. 2004. *Who Are We? The Challenges to America's National Identity*. New York: Simon and Schuster.

Jacoby, Tamar. 2006. "Immigration Nation." *Foreign Affairs* 85(6): 50–65.

Leach, Mark A., and Frank D. Bean. 2008. "The Structure and Dynamics of Mexican Migration to New Destinations in the United States." In *New Faces in New Places: The Changing Geography of American Immigration*, edited by Douglas S. Massey. New York: Russell Sage Foundation.

Lee, Jennifer, and Frank D. Bean. 2004. "America's Changing Color Lines: Immigration, Race/Ethnicity, and Multiracial Identification." *Annual Review of Sociology* 30: 221–42.

———. 2010. *The Diversity Paradox: Immigration and the Color Line in 21st Century America*. New York: Russell Sage Foundation.

Lopez-Sanders, Laura. 2011. "Is Brown the New Black? The Dynamics of Ethnic Labor Replacement in New Immigrant Destinations." Ph.D. diss., Stanford University.

Marrow, Helen B. 2011. *New Destination Dreaming: Immigration, Race, and Legal Status in the South*. Palo Alto, Calif.: Stanford University Press.

Massey, Douglas S., and Robert A. Sampson. 2009. "The Moynihan Report

Revisited: Lessons and Reflections After Four Decades." *Annals of the AAPSS* 621(January): 6–27.

Melville, Margarita B. 1988. "Mexicanas at Work in the United States." Houston, Tex.: Mexican American Studies Program, University of Houston.

Office of Immigration Statistics. 2007. *2006 Yearbook of Immigration Statistics*. Washington: U.S. Department of Homeland Security.

Ojeda de la Peña, Norma. 2007. "Transborder Families and Gendered Trajectories of Migration and Work." In *Women and Migration in the U.S.-Mexico Borderlands: A Reader*, edited by Denise A. Segura and Patricia Zavella. Durham, N.C.: Duke University Press.

Ottaviano, Gianmarco I. P., and Giovanni Peri. 2008. "Immigration and National Wages: Clarifying the Theory and the Empirics." *NBER* working paper 14188. Cambridge, Mass.: National Bureau of Economic Research. Available at:http://www.nber.org/papers/w14188 (accessed July 13, 2011).

Pagnini, Deanna L., and S. Philip Morgan. 1990. "Intermarriage and Social Distance Among U.S. Immigrants at the Turn of the Century." *American Journal of Sociology* 96(2): 405–32.

Peri, Giovanni. 2010. *The Impact of Immigrants in Recession and Economic Expansion*. Washington, D.C.: Migration Policy Institute. Available at: http://www.migrationpolicy.org/pubs/Peri-June2010.pdf (accessed July 13, 2011).

Piatt, Bill. 1997. *Black and Brown in America: The Case for Cooperation*. New York: New York University Press.

Reimers, David M. 1985. *Still the Golden Door: The Third World Comes to America*. New York: Columbia University Press.

———. 1998. *Unwelcome Strangers: American Identity and the Turn Against Immigration*. New York: Columbia University Press.

Reischauer, Robert D. 1989. "Immigration and the Underclass." *Annals of the AAPSS* 501: 120–31.

Rose, Peter I. 1997. *Tempest-Tost: Race, Immigration, and the Dilemmas of Diversity*. New York: Oxford University Press.

Ruggles, Steven, Matthew Sobek, Trent Alexander, Catherine A. Fitch, Ronald Goeken, Patricia Kelly Hall, Miriam King, and Chad Ronnander. 2009. *Integrated Public-Use Microdata Series: Version 4.0* [machine-readable database]. Produced and distributed by Minnesota Population Center, Minneapolis, Minnesota.

Ruiz, Vicki L. 1998. *From Out of the Shadows: Mexican Women in Twentieth-Century America*. New York: Oxford University Press.

Rumbaut, Rubén G., Douglas S. Massey, and Frank D. Bean. 2006. "Linguistic Life Expectancies: Immigrant Language Retention in Southern California." *Population and Development Review* 32(3): 447–60.

Sampson, Robert J. 2009. "Disparity and Diversity in the Contemporary

City: Social (Dis)Order Revisited." *British Journal of Sociology* 60(1): 1–31.

Segura, Denise A. 2007. "Working at Motherhood: Chicana and Mexican Immigrant Mothers and Employment." In *Women and Migration in the U.S.-Mexico Borderlands: A Reader*, edited by Denise A. Segura and Patricia Zavella. Durham, N.C.: Duke University Press.

Skrentny, John D. 2002. *The Minority Rights Revolution.* Cambridge, Mass.: Harvard University Press.

Smith, James P., and Barry Edmonston. 1997. *The New Americans: Economic, Demographic, and Fiscal Effects of Immigration.* Washington, D.C.: National Academy Press.

Somerville, Will, and Madeleine Sumption. 2009. *Immigration and the Labour Market: Theory, Evidence, and Policy.* Washington, D.C.: Migration Policy Institute / London: Equality and Human Rights Commission.

Suro, Roberto. 1998. *Strangers Among Us: How Latino Immigration Is Transforming America.* New York: Alfred A. Knopf.

Tafoya-Estrada, Rosaura. 2004. "The Unintended Consequences of Patriarchy: Mexican Immigrant Culture and Education among the Second Generation." Master's thesis, University of California, Irvine.

U.S. Bureau of the Census. 2007. *Current Population Survey: Annual Demographic Files.* Washington: U.S. Government Printing Office.

———. 2008. *Current Population Survey: Annual Demographic Files.* Washington: U.S. Government Printing Office.

Van Hook, Jennifer, and Frank D. Bean. 2009. "Explaining Mexican-Immigrant Welfare Behaviors: The Importance of Employment-Related Cultural Repertoires." *American Sociological Review* 74(3): 423–44.

Waldinger, Roger D. 1996. *Still the Promised City? African-Americans and New Immigrants in Postindustrial New York.* Cambridge, Mass.: Harvard University Press.

Western, Bruce, and Christopher Wildemann. 2009. "The Black Family and Mass Incarceration." *Annals of the AAPSS* 621 (January): 221–42.

Zolberg, Aristide R. 2006. *A Nation by Design: Immigration Policy in the Fashioning of America.* New York: Russell Sage Foundation / Cambridge, Mass: Harvard University Press.

Zúñiga, Victor, and Rubén Hernández-León. 2005. *New Destinations: Mexican Immigration in the United States.* New York: Russell Sage Foundation.

PART II

Politics

CHAPTER 2

Commonalities, Competition,
and Linked Fate

Michael Jones-Correa

Over the last three decades the Hispanic population in the United States has changed significantly. Compare, for instance, the census figures for 1980 and 2000: in 1980, this population was overwhelmingly native born, but by 2000 over 40 percent foreign born, and if one looks only at adults, over 60 percent. Second, in 1980, 90 percent of all Latinos lived in five states. In 2008, although these five states still held the majority of the Latino population, not even the top fifteen held 90 percent. Over the last two decades Latinos have become increasingly an immigrant population, increasingly diverse in terms of national origin, and increasingly dispersed throughout the United States.

In 2008 approximately 45 million persons of Hispanic origin lived in the United States, making Latinos the nation's largest minority ethnic-racial group. This has taken place over a relatively short period: the Hispanic population has increased rapidly over the last three decades, growing 63 percent between 1970 and 1980, 53 percent between 1980 and 1990, and another 58 percent between 1990 and 2000 (U.S. Bureau of the Census 1993).[1] Projections are that, if current trends continue, by 2050 Latinos will be 25 percent of the population and by 2100, 33 percent (Population Projection Program 2000).[2]

Much of this growth has taken place because of immigration. The Mexican-origin population, for instance, nearly doubled between 1970 and 1980, nearly doubled again between 1980 and 1990, and continued this double-digit growth rapidly throughout the next decade, largely because of immigration. Since 1970, at least 40 percent of the more than 1 million immigrants entering the United States in any given year have been from Latin America. The U.S. Census Current Population Survey indicates that in 2002, 52 percent of all first-generation immigrants living in the United States hailed from Latin America. Immigration has dramatically changed the composition of the Hispanic population. In 2008, slightly more than 60 percent of all Latino adults in the United States were first-generation immigrants. This means, for instance, that the Mexican-origin population is composed of large groups of first- and second-generation immigrants, but includes smaller cohorts of third-generation and succeeding generations of Americans.

Whereas in 2008 almost half of all Latinos still lived in two states—California and Texas—and made up a quarter or more of the populations of five states—Nevada (26 percent), New Mexico (45 percent), California (37 percent), Texas (37 percent), and Arizona (30 percent)—the Latino population in the fifteen states with the most Hispanic residents in 2010 is less than 90 percent of the Latino total. Hispanics in the United States are both concentrated and increasingly dispersed. Latinos in 2008 accounted for at least 5 percent of the population in thirty-two states, and by far the fastest growth over the last decade has been in the Southeast, Midwest, and West. States like Alabama, Arkansas, Georgia, North Carolina, Nebraska, Nevada, South Carolina, and Tennessee, for example, saw the number of their Hispanic residents leap at least threefold between 1990 and 2000.

These changes in Latino settlement patterns, driven largely by the movement of people from Latin America to the United States, and by secondary migrations of Latinos within the country, are the impetus for this chapter. Although these changes have been under way for at least two decades, they have attracted remarkably little attention from either scholars or policymakers (García and García 2002). This despite the fact that Latino migrants are moving into areas that have not previously experienced any sizeable immigration over the last hundred years, and that this migration raises a host of thorny issues and critical research questions. Will the settlement and integration of Latinos into new receiving areas differ from their integration into areas in which Latinos have a longer history of immigration and already a sizeable presence? How will the presence of Latinos in midwestern and southern cities and towns affect the balance of race relations between blacks and whites, and between these groups and the newcomers? Will the settlement and integration of Latinos play out differently in states with sizeable African American populations and in those with smaller native-born black populations?

LITERATURE ON RACE RELATIONS BETWEEN LATINOS AND BLACK-WHITE AMERICANS

Reflecting the demographic shifts in the population, researchers have recently begun to move beyond the black-white dichotomy in racial-ethnic group research, paying increasing attention to Latinos and Asian Americans in studies of interracial relations (Cummings and Lambert 1997; Taylor 1998; Welch and Sigelman 2000; Oliver and Wong 2003; Vaca 2004; McClain et al. 2006, 2007). This research, however, is still largely conceptualized in terms of threat and contact. Implicit in this framing is a concern with whites' racial attitudes toward minorities (Key 1949; Wright 1977; Fossett and Kiecolt 1989; Sigelman and Welch 1993; Sigelman et al. 1996; Taylor 1998). Despite considerable debate, the literature has been inconclusive on whether intergroup contact between majority and minority groups fosters hostility (Wright 1977; Glaser 1994; Taylor 1998) or increased racial-ethnic understanding (Ellison and Powers 1994; Sigelman and Welch 1993; Welch et al. 2001).

Some authors have worked to reconcile these attributes of race relations, noting the importance of context as a mechanism in determining contact between racial groups and its impact on individual behavior and perception. A small but growing body of literature has begun to focus on interethnic relations among minority group members. This departure from the traditional focus on black-white interactions more closely reflects the complex nature of contemporary race relations in the contemporary United States. Scholars who have examined black and Latino relations in particular have described interactions between the groups either as strained and in conflict or as cooperative, especially with regard to coalition building. Although it falls rather neatly into the traditional threat and contact framework, characterizing black and Latino relations as dichotomously in conflict or cooperation may not truly capture the nuances that make interactions between blacks and Latinos distinctive from their respective exchanges with whites.

This said, some scholars examining perceptions of commonality between Latinos and African Americans have found that Latinos perceive little in common with African Americans (Kaufmann 2007, 2003; Rodrigues and Segura 2006) and their relationships are largely competitive (McClain and Karnig 1990; McClain et al. 2007; Vaca

2004; Meier and Stewart 1991). Others examining the content of Latino attitudes toward African Americans have found that Latinos express stereotypical views of African Americans. Paula McClain and her colleagues (2006) found, for instance, that majorities of Latinos in their North Carolina study felt blacks did not work hard, were not easy to get along with, and were untrustworthy, feelings not reciprocated (or at least reported) by black respondents, majorities of whom reported they felt Latinos were hardworking and trustworthy. Latinos in the study also reported feeling more in common with whites than blacks. (Interestingly, a plurality of white respondents said they felt most in common with blacks, and a plurality of black respondents indicated they felt closest to Latinos.)

However, Latinos express more positive views of blacks than whites do (Oliver and Johnson 1984; Bobo and Johnson 2000; Mindiola, Niemann, and Rodriguez 2002; Oliver and Wong 2003; McClain et al. 2006). These scholars point to residential context, contact with African Americans, and perceptions of Latino linked fate as predictive of more positive views of African Americans. Income and education are critical to perceptions of conflict between Latinos and African Americans (Jackson, Gerber, and Cain 1994; Gay 2006; Betancur and Gills 2000; Borjas 1999). Claudine Gay's 2006 finding that the relative economic status of African Americans affects their perceptions of Latinos seems to hold for Latinos perceptions of conflict with African Americans. Scholars have also concluded that Latino linked fate as well as higher levels of acculturation are correlated with perceptions of commonality with African Americans (Sanchez 2008; Gay 2006; Bobo and Massagli 2001; Bobo et al. 1994; Mindiola, Niemann, and Rodriguez 2003; Cummings and Lambert 1997; Tedin and Murray 1994). In sum, the literature suggests that acculturation and time in the United States for Latinos leads to greater appreciation of commonalities with blacks—except when it doesn't. The historical literature, for instance, suggests that immigrant acculturation goes hand in hand with the adoption of greater distance from blacks (Roediger 1991; Jacobson 1999; Ignatiev 1995; Guglielmo 2003).

LITERATURE ON NEW
IMMIGRANT DESTINATIONS

The research on Latinos and interethnic relations has had a national rather than a regional, state, or local focus. The literature on new immigrant destinations, for its part, has focused to a large extent on the economic impacts of Latino immigrants, discussing either Latino immigration and the labor market more generally (Borjas 2004; Johnson-Webb 2002; Murphy, Blanchard, and Hill 2001), or their effect on particular industries (Donato, Bankston, and Robin 2001; Engstrom 2001; Hernández-León and Zúñiga 2000; Kandel and Parrado 2004). For example, several studies have looked at the impact of Latino immigration on the meat-processing industry in the South and Midwest (Broadway 1994; Gouveia and Stull 1995; Grey 1995; Griffith 1995; Guthey 2001). Because of their focus on labor issues, many of these studies touch only tangentially on questions of immigrant social and political settlement and integration, their impacts on race relations in these new receiving areas, or the differences in their experiences from that of their peers in either areas of historical immigrant settlement (like New York City) or areas of dense coethnic settlement (like parts of California).

Some recent collections of essays discussing recent Latino immigration (Massey 2008; Hernández-León and Zúñiga 2003, 2005; and Massey, Durand, and Malone 2002) have somewhat different emphases, dealing with themes of social dislocation, continuing transnational ties, and secondary migration. Other work has traced out the changing patterns of race and ethnicity in rural America (Zúñiga and Hernández-León 2005; Kandel 2003; Fennelley and Leitner 2002) and of increased residential segregation among Latinos in the South and Midwest (Cromartie and Kandel 2002; Kandel and Cromartie 2004). Helen Marrow (2007) and McClain and colleagues (2006) explore racial tensions between Latinos and blacks. Examples of this kind of work are increasing but still relatively few and far between. Despite Latinos' arriving in large numbers to the South and other areas of the country that have little experience with immigration, or with race relations beyond black and white, the implications of a rapidly growing Latino immigrant presence for race relations in the region are still largely unexplored.

STATE AND LOCAL VARIATION

The social incorporation of Hispanics across new receiving areas likely varies. One dimension along which incorporation might vary is whether Latinos are immigrating to a state with a sizeable native-born Latino population or to an area populated largely by first-generation immigrants. Latino arrivals to Iowa and Nebraska, for instance, settle where the majority of the Hispanic population is still native born (though the increase in the Latino population is largely driven by immigration). In states like Georgia and North Carolina, the overwhelming majority of the Latino population is recent, largely Mexican, immigrants. These distinct patterns are likely to have very different implications for the social and civic incorporation of new migrants. As the literature just reviewed suggests, it is also likely to matter if newcomers are arriving directly as immigrants, or indirectly as secondary migrants—after spending time, say, in a heavily Latino metropolitan area like Los Angeles.

Another factor that will likely help shape the social and civic incorporation of new migrants is that those living in areas with comparatively small Latino populations are likely to have significantly different social experiences than their counterparts in high-density Latino areas. Are Latino immigrants living in relative isolation, for instance, more likely to emphasize some form of ethnic identity, or to hold onto their transnational ties, or to give these up to better blend into their social surroundings? All in all, existing analyses fail to effectively capture these phenomena or allow for comparisons across receiving areas.

Latinos are arriving in new receiving areas that have existing patterns of racial relations. In the South, for instance, racial and ethnic identities are seen through the prism of black-white relations. In smaller towns in the rural Midwest, until the arrival of Latinos, most white residents may have had no experience dealing with such differences. And in other areas, such as suburbia anywhere, racial and ethnic differences may be subsumed under class differences. What implications does the racial context in each setting have for the incorporation of new migrants? How does the location to which migrants arrive affect their perceptions of discrimination and their views of American society? Do existing patterns of racial relations affect migrants' experience with housing, schooling, employment, and politics—in short, with their social and political integration? Rodney Hero (1998) makes this argument for state-level differences in racial outcomes in the United States. Does it hold true for new immigrants, and in new receiving areas, as well?

OPEN QUESTIONS

Numerous questions on the table about race relations between Latinos, whites, and African Americans remain unanswered. The contact-threat hypotheses are still unresolved, and the literature is divided when focusing on relations between blacks and Latinos, as the earlier discussion suggests, some scholars emphasizing negative views and stereotypes held by Latinos about blacks, and others pointing to evidence suggesting that Latino views of blacks are better than those they hold about whites, and that in any case these views ameliorate over time in the United States, and with rising levels of income and education. Any diagnosis of relations between Latinos and African Americans is complicated by the large foreign-born component to the Latino population in the United States, and by the fact that largely as the result of immigration Latinos have become more widely dispersed then ever, moving into new receiving destinations in the South, West, and Midwest. Race relations, then, are likely to vary across receiving contexts.

LATINO NATIONAL SURVEY: DESCRIPTION AND METHODOLOGY

To explore questions of relations between Latinos and blacks, and Latinos and whites, we turn to the 2006 Latino National Survey (LNS; Fraga et al. 2006).[3] The LNS contains 8,634 completed interviews of self-identified Latino Hispanic residents of the United States. Respondents were selected from a random sample of Latino households in the jurisdictions covered. The sample was drawn from a marketing database of approximately 11 million households in the United States identified as Latino or Hispanic. The survey, conducted by Interviewing Service of America in both English and Spanish, contains approximately 165 distinct items ranging from demographic descriptions to political attitudes and policy preferences, as well as a variety of social indicators and experiences. The Latino National Survey is state stratified and includes fifteen states and the Washington, D.C., metropolitan area (including counties and municipalities in Virginia and Maryland), with the universe of the analysis representing approximately 90 percent of the U.S. Hispanic population. The national margin of error is approximately ±1.05 percent.

The analysis presented here relies on both national and state-level analyses of the LNS data, and thus presenting the design of the state data in greater detail is merited. Table 2.1 reports each state, its Latino population, and the number of complete interviews. The sample is stratified by geographic designation, meaning that each state sam-

Table 2.1 Latino Population (2000) and Latino National
          Survey (2006) Sample Size

State	Latino Population	Sample Size
Arizona	1,295,617	400
Arkansas	86,666	400
California	10,966,556	1,200
Colorado	735,601	400
Florida	2,682,715	800
Georgia	435,227	400
Illinois	1,530,262	600
Iowa	82,473	400
Nebraska	94,425	400
Nevada	393,970	400
New Jersey	1,117,191	400
New Mexico	765,386	400
New York	2,867,583	800
North Carolina	378,963	400
Texas	6,669,666	800
Washington D.C., PSMA	432,003	400

Source: Author's compilation based on data from Therrien and Ramirez (2001) and
Fraga et al. (2006).

ple is a valid, stand-alone representation of that state's Latino population. The national margin of error is approximately ±1.05 percent.
The smallest sample size for any unit was 400, yielding a margin of
error of less than ±5 percent for each state.

DESCRIPTIVE DATA

The LNS data allow us to focus on three areas of Latino-black-white
relations: *commonalities*—respondents' sense of socioeconomic and
political commonalities with African Americans and whites; *competition*—respondents' impressions of competition in education, jobs
(including city and state government jobs), and political representation with African Americans; and, finally, *linked fate*—respondents'
perception that their well-being and that of other Latinos is linked to
that of African Americans. The tables presented here are a first step in
the analysis, comparing descriptive data in these three areas for Latinos in four new receiving states—Arkansas, Georgia, Iowa, and North
Carolina—with those in three traditional receiving states—California, New York, and Texas.

COMMONALITIES

The LNS asked a range of questions about feelings of closeness and perceptions of commonalities. These are the focus of the discussion in this section.

Socioeconomic commonalities.   LNS respondents were asked the following questions about socioeconomic commonalities between Latinos or Hispanics and other racial and ethnic groups: "Thinking about issues like job opportunities, educational attainment or income, how much do Latinos have in common with other racial groups in the United State today? Would you say Latinos have a lot in common, some in common, little in common, or nothing at all in common with African Americans?" The question was repeated for whites and in traditional receiving states for Asians, though we report findings only for responses for blacks and whites.

In all seven states, when asked about their socioeconomic commonalities with blacks or African Americans, more respondents say "some" or "a lot" than say "nothing" or "little" (see figure 2.1). However, as a whole, these numbers were higher in the traditional immigrant-receiving states of California (51 percent), Texas (54 percent), and New York (57 percent) than in the four emerging states, in which 50 percent or fewer respondents say they have "some" or "a lot" in common with African Americans. In all of the states, respondents felt they had more rather than less in common with African Americans, though the margin was wider in New York (57 percent versus 31 percent) than in Georgia (46.5 percent versus 40.5 percent) in favor of more commonalities.

When asked about socioeconomic commonalities between Latinos-Hispanics and whites, in every state fewer respondents felt they had "some" or "a lot" in common with whites than when the same question was asked about blacks. Likewise, in every state respondents were more likely to say they had "little" or "nothing" in common with whites than they did with black Americans. In general, as noted, feelings of commonalities were higher in traditional receiving states than in new ones, but the overall patterns of greater sense of commonalities with African Americans held across all states.

Political.   In terms of political commonalities between Latinos or Hispanics and other racial and ethnic groups, respondents were asked

Figure 2.1 Latino Perception of Socioeconomic
            Commonality

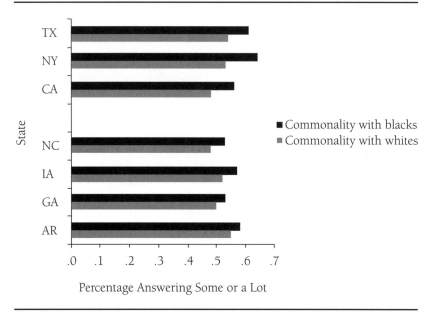

Source: Author's calculations based on Fraga et al. (2006).

the following question: "Now I'd like to ask you to think about the political situation of [selected ethnic term] in society. Thinking about things like government services and employment, political power and representation, how much do [selected ethnic term] have in common with other racial groups in the United States today? Would you say [selected ethnic term] have . . . in common [same choices as above]?"

There are obvious differences between traditional receiving states and emerging states as relates to respondents' feelings of commonalities in the political circumstances of Latinos and African Americans (see figure 2.2). Respondents from traditional receiving states like California (50 percent), Texas (52 percent), and New York (57 percent) are more likely to say that they have "some" or "a lot" in common politically with African Americans. By contrast, in three of four emerging states (with the exception of Iowa) more respondents indicated they shared "nothing" or "little" in political commonality with African Americans than "some" or "a lot." The pattern held for perceptions of political commonalities with whites as well: perceptions of common-

Figure 2.2 Latino Perception of Political Commonality

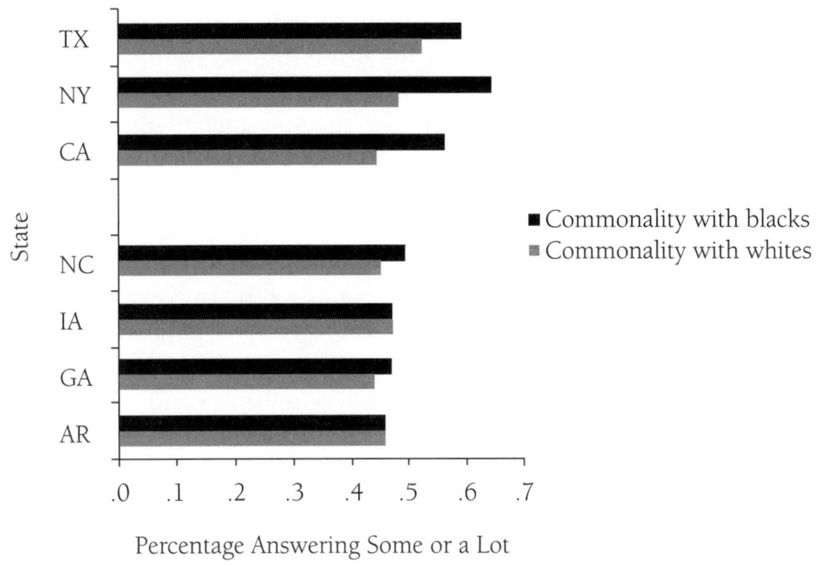

Percentage Answering Some or a Lot

Source: Author's calculations based on Fraga et al. (2006).

alities were higher in traditional receiving states (Texas was the only state in which respondents indicated they had "some" or "a lot" in common politically with whites rather than "nothing" or "little"). In figure 2.2, as in figure 2.1 for socioeconomic commonalities, perceptions of commonalities with whites were consistently lower than those with African Americans.

COMPETITION

Nontraditional receiving areas have emerged in part as a consequence of labor market opportunities available to new immigrants. As this new Latino population settles in these states, often relocating permanently from their home country or in secondary migration from another state, their decision to stay is based on several factors, including an assessment of how competitive the labor market and local political climates are in both emerging and traditional areas. The next set of questions asked respondents to reflect on competitive conditions in education, the labor market, local and state government employment, and political representation for Latinos and blacks. The questions gauging competition were as follows: "Some have suggested that Latinos or Hispanics are in competition with African-Americans. . . . Would you tell me if you believe there is strong competition, weak competition, or no competition at all with African-Americans [followed by specific queries about education, jobs, local and state government jobs, and political representation]?"

Education.   With respect to access to education and quality schools, the general pattern indicates that a plurality of Latinos viewed African Americans as "no competition at all" (41 to 51 percent) (see figure 2.3). The next most common perception was of blacks as "strong competition" (26 to 35 percent). In emerging states, close to half or more of respondents indicate that African Americans are "no competition at all" (47 to 52 percent), and just over a quarter of respondents that blacks are "strong competition" in gaining access to education (25 to 27 percent). Respondents in traditional receiving states—New York, Texas, and California—reported the highest levels of competition with African Americans in access to education.

Employment.   The outlook on competition in the job market is roughly similar to that for competition in access to education. In all seven states, roughly a quarter (25 to 28 percent) of respondents perceived blacks as strong competition and about 15 to 20 percent as weak competition. The plurality choice in every state was no competition (43 to 61 percent), but perceived competition was higher in the traditional receiving states. New York stood out in clearly having the highest proportion of respondents, 36 percent, indicating strong competition with African Americans in the workplace, and had the fewest respondents reporting no competition (43 percent). The exact opposite is true, however, of the new receiving states. In these states majorities of respondents reported no competition (Arkansas 61 percent, Iowa 57 percent, North Carolina 54 percent), with significantly lower levels reporting strong competition (Arkansas 22 percent, Iowa 24 percent, North Carolina 25 percent).

    In terms of competition over city or state government employment, a similar but less pronounced pattern emerged among new receiving states, in which 42 to 48 percent of respondents say no competition, and roughly 28 percent say strong competition, though

Figure 2.3 Latino Perceived Competition in Education
with African Americans

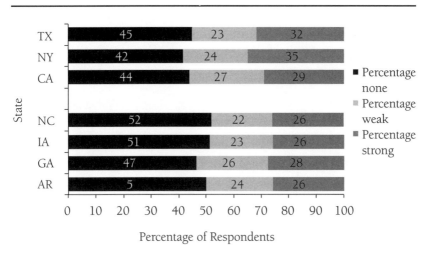

Source: Author's calculations based on Fraga et al. (2006).

Georgia stands out in this group, with 33 percent saying strong competition (see figure 2.4). In traditional receiving states, respondents
more often report strong competition with blacks for government
jobs (California 35 percent, Texas 33 percent, and, most strikingly,
New York 43 percent).

Political representation.   Figure 2.5 reflects competition over having
representatives in elected office. Respondents from new immigrant
destination states were most likely to report no competition (41, 39,
42, and 28 percent for Arkansas, Georgia, Iowa, and North Carolina,
respectively). Respondents in Georgia gave responses most similar to
those in traditional receiving states, with 36 percent indicating strong
competition to elect a Latino public official. Similar figures for traditional receiving states were higher: California (38 percent), Texas (38
percent), and New York (42 percent).

LINKED FATE

Linked fate is a measure of the recognition that the social, economic,
and political well-being of other racial or ethnic groups is linked to

Figure 2.4 Latino Perceived Job Competition with African Americans

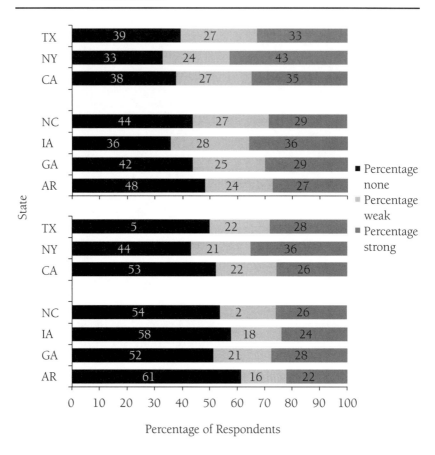

Source: Author's calculations based on Fraga et al. (2006).

the well-being of one's own group (Dawson 1995). LNS respondents were asked about linked fate with blacks with the following question: "How much does Latinos' doing well depend on African Americans' doing well?"

The results for this question suggest that a majority of respondents see a linked fate between blacks and Latinos in both traditional and new receiving states (see figure 2.6). Although more than half of all respondents say that African Americans' doing well has implications for Latinos, in the four emerging states the numbers range from 58

Figure 2.5 Latino Perceived Competition for Elected
Positions with African Americans

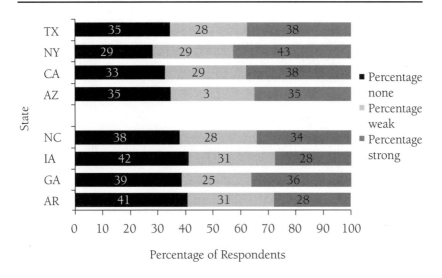

Source: Author's calculations based on Fraga et al. (2006).

Figure 2.6 Latino Perceived Linked Fate with African
Americans

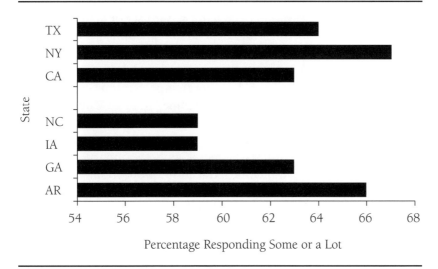

Source: Author's calculations based on Fraga et al. (2006).

percent in North Carolina to 65 percent in Arkansas. The results are more mixed in the traditional receiving states.

New York had the greatest percentage of respondents indicating that African Americans' doing well mattered some or a lot (67 percent) for the prospects of Latinos, but in California respondents essentially split, 53 percent saying it mattered some or a lot to Latinos, and 47 saying either not at all or only a little.

REGRESSION MODELS

These figures of descriptive data only take us so far. On the whole, they indicate that perceptions of cooperation between Latinos and African Americans are higher in traditional than in new receiving states, and that perceptions of competition are the other way around, with perceptions of competition higher in traditional receiving states and lower in the new states. Multivariate regression analyses give greater purchase on making sense of these results.

The following tables present the results for a number of different models. The first cluster, in table 2.2, have as dependent variables the same questions regarding perceptions of commonalities with blacks and whites, sense of linked fate with African Americans, and competition across a range of arenas—education, jobs, public-sector jobs, and electing coethnics to public office. A second cluster, in table 2.3, test models with the same dependent variables but include individual states as independent variables. Finally, a third set of tables have the same independent variables and dependent variables as table 2.2 but run for each state individually.

Given the findings in the literature thus far, and the results in the descriptive data sketched out, I expect that perceptions of commonality may increase with education, income, time in United States, generation in the United States, and English-language ability. In other words, I expect perceptions of commonality to increase with assimilation. This hypothesis is tested with the inclusion of variables for age, household income, education, proportion of life spent in the United States, a first-generation dummy variable, a Mexican-origin dummy variable (given that Mexican migrants are more likely to be recent arrivals, particularly in new receiving states), and citizenship.

The models also allow testing of other hypotheses as well. For example, it may be that participation in religious communities may shape one's attitudes toward other racial-ethnic groups. The models include variables for frequency of church attendance, a Catholic or non-Catholic dummy, as well as a dummy variable capturing whether respondents thought of themselves as born-again Christian.

It may also be the case that respondent's social networks shape racial perceptions as well. The LNS includes items on respondents' friendships. Three are included here: whether the respondent has some white friends, some black friends, and mostly Latino friends. The LNS also includes questions about the make-up of the respondent's workplace; the variables here are whether the workplace is mostly Latino, whether the respondent works with some whites, and whether the respondent works with some black coworkers. The LNS includes appended contextual data that allow some insight into the demographic composition of respondents' neighborhoods at the census tract level. The variables here are percentage Latino, percentage white, and percentage black, all measured at the tract level. The models also include a variable indicating whether a respondent has children in public schools.

The models also include controls for perceptions of discrimination. The two variables included are whether this discrimination was seen as coming at the hands of blacks or of whites. If the respondent was a victim of a crime, a variable indicates whether the perpetrator was black. Finally, respondents were asked if they believed that the police treated Latinos unfairly.

Apart from these variables, a few others were added to control for gender, marital status, respondents' identification with the white racial category, and their self-placement on a skin tone scale (a 5-point scale from dark to light).

FINDINGS FROM THE REGRESSION MODELS

The findings from the probit models follow. To keep the discussion of the models brief, I limit myself to discussing only variables that are significant in the models.

Commonalities with whites. The results presented in table 2.2 indicate that Latinos perceived fewer commonalities with whites (both in general and in politics more specifically) if they were female, if they had spent less time in the United States, if they had black friends, if

Table 2.2　Probit Regression Models

	Commonalities with Blacks	Commonalities with Whites	Political Commonalities with Blacks	Political Commonalities with Whites
R age		0.0000728***	0.0000488**	0.00015834***
Household income				
Gender	0.089139**	–0.09734*		–0.10795*
Married				
Education				–0.14855***
White		0.28372***		0.19941***
Skin tone		0.0834***		
Employed				
Proportion life in U.S.		–0.23474*		–0.30054**
First generation	–0.219353*		–0.17622*	
English speaking	0.43871***	0.24424***	0.33797***	0.18402***
Church attendance				
Non-Catholic				
Born-again	0.1484***	0.10451*	0.109333*	0.12305**
Citizen				
Mexican national origin	–0.10587**		–0.16503***	
Kids in school	0.10152**			
Have black friends		–0.49165***		–0.35266***
Have black coworkers				
Percent black in neighborhood	0.00521**			
Have white friends	–0.39121***		–0.322888***	
Have white coworkers				
Percent white in neighborhood				
Mostly Latino friends	–0.28519***	–0.28783***	–0.29406***	–0.3176***
Mostly Latino coworkers	–0.1449**	–0.19387**		
Percent Latino in neighborhood			0.002149**	0.00187**
Victim of crime with black perpetrator				
Discriminated against by black				
Discriminated against by white		–0.22628**		–0.21407*
Latino maltreatment by police				

Source: Author's compilation based on Fraga et al. (2006).
*p < .05; **p < .01; ***p < .001.

Linked Fate with African Americans	Job Competition with Blacks	Competition with Blacks over Access to Education	Competition with Blacks over Government Jobs	Competition with Blacks over Election to Public Office
0.0000576***		0.0000366*		
		−0.1263**	−0.09291*	794E-06**
	−0.13599**			
		−0.0955598**		
	0.28233***	−0.25605***		
−0.74927***		0.13821**		
		−0.10704**		−0.086093*
−0.1408*		−0.123478**	−0.096357*	−0.111137*
0.24386***	0.1067959*	0.098388*	0.11294**	0.118814**
	0.130676*			0.13148*
−0.109698*	−0.32023***	−0.151255**	−0.31625***	−0.200644***
0.2302356*	0.326082**		0.344002**	
	0.363651**	0.321584**		
−0.151879**	0.131193*		0.145611**	
0.13882**		0.134423*		
−0.14458**	0.17485**		0.20642***	
		0.1199105*		
0.001444*	0.0018833**	0.0014154*	0.002668***	0.002493***
−0.146807*				
				0.1847*
0.15391***				

Table 2.3 Latino Perceived Commonalities

	Economic				Political			
	with Blacks		with Whites		with Blacks		with Whites	
Age squared	0.000	0.000	0.000***	0.000	0.000**	0.000	0.000***	0.000
Household income	0.000	0.000	0.000	0.000	0.000	0.000	0.000	0.000
Sex (female)	-0.084	-0.046	-0.098*	-0.045	-0.057	-0.046	-0.111**	-0.045
Married	0.062	-0.062	0.081	-0.061	0.051	-0.063	0.066	-0.061
Education	0.024	(-0.355)	0.063	-0.359	0.064	-0.036	-0.156***	-0.356
White	-0.039	(-0.052)	0.283***	-0.051	0.013	-0.053	0.201***	-0.051
Skintone	-0.017	-0.022	0.083***	-0.022	-0.025	-0.023	0.031	-0.022
Employed	-0.007	-0.054	-0.022	-0.053	-0.009	-0.054	0.001	-0.053
English	0.487***	-0.054	0.249***	-0.054	0.405***	-0.056	0.173***	-0.055
Born-again	0.146**	-0.045	0.101*	-0.046	0.107*	-0.046	0.121**	-0.046
Citizen	0.228***	-0.055	0.02	-0.056	0.237***	-0.056	0.008	-0.055
Latin spouse	-0.156**	-0.062	-0.019	-0.059	-0.024	-0.062	-0.047	-0.06
Child in school	0.101*	-0.048	0.02	-0.048	-0.002	-0.049	-0.006	-0.048
Black friend	0.189	-0.111	-0.487***	-0.111	0.225*	-0.101	-0.347	-0.11
Black coworker	0.068	-0.112	-0.14	-0.11	0.022	-0.108	-0.128	-0.115
Percentage black in tract	0.007**	-0.003	0.001	-0.003	0.002	-0.003	0.002	-0.003
White friend	-0.389***	-0.06	0.081	-0.059	-0.329***	-0.061	-0.032	-0.059
White coworker	0.026	-0.057	0.03	-0.057	0.063	-0.058	0.08	-0.057
Percentage white in tract	0.005*	-0.002	0.001	-0.002	0.001	-0.002	0.001	-0.002
Latino friend	-0.283***	-0.061	-0.275***	-0.061	-0.309***	-0.062	-0.299***	-0.061
Latino coworker	-0.154*	-0.064	-0.194***	-0.064	-0.045	-0.065	-0.083	-0.064
Percentage Latino in tract	0.000	-0.001	0.000	-0.001	0.002*	-0.001	0.002	-0.001
Victim of crime, black perpetrator	0.126*	-0.061	-0.007	-0.059	0.088	-0.062	0.028	-0.06

Black discrimination	-0.046	-0.093	0.033	-0.086	-0.032	-0.091	0.061	-0.092
White discrimination	0.063	-0.09	-0.232**	-0.082	0.007	-0.088	-0.223**	-0.089
Perceive police unfair	0.023	-0.045	-0.076	-0.044	0.028	-0.045	-0.053	-0.045
AR	-0.003	-0.121	0.169	-0.116	-0.197	-0.124	0.083	-0.122
CO	-0.063	-0.107	0.169	-0.112	-0.025	-0.114	0.19	-0.112
DC	0.212	-0.237	0.156	-0.218	0.188	-0.243	0.275	-0.225
FL	-0.118	-0.103	0.246**	-0.099	-0.127	-0.102	0.266**	-0.1
GA	-0.204	-0.121	0.0337	-0.12	-0.270*	-0.124	0.058	-0.121
IL	-0.167	-0.093	-0.047	-0.098	-0.101	-0.095	0.012	-0.101
IA	-0.118	-0.117	0.004	-0.115	0.068	-0.119	0.078	-0.12
MD	-0.160	-0.16	-0.160	-0.153	-0.039	-0.169	-0.098	-0.169
NV	-0.299**	-0.111	0.041	-0.107	-0.259*	-0.108	0.125	-0.114
NJ	0.250*	-0.119	0.128	-0.113	0.072	-0.121	0.216*	-0.111
NM	0.067	-0.104	0.118	-0.11	-0.162	-0.105	0.317***	-0.11
NY	0.102	-0.102	0.044	-0.1	0.119	-0.105	0.032	-0.102
NC	-0.176	-0.126	-0.035	-0.121	-0.168	-0.129	0.085	-0.125
TX	-0.007	-0.088	0.05	-0.087	0.01	-0.088	0.101	-0.088
VA	0.098	-0.178	0.463**	-0.187	0.165	-0.182	0.338*	-0.176
WA	-0.001	-0.115	0.079	-0.112	-0.08	-0.113	0.095	-0.112
Intercept 1	-1.338***	-0.309	-1.255***	-0.305	-1.72***	-0.306	-1.660***	-0.307
Intercept 2	-0.038	-0.309	0.243	-0.305	-0.168	-0.305	-0.026	-0.306
Intercept 3	1.611***	-0.311	1.855***	-0.306	1.519***	-0.306	1.575***	-0.308
N	7,267		7,402		7,217		7,301	

Source: Author's calculation based on Fraga et al. (2006).

Note: Standard errors in parentheses.

*p < .05; **p < .01; ***p < .001.

their friends were mostly Latino, and if their coworkers were mostly Latino. They were more likely to perceive commonalities with whites if they themselves identified as white, if they were English speaking, or if they were born-again Christian.

Commonalities and linked fate with blacks.   The results presented in table 2.2 for the regression models for commonalities with black Americans (in general and in politics specifically) suggest that Latinos are less likely to perceive commonalities with African Americans if they were foreign born, if they were Mexican, if they had white friends, if most of their friends were Latino, and if most of their coworkers were Latino. Latinos were more likely to see commonalities with African Americans if they were English speaking, if they were male, if they were born-again, and if they saw themselves as darker skinned. A greater sense of commonality is also positively and significantly correlated with living with African Americans in respondents' neighborhoods, having children in the public schools (presumably resulting in cross-racial friendships through one's children), having black friends, and having a negative view of police treatment of Latinos. Perceiving a linked fate with blacks follows the same pattern, though having been the victim of a crime with a black perpetrator reduces the likelihood of indicating a linked fate with African Americans.

Competition with blacks.   Table 2.2 presents the results for four dependent variables measuring perceptions of competition with blacks in four distinct arenas: private-sector jobs, access to education, public-sector jobs, and running for public office.

Perceptions of competition for private-sector jobs were greater if respondents were citizens and, interestingly, if they were born-again. The view that they competed for jobs was also more likely when the respondent had black friends or coworkers, white friends, or mostly Latino friends or lived in a neighborhood with a greater percentage of Latinos. These perceptions of competition over jobs was lower if respondents were first-generation foreign-born immigrants, if they were Mexican, and if they were married.

Respondents were more likely to see competition with African Americans for access to education if they were older, spoke English, or were born-again. They were also more likely to perceive competition if they worked in jobs with black or white coworkers. Alternatively, they saw greater competition if they worked in jobs with mostly Latino coworkers or lived in neighborhoods with more Latinos. Respondents were less likely to view their relations with blacks as competitive in the educational arena if they were male, more educated, went to church more often, or were non-Catholic. Foreign-born and Mexican-origin respondents also perceived less competition.

In the area of public-sector jobs, perceptions of greater competition with blacks was positively correlated with social networks (black friends, white friends, or mostly Latino friends), living in a neighborhood with a greater percentage of Latinos, and being born-again. Competition for public-sector jobs was seen as less competitive with blacks if respondents were male, non-Catholic, or Mexican.

Finally, competition with blacks over the election of coethnics to public office was perceived as greater by men, citizens, those who saw themselves as born-again, those who perceived discrimination by whites, and those living in neighborhoods with a greater percentage of Latinos. Mexican-origin respondents, those going to church more frequently, and non-Catholics perceived less competition with blacks in this arena.

State-level differences.   Tables 2.3 and 2.4 have similar models, with similar results for most of the independent variables, but add an additional set of control variables for each state covered by the LNS. These were included to test the possibility that respondents in new receiving states might be less likely to perceive commonalities with blacks, and more likely to perceive competition, than those living in traditional receiving states (as suggested by some of the recent literature on race relations in the new receiving states). Alternatively, the models might indicate support for the findings from the descriptive data showing a pattern of greater appreciation of commonalities and less perceived competition in new receiving versus traditional receiving states.

However, on the whole, the models do not seem to indicate any statistically significant pattern. For instance, Latino residents in Nevada and Georgia, two new receiving states, perceived less economic and political commonalities with blacks, whereas respondents from New Jersey perceived more economic commonalities. Respondents from Florida had significantly more positive views of their economic and political commonalities with whites (along with Latino residents

Table 2.4 Perceived Competition between Latinos and Blacks

	Linked Fate		Nongovernment Jobs		Education		Government Jobs		Public Office	
Age squared	0.000***	0.000	0.000	0.000	0.000*	0.000	0.000	0.000	0.000	0.000
Household income	0.000**	0.000	0.000	0.000	0.000	0.000	0.000	0.000	0.000	0.000
Sex (female)	-0.041	-0.044	-0.061	(0.046)	-0.124**	(0.044)	-0.91*	(0.044)	-0.125***	(0.044)
Married	-0.05	-0.059	-0.086	(0.059)	-0.064	(0.060)	-0.042	(0.060)	-0.055	(0.060)
Education	-0.042	-0.034	-0.012	(0.355)	-0.094**	(0.034)	0.03	(0.035)	0.019	(0.034)
White	-0.004	-0.051	0.072	(0.052)	0.096	(0.051)	0.043	(0.051)	0.04	(0.050)
Skintone	0.018	-0.021	-0.026	(0.022)	-0.019	(0.021)	0.016	(0.021)	0.023	(0.020)
Employed	0.056	-0.05	-0.015	(0.053)	0.023	(0.052)	0.04	(0.052)	0.059	(0.051)
English	-0.809***	-0.053	0.220***	(0.054)	0.199***	(0.053)	-0.008	(0.053)	-0.004	(0.053)
Church	0.009	-0.065	-0.113	(0.066)	-0.188***	(0.066)	-0.159*	(0.065)	-0.201***	(0.064)
Non-Catholic	-0.153***	-0.051	-0.033	(0.052)	-0.078	(0.052)	-0.038	(0.050)	-0.061	(0.050)
Born-again	0.245***	-0.044	0.109*	(0.046)	0.1	(0.045)	0.119**	(0.045)	0.124**	(0.044)
Very religious	0.054	-0.097	-0.112	(0.100)	-0.174	(0.099)	-0.254**	(0.098)	-0.227	(0.096)
Citizen	-0.071	-0.053	0.217***	(0.056)	0.106*	(0.054)	0.113*	(0.053)	0.071	(0.054)
Mexico	-0.115*	-0.059	-0.287***	(0.063)	-0.14*	(0.061)	-0.291***	(0.061)	-0.195***	(0.060)
Latin spouse	0.069	-0.059	-0.092	(0.059)	-0.009	(0.060)	-0.035	(0.060)	0.014	(0.059)
Child in school	0.042	-0.047	-0.077	(0.049)	-0.099*	(0.048)	-0.033	(0.047)	0.015	(0.046)
Black friend	0.229*	-0.102	0.325**	(0.116)	0.075	(0.112)	0.328***	(0.107)	0.148	(0.108)
Black coworker	0.004	-0.107	0.354***	(0.119)	0.316**	(0.113)	0.077	(0.113)	0.177	(0.107)
Percentage black in tract	0.001	-0.003	0.003	(0.003)	0.001	(0.003)	0.003	(0.003)	0.003	(0.003)
White friend	-0.150**	-0.058	0.133*	(0.059)	0.103	(0.058)	0.145**	(0.059)	0.046	(0.057)
White coworker	0.142**	0.056	0.116	(0.058)	0.152**	(0.058)	0.103	(0.057)	0.085	-0.056
Percentage white in tract	0.001	-0.002	0.003	(0.002)	0.000	(0.002)	0.002	(0.002)	0.001	(0.002)
Latino friend	-0.142*	-0.058	0.173**	(0.061)	0.078	(0.059)	0.192***	(0.059)	0.041	(0.059)
Latino coworker	-0.016	-0.061	0.062	(0.065)	0.122*	(0.063)	0.026	(0.062)	0.022	(0.062)

Percent Latino in tract	0.001	(0.001)	0.002	(0.001)	0.001	(0.001)	0.002**	(0.001)	0.002 (0.001)
Victim of crime, black perpetrator	−0.169**	(0.061)	0.037	(0.060)	0.005	(0.060)	0.02	(0.061)	−0.043 (0.060)
Black discrimination	−0.002	(0.087)	0.136	(0.092)	0.111	(0.091)	0.073	(0.091)	−0.069 (0.087)
White discrimination	0.035	(0.084)	−0.065	(0.089)	0.099	(0.087)	0.117	(0.087)	0.190* (0.083)
Perceive police unfair	0.150***	(0.043)	0.036	(0.045)	0.025	(0.043)	0.012	(0.043)	0.023 (0.043)
AR	−0.083	(0.118)	−0.281*	(0.125)	−0.188	(0.116)	−0.303**	(0.115)	−0.360*** (0.110)
CO	−0.036	(0.103)	−0.218*	(0.109)	−0.18	(0.108)	−0.288**	(0.109)	−0.330*** (0.104)
DC	0.138	(0.274)	−0.123	(0.257)	0.02	(0.266)	0.015	(0.241)	0.006 (0.223)
FL	−0.194*	(0.1)	−0.237*	(0.102)	0.266**	(0.100)	−0.269**	(0.099)	−0.256** (0.098)
GA	−0.192	(0.112)	0.162	(0.119)	0.009	(0.115)	−0.014	(0.117)	−0.148 (0.119)
IL	−0.221**	(0.09)	−0.065	(0.096)	−0.048	(0.093)	0.06	(0.091)	0.037 (0.090)
IA	−0.260*	(0.114)	−0.155	(0.120)	−0.245*	(0.115)	−0.281*	(0.116)	−0.361 (0.112)
MD	0.228	(0.164)	0.174	(0.160)	0.066	(0.151)	0.017	(0.156)	−0.094 (0.157)
NV	0.1	(0.113)	−0.263*	(0.114)	−0.232*	(0.113)	−0.047	(0.108)	−0.113 (0.105)
NJ	−0.15	(0.111)	0.01	(0.121)	−0.036	(0.114)	−0.043	(0.113)	−0.04 (0.117)
NM	−0.19	(0.104)	−0.039	(0.106)	−0.15	(0.110)	−0.302**	(0.111)	−0.220* (0.109)
NY	0.012	(0.097)	0.193*	(0.102)	0.085	(0.098)	0.113	(0.099)	0.066 (0.098)
NC	−0.398***	(0.114)	0.007	(0.122)	−0.196	(0.119)	−0.152	(0.116)	−0.156 (0.119)
TX	−0.066	(0.082)	0.039	(0.088)	0.044	(0.086)	−0.054	(0.084)	−0.032 (0.087)
VA	−0.036	(0.171)	0.07	(0.167)	0.193	(0.169)	0.074	(0.165)	−0.088 (0.161)
WA	−0.218*	(0.109)	−0.065	(0.113)	−0.09	(0.111)	−0.18	(0.109)	−0.087 (0.109)
Intercept 1	−1.896***	(0.292)	0.087	(0.300)	−.653*	(0.293)	−0.441	(0.295)	−1.010*** (0.292)
Intercept 2	−0.890***	(0.292)	1.041***	(0.301)	0.402	(0.293)	0.650*	(0.296)	0.241 (0.292)
Intercept 3	0.298	(0.291)							
N	8,137		8,137		8,137		8,137		8,137

Source: Author's calculation based on Fraga et al. (2006).

Note: Standard errors in parentheses.

*p < .05; **p < .01; ***p < .001.

of New Jersey and Texas in the political realm). Respondents in Florida, Illinois, Iowa, North Carolina, and Washington state perceived, on average, lower levels of linked fate with African Americans than respondents in the omitted state, California. Some of these were new receiving states—Iowa, North Carolina, and Washington—but two are not. Only in Florida—home of a significantly more conservative Cuban American Latino community—were Latinos less positive in their views of their commonalities with, and perception of linked fate with, African Americans.

Respondents in Arkansas, Colorado, Florida, Iowa, Nevada, and New Mexico on average perceived less competition across a number of arenas than their counterparts in California, whereas in only two states—New York (in the area of competition over jobs) and Florida (in the area of competition over access to education)—did Latinos perceive more competition with blacks than their peers in California. Again, among the states with lower levels of perceived competition were both old (Colorado, Florida, and New Mexico) and new (Arkansas, Iowa, and Nevada) receiving states, so there is no clear pattern here. It is of interest that the two states with indications of greater perceived competition by Latinos were traditional receiving states (New York and Florida).

One possibility is that framing the discussion in terms of new and traditional receiving states obscures what is going on, and the more pertinent difference might be states with higher or lower percentages of African American population. This isn't borne out in the data at the neighborhood level—the variable for percentage African American population in the respondents' census tract is never significant—nor does it seem to be borne out at the state level. Table 2.5 gives an indication of the models' results by state, ranked by African American population.

From the table there is no clear relationship between the percentage black in a state's population and the likelihood that Latino residents in that state perceived a greater or lesser sense of commonality or competition with African Americans.

DISCUSSION AND CONCLUSION

Latinos have become a national racial-ethnic minority, with a population growth driven by immigration, and immigrant settlement no lon-

Table 2.5 LNS States Ranked by Percentage Black Population

	Percentage Black	State Rank	Linked Fate with Blacks	Competition with Blacks
District of Columbia	55.2	(NA)		
Georgia	30.0	3		
Maryland	29.5	4		
North Carolina	21.7	7	<	
Virginia	19.9	9		
New York	17.4	10		>
Florida	15.9	12	<	<
Arkansas	15.8	13		<
Illinois	15.0	14	<	
New Jersey	14.5	15		
Texas	12.0	18		
Nevada	8.0	23		<
California (omitted)	6.7	27		
Colorado	4.2	33		
Arizona	4.0	35		<
Washington	3.6	36	<	
New Mexico	2.9	39		<
Iowa	2.6	40	<	<

Source: Author's compilation based on Fraga et al. (2006).

ger confined to traditional receiving states like California or Texas, but instead dispersed across wide swaths of the Midwest, Southeast, and Northeast as well. This chapter has sought to lay out some of the key questions these new settlement patterns raise, particularly for interracial relations in new receiving versus traditional receiving states.

Perhaps surprisingly, across a number of areas—perceptions of cooperation and competition in a number of different arenas, perceptions of linked fate, and evaluations of attitudes toward Latino immigrants—Latinos in new receiving areas evaluate race relations with both blacks and whites as positively as do their counterparts in traditional receiving states, and both the descriptive data and the multivariate regression models indicate that respondents in traditional receiving states perceive higher levels of competition than their peers in new receiving areas.

In the multivariate regressions, the patterns that emerge indicate that perceptions of commonality are higher among those who are more integrated in American society, as suggested by the existing literature, with respondents who speak English and are citizens more likely to see greater commonalities with blacks (and whites). Latinos' social networks matter too: respondents are more likely to report greater commonalities with blacks if they have black friends, and less likely to do so if they have white or mostly Latino friends. Of course, if they have mostly Latino friends, they are less likely to report commonalities with whites as well. On the whole, indicators of integration are correlated with greater perception of commonalities, whereas being foreign born or of Mexican origin, both arguably indicators of recent arrival or lack of integration, signal distance from blacks and whites both.

These findings reverse themselves in the competition models. Here, variables indicating integration are correlated with higher perceptions of competition, and social networks such as friendships and shared workplaces, which are positively correlated with perceptions of commonality, are more likely to be negatively correlated with perceptions of competition. This suggests that integration, close contact, and social relationships may in fact go hand in hand with perceptions of competition. Intuitively this makes some sense: recent arrivals, who have little in the way of social networks, feel neither anything in common nor any sense of competition with whites or blacks. It is more integrated Latinos, who have social networks that include members of other races, who are more likely to feel competitive with them. Closeness, in a sense, breeds competition.

What these findings suggest is that in new receiving areas Latino immigrants who have not yet established social networks with blacks or whites (or both) are also less likely to feel either close to other racial-ethnic groups or competitive with them. Where Latinos have been settled for longer—over time and over generations—they are more likely to live among, work with, and have friendships and other social ties with both blacks and whites. With very few exceptions, the state-level data indicate that Latinos feel closer to blacks than to whites. This does not mean that Latinos do not feel competition with blacks; indeed the data suggest that competition is most likely among racial-ethnic groups when they have contact, and feel a sense of closeness, with one another.

NOTES

1. Figures for 2000 are from "Population by Race and Hispanic or Latino Origin for the US: 1990 and 2000 (PHC-T-1)," available at http://www.census.gov/population/www/cen2000/phc-t1.html (accessed July 20, 2011).
2. See census estimates of population trends at http://www.census.gov/population/www/projections/2009cnmsSumTabs.html (accessed July 20, 2011).
3. For a detailed description of the LNS and its methods, see http://depts.washington.edu/uwiser/LNS.shtml. The data are publicly available at http://www.icpsr.umich.edu/cocoon/MDRC/STUDY/20862.xml (accessed July 20, 2011). For key questions from the LNS Survey, see online appendix 2.A1, available at: http://www.russellsage.org/telles_sawyer_online_appendix.pdf.

REFERENCES

Betancur, John, and Douglas C. Gills, eds. 2000. *The Collaborative City: Opportunities and Struggles for Blacks and Latinos in U.S. Cities*. New York: Garland Publishing.

Bobo, Lawrence D., and Devon Johnson. 2000. "Racial Attitudes in the Prismatic Metropolis: Identity, Stereotypes, and Perceived Group Competition in Los Angeles." In *Prismatic Metropolis: Inequality in Los Angeles*, edited by Lawrence D. Bobo, Melvin L. Oliver, James H. Johnson Jr., and Abel Valenzuela. New York: Russell Sage Foundation.

Bobo, Lawrence D., and Michael P. Massagli. 2001. "Stereotypes and Urban Inequality." In *Urban Inequality: Evidence from Four Cities*, edited by Alice O'Connor, Chris Tilly, and Lawrence D. Bobo. New York: Russell Sage Foundation.

Bobo, Lawrence D., Camille L. Zubrinsky, James H. Johnson Jr., and Melvin L. Oliver. 1994. "Public Opinion Before and After a Spring of Discontent." In *The Los Angeles Riots: Lessons for the Urban Future*, edited by Mark Baldassare. New York: Westview Press.

Borjas, George. 1999. *Heaven's Door: Immigration Policy and the American Economy*. Princeton, N.J.: Princeton University Press.

———. 2004. "The Rise of Low-Skill Immigration in the South." *Center for Poverty Research* working paper DP 2004–01. Lexington: University of Kentucky. Available at: http://www.ukcpr.org-Publications-Immigration_in_the_South_1.pdf (accessed July 20, 2011).

Broadway, Michael J. 1994. "Hogtowns and Rural Development." *Rural Development Perspectives* 9(2): 40–46.

Cromartie, John, and William Kandel. 2002. "Did Residential Segregation in Rural America Increase with Recent Hispanic Population Growth?" Poster presented at the meetings of the Population Association of America. Atlanta, Ga. (May 8–11, 2002).

Cummings, Scott, and Thomas Lambert. 1997. "Anti-Hispanic and Anti-Asian Sentiments Among African Americans." *Social Science Quarterly* 78(2): 338–53.

Dawson, Michael. 1995. *Behind the Mule: Race and Class in African American Politics.* Princeton, N.J.: Princeton University Press.

Donato, Katharine, Carl L. Bankston, and Dawn T. Robinson. 2001. "Immigration and the Organization of the Onshore Oil Industry: Southern Louisiana in the Late 1990s." In *Latino Workers in the Contemporary South,* edited by Arthur D. Murphy, Colleen Blanchard, and Jennifer A. Hill. Athens: University of Georgia Press.

Ellison, Christopher G., and Daniel A. Powers, 1994. "The Contact Hypothesis and Racial Attitudes among Black Americans." *Social Science Quarterly* 75(2): 385–400.

Engstrom, James D. 2001. "Industry and Immigration in Dalton, Georgia." In *Latino Workers in the Contemporary South,* edited by Arthur D. Murphy, Colleen Blanchard, and Jennifer A. Hill. Athens: University of Georgia Press.

Fennelly, Katherine, and Helga Leitner. 2002. "How the Food Processing Industry Is Diversifying Rural Minnesota." *Julien Samora Research Institute* working paper 59. East Lansing: Michigan State University.

Fossett, Mark A., and K. Jill Kiecolt. 1989. "The Relative Size of Minority Populations and White Racial Attitudes." *Social Science Quarterly* 70(4): 820–35.

Fraga, Luis R., John A. García, Rodney Hero, Michael Jones-Correa, Valerie Martinez-Ebers, and Gary M. Segura. 2006. *Latino National Survey* (LNS), 2006 [Computer file]. ICPSR20862-v1. Ann Arbor, Mich.: Inter-University Consortium for Political and Social Research [distributor], 2008-05-27. doi:10.3886-ICPSR20862.

García, Gilberto, and Jerry García. 2002. *The Illusion of Borders: The National Presence of Mexicanos in the United States.* Dubuque, Iowa: Kendall-Hunt.

Gay, Claudine. 2006. "Seeing Difference: The Effect of Economic Disparity on Black Attitudes toward Latinos." *American Journal of Political Science* 50(4): 982–97.

Glaser, James. 1994. "Back to the Black Belt: Racial Environment and White Racial Attitudes in the South." *Journal of Politics* 56(1): 21–41.

Gouveia, Lourdes, and Donald Stull. 1995. "Dances with Cows: Beefpacking's Impact on Garden City, KS, and Lexington, NE." In *Any Way You Cut It: Meat Processing and Small-Town America,* edited by Donald D. Stull,

Michael J. Broadway, and David Griffith. Lawrence: University Press of Kansas.

Grey, Mark A. 1995. "Pork, Poultry, and Newcomers in Storm Lake, Iowa." In *Any Way You Cut It: Meat Processing and Small-Town America*, edited by Donald D. Stull, Michael J. Broadway, and David Griffith. Lawrence: University Press of Kansas.

Griffith, David. 1995. "New Immigrants in an Old Industry: Blue Crab Processing in Pamlico County, North Carolina." In *Any Way You Cut It: Meat Processing and Small-Town America*, edited by Donald D. Stull, Michael J. Broadway, and David Griffith. Lawrence: University Press of Kansas.

Guglielmo, Thomas. 2003. *White on Arrival: Italians, Race, Color, and Power in Chicago, 1890–1945*. Oxford: Oxford University Press.

Guthey, Greg. 2001. "Mexican Places in Southern Spaces: Globalization, Work, and Daily Life in and around the North Georgia Poultry Industry." In *Latino Workers in the Contemporary South*, edited by Arthur D. Murphy, Colleen Blanchard, and Jennifer A. Hill. Athens: University of Georgia Press.

Hernández-León, Rubén, and Victor Zúñiga. 2000. 'Making Carpet by the Mile': The Emergence of a Mexican Immigrant Community in an Industrial Region of the U.S. Historic South." *Social Science Quarterly* 81(1): 49–66.

———. 2003. "Mexican Communities in the South and Social Capital: The Case of Dalton, Georgia." *Southern Rural Sociology* 19(1): 20–45.

———, eds. 2005. *New Destinations of Mexican Immigration in the United States*. New York: Russell Sage Foundation.

Hero, Rodney E. 1998. *Faces of Inequality: Social Diversity in American Politics*. New York: Oxford University Press.

Ignatiev, Noel. 1995. *How the Irish Became White*. New York: Routledge.

Jackson, Byran, Elizabeth Gerber, and Bruce Cain. 1994. "Coalitional Prospects in a Multi-racial Society: African-American Attitudes towards Other Minority Groups." *Political Research Quarterly* 47(2): 277–94.

Jacobson, Matthew Frye. 1999. *Whiteness of a Different Color: European Immigrants and the Alchemy of Race*. Cambridge, Mass.: Harvard University Press.

Johnson-Webb, Karen D. 2002. "Employer Recruitment and Hispanic Labor Migration: North Carolina Urban Areas at the End of the Millennium." *Professional Geographer* 54(3): 406–21.

Kandel, William. 2003. "Race and Ethnicity in Rural America." Washington: Economic Research Service, U.S. Department of Agriculture. Available at: http://www.soc.iastate.edu/sapp/Race%20and%20Ethnicity.pdf (accessed July 20, 2011).

Kandel, William, and John Cromartie. 2004. *New Patterns of Hispanic Settle-*

ment in Rural America. Rural Development and Research Report 99. Washington: U.S. Department of Agriculture.

Kandel, William, and Emilio Parrado. 2004. "Industrial Transformation and Hispanic Migration to the American South: The Case of the Poultry Industry." In Hispanic Spaces, Latino Places: A Geography of Regional and Cultural Diversity, edited by Daniel D. Arreola. Austin: University of Texas Press.

Kaufmann, Karen. 2003. "Cracks in the Rainbow: Group Commonality as a Basis for Latino and African-American Political Coalitions." Political Research Quarterly 56(2): 199–210.

———. 2007. "Immigration and the Future of Black Power in American Cities." Du Bois Review 4(1): 79–96.

Key, V. O. 1949. Southern Politics in State and Nation. New York: Alfred A. Knopf.

Marrow, Helen. 2007. "Southern Becoming: Immigrant Incorporation and Race Relations in the Rural U.S. South." Ph.D. diss., Harvard University.

Massey, Douglas S., ed. 2008. New Faces in New Places: The New Geography of American Immigration. New York: Russell Sage Foundation.

Massey, Douglas S., Jorge Durand, and Nolan Malone. 2002. Beyond Smoke and Mirrors: Mexican Immigration in an Era of Economic Integration. New York: Russell Sage Foundation.

McClain, Paula D., Niambi M. Carter, Victoria M. DeFrancesco Soto, Monique L. Lyle, Jeffrey D. Grynaviski, Shayla C. Nunnally, Thomas J. Scotto, J. Alan Kendrick, Gerald F. Lackey, and Kendra Davenport Cotton. 2006. "Racial Distancing in a Southern City: Latino Immigrants' Views of Black Americans." Journal of Politics 68(3): 571–84.

McClain, Paula D., and Albert K. Karnig. 1990. "Black and Hispanic Socioeconomic and Political Competition." American Political Science Review 84(2): 535–45.

McClain, Paula D., Monique L. Lyle, Niambi M. Carter, Victoria M. DeFrancesco Soto, Gerald F. Lackey, Kendra Davenport Cotton, Shayla C. Nunnally, Thomas J. Scotto, Jeffrey D. Grynaviski, and J. Alan Kendrick. 2007. "Black Americans and Latino Immigrants in a Southern City: Friendly Neighbors or Economic Competitors?" Du Bois Review 4(1): 97–117.

Meier, Kenneth J., and Joseph Stewart Jr. 1991. "Cooperation and Conflict in Multiracial School Districts." Journal of Politics 53(4): 1123–33.

Mindiola, Tatcho, Jr., Yolanda Flores Niemann, and Nestor Rodriguez. 2003. Black-Brown Relations and Stereotypes. Austin: University of Texas Press.

Murphy, Arthur, Colleen Blanchard, and Jennifer Hill, eds. 2001. Latino Workers in the Contemporary South. Athens: University of Georgia Press.

Oliver, Melvin L., and James H. Johnson Jr. 1984. "Interethnic Conflict in an Urban Ghetto: The Case of Blacks and Latinos in Los Angeles." Social Movements, Conflicts, and Change 6(1): 57–94.

Oliver, J. Eric, and Janelle Wong. 2003. "Intergroup Prejudice in Multiethnic Settings." *American Journal of Political Science* 47(4): 567–82.

Population Projection Program. 2000. "Population Projections of the United States by Age, Sex, Race, Hispanic Origin, and Nativity: 1999 to 2100." Washington: U.S. Bureau of the Census.

Rodrigues, Helena Alves, and Gary M. Segura. 2006. "Comparative Ethnic Politics in the United States: Beyond Black and White." *Annual Review of Political Science* 9: 375–95.

Roediger, David R. 1991. *The Wages of Whiteness: Race and the Making of the American Working Class.* New York: Verso.

Sanchez, Gabriel. 2008. "Latino Group Consciousness and Perceptions of Commonality with African Americans." *Social Science Quarterly* 89(2): 428–44.

Sigelman, Lee, Timothy Bledsoe, Susan Welch, and Michael Combs. 1996. "Making Contact? Black-White Social Interaction in an Urban Setting." *American Journal of Sociology* 101(5): 1306–332.

Sigelman, Lee, and Susan Welch. 1993. "The Contact Hypothesis Revisited: Black-White Interaction and Positive Racial Attitudes." *Social Forces* 71(3): 781–95.

Taylor, Marylee C. 1998. "How White Attitudes Vary with the Racial Composition of Local Populations: Numbers Count." *American Sociological Review* 63(4): 512–35.

Tedin, Kent L., and Richard W. Murray. 1994. "Support for Biracial Coalitions Among Blacks and Hispanics." *Social Science Quarterly* 75(4): 705–40.

Therrien, Melissa, and Roberto R. Ramirez. 2001. "The Hispanic Population in the United States: Population Characteristics." *Current Population Report* P20-535. Washington: U.S. Census Bureau (March).

U.S. Bureau of the Census. 1993. *We the American . . . Hispanics.* Washington: Government Printing Office.

Vaca, Nicolás C. 2004. *The Presumed Alliance: The Unspoken Conflict Between Latinos and Blacks and What It Means for America.* New York: HarperCollins.

Welch, Susan, and Lee Sigelman. 2000. "Getting to Know You? Latino-Anglo Social Contact." *Social Science Quarterly* 81(1): 67–83.

Welch, Susan, Lee Sigelman, Tim Bledsoe, and Michael Combs. 2001. *Race and Place: Residence and Race Relations in an American City.* Cambridge: Cambridge University Press.

Wright, Gerald. 1977. "Contextual Models of Electoral Behavior: The Southern Wallace Vote." *American Political Science Review* 71(2): 497–508.

Zúñiga, Victor, and Rubén Hernández-León, eds. 2005. "Appalachia Meets Aztlán: Mexican Immigration and Inter-Group Relations in Dalton, Georgia." In *New Destinations: Mexican Immigration in the United States.* New York: Russell Sage Foundation.

CHAPTER 3

Perceptions of Competition

Jason L. Morin, Gabriel R. Sanchez,
and Matt A. Barreto

The demographics of the United States are undergoing significant changes, largely based on the rapid growth and dispersion of the Latino population.[1] Between 1990 and 2000, for example, the Latino population grew from approximately 22 million to 35 million, an increase of 57.9 percent (Guzman 2001). Today, the number of Latinos living in the United States is estimated at nearly 45 million, and in the coming years an additional 67 million are expected to emigrate from Latin America (Passel and Cohn 2008). Subsequently, demographers project the Latino population to approximate 438 million by 2050 (Passel and Cohn 2008). It is not just the well-noted growth of the Latino population that has captured the interests of many academics and pundits, but also the movement of Latino populations, particularly immigrants, into regions of the country previously not associated with Latinos or Hispanics. In 1990 Hispanics were less than 2 percent of the population in twenty-two states but by 2000, in only eleven states (Garcia and Sanchez 2008). Today, at least one thousand Hispanics live in each of the fifty states. This demographic shift has been most pronounced in the southern United States, as Latinos have almost doubled in that region—from 6.8 million to almost 12 million (Guzman 2001). In fact, according to the Pew Hispanic Center, "the Hispanic population is growing faster in much of the South than anywhere else in the United States" (Kochhar, Suro, and Tafoya 2005, i).

In this chapter, we investigate the impact this demographic transformation has had on the relationship between the two largest racial and ethnic populations in the United States, Latinos and African Americans. Our analysis intends to shed some new light on this subject by investigating Latino perceptions of competition with African Americans. Our focus in this analysis is multifaceted. We intend to explore Latino attitudes toward African Americans across several dimensions within the Latino population using the most recent and comprehensive data available to measure Latino public opinion, the Latino National Survey (LNS). We contend that when attempting to measure Latino attitudes toward African Americans it is necessary to take into account the propensity of Latinos to view other groups as competitors as well—including coethnics. In their analysis using the LNS, Matt Barreto and Gabriel Sanchez (2008) identified that a key advantage of the LNS data is that they provide the opportunity to isolate Latino perceptions of competition with African Americans while accounting for perceptions of overall competition. We build on the Barreto and Sanchez study and illustrate the depth of the LNS by examining Latino perceptions of competition with blacks relative to perceptions of competition with other Latinos across two segments of the Latino population: Latino immigrants and those living in the South. Focusing on the impact of region on Latino attitudes toward African Americans provides a nice complement to chapter 7 of this volume, which also focuses on the South.

Results from the full LNS sample suggest that Latinos actually view coethnics as a greater source of competition than blacks when a standardized measure is used to interpret Latino perceptions of competition with African Americans relative to other Latinos. We expand on this initial finding by isolating Latino immigrants and Latinos who live in the southern region of the United States in the LNS sample and find that though immigrants are more likely to perceive competition with coethnics, Latinos living in the South are more likely to see African Americans as competitors. This multidimensional approach adds significantly to the discussion of Latino attitudes toward African Americans by exploring how these attitudes vary across the diverse Latino population, and how perceptions of competition toward blacks compare with those of coethnic competition.

NATIVITY AND LATINO PERCEPTIONS OF COMPETITION

Scholars have examined intergroup attitudes for some time, often questioning whether the views between Latinos and African Americans are obstacles to coalitions between them, the nation's two largest minority groups. For example, studies using public opinion data to examine intergroup attitudes have found that a large segment of African Americans either distrust or feel competitive toward Latinos (Bobo and Massagli 2001; Bobo et al. 1994; Dyer, Vedlitz, and Worchel 1989; Mindiola, Niemann, and Rodriguez 2003; Kaufmann 2005; Oliver and Wong 2003), and that these feelings and attitudes are reciprocated (Bobo and Hutchings 1996; Johnson Farrell, and Guinn 1997; Oliver and Johnson 1984; Johnson and Oliver 1989). Although most of the extant literature in this area focuses on African American attitudes toward Latinos, an emerging literature is developing that focuses on Latino attitudes toward African Americans.

Among this scholarship, Lawrence Bobo and Vincent Hutchings (1996) found that Latinos were surpassed only by African Americans in their propensity to view other racial-ethnic groups as competitors. In addition to perceptions of competition, scholarship in this area has also suggested that Latinos tend to maintain negative stereotypes of African Americans. For instance, James Johnson, Walter Farrell, and Chandra Guinn (1997) found that a majority of Asian Americans and a large percentage of Latinos viewed blacks as less intelligent and more welfare dependent than their own groups. More recently, the study of Latinos in North Carolina by Paula McClain and her colleagues found that the stereotypes of blacks by Latinos were more negative than those of whites. Specifically, nearly 57 percent of Latinos in this study felt that few or almost no blacks could be trusted and nearly 59 percent believed that few or almost no blacks are hard working (McClain et al. 2006, 578). Particularly when contrasted with the more positive perceptions of whites in the study, it appears as though Latinos, at least those in North Carolina, do not have strong feelings of commonality with blacks. This supports earlier work that suggests both African Americans and Latinos feel closer to whites than to each other (Dyer, Vedlitz, and Worchel 1989).

Negative stereotypes and perceptions of competition among Latinos toward blacks seem to be even more intensified in the foreign-born population, as demographic trends and existing attitudes regarding race may heighten perceptions of competition among Latino immigrants. During the 1980s, many of the nation's major cities went through rapid demographic transformations, and government cutbacks left new immigrants and older residents in poor sections of these cities directly engaged in competition for scarce resources (Jones-Correa 2001). The upward concentration of wealth in the United States over the last two decades has been coupled with declines in real wages and lack of investments in urban neighborhoods, putting the black and Latino working class in a disadvantaged position (Jennings 2003). Moreover, scholars have argued that due to the prevalence of racial discrimination and stereotypes in Latin America some immigrants may enter the United States with negative attitudes toward blacks (de la Cadena 2001; Dulitzky 2005; Guimaraes 2001; Hanchard 1994; Mörner 1967; Sweet 1997; Wade 1993, 1997; Winant 1992). Consequently, foreign-born Latinos have been found to perceive greater competition with African Americans than do their native-born counterparts (Bobo and Hutchings 1996; Rodrigues and Segura 2004; Jones-Correa 2001; McClain et al. 2006). These trends among the foreign-born population motivate our decision to isolate this segment of the Latino community in our analysis.

Although the extant literature seems to indicate that Latinos have antiblack attitudes, this research has not been able to control for more general perceptions of conflict or competition. We contend that although it is plausible that Latino immigrants have high levels of perceived competition with blacks, this trend may be tempered by perceptions of competition in general—including internal competition. Research interested in the contextual determinants of racial animosity among whites has found that individuals faced with economic adversity tend to exhibit not only a generic distrust of outgroups but also feelings of relative deprivation, anxiety, and alienation (Oliver and Mendelberg 2000). Similarly, African Americans in urban ghettos tend to have a "deep suspicion of the motives of others, a marked lack of trust in the benevolent intentions of people and institutions" (Massey and Denton 1993, 172). Claudine Gay (2004) has also found that African Americans living in low-income neighborhoods tend to believe that racism limits their individual life chances, as well as the overall socioeconomic attainment of blacks as a group. We contend that it is likely that Latinos, primarily the foreign born, may have similar worldviews marked by perceptions of competition with multiple groups, including other Latinos. Thus there is reason to believe that Latino perceptions of internal competition will be similar to perceptions of competition toward African Americans.

Our contention is supported by social contact theory. The social interaction explanation of group competition reasons that perceptions of zero-sum competition are conditions associated with the geographic and social proximity of two or more groups (Alozie and Ramirez 1999; Kerr, Miller, and Reid 2000; Betancur and Gills 2000).

Although there is debate regarding whether greater interaction leads to more conflict among groups, the evidence is clear that greater interaction among groups influences intergroup attitudes (Frisbie and Niedert 1977; Glaser 1994; Taylor 1998; Wright 1977; Sigelman and Welch 1993; Welch et al. 2001; Powers and Ellison 1995). We approach this analysis from the standpoint that the level of interaction between Latinos and African Americans is significantly lower than that among coethnics, particularly within settings that lend themselves to competition. Being new to the United States causes the foreign-born population in particular to seek out coethnics for social connections (Keefe and Padilla 1987), with English-language ability being critical because it sets social and formal parameters of interaction.

Research has suggested that perceptions of internal competition may be high within the Latino community, a trend that our measure of relative competition is well designed to capture. For example, David Gutiérrez (1995) states, "Despite the cultural affinities Mexican Americans may have felt toward immigrants of Mexico, as their numbers grew, many Mexican Americans began to worry that the recent arrivals were depressing wages, competing with them for scarce jobs and housing, and undercutting their efforts to achieve better working conditions" (59). This was reinforced by the work of Nestor Rodriguez and Rogelio Nuñez (1986), whose survey indicated that U.S.-born Chicanos often viewed Mexican immigrants as rate busters who would take harder, more dangerous, and dirtier jobs than Chicanos, and also felt that Mexican immigrants received preferential treatment in consideration of social services.

By isolating the foreign-born population in the LNS data, we are able to determine any potential sources of perceived competition with blacks among this important demographic group. We do not deny that the economic conditions facing both groups can and often do lead to competition for scarce resources, and consequently perceptions of competition. At the same time, we believe that the extant literature may overstate the extent of these issues by not accounting for more general perceptions of competition among these groups. We contend in the next section that when considered in the context of relative competition with other Latinos, any observed competition with African Americans among Latino immigrants will be tempered significantly. This theoretical discussion motivates the following formal hypotheses:

Relative competition hypothesis. Among Latino immigrants, we anticipate finding that perceptions of competition with blacks will become significantly tempered when perceptions of competition with other groups are taken into account.

Latino immigrant competition hypothesis. Given higher rates of interaction with other Latinos, we anticipate that Latino immigrants will have particularly high rates of perceived internal competition and consequently lower levels of perceived competition with blacks.

REGION AND PERCEPTIONS OF COMPETITION

We also examine the importance of regional dynamics and its influence on perceptions of competition among Latinos. The Latino immigrant population has increased rapidly throughout the southern United States, where race has defined the political, economic, and social context of the region. According to the Pew Hispanic Center, "The Hispanic population is growing faster in much of the South than anywhere else in the United States" (Kochhar, Suro, and Tafoya 2005, i). Between 1990 and 2000, for example, the Latino population grew by an average of 308 percent in Arkansas, North Carolina, Georgia, Tennessee, South Carolina, and Alabama (Kochhar, Suro, and Tafoya 2005). Consequently, the cultural context of the South is beginning to change as the area incorporates this new ethnic group into the racial-ethnic paradigm historically defined by black and white.

The influx of Latinos entering the South can be explained by the region's fairly recent economic success. Compared with other regions of the United States, employment in the South increased in six states by an average of 2.4 percent—larger than the national employment average (Kochhar, Suro, and Tafoya 2005). Given this employment rate, employers across a variety of industries sought unskilled and inexpensive labor (Torres 2000). Although the majority of Latinos took jobs performing services, expansions in manufacturing and construction provided additional opportunities (Kochhar, Suro, and Tafoya 2005). In South Carolina, for example, "Latinos held 20 percent of the state's meat industry jobs" (Torres 2000, 6). Furthermore, "in North Carolina and Georgia, increased labor demands in industry and construction led to a 75 percent increase in the Latino population" (Torres 2000, 6). Creating more than 400,000 new jobs for Latinos in manufacturing, construction, and services, the South provided job opportunities not available elsewhere in the United States (Kochhar, Suro, and Tafoya 2005).

The regional dynamics of the South provide a unique opportunity to examine perceptions of competition among Latinos and African Americans. Unlike other areas of the country, the South is populated by a large number of blacks but few Latinos. Given the rate at which Latinos are entering the region, social interaction between both groups is likely to be higher than in areas with more traditional Latino neighborhoods. More important, the South is a region where race has historically defined social, economic, and political life (McClain et al. 2006). We believe that the unique cultural dynamics associated with the South, as well as the recent Latino influx, may heighten real and perceived competition among Latinos and African Americans. Given the size of the nationwide sample, the LNS provides an opportunity to examine Latino perceptions of competition across several southern states, and samples are large enough to account for important factors, such as nativity, in a multivariate analysis. We therefore isolate this segment of the Latino community to explore the following hypotheses:

Southern hypothesis. Latinos living in the South will have higher perceptions of competition with African Americans than Latinos living outside of the South.

Social contact in the South hypothesis. Social contact with African Americans in the South will increase Latino perceptions of competition with African Americans.

DATA AND METHODS

The data for this study are from the 2006 Latino National Survey. The LNS is a national telephone survey of 8,600 Latino residents of the United States that seeks a broad understanding of the qualitative nature of Latino political and social life in America. With its ability to account for perceptions of competition across various contexts and to analyze perceptions of competition with African Americans relative to other Latinos, the LNS is the only data set available to address the research questions driving this analysis. To take advantage of the unique approach and rich sample sizes, we perform a wide range of statistical analyses to provide a comprehensive investigation of Latino immigrants' perceptions of social and political competition. The universe of the LNS is all adult Latinos (eighteen years of age and older), with surveys conducted in the preferred language of the respondent (English, Spanish, or both). The sample design was stratified to create stand-alone samples in fifteen states and the Washington, D.C., metro area, allowing for statistically sound analysis in each context. The majority of our analyses use national data instead of state-by-state data. The weight of the sample is therefore nationally proportionate to the Latino population. However, for the South-specific analysis we use unweighted data because we are working with neither individual states nor the national sample.

The first stage of the analysis consists of a series of descriptive statistics to determine the degree to which Latino immigrants and Latinos living in the South perceive African Americans and coethnics to be competitors for economic and political resources. We then explore perceived competition across the subsamples of Latino immigrants and Latinos living in the South. We specifically define the South in our study as the southern states available for analysis in the LNS: Arkansas, Virginia, Georgia, and North Carolina.[2] Because of the large overall sample size in the LNS, we are able to observe statistically significant relationships between subgroups even with descriptive analysis. Afterward, we present results from two sets of multivariate regression models: one focused on identifying factors that contribute to perceptions of competition among Latino immigrants, and the other focused on the same phenomenon among Latinos in the South. In both cases, we present two sets of results. The first set of results uses a dependent variable isolating perceptions of competition with blacks alone. The second set uses our new measure of relative competition, where perceptions of competition with coethnics is used as a benchmark.

Dependent Variable Construction: Our Relative Measure

One of the most important contributions of this chapter is the construction of the dependent variable. Most studies cited in this study rely on a single measure or an index of black-brown conflict that focuses on how Latinos perceive blacks or how blacks perceive Latinos.

However, understanding one group's perceptions of another are meaningless without also having a group for comparison. In this study, we add to the literature by constructing a relative scale of black-brown competition that measures Latinos' relative perceptions of competition with African Americans and other Latinos. For example, if the dependent variable were social trust, and on a 0 to 10 scale a respondent assigned trust in blacks a value of 3, on its face that would appear to be very low, and may appear to be an antiblack attitude. However, if we asked about the same respondent's trust in other Latinos, and he or she also reported a value of 3, the full context illustrates that the attitudes are not antiblack, but rather that the person has low levels of trust in general, for both in-group and an out-group. In this project, we take advantage of two series of questions on the LNS and create a relative measure of black-brown competition, a significant improvement in understanding race relations.

First, respondents were asked, "Some have suggested that Latinos are in competition with African Americans. After each of the next items, would you tell me if you believe there is strong competition, weak competition, or no competition at all with African Americans?"

- getting jobs
- having access to education and quality schools
- getting jobs with the city or state government
- having Latino representatives in elected office

From these four questions, we created an overall index of perceived competition with African Americans. However, this is only half the story. We are interested in knowing whether the perceived competition is a unique brown-versus-black phenomenon or whether competition is also perceived with other Latinos. Thus, we used the same series of questions for Latinos: "Some have suggested that [insert country of ancestry[3]] are in competition with other Latinos. After each of the next items, would you tell me if you believe there is strong competition, weak competition, or no competition at all with other Latinos" and the same four items were used: jobs, education, government jobs, and elected representation. By combining the black competition index with the Latino competition index, we are able to arrive at an overall relative measure of black-brown competition. The combined index ranges from –8 to +8, where a value of –8 represents high competition with Latinos and low competition with blacks. In contrast, a value of +8 represents high competition with blacks and low competition with Latinos. Respondents who had the same value for both groups, regardless of that value, are scored as a zero because they see no difference in the amount of competition between blacks and Latinos.

INDEPENDENT VARIABLES

We rely on a variety of well-used and several new independent variables in predicting black-brown competition. Our variables all intend to gauge the extent and nature of social interaction between Latinos and blacks: *Black Population, Black Friends, Black Workers, Black Crime,* and *Black Discrimination.* We include these variables to determine whether exposure to the black community has a positive or negative impact on how Latinos view competition with blacks. To account for contextual factors that influence perceptions of competition, we also control for the black population of a respondent's county. *Black Population* is the percentage of African Americans living within the surrounding county taken from the U.S. census. *Black Friends* and *Black Workers* are dichotomous variables and measure whether the respondent's friends or coworkers are mostly black or mixed black and Latino. In contrast to these two social interaction variables, two additional variables relate to self-reported negative experiences with African Americans: whether the respondent has been the victim of a crime or experienced discrimination by an African American.

Our next cluster of variables measures how much Latinos feel they have in common with African Americans. *Black Commonality* measures how much Latinos feel they have in common with blacks. *Rank Blacks* is an ordinal measure, ranging from 1 to 8, which takes into account Latinos' perception of commonality with African Americans relative to other racial and ethnic groups. For instance, if a Latino respondent had 5 out of 8 commonalities with blacks, but had 4 of 8 for Asians, 3 of 8 for whites, and 6 of 8 for other Latinos, blacks would be ranked second in terms of commonality. In full, we use eight variables specifically related to race. Finally, we include a new measure that controls for the respondent's self-identified phenotype—an interesting question rarely included on surveys of Latinos (Sawyer, Peña, and Sidanius 2004). *Black Skin* is a dummy variable that measures whether Latino respondents described themselves as having very dark or dark skin.

In addition to measures of social interaction and group commonality, we also include many standard variables employed in racial and ethnic politics to test cultural-based hypotheses, which include religion (*Catholic*), *Immigrant Generation*, *Immigrant Neighborhood*, *Spanish Usage*, *Latino Linked Fate*, importance of *Maintaining Latino Culture*, and *Identification as American*. With respect to political variables, we include *Interest in Politics*, *Political Knowledge Index*, and *Party Identification*. Standard demographic and resource variables, such as *Age*, *Education*, *Income*, *Gender*, *Marital Status*, and *Home Owner* status, are included in our models. Here, we are particularly interested in class-based variables such as income and also evaluation of personal financial situation and employment status. Additionally, we include Latino national origin to account for differences among the major nationalities represented in the LNS sample. Specifically, we control for Mexican, Cuban, and Puerto Rican. Finally, we control for state-level variables in the South-only model to capture variation in immigrant perceptions of African Americans and other Latinos. Using North Carolina as a baseline, we control for Arkansas, Georgia, and Virginia. Complete coding instructions for all independent variables can be found in the appendix for this chapter (available online at http://www.russellsage.org/telles_sawyer_online_appendix.pdf).

DESCRIPTIVE RESULTS: RELATIVE MEASURE OF PERCEIVED COMPETITION TRENDS

We begin our investigation by examining the descriptive frequencies of our relative black-brown competition measure for Latino immigrants. Figure 3.1 strongly suggests that the relative competition measure provides a clearer picture of black-brown competition than those used previously. For example, a greater segment of the immigrant population views other Latinos as a source of competition (43 percent) than they do African Americans (32 percent), with a quarter of the sample seeing no difference between the two. When analyzing perceptions of competition across generational status, as depicted in figure 3.2, we find a clear linear pattern whereby foreign-born noncitizens perceive the least competition with blacks. As Latinos be-

Figure 3.1   Relative Scale of Black-Brown Competition
Among Latino Immigrants

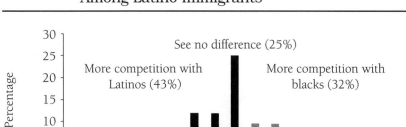

Source: Authors' calculations based on data from the 2006 Latino National Survey (Fraga et al. 2006).

come more assimilated and move away from the immigrant experience, however, perceptions of competition toward African Americans begin to increase, with fourth-generation Latinos perceiving the most competition with blacks. This preliminary finding contradicts several extant theories cited in our literature which contend that Latino immigrants tend to have more negative attitudes toward blacks than their native-born counterparts.

Providing preliminary support for our relative competition and immigrant competition hypotheses, and supporting the trends from figures 3.1 and 3.2, comparisons of means based on nativity show differences between foreign- and native-born Latinos as well. Using the nonrelative measure, the average response for native- and foreign-born Latinos is 7.7 and 7.4, respectively, suggesting that competition with African Americans is moderately high across both groups. However, once in-group competition is taken into consideration with respect to competition with African Americans, Latino perceptions with African Americans become significantly tempered. In fact, the results demonstrate that immigrants are more likely to perceive competition with other Latinos than with African Americans. Overall, these initial findings from the LNS data set strongly support our relative competition and immigration hypotheses.

Figure 3.2 Perception of Black-Brown Competition (Mean)

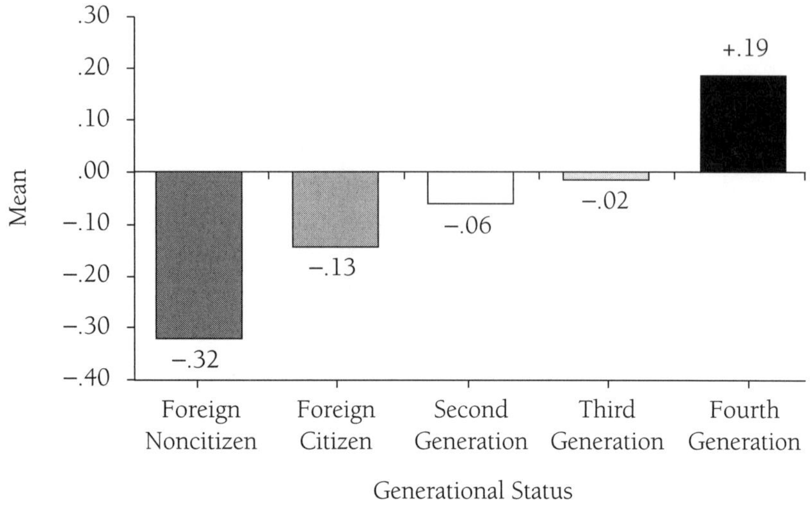

Source: Authors' calculations based on data from the 2006 Latino National Survey (Fraga et al. 2006).

MULTIVARIATE RESULTS: PERCEIVED COMPETITION AMONG LATINO IMMIGRANTS

The next stage of our analysis focuses on explaining immigrant perceptions of competition, a segment of the Latino population that the literature suggests to have more stereotypical views toward African Americans. Online appendix table 3.A2 contains results for two OLS regression models. The first regression in column 1 uses the nonrelative measure of competition—that is, only perceived competition with blacks, without taking perceived competition with Latinos into account. The second regression in column 2 is of primary interest because it uses the relative measure of competition that ranges from −8 to +8.

The models comparing the two measures of competition among Latino immigrants reveal some notable differences. In the relative model of black-brown competition (column 2), *Black Worker* is significant and positive. Latino immigrants with greater numbers of black coworkers are more likely to perceive competition with African

Americans. Highlighting this relationship, for example, figure 3.3, shows that the probability of greater perceptions of competition toward African Americans is about 65 percent higher for Latino immigrants who work with African Americans than for foreign-born Latinos who do not. Although the social interactions of a shared work environment between blacks and Latinos promote competitiveness between racial groups, we contend that this does not necessarily lead to negative stereotypes or conflict. In fact, it makes intuitive sense that Latino immigrants who work in labor markets alongside African Americans are more likely to view African Americans as a source of competition, just as lawyers are likely to see other lawyers as competitors.

This finding is reinforced by the relationship between perceived commonality and perceptions of competition. For example, *Black Commonality* is significant and positive (columns 1 and 2). Latino immigrants who say that they have a great deal in common with blacks in the areas of jobs, education, income, and politics are more likely to perceive competition with African Americans. This finding is further supported by figure 3.4, which demonstrates a strong progression in the predicted probability between immigrants' perceptions of commonality with African Americans and our relative competition measure. Specifically, as perceptions of commonality with African Americans increase, the predicted probability moves from −.79 to .059 suggesting that the probability of perceiving competition with African Americans is much greater for immigrants who say they have a lot in common with other African Americans than for those who say they have some, little, or none at all. *Rank Black* is also significant in both models. In the nonrelative competition model, Latino immigrants who feel they are closer to African Americans relative to other racial and ethnic groups are more likely to perceive competition with African Americans. We speak more about the implications of these findings in our concluding remarks. The relative model of competition, however, demonstrates that perceptions of competition toward African Americans become significantly tempered once competition with other Latinos is taken into account. In fact, perceptions of closeness with African Americans decrease perceptions of competition with other African Americans.

Cultural variables also highlight the importance of including a relative measure of competition as well. For example, *Linked Fate* is

Figure 3.3 Probability of Black-Brown Competition Among Immigrants, by Black Coworkers

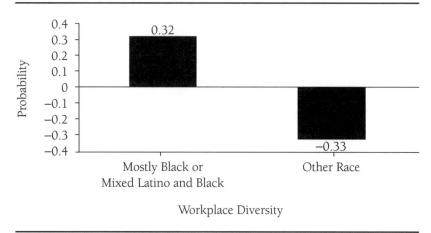

Source: Authors' calculations based on data from the 2006 Latino National Survey (Fraga et al. 2006).

Figure 3.4 Probability of Black-Brown Competition Among Immigrants, by Perceptions of Commonality with African Americans

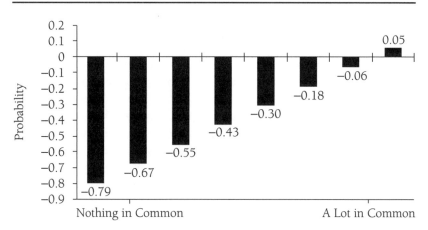

Source: Authors' calculations based on data from the 2006 Latino National Survey (Fraga et al. 2006).

PERCEPTIONS OF COMPETITION

significant in both models, but has differing effects in each. Latinos with a strong sense of linked fate have high perceptions of competition with blacks when competition with blacks is isolated. In the relative competition model however, *Linked Fate* becomes negative, suggesting that Latinos with a strong sense of linked fate are less likely to view competition with African Americans relative to perceived competition with other Latinos. This finding directly confirms our relative competition hypothesis and our more general argument that the relative perceived competition measure adds significantly to our working understanding of intergroup attitudes among Latinos and African Americans. Similarly, the sign of the coefficient for our *American ID* measure switches as well from model 1 to model 2. In the first regression model, Latino immigrants with a high sense of American identity are more likely to view competition with blacks. However, in the relative competition model, identifying primarily as American results in less perceived competition with blacks than with other Latinos. Although insignificant in the nonrelative model, *Catholic* is significant and positive once in-group competition is taken into consideration. Latinos who identify themselves as Catholic are more likely to maintain heightened perceptions of competition with African Americans than with Latinos. Finally, a number of cultural variables are significant in the nonrelative model (column 1) but fail to achieve significance in the relative competition model. For instance, *Maintain Culture* is significant and positive, suggesting that Latino immigrants who believe it is important to maintain the Spanish culture are more likely to hold perceptions of competition with other Latinos. Likewise, immigrants who are more affluent in the Spanish language and Latinos who have more Spanish services in their communities are more likely to perceive heightened levels of competition with African Americans. These last findings suggest that when multiple groups are taken into consideration, perceptions of competition with African Americans are not as strongly held as originally thought.

In addition to cultural factors, online appendix table 3.A1 reveals that, with the exception of *Party ID* in the nonrelative model of competition, none of the political factors are significantly correlated with perceptions of competition in either context. Still, *Party ID* presents an interesting outcome, as those who identify more strongly with the Democratic Party are more likely to perceive a sense of competition with African Americans. The finding makes intuitive sense, as well

Figure 3.5 Probability of Black-Brown Competition Among Immigrants, by Region

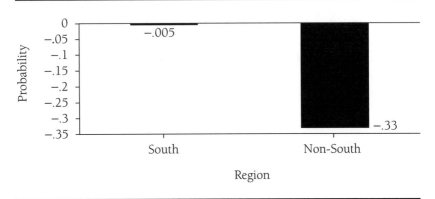

Source: Authors' calculations based on data from the 2006 Latino National Survey (Fraga et al. 2006).

over 80 percent of African Americans identify themselves as being affiliated with the Democratic Party. Similar to common economic circumstances, individuals who share political interests and goals are likely to see one another as competitors for scarce resources.

The model also shows support for the southern hypothesis, which states that the unique demography and racialized history of the southern region will heighten perceptions of completion for Latinos in those states. Confirming the study by McClain and her colleagues (2006) of immigrants in North Carolina, the relative model of competition reveals a significant relationship for the *South* variable, indicating that Latino immigrants in this region are more likely to maintain perceptions of competition with blacks. Illustrating this finding in further detail, figure 3.5 shows that perceptions of competition toward African Americans are much (.33) higher for Latino immigrants living in the South than for immigrants living across other regions of the United States. Not only do these results fall in line with the major McClain findings, but the relative measure of group competition provides a more exhaustive test for understanding group dynamics in the South.

Last, we examine the impact of resource variables on the perceptions of competition among Latino immigrants. In the nonrelative competition model (column 1), *Age* is significant and positive, suggesting that perceived competition with blacks is greater among older

Latinos. *Married* is also significant, but the sign of the coefficient is negative, suggesting that perceptions of competition with African Americans are less among those who are married. Important differences occur, however, when we include perceptions of competition with coethnics in our relative competition model depicted in column 2. Although *Age* and *Married* are found to be insignificant, the results from the relative competition model also indicate that several resource variables that were not significantly correlated with Latino immigrant perceptions of competition when African Americans were isolated are now meaningful. For example, *Education* is significant and negative, suggesting that Latinos with higher levels of education are more likely to view fellow Latinos as competitors, and, conversely, perceptions of competition with African Americans are more likely among Latinos with lower levels of education. The relative competition model also shows that *Financial Situation* is significant and positive. Therefore, Latino immigrants who indicate that their financial situation has improved recently are more likely to perceive competition with African Americans than with other Latinos.

Finally, important differences occur between national-origin subgroups. In both models of competition *Mexican* is significant and negative, indicating that this group is less likely to view blacks as a source of competition than are Latinos from other backgrounds. In fact, once in-group competition is taken into account (model 2), the results show that Mexicans are more likely to perceive competition with other Latinos relative to competition with blacks. These findings make intuitive sense given the proximity of the Mexican border to regions of the United States, where fewer African Americans typically live. *Cuban* is also significant in both models of competition. In the nonrelative model, Cubans are less likely to perceive competition with African Americans relative to other Latinos. In the nonrelative competition model, however, the positive coefficient suggests that Cubans are more likely to perceive competition with African Americans relative to other Latinos.

LATINO PERCEPTIONS OF COMPETITION IN THE SOUTH

In the next stage of the analysis, we turn our attention to Latino perceptions of competition with African Americans relative to other Latinos in the South—where the Latino population is growing rapidly.

The descriptive analysis discussed to this point has indicated that Latino immigrants are more likely to view coethnics as a source of competition than blacks. However, figure 3.6 reveals that perceptions of competition among Latinos differ in the South, where they are more likely to view African Americans as competitors than other Latinos. Specifically, 38 percent of southern Latinos perceive more competition with African Americans, 37 percent perceive more competition with other Latinos, and the remaining 25 percent see no difference in competition between both groups. Using both measures of competition, table 3.1 compares the average perceptions of competition among Latinos in the South with Latinos living elsewhere in the United States. In line with the southern hypothesis and the results of the immigrant model, the results indicate significant differences based on region, as Latinos living in the southern states are more likely to view African Americans as competitors. Perceptions of competition also vary in important ways by state. Compared with other states across the country, Latinos living in Arkansas and North Carolina are more likely to view African Americans as competitors. The discussion of the sociopolitical histories of both states in chapter 7 of this volume is particularly helpful in understanding the context behind the trends we find here.

Figure 3.6 Relative Scale of Black-Brown Competition
        Among Latino Immigrants in the South

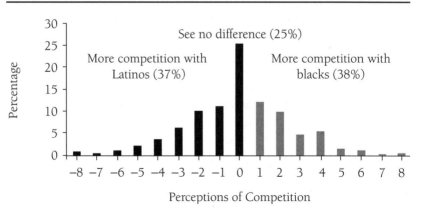

Source: Authors' calculations based on data from the 2006 Latino National Survey (Fraga et al. 2006).

Table 3.1 Perception of Black-Brown Competition, Mean

All South	0.0537***
Arkansas	0.1296***
Georgia	–0.0225
North Carolina	0.1546**
Virginia	–0.1761
Non-South	–0.2279***
Arizona	–0.5800***
California	–0.2948
District of Colombia	–0.1129
Florida	–0.0800
New York	–0.07
Texas	–0.5006***

Source: Authors' calculations based on data from the 2006 Latino National Survey (Fraga et al. 2006).
Note: We test for significance differences between the South and Non-South as well as differences between each state.
$*p < .10; **p < .05, ***p < .01.$

Online appendix table 3.A3 presents results for ordinary least squares (OLS) regressions for all Latinos living in the South. The first regression in column 1 again uses the nonrelative measure of competition that focuses only on perceived competition with blacks. The second regression in column 2 uses the relative measure of competition, which takes into account perceptions of competition with other Latinos and African Americans. When moving from the model isolating perceptions of competition among blacks (column 1) to the relative measure of competition (column 2), several interesting trends emerge.

The nonrelative competition model shows that *Black Workers* and *Black Crime* are significant and positive, suggesting that Latinos who work predominately with blacks or who are victims of a crime committed by an African American are more likely to perceive competition with blacks. Once competition with other Latinos is taken into account, however, these indicators of social interaction are no longer statistically significant. The relative competition model further demonstrates that perceptions of competition depend on the quality or type of social interaction. Interestingly, *Black Friends* has a significant and negative relationship with perceptions of competition (model 2). Whereas *Black Workers* and *Black Crime* are associated with more negative experiences with blacks, friendly interactions with African Americans significantly temper negative attitudes and heighten per-

Figure 3.7 Probability of Black-Brown Competition Among Latinos in the South, by Black Friends

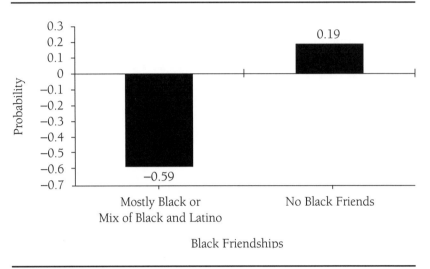

Black Friendships

Source: Authors' calculations based on data from the 2006 Latino National Survey (Fraga et al. 2006).

ceptions of competition with other Latinos. As figure 3.7 illustrates, friendships with African Americans can have a significant and important effect on perceptions of competition with African Americans and Latinos in the South. For example, the graph suggests that the probability of perceiving competition with African Americans is much higher for Latinos who say they have no black friends than for Latinos who do. The results also demonstrate that perceptions of commonality with African Americans also matter, but lose their effect once perceptions of competition with Latinos are taken into consideration. In the nonrelative competition model, *Black Commonality* is significant and positive. Latinos who feel that they have more in common with African Americans are more likely to perceive competition with other African Americans. Likewise, the finding is supported by the significant and positive association between *Rank Black* and perceived competition, as Latinos who feel closer to African Americans are more likely to perceive competition with other blacks.

In addition to indicators of social interaction with African Americans, cultural variables also matter, but vary according to measure of competition. For instance, *Latino Linked Fate* is significant and positive in the nonrelative competition model but fails to achieve statistical significance once in-group competition is taken into account. Thus Latinos who feel that doing well depends on other Latinos doing well are more likely to view more competition with African Americans. *American ID* is also significant, but only in the relative competition model, which considers competition with both Latinos and African Americans. The negative coefficient suggests that Latinos who identify strongly as being American are more likely to perceive competition with Latinos.

Resource variables also matter, but once again vary according to which measure of competition is used. In the nonrelative model of competition, *Married* is significant and negative, suggesting that Latinos who identify as being married are more likely to perceive competition with African Americans. *Years Address* is also significant, but only after competition with other Latinos is taken into consideration. Capturing financial stability, the positive coefficient suggests that perceptions of competition with African Americans are more likely to increase the longer Latinos live in their home. Among national-origin variables, *Mexican* and *Cuban* are significant and negative in the nonrelative competition model. Thus Latinos who identify as Mexican or Cuban in the South are less likely to maintain perceptions of competition with African Americans. In the relative competition model, only *Mexican* remains significant. Thus, similar to our foreign-only sample, Latinos who identify as Mexican are more likely to hold perceptions of competition with other Latinos.

Finally, we control for differences between states within the southern region of the United States. Given the findings of McClain and colleagues (2006) in North Carolina, as well as our descriptive statistics showing Latinos in North Carolina to have the highest perceptions of competition across the South, we decided to use North Carolina as a baseline. The purpose of this comparison is to examine whether perceptions of competition in North Carolina are representative of other states in the South. In the nonrelative competition model, all state-related variables are insignificant, and in the relative competition model, Latino perceptions of competition in Arkansas and Georgia do not significantly differ from Latino attitudes in North Carolina. However, *Virginia* is significant and negative, presenting itself as a unique case. Despite having a large African American population, the results from the South-only model demonstrate that Latinos in Virginia are more likely than those in

North Carolina to perceive competition with other Latinos than with African Americans. These trends make it clear that it is not only imperative for scholars to control for region when exploring intergroup relations, it is also necessary to account for individual states whenever possible.

CONCLUSION AND DISCUSSION

The relationships between Latinos and African Americans have become more critical as changing demographics have increased interactions among the nation's two largest minority groups. The 2008 presidential election highlighted the impact that black-brown attitudes can have on political outcomes. At the outset of the contest, misguided observers speculated that Latinos would not vote for a black candidate because of the simmering tensions and competition between the two groups. The primary election results helped fuel this rhetoric among political pundits, and Barack Obama lost by large numbers in several states with high Latino populations. In the end, this sense of black-brown competition proved both fabricated and exaggerated. Latino voters preferred Hillary Clinton, in large part because of her high name recognition, extensive Latino outreach, and prominent endorsements from Latino officials.[4] After the final votes had been cast, the media noted that Hispanic voters had been critical to the Obama victory, delivering a 70 percent vote share to the Democratic candidate, noticeably more than the two previous Democrats running for president had garnered. In this chapter, we argue that claims of mounting competition over public policy, elected office, jobs, and education are far overstated. Using the most comprehensive data set of Latino adults to date—the Latino National Survey—we demonstrate that traditional measures of black-brown competition are flawed because they lack a basis for comparison.

In our view, the most significant contribution from this analysis is the implementation of the relative competition measure. Our results strongly suggest that observed competitive attitudes toward blacks among Latinos are muted significantly when Latino perceptions of competition with African Americans are viewed in light of perceptions of internal competition. Frequencies of our relative competition dependent variable for the Latino immigrant sample indicate that Latinos see coethnics as a greater source of competition than African Americans. Trends from our multivariate models also indicate that the relative measure of competition provides a more clear interpretation of factors that contribute to intergroup attitudes. Several variables that appear to lead to greater perceptions of competition with blacks when a comparison group is not included either become insignificant or switch direction when perceptions of competition with other Latinos are accounted for. This we believe adds significantly to our working knowledge of black-brown relations by strongly suggesting that Latino attitudes toward African Americans are not as hostile as once thought.

Although it is clear that Latinos do have some sense of competition with African Americans, they also have a good deal of commonality. Furthermore, the relationship between these two attitudes is positive, in that Latinos who see more commonality between Latinos and African Americans are also more likely to perceive competition with blacks. We believe this to be evidence that perceived competition is not racially motivated or necessarily negative, but rather a realistic observation of a political and social environment. Thus, we believe that perceptions of competition should not be viewed as inherently negative, but as a somewhat natural outcome of increased interaction and shared disadvantaged status. The overall success of the Obama campaign, and the specific success of the Latino outreach, highlighted the possibility of a broad minority coalition based on these shared interests and circumstances.

Relying on the rich sample sizes and depth of the LNS, our analysis reveals several interesting trends that contribute to our knowledge of black-brown relations. For example, we find that Latino immigrants are actually more likely to perceive high levels of competition with other Latinos than with African Americans. This, we believe, helps clarify the relationship between nativity and racial attitudes often discussed in the literature. Finally, it appears as though black-brown relations in the South are distinct from those in other regions. Our results from the LNS therefore tend to support the work being done by Paula McClain and others interested in the demographic changes taking place in the South, in that we find that Latinos in southern states view blacks as a greater source of competition than other Latinos. However, results from our South-only model suggest that these perceptions of competition can be overcome with positive social interactions, such as having black friends. Given the changing demographics and historical racial paradigm in that region, scholars interested in black-brown relations should continue to explore these dynamics.

Finally, although we believe our new measure has tremendous implications on future work exploring intergroup relations, this chapter has focused largely on subgroups of the Latino population, specifically the foreign-born and immigrant segments. More important, we have examined only the viewpoints of Latinos toward blacks. Because Latinos are now the largest minority group in America, surpassing African Americans in thirty states, it may be that blacks actually view more competition with Latinos than Latinos do with blacks. Further, as the racial and ethnic demography of the country continues to evolve, it will be critical to include other populations, including Asians, in these discussions. Although lack of reliable data is an obstacle, future studies should use measures similar to that we introduce here to provide a frame of reference for intergroup attitudes whenever possible, as well as to examine multiple groups simultaneously to fully understand the ever-evolving dynamics of race relations in the United States.

NOTES

1. We use the terms *Latino* and *Hispanic* interchangeably throughout the chapter.
2. Although Florida could arguably be included among other southern states in our analysis, we decided to remove this state due to the high concentration of the LNS Florida sample coming from the Miami metropolitan area. We believe that the demographic and historical realties of this area do not lend themselves to a test of southern regional dynamics.
3. For example, the question might have read, "Some have suggested that Puerto Ricans are in competition with other Latinos. After each of the next items, would you tell me if you believe there is strong competition, weak competition, or no competition at all with other Latinos."
4. Matt Barreto and Ricardo Ramirez, "The Clinton Vote Is Pro-Clinton, not Anti-Obama," *Los Angeles Times*, February 7, 2008 (available at: http://www.latimes.com/news/opinion/la-oew-barreto7feb07,0,6253659.story [accessed May 9, 2011]); Barreto et al. 2008).

REFERENCES

Alozie, Nicholas O., and Enrique Ramirez. 1999. "'A Piece of the Pie' and More: Competition and Hispanic Employment on Urban Police Forces." *Urban Affairs Review* 34(3): 456–75.
Barreto, Matt, Luis Fraga, Sylvia Manzano, Valerie Martinez-Ebers, and Gary Segura. 2008. "Should They Dance with the One Who Brung 'Em? Lati-

nos and the 2008 Presidential Election." *PS: Political Science and Politics* 41(4): 753–60.

Barreto, Matt, and Gabriel Sanchez. 2008. "Social and Political Competition Between Latinos and Blacks: Exposing Myths, Uncovering New Realities." Paper presented at the Latino National Survey Conference. Cornell University (November 2–3, 2007).

Betancur, John J., and Douglas C. Gills, eds. 2000. *The Collaborative City: Opportunities and Struggles for Blacks and Latinos in U.S. Cities.* New York: Garland Publishing.

Bobo, Lawrence D., and Vincent Hutchings. 1996. "Perceptions of Racial Group Competition: Extending Blumer's Theory of Group Position to a Multiracial Social Context." *American Sociological Review* 61(6): 951–72.

Bobo, Lawrence D., and Michael P. Massagli. 2001. "Stereotyping and Urban Inequality." In *Urban Inequality*, edited by Alice O'Connor, Chris Tilly, and Lawrence D. Bobo. New York: Russell Sage Foundation.

Bobo, Lawrence D., Camile L. Zubrinsky, James Johnson, and Melvin L. Oliver. 1994. "Public Opinion Before and After a Spring of Discontent." In *The Los Angeles Riots: Lessons from the Urban Future*, edited by Mark Baldassare. Boulder, Colo.: Westview Press.

de la Cadena, Marisol. 2001. "Reconstructing Race: Racism, Culture, and Mestizaje in Latin America." *NACLA Report on the Americas* 34(6): 16–23.

Dulitzky, Ariel E. 2005. "A Region in Denial: Racial Discrimination and Racism in Latin America." In *Neither Enemies nor Friends: Latinos, Blacks, Afro-Latinos*, edited by Anani Dzidzienyo and Suzanne Oboler. New York: Palgrave-Macmillan.

Dyer, James, Arnold Vedlitz, and Stephen Worchel. 1989. "Social Distance Among Racial and Ethnic Groups." *Social Science Quarterly* 70(3): 607–16.

Fraga, Luis R., John A. Garcia, Rodney Hero, Michael Jones-Correa, Valerie Martinez-Ebers, and Gary M. Segura. 2006. *Latino National Survey (LNS), 2006* [Computer file]. ICPSR20862-v4. Ann Arbor, Mich.: Inter-university Consortium for Political and Social Research [distributor]. Available at http://dx.doi.org/10.3886/ICPSR20862 (accessed September 19, 2009).

Frisbie, W. Parker, and Lisa J. Niedert. 1977. "Inequality and the Relative Size of Minority Populations: A Comparative Analysis." *American Journal of Sociology* 82(5): 1007–30.

Garcia, F. Chris, and Gabriel R. Sanchez. 2008. *Hispanics and the U.S. Political System.* Upper Saddle River, N.J.: Prentice Hall.

Gay, Claudine. 2004. "Putting Race in Context: Identifying the Environmental Determinants of Black Racial Attitudes." *American Political Science Review* 98(4): 547–62.

Glaser, James. 1994. "Back to the Black Belt: Racial Environment and White Racial Hostility in the South." *Journal of Politics* 56(1): 21–41.

Guimaraes, Antonio Sergio. 2001. "Race, Class, and Color: Behind Brazil's 'Racial Democracy.'" *NACLA Report on the Americas* 34(6): 38–41.

Gutiérrez, David. 1995. *Walls and Mirrors: Mexican Americans, Mexican Immigrants, and the Politics of Ethnicity*. Berkeley: University of California Press.

Guzman, Betsy. 2001. *The Hispanic Population: Census 2000 Brief.* Washington: U.S. Department of Commerce. Available at: http://www.census.gov/prod/2001pubs/c2kbr01-3.pdf (accessed July 20, 2011).

Hanchard, Michael G. 1994. *Orpheus and Power: The Movimento Negro of Rio de Janeiro and São Paulo, Brazil, 1945–1988*. Princeton, N.J.: Princeton University Press.

Jennings, James. 2003. *Welfare Reform and the Revitalization of Inner City Neighborhoods*. East Lansing: Michigan State University Press.

Johnson, James H., Jr., Walter C. Farrell Jr., and Chandra Guinn. 1997. "Immigration Reform and the Browning of America: Tensions, Conflicts, and Community Instability in Metropolitan Los Angeles." *International Migration Review* 31(4): 1055–95.

Johnson, James, and Melvin Oliver. 1989. "Interethnic Minority Conflict in Urban America: The Effects of Economic and Social Dislocations." *Urban Geography* 10(5): 449–63.

Jones-Correa, Michael. 2001. "Institutional and Contextual Factors in Immigrant Naturalization and Voting." *Citizenship Studies* 5(1): 41–56.

Kaufmann, Karen. 2005. "Divided We Stand: Mass Attitudes and the Prospects for Black-Latina/o Urban Political Coalitions." In *Black and Latina/o Politics: Issues in Political Development in the United States*, edited by William E. Nelson Jr. and Jessica Pérez-Monforti. Miami, Fla.: Barnhardt and Ashe Publishing.

Keefe, Susan, and Amado Padilla. 1987. *Chicano Ethnicity*. Albuquerque: University of New Mexico Press.

Kerr, Brinck, Will Miller, and Margeret Reid. 2000. "The Changing Face of Urban Bureaucracy: Is There Inter-Ethnic Competition for Municipal Government Jobs?" *Urban Affairs Review* 35(6): 770–93.

Kochhar, Rakesh, Roberto Suro, and Sonya Tafoya. 2005. "The New Latino South: The Context and Consequences of Rapid Population Growth." Pew Hispanic Center Report. Washington, D.C.: Pew Research Center.

Massey, Douglas S., and Nancy A. Denton. 1993. *American Apartheid*. Cambridge, Mass.: Harvard University Press.

McClain, Paula D., Niambi M. Carter, Victoria M. DeFrancesco Soto, Monique L. Lyle, Jeffrey D. Grynaviski, Shayla C. Nunnally, Thomas J. Scotto, J. Alan Kendrick, Gerald F. Lackey, and Kendra Davenport Cotton. 2006. "Racial Distancing in a Southern City: Latino Immigrants' Views of Black Americans." *Journal of Politics* 68(3): 571–84.

Mindiola, Tatcho, Jr., Yolanda Flores Niemann, and Nestor Rodriguez. 2003. *Black-Brown Relations and Stereotypes*. Austin: University of Texas Press.

Mörner, Magnus, ed. 1967. *Race Mixture in the History of Latin America*. Boston, Mass.: Little, Brown.

Oliver, Melvin L., and James H. Johnson Jr. 1984. "Interethnic Conflict in an Urban Ghetto: The Case of Blacks and Latinos in Los Angeles." *Research in Social Movements, Conflict, and Change* 6(1): 57–94.

Oliver, J. Eric, and Tali Mendelberg. 2000. "Reconsidering the Environmental Determinants of White Racial Attitudes." *American Journal of Political Science* 44(3): 574–89.

Oliver, J. Eric, and Janelle Wong. 2003. "Intergroup Prejudice in Multiethnic Settings." *American Journal of Political Science* 47(4): 567–82.

Passel, Jeffrey S., and D'Vera Cohn. 2008. "U.S. Population Projections: 2005–2050." Washington, D.C.: Pew Research Center. Available at: http://www.pewhispanic.org/files/reports/85.pdf (accessed July 20, 2011).

Powers, Daniel A., and Christopher G. Ellison. 1995. "Interracial Contact and Black Racial Attitudes: The Contact Hypothesis and Selectivity Bias." *Social Forces* 74(1): 205–26.

Rodrigues, Helena Alves, and Gary M. Segura. 2004. "A Place at the Lunch Counter: Latinos, African-Americans, and the Dynamics of American Race Politics." Presented at the conference Latino Politics: The State of the Discipline. Texas A&M University (April 30–May 1, 2004).

Rodriguez, Nestor, and Rogelio T. Nuñez. 1986. "An Exploration of Factors That Contribute to Differentiation Between Chicanos and Indocumentados." In *Mexican Immigrants and Mexican Americans: An Evolving Relation*, edited by Harley L. Browning and Rodolfo O. de la Garza. Austin: University of Texas Press.

Sawyer, Mark Q., Yesilernis Peña, and James Sidanius. 2004. "Cuban Exceptionalism: Group-Based Hierarchy and the Dynamics of Patriotism in Puerto Rico, the Dominican Republic, and Cuba." *Du Bois Review* 1(1): 93–114.

Sigelman, Lee, and Susan Welch. 1993. "The Contact Hypothesis Revisited: Black-White Interaction and Positive Racial Attitudes." *Social Forces* 71(3): 781–95.

Sweet, James H. 1997. "The Iberian Roots of American Racist Thought." *William and Mary Quarterly* 54(1): 143–66.

Taylor, Marylee C. 1998. "How White Attitudes Vary with the Racial Composition of Local Populations: Numbers Count." *American Sociological Review* 63(4): 512–35.

Torres, Cruz C. 2000. "Emerging Latino Communities: A New Challenge for the Rural South." *Southern Rural Development Center* 12(August): 1–8.

Wade, Peter. 1993. *Blackness and Race Mixture: The Dynamics of Racial Identity in Colombia*. Baltimore, Md.: Johns Hopkins University Press.

———. 1997. *Race and Ethnicity in Latin America*. London: Pluto Press.

Welch, Susan, Lee Sigelman, Timothy Bledsoe, and Michael Combs. 2001. *Race and Place: Race Relations in an American City*. New York: Cambridge University Press.

Winant, Howard. 1992. "Rethinking Race in Brazil." *Journal of Latin American Studies* 24(1): 173–92.

Wright, Gerald. 1977. "Contextual Models of Electoral Behavior: The Southern Wallace Vote." *American Political Science Review* 71(2): 497–508.

CHAPTER 4

Elite Messages and Perceptions of Commonality

Kevin Wallsten and Tatishe M. Nteta

Like much of the twentieth century, the first decade of the twenty-first witnessed a number of conflicts between African Americans and Latinos over scarce resources such as private- and public-sector employment, political power, schools, and housing. Many of these conflicts took place in America's urban centers, which have experienced a number of divisive and at times violent incidents involving African Americans and Latinos in city council meetings, school board gatherings, and political campaigns (McClain and Karnig 1990; Meier and Stewart 1991; Meier et al. 2004; Vaca 2004).

Unsurprisingly, the evolving relationship between the Latino and African American communities has attracted the attention of political leaders from across the ideological spectrum. What is somewhat surprising, however, are the clear differences in the way liberal and conservative elites address the increasingly complex interactions between these two groups. In an attempt to downplay and potentially diffuse conflicts between Latinos and African Americans, liberal political elites have chosen to focus attention on the shared circumstances, issues, and interests of the two communities. In a 2008 campaign speech to the National Association of Latino Elected and Appointed Officials, for example, Barack Obama said,

> We [African Americans and Latinos] stood together when I was an organizer, lifting up neighborhoods in Chicago that had been devastated when the local steel plants closed. We stood together when I was a civil rights attorney, working with MALDEF and local Latino elected officials to ensure that Latinos were being well represented in Chicago. And we marched together in the streets of Chicago to fix our broken immigration system. That's why you can trust me when I say that I'll be your partner in the White House.

Similarly, Sonia Perez, then deputy vice president for research at the National Council of La Raza, claimed, "Rather than comparing groups we should be looking at the status of communities. When you look at Latino and African-American communities, the elements of the agendas are not that different. We share many of the same issues, interests and values."[1] Echoing these sentiments, Hector Flores, president of the League of United Latin American Citizens, said, "We're [Latinos and African Americans] compatible in the things we are seeking: equal opportunities, better education for our children, the right to buy a home, affirmative action, justice."[2] As table 4.1 further illustrates, high-profile political leaders on the left have consistently used their rhetoric to emphasize the socioeconomic and political similarities between Latinos and African Americans.

Standing in marked contrast to the approach of liberal political leaders, conservative elites have frequently used their words to paint a picture of Latino-black relations characterized by conflict, competition, and division. For instance, Linda Chavez, a conservative media commentator, wrote,

> Hispanics are steadily moving into the social and economic mainstream. They have leapfrogged blacks on almost every measure of social and economic status. Yet Hispanic leaders seem more intent on vying with blacks for permanent victim status than they do on acknowledging genuine Hispanic achievement. . . . The Hispanic future lies in recognizing that the vast majority of Hispanics can—and do— make it in this country. It is a future that increasingly has little to do with the civil rights rhetoric of a bygone era. (1990, 16)

A similar view was expressed by Didi Lima, the former Republican communications director of Clark County in Nevada and co-chair of Senator John McCain's Nevada Hispanic Leadership Team, when she claimed, "We don't want [Latinos] to become the new African American community. And that's what the Democratic Party is going to do to them [Latinos], create more programs and give them handouts, food stamps, and checks for this and checks for that. We don't want that."[3] In a somewhat more laconic statement of this view, Fernando de Baca, the former chairman of the Republican Party in Bernalillo County in New Mexico, asserted that "the truth is that Hispanics came here as conquerors. African Americans came here as slaves."[4]

Table 4.1 Liberal Political Elites on Commonality Between Latino and African American Communities

Reverend. Martin Luther King Jr.	"Our separate struggles are really one–a struggle for freedom, for dignity, and for humanity."
Hilary Shelton, director of the Washington bureau of the NAACP	"We have as much or more in common than any two ethnic or racial groups in the country, and that's because of the phenomenon of racial discrimination and how it affects our community."
Antonio Villaraigosa, mayor of Los Angeles	"I'm just another shade of brown."
Al Sharpton, former presidential candidate	"We are not each other's enemies. We're not even each other's friends. We are the same family. We may speak a different language, have a different skin texture, but we are in the same house. And if the house burns down we are all going to die together."
Governor Bill Richardson	"Parties think well they [African Americans and Latinos] only care about immigration or civil rights or affirmative action. I think what is one of the most fundamental misconceptions about minorities is that we care about all issues. We care about health care and education. We care about moving this country forward."
Senator John Edwards 2007	"I think we have a wall that's been built around Washington, D.C. And no one understands that wall better than African Americans and Latinos in America. Because you have been left on the outside of that wall. And that wall has been built by people with money and power to protect their own interests. And to make sure that their interests are taken care of and not the interests of the vast majority of the American people."

Table 4.1 (*cont.*)

Julian Bond, former NAACP chairman	"It's obvious that there is a growing population of Hispanics in the United States and they have been and will be allies and partners in the fight for civil rights."
Senator Bob Menendez (Democrat, New Jersey)	Today, all students do not have an equal chance to attend college. Latinos and African Americans are less likely to be able to afford college, and are 40 to 60 percent less likely to earn a bachelor's degree in their lifetime than white students. By expanding federal aid opportunities for minorities, this bill will help improve those numbers and close a critical gap in higher education.
Ana Yaez-Correa, acting executive director of Texas LULAC	"Our socioeconomic conditions are on the same kinds of levels. Academically, our children are in trouble. Both populations are [disproportionately] in prison. We're dropping out [of school] the most. We don't have the means and the resources."

Source: Authors' compilation.

Each of these statements (as well as those made by other conservative political leaders listed in table 4.2) emphasizes the belief that Latinos have little in common with African Americans, that notions of commonality have been fabricated by liberal elites, and that the Latino community would be best served by severing any ties with the African American community.

These competing perspectives concerning commonality with African Americans presented by Latino political elites raise the question of whether elite rhetoric about commonality with African Americans influences the attitudes of the Latino community. Unfortunately, little research has explored the extent to which such assertions are picked up by Latinos in the general public. Indeed, a number of studies have addressed the individual-level determinants of Latino perceptions of commonality with African Americans (Kaufmann 2003a; Rodrigues and Segura 2003; Sanchez 2004; Nicholson, Pantoja, and Segura 2005); and in this volume chapter 2 examines the impact of acculturation and state residence (new immigrant-receiving state versus traditional immigrant-receiving state) on Latino perceptions of com-

Table 4.2 Conservative Political Elites on Commonality Between Latino and African American Communities

Orlando Sanchez, Republican candidate for mayor of Houston	"And on everyday issues, I think that Republicans and Hispanics are in lock step. . . . [Blacks] have voted as a bloc and been stuck in the promises of the Great Society and told that it is taboo to break out of that pack."
Orlando Sanchez, former Republican candidate for mayor of Houston	"They see the pie as finite and limited. If an Hispanic gets in, they see a diminution of services, but it really isn't that way at all."
Clara Nibot, head of the Bergen County Hispanic Republican Organization	"African Americans have drawn the line in the sand." "If there was ever any doubt about their intentions to work with us and support us, there isn't a doubt any longer. This is a competition; now it's clear."
Fernando Oaxaca, founder of the National Hispanic Republican Assembly	"To me, the Hispanic mentality, the view of the world, is more in sync with Republicans right now, while blacks are now a large part of the middle class but don't seem to be voting Republican,"
Dan Stein, executive director of the Federation for American Immigration Reform	"The surge in Latino numbers comes at the expense of other minority groups, especially black people, who have worked for 200 years to get a level playing field, a fair shot."
Vincente Fox, former president of Mexico	"There is no doubt that Mexicans, filled with dignity, willingness and ability to work, are doing jobs that not even blacks want to do there in the United States."
Fernando de Baca, former chairman of the Republican Party in Bernalillo County in New Mexico	"I feel strongly that Hispanics will not support, in my generation and the generation around my age, are not going to support the Democratic candidate for president primarily because there is a strong feeling that African Americans during the civil rights movement took advantage, full advantage, of all the benefits and programs that the government offered, that were supposed to be offered to all minorities. But we were left behind, we were

Table 4.2 (*cont.*)

	left sucking air, and we resented that ever since the 60s, and I don't see how a black president is going to change that."
David Hill, a GOP pollster for the Cornyn campaign	There is "a natural competition between blacks and Hispanics for power."

Source: Authors' compilation.

monality with African Americans. However, little attention has been paid to the role that cues provided by Latino political elites may be playing in structuring perceptions of commonality with African Americans. The absence of research assessing the impact that elite discourse may have on perceptions of commonality is particularly surprising given that the so-called elite opinion hypothesis—which states that the actions and statements of political elites exert an overwhelming influence on mass political attitudes—has come to dominate the public opinion literature (Lee 2002).

In this chapter, we provide a systematic empirical assessment of the impact that elite messages have on perceptions of economic and political commonality by using the unique data provided by the Latino National Survey (LNS). Testing propositions from John Zaller's (1992) Reception-Acceptance-Sample (RAS) model, we find strong evidence that elite messages play an important role in structuring how Latinos view their relationship with African Americans. In addition to showing that politically aware Latinos, regardless of ideological leanings, are more likely to form opinions on commonality with African Americans, we also demonstrate that exposure to elite messages polarizes self-identified liberals and conservatives—with politically aware liberals seeing more in common with African Americans and politically aware conservatives seeing less.

LITERATURE REVIEW

The remainder of this chapter examines the nascent literature on Latino perceptions of commonality with African Americans as well as the literature on elite opinion theory.

COMMONALITY

Do Latinos perceive a high degree of economic and political commonality with African Americans, and, if so, what are the key determinants of these views? These questions have historically been overlooked in the social sciences, but recently a number of political scientists have begun to examine support for perceptions of commonality held by Latinos toward African Americans. Using the 1999 Washington Post/Kaiser Foundation/Harvard University National Survey on Latinos in America survey, a number of scholars have discovered that Latinos view similar levels of commonality with both African Americans and whites (Kaufmann 2003b; Nicholson, Pantoja, and Segura 2005; Rodrigues and Segura 2003; Sanchez 2008). These scholars point to a number of key individual-level determinants of Latino perceptions of greater commonality with African Americans that include the following measures: Latino linked fate (Kaufmann 2003a; McClain et al. 2006; Rodrigues and Segura 2003; Sanchez 2008); racial identification as black (Kaufmann 2003b; Nicholson, Pantoja, and Segura 2005); ethnic identification with nations with large Afro-Latino populations (Kaufmann 2003a; Rodrigues and Segura 2003; Sanchez 2008); commonality with whites (Rodrigues and Segura 2003); contact (McClain et al. 2006); and acculturation (Kaufmann 2003b; Rodrigues and Segura 2003; Sanchez 2008). Most recently, Michael Jones-Correa (chapter 2, this volume) finds that Latinos who are more integrated into American society are more likely to see commonality with African Americans.

Despite the insights these studies provide, the literature to date has been plagued by a number of key problems that we believe unnecessarily limit our understanding of how Latinos view their relationship with African Americans. First, the bulk of these studies rely on survey data from the 1990s and thus do not present a contemporary view of Latino perceptions of commonality with African Americans in a period in which Latinos are the largest minority group in the nation and are increasingly clashing with African Americans for scarce sociopolitical resources and power (Vaca 2004). Second, many of these studies narrowly focus their attention on a single city rather than the nation, which elicits concerns about the generalizability of the findings. As a result of the increased dispersion of the growing Latino community throughout the United States, we believe that studies should expand their focus beyond specific geographic regions. Finally, and most important, these studies focus solely on individual-level factors in accounting for Latino perceptions of commonality. In doing so, they fail to recognize the potential impact that contextual dynamics, most notably elite messages, may have on Latino perceptions of economic and political commonality with African Americans. We believe it is time for scholars to "bring politics back in" to their analyses of how the Latino mass public forms their opinions on the nature of intergroup relations.

Elite Messaging and Public Opinion

The lack of attention to the impact of elite messages on Latino opinion is surprising given the vaunted position that elite opinion theory has achieved in the study of public opinion. The consensus in political science research that information, ideas, and issue frames follow a one-way path from political elites and mainstream media to the mass public is long standing. Beginning with the early work of Bernard Berelson, Paul Lazasfeld, and William McPhee (1954) and Anthony Downs (1957), numerous scholars have hypothesized that the "rational ignorance" of ordinary citizens leads them to pay little attention to political affairs and to rely instead on cues from political elites when forming their political judgments. As suggested, this approach to studying the dynamics of attitude formation and change, which implies that public opinion is essentially top down and elite driven, has come to dominate the contemporary literature on public opinion (see Brody 1991; Erikson, MacKuen, and Stimson 2003; Gerber and Jackson 1993; Lupia and McCubbins 1998; Page and Shapiro 1992; Popkin 1991; Stimson 1991; Zaller 1992; Karp 1998; for a critique, see Lee 2002). Echoing this sentiment, in their review of recent works on heuristics, Martin Gilens and Naomi Murakawa write that "among political scientists, the heuristic that has attracted the greatest attention is the use of elite cues as aids in political decision making" (2002, 18).

Given the central role that elite opinion theory accords to political elites in determining public opinion the key question, of course, becomes who these elites are. Elite opinion theory approaches are likely to adopt a rather broad definition that includes almost anyone engaged primarily in political activity—whether operating inside or outside formal political channels and institutions. Elite opinion theory's leading scholar, John Zaller, for example, defines elites as "persons who devote themselves full time to some aspect of politics or public affairs. . . . These elites include politicians, higher level government officials, journalists, some activists and many kinds of experts and policy specialists" (1992, 6). Similarly, Edward Carmines and James Kuklinski draw a distinction between elites, "those whose primary business is governing the nation," and nonelites, "those for whom politics is secondary" (1990, 9).

If elite opinion theory focuses on political elites as the primary contextual influence on public opinion, what is it these political elites do to exert their influence? Here elite opinion approaches also adopt a broad definition. In most elite opinion research, almost anything a particular elite or group of elites says or does can influence public opinion. Researchers have pointed to a change in party platforms (Gerber and Jackson 1993), important speeches and books written by political elites (Zaller 1992), the influence of formal institutional events such as Supreme Court cases (Persily, Citrin, and Egan 2008; Unger 2008), key pieces of legislation (Lee 2002), and statements by congressional leaders (Carmines and Kuklinski 1990) as the key independent variables in explaining mass political attitudes. For Benjamin Page and Robert Shapiro (1992), elites can influence public opinion merely by appearing in a sound bite for a news story about a given political issue. Indeed, almost anything an elite actor says or does is a potential influence on public opinion for an elite opinion theorist; more important, all these various activities are presumed to have a similar causal impact on mass preferences. No distinction is drawn in the literature between times where elites consciously try to influence public opinion, as in campaigns or speeches, and when they simply act or speak, as in Supreme Court cases or legislation, and end up changing attitudes through the sheer strength of their voice. In fact, the only requirement seems to be that the activity or message is publicized and available to members of the public. Thus, elite opinion theory can be seen to be very inclusive in both its definition of elites and in its definition of what these elites actually do to exert their influence.

Although elite activity has been declared the central macro-level independent variable in explaining changes in mass public opinion, it is important that not all members of the public are equally influenced by elite messages. Zaller outlines the differential impact of elite messages in his RAS model of opinion formation (1992). According to him, the RAS model has two basic steps: input (how information is received and processed) and output (survey responses or "opinion statements"). In Zaller's formulation, the input step depends on two separate events: receiving the message (influenced by an individual's level of political awareness) and accepting the message (influenced by an individual's predispositions). More specifically, Zaller argues that more politically aware people will be more likely to receive political communications than less aware people and, for those who receive these communications, acceptance will increase when the message is consistent with the individual's predispositions—broadly defined as an individual's "interest, values and experiences" (22).

A key aspect of the RAS model, and elite opinion theory in general, concerns the characteristics of elite messages. According to Zaller, when elite messages are unified (that is, all elites are in agreement concerning an issue at hand), all politically aware members of the public will receive the message, and this message will shape their individual opinion. On the other hand, when the elites present conflicting messages on the same issue, then the opinion of politically aware members of the public reflects the elite message that is most in line with partisan or ideological identifications of the individual in question. Zaller says of the characteristics of elite messages, "When elites uphold a clear picture of what should be done, the public tends to see events from that point of view. . . . When elites divide, members of the public tend to follow the elites sharing their general ideological or partisan predisposition" (1992, 8). Thus, an environment characterized by polarized elite messages regarding commonality with African Americans may elicit polarized opinions on this issue among politically aware Latinos with strong ideological attachments.

Elite opinion theory has typically been used to explain opinion shifts on remote and complex issues, where there are good a priori reasons to expect that elites matter, but surprisingly little research has addressed elite influence on issues that have more direct and immediate relevance to the day-to-day lives of citizens (Paul and Brown 2001). In testing his RAS model, for example, Zaller focuses on low salience cases, such as defense spending and aid to the Contras, issues that have little significance to the daily lives of most individuals (1992). Similarly, Jeffrey Karp analyzes elite influence on the issue of term limits—an issue that is also fairly abstract and remote for many citizens (1998). As a result of this lopsided attention, important questions such as whether elites exert influence on issues where citizens can easily become informed and whether elites can shape opinions when individuals have firsthand experience with an issue have been ignored. To state the issue in Carmines and Stimson's terms, we do not know whether elites can influence public opinion on "easy" issues or whether their influence is limited to "hard" issues (1980, 78). Although it is easy to imagine that elites may only be capable of persuading the public on hard issues, we believe that this is a question that needs to be subjected to empirical analysis and not left solely to presumptive speculation.

ELITE OPINION THEORY AND MINORITY COMMUNITIES

Although broad definitions of elites, such as the ones provided, are relatively standard fare in studies of national public opinion, they are also a prerequisite to accurately assessing the dynamics of attitude change in minority communities. The necessity of employing an inclusive conception of elites stems in large measure from the fact that relatively few members of minority groups occupy positions of power in formal political institutions. For instance, in the 111th Congress, the twenty-seven Latino members make up 5 percent of the total and 455 non-Hispanic whites make up close to 86 percent.[5] If members of minority groups are likely to look to leaders who share their racial or ethnic background for guidance about political issues, they are looking beyond the halls of Congress. As a result, Taeku Lee (2002) and Paula McClain and her colleagues (2008) argue that studies of opinion dynamics within minority communities must define elites in a way that includes not only political actors who are part of the formal institutions of local, state, and national government, but also individuals, such as community organizers, church leaders, media personalities, and heads of interest groups, who have historically been influential by operating outside of these channels.[6]

All of the individuals quoted in tables 4.1 and 4.2 fit the standard definitions of elites, such as those provided by Zaller (1992) and Carmines and Stimson (1980), and the requirements spelled out by Lee (2002) and McClain et al. (2008) quite well. We are therefore confident that the pronouncements of these elites represent both the liberal and conservative viewpoints on the levels of commonality between Latinos and African Americans.

RESEARCH QUESTIONS

Given the lack of inclusion of contextual influences, most notably elite messages, in the literature on commonality, our chapter investigates the impact of elite rhetoric on Latino perceptions of economic and political commonality with African Americans. More specifically, we ask three central questions. First, are politically attentive Latinos more likely to form opinions on commonality than politically inattentive Latinos? Second, is the conflicting nature of elite messages on commonality reflected in the perceptions of commonality among attentive Latinos? Last, does the interaction of attentiveness and ideology, when tested alongside traditional predictors of Latino opinion on commonality, predict opinion on commonality with African Americans among Latino respondents?

HYPOTHESES

Coupling the strong ideological divide illustrated by the statements of liberal and conservative elites with the propositions of elite opinion theory and the RAS model, we were able to specify three testable hypotheses regarding Latino perceptions of economic and political commonality with African Americans:

> The most politically aware Latinos, who are more likely to receive elite messages on relations with African Americans, will be more likely to have an opinion on economic and political commonality with African Americans.

> Politically attentive liberals, who are likely to receive and accept messages from liberal elites, will express more economic and political commonality with African Americans than politically attentive conservatives, who are likely to receive and accept messages from conservative elites.

> The interaction of ideological self-identification and political attentiveness will predict support for economic and political commonality even after controlling for all other potential influences

on Latino attitudes toward relationships with African Americans.

DATA

To test our hypotheses about the influence of elite messages on Latino perceptions of commonality with African Americans, we use the 2006 Latino National Survey. This survey was selected for analysis for three reasons. First, it provides a contemporary view of Latino perceptions of commonality with African Americans, which is particularly important given our criticism of previous work based on data derived from the 1990s. Second, the LNS contains a substantial number of measures of explanatory and dependent variables of interest missing in previous surveys of interracial attitudes that include measures of political and economic commonality with African Americans, political attentiveness, contact, and ethnic, racial, and national identification. Finally, the LNS samples a large number of Latino respondents (N = 8,634) living in fifteen states and Washington, D.C. Selected in large part based on the overall size of the Latino population in the United States, these states account for 87.5 percent of the U.S. Latino population. The LNS thus provides a large and national picture of Latino attitudes about commonality with African Americans.

RESULTS

The reception axiom of Zaller's model suggests that more politically aware individuals will be more likely to pick up on elite cues related to economic and political commonality with African Americans than those with less political awareness.[7] Thus, in this chapter, in line with much of the literature on the impact of elite messages, we use a respondent's level of political awareness as a proxy for reception of elite messages related to commonality (Dobrzynska and Blais 2007; Krosnick and Brannon 1993; Marquis and Sciarini 1999; Zaller 1992). As a result, we hypothesized that the members of our sample with the most political awareness would be more likely to form and express opinions on commonality between Latinos and African Americans because they were more likely to have been exposed to and accepted messages related to commonality from like-minded elites. To deter-

Table 4.3 Latino "Don't Know" Responses to Commonality Questions about Blacks

	Economic	Political	Political and Economic
No political awareness	17.0%	19.9%	11.5%
Low political awareness	9.8%	10.2%	4.8%
Moderate political awareness	6.6%	5.6%	2.6%
High political awareness	4.1%	4.3%	1.6%
Total	10.9%	11.9%	6.3%
N	10,009	10,010	10,011

Source: Authors' calculations based on data from the 2006 Latino National Survey (Fraga et al. 2006).

mine the validity of our hypothesis, we explored the extent to which more politically aware Latinos gave valid responses to the LNS questions on commonality.[8] Table 4.3 reports these findings.

A significant number of Latinos seem to have no opinions about commonality with African Americans. Nearly 11 percent of Latinos responded Don't know to the question about economic commonality, almost 12 percent responded Don't know to the question about political commonality, and over 6 percent responded Don't know to both questions. As table 4.3 also indicates, the politically unaware are vastly more likely to have no opinion on economic and political commonality with African Americans than those who are politically aware. In other words, the more likely an individual is to receive elite messages, the more likely he or she is to have an opinion about the presence (or absence) of commonality with African Americans.

As discussed, the RAS model also supplies us with expectations about the reception stage of opinion formation. Positing an interaction between ideological predispositions and awareness, Zaller's model predicts that opinions on political issues will be polarized according to ideology among the political aware, but not among the less informed, when liberal and conservative elites send conflicting messages. Given the divisions between liberal and conservative leaders regarding economic and political relations between Latinos and African Americans, we hypothesized that ideology would play an important role in structuring perceptions of commonality among aware—but not unaware—members of our sample. Specifically, we predicted that politically aware liberals, who are likely to both receive

Figure 4.1 Mean Scores on Economic Commonality

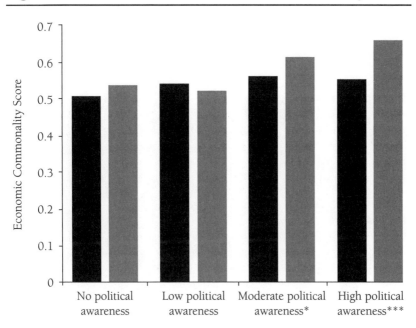

Source: Authors' calculations based on data from the 2006 Latino National Survey (Fraga et al. 2006).
* $p < .05$ ** $p < .01$ *** $p < .001$.

and accept the messages from liberal leaders that encourage perceptions of commonality, would be more likely to express feelings of commonality with African Americans than their conservative counterparts, who are likely to both receive and accept messages from conservative leaders that discourage such perceptions.

To test our predictions, we conducted difference of means tests for the questions on economic and political commonality—comparing the opinions of liberals and conservatives at all four levels of political awareness. As figures 4.1 and 4.2 show, there were no significant differences in perceptions of commonality between liberals and conservatives at lower levels of political awareness. Among those who were highly politically aware, however, conservatives were significantly less likely to express strong feelings of economic and political com-

Figure 4.2 Mean Scores on Political Commonality

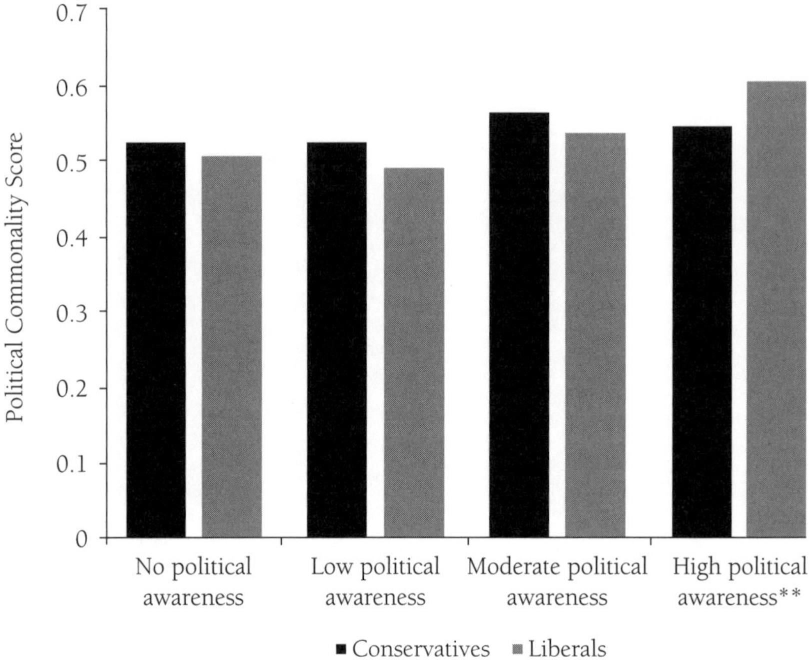

Source: Authors' calculations based on data from the 2006 Latino National Survey (Fraga et al. 2006).
* $p < .05$ ** $p < .01$ *** $p < .001$.

monality than liberals were. These findings support the idea that ideology and political awareness interact in structuring attitudes and are consistent with our claim that elite cues are influencing Latino perceptions of commonality with African Americans.

Although the results of the difference of means tests provide initial evidence that elite messages influence the way Latinos think about their relationship with African Americans, a more sophisticated analysis is needed to control for the influence that other factors may have. As a result, we use ordinary least square (OLS) regression to predict responses to our two measures of commonality.[9] The primary independent variable in each model is an interaction term between ideology and political awareness—which is designed to measure reception and acceptance of messages from political elites, thereby measuring the extent of elite influence (Dobrzynska and Blais 2007). Consistent with the research discussed earlier, the OLS models predicting perceptions of commonality with African Americans also include measures of demographic characteristics (age, gender, and country of ancestry), long-term social characteristics (income and education), acculturation (language of interview and nativity), contact with African Americans (the extent to which the respondent has mostly black friends and coworkers), Latino group consciousness (a series of questions about economic and political commonality with other Latinos),[10] and perceptions of commonality with whites.[11] A list of each of the survey items used in the regression analysis can be found in online appendix 4.A1 (available at: http://www.russellsage.org/telles _sawyer_online_appendix.pdf).

As table 4.4 shows, perceptions of economic and political commonality grow from a number of common sources. First, the extent to which an individual feels economic and political commonality with whites has an important influence on whether the individual feels similarly about African Americans. Indeed, as table 4.4 makes clear, feeling a stronger sense of commonality with whites is predicted to dramatically increase the feeling of commonality with African Americans. Second, feelings of commonality with other Latinos also influence perceptions of economic and political commonality with African Americans. To be more precise, a strong sense of commonality with Latinos leads to stronger feelings of economic and political commonality with African Americans. Third, having mostly black friends has a large, positive impact on perceptions of economic and political commonality with African Americans. Finally, acculturation—measured by the language that the respondent chose to be interviewed in—exerts a significant, positive influence on feelings toward African Americans.

More germane here, we also find that the interaction between ideology and political attentiveness is a strong and statistically significant predictor of perceptions of both economic and political commonality. To better illustrate the influence that elite messages have on Latino assessments of economic and political commonality with African Americans, we used the coefficients in table 4.4 to generate predicted values for strong ideologues on both of our dependent variables.[12] The predicted values are presented in figures 4.3 and 4.4.[13] As each of these figures shows, strong conservatives with no political awareness are actually predicted to feel more in common economically and politically with African Americans than strong liberals with

Table 4.4 OLS Regression Analysis

	Economic Commonality		Political Commonality	
	b	SE	b	SE
Age	.00	.00*	.00	.00
Education	−.02	.03	.01	.03
Male	.02	.01	.02	.01
Income	.05	.02*	.05	.02*
Interview in English	.10	.02***	.04	.02**
First generation	.05	.04	.02	.04
Born in the United States	.08	.03*	.06	.03
Commonality with whites	.29	.02***	.17	.02***
Commonality with Latinos	.08	.02***	.12	.02***
Political awareness	−.08	.03**	−.07	.03*
Party Identification	.01	.02	.02	.02
Ideology	−.09	.03**	−.07	.03*
Ideology × political awareness	.20	.05***	.14	.05**
Black friends	.26	.07***	.16	.07*
Black coworkers	.03	.05	.05	.05
Mexican	−.01	.02	−.01	.02
Cuban	−.05	.03	−.02	.03
Dominican	.08	.03*	.09	.03*
Puerto Rican	.06	.03*	.06	.03*
(Constant)	.30	.05***	.29	.05***
N		2,445		2,441
R^2		.16		.08

Source: Authors' calculations based on data from the 2006 Latino National Survey (Fraga et al. 2006).
* $p < .05$ ** $p < .01$ *** $p < .001$.

no political awareness. As the figures also show, however, increasing political awareness is predicted to considerably increase perceptions of commonality for strong liberals and considerably decreasing them for strong conservatives. Figure 4.3, for example, shows that although politically unaware conservatives are predicted to feel more in common economically with African Americans than unaware liberals, politically aware liberals are predicted to feel more than .12 points more in common with African Americans than their conserva-

Figure 4.3 Predicted Values for Perceptions of Economic
Commonality

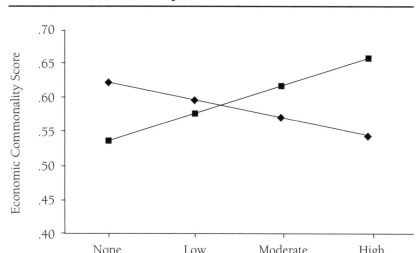

Source: Authors' calculations based on data from the 2006 Latino National Survey (Fraga et al. 2006).

tive counterparts. In short, high levels of exposure to elite messages appear to lead liberal and conservative Latinos down very different paths—with liberals seeing more in common with African Americans and conservatives seeing less in common.

CONCLUSION

What impact do elite messages regarding commonality with African Americans have on the Latino community? We find that politically aware Latinos, the individuals most likely to receive elite messages, are more likely to have an opinion on commonality with African Americans than are their less aware brethren. More important, and in line with the predictions of elite opinion theory, we find that politically aware liberals express higher levels of commonality with African Americans than their conservative counterparts do. This finding indicates that the opinions of politically aware liberals and conservatives reflect those of political elites. Finally, we find that the interaction of ideology and political attentiveness remains a significant

Figure 4.4   Predicted Values for Perceptions of Political Commonality

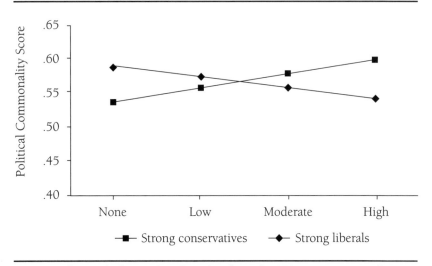

Source: Authors' calculations based on data from the 2006 Latino National Survey (Fraga et al. 2006).

predictor of perceptions of economic and political commonality with African Americans. We interpret these descriptive and explanatory findings to indicate that exposure and acceptance of elite discourse is central to the process by which Latinos form their opinions on commonality with African Americans.

The findings presented here make a number of key contributions to the literature on commonality, public opinion, multiracial coalitions, and interracial conflict. First, unlike many studies that focus exclusively on individual-level determinants of commonality, ours finds clear evidence that liberal and conservative elites send different signals and that these signals influence Latino perceptions of commonality. Yet much of the current work on the relationship between Latino elites and the Latino mass public focuses attention on the representative quality of Latino representatives (Bratton 2006; Kerr and Miller 1997; Hero and Tolbert 1995), the impact of Latino candidates on Latino voting behavior (Baretto 2007; Leighley 2001; Pantoja and Segura 2003), or the mobilization of the Latino electorate by Latino elites (Shaw, de la Garza, and Lee 2000; Ramirez 2007; Wrinkle et al. 1996). We hope the conclusions presented here help expand the boundaries of the literature on Latino public opinion and political behavior to include studies that examine the direct impact that elite rhetoric may have on the contours of Latino political attitudes. Elites, in other words, need to be "brought back in" to studies of Latino politics.

The second contribution this study makes is to those of public opinion more generally, by testing the application of Zaller's model for a new population—Latinos—and for a new issue—commonality. As suggested, the question about how far elite influence will extend remains (Paul and Brown 2001). Most studies of elite influence have focused attention on issues that are abstract and complex, based on the assumption that elite influence is greater on these issues, given the public's proclivity for rational ignorance in the realm of politics. We find, however, that elite influence extends to perceptions of commonality with African Americans, an issue that Latinos can become easily informed about on their own and that many Latinos have direct experiences with in their daily lives (Meier et al. 2004; Mindiola, Niemann, and Rodriguez 2003; Vaca 2004). It appears, therefore, that elites can shape perceptions of everyday life by framing group dynamics in a particular way.

Third, these findings further expand our understanding of the role that elites may play in the formation of multiracial coalitions between America's two largest minority groups. Studies have pointed to a number of conditions necessary to creating successful multiracial coalitions—including shared interests, ideology, and circumstances (Browning, Marshall, and Tabb 1984; Sonenshein 2003; Wilson 1999). Although this literature has significantly expanded our knowledge about cooperation between African Americans and Latinos, much of the existing research tells us painfully little about the underlying attitudinal foundations on which multiracial coalitions might be built. To be more precise, existing studies of multiracial coalitions between African Americans and Latinos focus too heavily on objective measures of socioeconomic, experiential, and partisan similarities and largely ignore the significant role that perceptions of commonality are likely to play. We hope that the results of this analysis will refocus attention on the importance of feelings of economic and political commonality in coalition formation and, more important, remind scholars of the primacy of political leadership in forging bonds of cooperation across racial and ethnic lines.

Finally, our findings shed light on potential solutions to the increasingly frequent and, at times, violent conflicts between African Americans and Latinos in America's urban centers (McClain and Karnig 1990; Meier and Stewart 1991; Meier et al. 2004; Vaca 2004). The results presented imply that many of the more contentious disagreements may be driven by a combination of politically inattentive liberals and politically attentive conservatives. If so, then elites from both ends of the ideological spectrum could play an important role in quelling the violence between these communities. On the one hand, liberal elites can mollify tensions by amplifying their messages of commonality to the point that it reaches even the most politically inattentive members of the Latino community. On the other, conservative elites can diminish the antagonism by softening their more divisive language and by devoting more rhetorical attention to the common socioeconomic and political circumstances the two communities face. To cast this in slightly different terms, our findings suggest that there is no single path that Latino–African American relations must travel and that the actions and statements of political elites will play a large role in charting the course of interactions by shaping the ways Latinos and African Americans view each other.

Although we believe our findings make a strong initial case for the centrality of elite discourse in race relations, we also believe that there is much more to be done. Future research should more systematically examine the content of elite messages on both economic and political commonality with African Americans to get a more complete picture of the nature of elite rhetoric on this issue, for example, whether communication is unified or polarized. In line with the argument in chapter 3 of this volume, we believe that future work should seek to develop more relational measures of commonality that place Latino's perceptions of commonality with other groups alongside their feelings about other Latinos. We also believe that new measures of commonality should reflect not only the social, political, and economic similarities between groups, but also the philosophical aspects that speak to a sense of belonging and identification, a degree of especial mutual concern among members, and a sense of linked fate, mutual trust, and loyalty (see Shelby 2005; Blum 2007). Future studies might also explore the role political elites play in fostering perceptions of competition between groups. Until work on these questions is done, definitive answers about the extent to which the mass public is simply following elite directives on interminority race relations will remain elusive.

NOTES

1. Lynette Clemetson, "Hispanics Now Largest Minority, Census Shows," New York Times, January 22, 2003, A1.
2. Cindy Rodriguez, "Black Enclaves See Latino Influx," Boston Globe, May 4, 2003, A10.
3. "GOP Official Removed for Racial Remarks," USA Today, September 28, 2008 (available at: http://www.usatoday.com/news/politics/election 2008/2008-09-28-gop-remarks_N.htm; accessed January 10, 2009).
4. "Republican Quits in Hispanic Row," BBC News, September 20, 2008 (available at: http://news.bbc.co.uk/2/hi/americas/7639111.stm; accessed January 10, 2009).
5. In comparison, African Americans hold 8 percent, Asian Americans 1.25 percent, and Native Americans less than 1 percent of the total congressional makeup.
6. Charlie Brennan and Myung Oak Kim, "Media Might—En Espanol; From Radio to TV to Newspapers, Spanish Journalism Has Clout," Rocky Mountain News, April 1, 2006; Hammerback, Jensen, and Gutierrez 1985; Marquez and Jennings 2001.
7. An emerging consensus holds that factual knowledge about politics is the best method to measure political awareness (Delli Carpini and Keeter 1993; Price and Zaller 1993). As a result, to measure political awareness in this chapter, we use an index composed of responses to several questions measuring the respondents' factual knowledge about American politics. This measure of political awareness is similar to Zaller's (1992) index of factual information—which counts the number of correct answers the respondent has given to factual questions about elite-level politics at the federal level. A list of the items used to construct the political awareness index is provided in online appendix 4.A1.
8. The exact wording of these questions is provided in online appendix 4.A1.
9. Ordered probit model is available on request. The results of the ordered probit model mirror that of the OLS model, and for ease of interpretation the authors present an OLS model.
10. Perceptions of economic commonality with other Latinos were used to predict perceptions of economic commonality with blacks, while perceptions of political commonality with other Latinos were used to predict perceptions of political commonality with blacks.
11. Perceptions of economic commonality with whites were used to predict perceptions of economic commonality with blacks, while perceptions of political commonality with whites were used to predict perceptions of political commonality with blacks.

12. The predicted values give the predicted outcome of the dependent variable for different scores of the interaction term while holding all other variables constant at their mean.
13. The predicted values for weak liberals and weak conservatives (not shown here) display a similar pattern to that of strong liberals and strong conservatives.

REFERENCES

Barreto, Matt. 2007. "Si Se Puede! Latino Candidates and the Mobilization of Latino Voters." *American Political Science Review* 101(3): 425–41.

Berelson, Bernard, Paul Lazarsfeld, and William McPhee. 1954. *Voting: A Study of Opinion Formation in a Presidential Campaign.* Chicago: University of Chicago Press.

Blum, Lawrence. 2007. "Three Kinds of Race-Related Solidarity." *Journal of Social Philosophy* 38(1): 53–72.

Bratton, Kathleen A. 2006. "The Behavior and Success of Latino Legislators: Evidence from the States." *Social Science Quarterly* 87(1): 1136–57.

Brody, Richard A. 1991. *Assessing the President: The Media, Elite Opinion, and Public Support.* Stanford, Calif.: Stanford University Press.

Browning, Rufus, Dale Rogers Marshall, and David Tabb. 1984. *Protest Is Not Enough: The Struggle of Blacks and Hispanics for Equality in Urban Politics.* Berkeley: University of California Press.

Carmines, Edward G., and James H. Kuklinski. 1990. "Incentives, Opportunities, and the Logic of Public Opinion in American Political Representation." In *Information and Democratic Processes*, edited by John A. Ferejohn and James H. Kuklinski. Urbana: University of Illinois Press.

Carmines, Edward G., and James A. Stimson. 1980. "The Two Faces of Issue Voting." *American Political Science Review* 74(1): 78–91.

Chavez, Linda. 1990. "Rainbow Collision." *New Republic*, November 19, 14–16.

Delli Carpini, Michael X., and Scott Keeter. 1996. *What Americas Know about Politics and Why It Matters.* New Haven, Conn.: Yale University Press.

Dobrzynska, Agnieszka, and André Blais. 2007. "Testing Zaller's Reception and Acceptance Model in an Intense Election Campaign." *Political Behavior* 30(2): 259–76.

Downs, Anthony. 1957. *An Economic Theory of Democracy.* New York: Harper.

Erikson, Robert, Michael B. MacKuen, and James Stimson. 2002. *The Macro Polity.* New York: Cambridge University Press.

Fraga, Luis R., John A. Garcia, Rodney Hero, Michael Jones-Correa, Valerie Martinez-Ebers, and Gary M. Segura. 2006. *Latino National Survey (LNS), 2006* [Computer file]. ICPSR20862-v4. Ann Arbor, Mich.: Inter-university Consortium for Political and Social Research [distributor]. Available at: http://dx.doi.org/10.3886/ICPSR20862 (accessed September 19, 2009).

Gerber, Elisabeth R., and John E. Jackson. 1993. "Endogenous Preferences and the Study of Institutions." *American Political Science Review* 87(3): 639–56.

Gilens, Martin, and Naomi Murakawa. 2002. "Elite Cues and Political Decision Making." In *Political Decision Making, Deliberation, and Participation*, edited by Michael Delli Carpini, Leonie Huddy, and Robert Shapiro. Philadelphia, Pa.: Elsevier Science.

Hammerback, John, Richard J. Jensen, and Jose Angel Gutierrez. 1985. *A War of Words: Chicano Protest in the 1960s and 1970s*. Westport, Conn.: Greenwood Press.

Hero, Rodney E., and Caroline J. Tolbert. 1995. "Latinos and Substantive Representation in the U.S. House of Representatives: Direct, Indirect, or Nonexistent?" *American Journal of Political Science* 39(3): 640–52.

Karp, Jeffrey A. 1998. "The Influence of Elite Endorsements in Initiative Campaigns." In *Citizens as Legislators*, edited by Shaun Bowler, Todd Donovan, and Caroline Tolbert. Athens: Ohio University Press.

Kaufmann, Karen M. 2003a. "Black and Latino Voters in Denver: Responses to Each Other's Political Leadership." *Political Science Quarterly* 118(1): 107–25.

———. 2003b. "Cracks in the Rainbow: Group Commonality as a Basis for Latino and African-American Political Coalitions." *Political Research Quarterly* 56(2): 199–210.

Kerr, Brinck, and Will Miller. 1997. "Latino Representation, It's Direct and Indirect." *American Journal of Political Science* 41(3): 1066–71.

Krosnick, Jon, and Laura A. Brannon. 1993. "The Media and the Foundations of Presidential Support: George Bush and the Persian Gulf Conflict." *Journal of Social Issues* 49(4): 167–82.

Lee, Taeku. 2002. *Mobilizing Public Opinion: Black Insurgency and the Civil Rights Movement*. Chicago: University of Chicago Press.

Leighley, Jan E. 2001. *Strength in Numbers: The Political Mobilization of Racial and Ethnic Minorities*. Princeton, N.J.: Princeton University Press.

Lupia, Arthur, and Matthew D. McCubbins. 1998. *The Democratic Dilemma: Can Citizens Learn What They Need to Know?* Cambridge: Cambridge University Press.

Marquez, Benjamin, and James Jennings. 2001. "Representation by Other Means: Mexican American and Puerto Rican Social Movement Organizations." *PS: Political Science and Politics* 37(3): 547–54.

Marquis, Lionel, and Pascal Sciarini. 1999. "Opinion Formation in Foreign Policy: The Swiss Experience." *Electoral Studies* 18(4): 453–71.

McClain, Paula D., Niambi M. Carter, Victoria M. DeFrancesco Soto, Monique L. Lyle, Jeffrey D. Grynaviski, Shayla C. Nunnally, Thomas J. Scotto,

J. Alan Kendrick, Gerald F. Lackey, and Kendra Davenport Cotton. 2006. "Racial Distancing in a Southern City: Latino Immigrants' Views of Black Americans." *Journal of Politics* 68(3): 571–84.

McClain, Paula D., and Albert Karnig. 1990. "Black and Hispanic Socioeconomic and Political Competition." *American Political Science Review* 84(2): 535–45.

Meier, Kenneth J., Paula D. McClain, J. L. Polinard, and Robert D. Wrinkle. 2004. "Divided or Together? Conflict and Cooperation between African Americans and Latinos." *Political Research Quarterly* 57(3): 399–409.

Meier, Kenneth, and Joseph Stewart. 1991. "Cooperation and Conflict in Multiracial School Districts." *Journal of Politics* 53(4): 1123–33.

Mindiola, Tatcho, Jr., Yolanda F. Niemann, and Nestor Rodriguez. 2003. *Black-Brown Relations and Stereotypes*. Austin: University of Texas Press.

Nicholson, Stephen, Adrian Pantoja, and Gary Segura. 2005. "Race Matters: Latino Racial Identities and Political Beliefs." Paper presented at the 2005 annual meeting of the American Political Science Association. Washington, D.C. (August 31–September 3).

Obama, Barack. 2008. "Speech at NALEO on Immigration." Available at: http://www. cfr.org/immigration/obamas-speech-naleo-immigration/p166 89 (accessed March 23, 2011).

Page, Benjamin, and Robert Shapiro. 1992. *The Rational Public: Fifty Years of Trends in Americans' Policy Preferences*. Chicago: University of Chicago Press.

Pantoja, Adrian D., and Gary M. Segura. 2003. "Does Ethnicity Matter? Descriptive Representation in Legislatures and Political Alienation Among Latinos." *Social Science Quarterly* 84(2): 441–60.

Paul, David M., and Clyde Brown. 2001. "Testing the Limits of Elite Influence on Public Opinion: An Examination of Sports Facility Referendums." *Political Research Quarterly* 54(4): 871–88.

Persily, Nathan, Jack Citrin, and Patrick Egan, eds.. 2008. *Public Opinion and Constitutional Controversy*. New York: Oxford University Press.

Popkin, Samuel L. 1991. *The Reasoning Voter: Communication and Persuasion in Presidential Campaigns*. Chicago: University of Chicago Press.

Price, Vincent, and John Zaller. 1993. "Who Gets the News? Measuring Individual Differences in Likelihood of News Reception." *Public Opinion Quarterly* 57(2): 133–64.

Ramírez, Ricardo. 2007. "Segmented Mobilization: Latino Nonpartisan Get-Out-the-Vote Efforts in the 2000 General Election." *American Politics Research* 35(2): 155–75.

Rodrigues, Helena Alves, and Gary Segura. 2003. "Attitudinal Underpinnings of Black-Brown Coalitions: Latino Perceptions of Commonality with African Americans and Anglos." Unpublished paper.

Sanchez, Gabriel. 2004. "Building a Foundation for Coalitions Among Latinos and African Americans: The Impact of Latino Group Consciousness on Perceptions of Commonality with African Americans." Paper delivered at the 2004 annual meeting of the American Political Science Association. Chicago, Ill. (September 2–5).

———. 2008. "Latino Group Consciousness and Perceptions of Commonality with African Americans." *Social Science Quarterly* 89(2): 428–44.

Shaw, Daron, Rodolfo O. de la Garza, and Jongho Lee. 2000. "Examining Latino Turnout in 1996: A Three-State, Validated Survey Approach." *American Journal of Political Science* 44(2): 332–40.

Shelby, Tommie. 2005. *We Who Are Dark: The Philosophical Foundations of Black Solidarity.* Cambridge, Mass.: Harvard University Press.

Sonenshein, Raphael J. 2003. "The Prospects for Multiracial Coalitions: Lessons from America's Three Largest Cities." In *Racial Politics in American Cities,* edited by Rufus P. Browning, Dale Rogers Marshall, and David H. Tabb. New York: Longman.

Stimson, James A. 1991. *Public Opinion in America: Moods, Cycles, and Swings.* Boulder, Colo.: Westview Press.

Unger, Michael A. 2008. "After the Supreme Word: The Effect of McCreary County v. ACLU (2005) and Van Orden v. Perry (2005) on Support for Public Displays of the Ten Commandments." *American Politics Research* 36(5): 750–75.

Vaca, Nicolás C. 2004. *The Presumed Alliance: The Unspoken Conflict between Latinos and Blacks and What It Means for America.* New York: HarperCollins.

Wilson, William. 1999. *The Bridge over the Racial Divide: Rising Inequality and Coalition Politics.* Berkeley: University of California Press.

Wrinkle, Robert, Joseph Steward, Jerry Polinard, Ken Meier, and John Arvizu. 1996. "Ethnicity and Nonelectoral Political Participation." *Hispanic Journal of Behavioral Sciences* 18(2): 142–53.

Zaller, John. 1992. *The Nature and Origins of Mass Opinion.* Cambridge: Cambridge University Press.

PART III

Urban Profiles

CHAPTER 5

Intergroup Perceptions and Relations in Houston

Nestor Rodriguez and Tatcho Mindiola Jr.

A major development in U.S. society at the beginning of the twenty-first century concerns the racial and ethnic recomposition of many communities across the country, attributable primarily to immigration. One dimension of this change is the simultaneously growing concentration of African Americans and Latinos in the same urban areas. In several of the largest cities (New York, Chicago, Los Angeles, and the like), for example, the combined population of Hispanics and African Americans is now the majority. Natural population growth in both groups and high immigration levels in the former are contributing to this development. Out-migration of non-Latino whites to the suburbs contributes to the shift in central cities. The simultaneous concentration of African Americans and Latinos raises important questions about the future dynamics of the affected social settings. Given that these settings include the largest population concentrations in the country, it is not an exaggeration to say that relations between African Americans and Latinos will significantly affect the future of large U.S. urban areas throughout the course of the twenty-first century.

In this chapter, we address questions about evolving relations between African Americans and Latinos from the perspective of survey research conducted in the Houston area since 1996. Our focus is on perceptions among African Americans and Latinos regarding their intergroup relations, as well as political, educational, corporate, and residential developments that affect interactions between the two groups. One key topic concerns immigration and related issues, such as employment, the impact of the Spanish language, and what constitutes an American identity. Although economic factors are assumed to play an important role in perceptions and relations between African Americans and Latinos, we assume that the full range of influ-

155

ences transcends the economic sphere to include social, cultural, and spatial conditions as well.

HOUSTON BACKGROUND

The Houston area has become a major setting for African American and Latino concentrations. In 2009, the two populations accounted for 51 percent of the metropolitan population and 65 percent of the central city population (see table 5.1). Regionally, this is the largest population of both African Americans and Latinos in the country (Atlanta has the largest metropolitan population of African Americans in the South). Also in 2009 the Houston metropolitan area had an estimated 863,953 Latin American immigrants, of whom 68 percent had emigrated from Mexico (U.S. Census Bureau 2010). This is the largest foreign-born Latino population in the southern region. Immigrants accounted for 43 percent of Latinos in the Houston metropolitan area in 2008, but for only 6 percent of African Americans (U.S. Census Bureau 2010). In sum, the Houston area is a dynamic setting of evolving intergroup relations between African Americans and Latinos.

Historically, African American neighborhoods developed in three large areas (wards) surrounding the downtown area. Latino-origin (that is, Mexican) neighborhoods also developed in mainly three large neighborhood areas, one of which was adjacent to downtown and two of which were a few miles away. Both the African American and Latino communities originated in the eastern half of the city. African American neighborhoods, which developed during the Jim Crow era, had rigid boundaries of racial segregation, and Latino neighborhoods also became fairly separated from others. With the exception of Houston Heights, a neighborhood several miles northwest of downtown, these conditions held until the 1960s and 1970s, when large numbers of African Americans and Latinos started settling in western and southwestern sectors of the city (Mindiola, Niemann, and Rodriguez 2003).

Two factors affected the expansion of African American and Latinos into the western and southwestern sectors of the city. One was that the growth of the two populations could no longer be accommodated in the housing markets on the east side. Particularly in the late 1970s and 1980s, new large-scale immigration from Mexico and Central America created a Latino demand for housing greatly dispro-

Table 5.1 Houston Area Population Estimates, 2009

Population	Central City	Metropolitan Area
Total	2,260,918	5,865,086
Non-Latino	1,301,235	3,849,558
White alone	639,304	2,443,815
African American alone	502,199	967,026
Asian alone	131,787	351,226
Native American–Alaskan Native alone	3,478	10,222
Native Hawaiian–Pacific Islander alone	1,816	4,385
Some other race alone	5,016	13,884
Two or more races	17,635	59,000
Latino	959,683	2,015,528
White alone	731,061	1,519,608
African American alone	11,250	19,981
Asian alone	2,346	3,977
Native American–Alaskan Native alone	8,761	14,720
Native Hawaiian–Pacific Islander alone	80	379
Some other race alone	193,556	414,067
Two or more races	12,629	42,796

Source: Authors' calculations based on data from U.S. Census Bureau 2010.

portionate to what could be found in the established east-side barrios (Rodriguez 1993). The second factor was a crisis in apartment real estate capital in the early 1980s, which developed as the Houston oil-centered economy entered a recession with the fall of oil prices in the world market (Feagin 1988). Real estate capital had overbuilt the apartment market, and the out-migration of thousands of unemployed white workers during the recession left many apartment complexes abandoned in the mostly white west side of the city. In response, real estate capital seized on the strategy of lowering rental prices and recruiting the arriving Latino immigrants and other minorities as the new tenants (Rodriguez and Hagan 1992).

Whether in the old east-side neighborhoods or in the new settlements in the western and southwestern sectors, African Americans and Latinos in the Houston area have not experienced the level of intergroup conflict reported for other areas, such as for the Los Angeles suburb of Compton (see Johnson, Farrell, and Guinn 1997). The most visible tensions have involved mainly the Houston Independent School District and police incidents. In one case, Latino leaders reacted against the school board for selecting an African American school board member to be the new superintendent without considering other candidates, especially a Latino one, given the fast-growing Latino student population in the school district. In a second case, African American leaders expressed strong opposition to a school-improvements bond proposal made by a Mexican American superintendent without much community input (Mindiola, Niemann, and Rodriguez 2003). A number of Latino organizations supported the bond, but African American leaders contended that the bond proposal was unfair to African American children (*African American News & Issues* 2007). Apart from the educational arena, two incidents involving fatal police encounters between African Americans and Latinos received high-profile coverage in the local media. One involved the killing of an African American driver by a Latino police officer, and the second the killing of an African American constable by a Latino immigrant. Both incidents received wide attention in the city, but they were not framed in terms of problematic relations between African Americans and Latinos.[1]

Although tension and conflict do not characterize relations between African Americans and Latinos, issues about Latino development do concern large percentages of African Americans in the Houston area, as the discussion in the next section indicates. These issues involve Latino immigration–related conditions and related developments, such as competition for jobs and the growing use of the Spanish language in the area.

RESEARCH METHODS

This analysis is based on two surveys conducted in Harris County, which includes most of the city of Houston. One, by the Center for Mexican American Studies (CMAS) at the University of Houston in 1996, was conducted by telephone interview with a random selection of 1,200 African American and Latino respondents, 600 African Americans and 600 Latinos. The Latino participants—252 U.S. born and 348 foreign born—were interviewed in English or Spanish. Questions were framed to determine the degree of social distance between African Americans and Latinos based on the answers about how often they interacted with members of the other group (African American or Latino) and how they perceived the characteristics of that group. A series of questions were also asked about intergroup issues, such as the impacts of immigration, competition for jobs, impacts of the Spanish language, intergroup prejudice and discrimination, and willingness to support immigrants with public assistance. Another series gauged how much or how little the two groups came together on a variety of social issues such as prayer and sex education in schools (Mindiola, Niemann, and Rodriguez 2003).

The second survey is the Houston Area Survey (HAS), which has been conducted annually in Harris County since 1982 at Rice University. From 1982 to 2010, the HAS was housed in the Urban Research Center at Rice University, which in 2010 was reorganized into the Institute for Urban Research. The HAS covers a range of social, economic, and political topics affecting residents of the Houston area and conducts interviews with Anglos, African Americans, Asians, and Latinos. Basically, the survey obtains annual assessments of how residents view the quality of life in the Houston area, operationally defined in the survey as Harris County. The survey questions address topics such as the quality of local economic conditions, ethnic relations, prejudice and discrimination, the local urban environment, poverty, immigration, crime and public safety, and politics. New topics are added periodically. Since 1990, the number of survey respondents has been set at 650, all residents, age eighteen or older, contacted through random telephone interviews. Since 1995, with the exception of 1996, the basic survey has included an oversampling of African Americans and Latinos to reach approximately 500 of each, the number of non-Hispanic white respondents. Interviews of Latinos are conducted in either English or Spanish, depending on the respondent's preference, and in 1995 and 2002 Asians were similarly interviewed, in either English or the Asian language of choice.

Although the CMAS survey and HAS overlap, the two surveys are not identical. The CMAS survey interviewed African Americans and Latinos exclusively, and mostly on issues of intergroup perceptions and relations in the Houston area, whereas the HAS interviewed Anglos and Asians as well and covers a much broader range of social topics over a wide range of years. For this analysis, we use selected years of the HAS that correspond with the time or issues addressed in the CMAS survey. The items concern those addressed by the over-samples of African Americans and Latinos on intergroup issues and perceptions.

IMMIGRATION

Immigration is particularly relevant in evolving relations between Latinos and African Americans for at least two reasons. One, it is a primary source of Latino population growth in many areas of African American concentration. Two, it is perceived as increasing the labor market competition, if not actual displacement, of African Americans (Borjas 1998; Rosenfeld and Tienda 1999). If Latinos and African Americans are perceived as having a zero-sum game relationship, in which the economic gains of one group occurs at the expense of the other, then African Americans have nothing to gain and actually lose from Latin American immigration (in which African-origin migrants are only a small portion), because immigration increases the inflow of immigrant workers. From this standpoint, the analysis of the survey data described should anticipate finding anti-immigration and anti-immigrant sentiments among the African American responses. Using the same logic, the analysis also should find anti–African American attitudes among the Latino respondents, given that Latinos would view African Americans as competitors for social resources (housing, jobs, and the like) as well.

The 1996 CMAS survey findings indicate that all African Americans do not perceive a zero-sum game relationship with Latino immigrants. On the question of whether immigrants take jobs from blacks, 54 percent of African Americans believed this to be the case, but 39 percent disagreed (see table 5.2). The analysis of the survey data found that responses varied according to income and educational characteristics of the respondents. Those with lower incomes and levels of education were more likely to believe that immigrants take jobs from African Americans.

Findings reported in chapter 8 of this volume also indicate that African American perceptions of Latino immigrants vary by social differentials. Monica McDermott's fieldwork in Greenville, North Carolina, finds the opposite of the Houston survey results, that is, that it was lower-class African Americans who had more favorable attitudes toward Latino immigrants than their middle-class counterparts. The survey and ethnographic findings thus indicate that there

Table 5.2 Houston-Area Perceptions, 1996 and 2010

	African Americans	U.S.-Born Latinos	Foreign-Born Latinos
"Immigrants take jobs from African Americans"*	(n = 600)	(n = 252)	(n = 348)
Agree	54%	25%	13%
Disagree	39	71	83
No opinion	7	4	4
"Legalization for undocumented immigrants who speak English and have no criminal record"**	(n = 496)	(n = 378)	(n = 102)
For it	65%	77%	84%
Against it	30	23	16
No response	5	0	0
"Impact of immigrants in the Houston area"*	(n = 600)	(n = 252)	(n = 348)
Good	36%	56%	63%
Bad	54	36	21
Don't know/No response	10	8	16
"How serious a problem that many undocumented migrants come to Houston?"**	(n = 477)	(n = 390)	(n = 103)
Not much of a problem	15%	24%	41%
Somewhat of a problem	31	31	36
Very serious problem	54	44	23
"Build a border fence to stop undocumented immigration"**	(n = 468)	(n = 367)	(n = 98)
Favor	72%	54%	36%
Oppose	28	46	64
"Impact of the Spanish language in the United States"*	(n = 600)	(n = 252)	(n = 348)
Good	43%	78%	76%
Bad	46	17	19
Don't know/No response	11	5	5

Source: Authors' compilation based on Intergroup Relations Survey (Center for Mexican American Studies 1996) and Houston Area Survey (Kinder Institute for Urban Research 2010).
*Intergroup Relations Survey, 1996, Center for Mexican American Studies, University of Houston.
**Houston Area Survey, 2010, Institute for Urban Research, Rice University.

is no clear-cut perception among African Americans regarding the impact of Latino immigration on African American employment. The issue becomes more complicated when we consider the finding reported in chapter 1 of this volume, that national census data indicate that the presence and growth of the immigrant Latino population has either no or at most a minimal effect on African American employment rates and wages. As the authors explain, the labor force participation of African Americans and Latinos may be contextualized by racial and ethnic segmentation in the labor market, which serves to minimize intergroup job impacts.

Analysis of HAS data indicates, moreover, that African Americans do not consider job loss to be the biggest problem of undocumented immigration. Responding to a question in the 2010 survey on this topic, a plurality of African American respondents ranked an increase in crime (30 percent) and a strain on public services (28 percent) as the two most important problems, and taking American jobs (23 percent) the third most important. Latino respondents concurred on the three issues, but cited strain on public services as the most important (42 percent). The response did not differ by gender but did differ—significantly—by income: lower-income respondents were more likely than their higher-income counterparts to report American jobs as the most important problem.

To be sure, the responses that undocumented immigrants are a strain on public services are ironic, because federal laws restrict undocumented immigrants from using all but emergency public services but do not restrict the U.S.-born children of undocumented immigrants from using these services. It is possible that the responses that undocumented immigrants strain public services reflect wider public perceptions that undocumented immigrants come to the United States to get on welfare. Social research has not found evidence of such usage; instead, some immigrants who qualify for public services appear to shy away, either because they don't have reliable information about them or out of fear that they will be disqualified later for citizenship because they used the services (Hagan et al. 2003).

In a number of other survey questions, African Americans and Hispanics agree or come close to agreement on immigration-related issues. For example, 70 percent of African Americans and 67 percent of Hispanics agreed in the 2010 HAS that something should be done to reduce the number of new immigrants coming to the country.

These responses did not differ significantly by gender, income status, or even by U.S-born or foreign-born status. But the agreement in the Houston area is not solely in favor of restriction. For example, large majorities of African Americans (65 percent) and Latinos (78 percent) agreed in the 2010 HAS on granting "illegal aliens in the U.S. a path to citizenship" if they spoke English and had no criminal record (see table 5.2). Hispanic, female, and foreign-born respondents tended to agree at significantly higher rates, but the rates did not differ across income levels. A majority of African Americans (86 percent) and Latinos (92 percent) also agreed with allowing undocumented immigrant children to become citizens if they graduated from college or served in the military. Hispanics and foreign-born respondents agreed at higher rates, but these rates did not differ significantly by gender or income level.

African Americans and Hispanics also disagree, however, on a number of immigration-related issues. For example, a majority of African Americans in the 1996 CMAS survey stated that the impact of immigrants in the Houston area was bad, whereas a majority of Hispanics said that it was good (see table 5.2). Concerning particularly the impact of undocumented immigration in the Houston area, African Americans and Hispanics also differed a decade later. A majority of blacks in the 2006 HAS saw the impact as a very serious problem, whereas the majority of U.S.-born and foreign-born Latinos saw it as either not much of a problem or just somewhat of one. This contrast was repeated in the 2010 HAS (table 5.2), in which the responses to the question varied by U.S.- and foreign-born status, but not by gender or income level. In a somewhat similar pattern, a majority of African Americans (58 percent) stated that immigrants "take more" than they contribute to the U.S. economy, and a majority of Hispanics (60 percent) that they "contribute more." The responses did not differ by gender, but foreign-born and higher-income respondents were more likely to say that immigrants contribute more.

African Americans and Hispanics also disagreed in the 2010 HAS on favoring or opposing the construction of a security fence at the U.S.-Mexico border "to stop all undocumented immigrants." Almost three-fourths of African Americans were in favor of the fence, almost two-thirds of foreign-born Hispanics opposed it (see table 5.2). Foreign-born Hispanics opposed the fence significantly more than U.S.-born Hispanics did, but the total responses in the survey did not vary by gender or income level.

Finally, African Americans and Hispanics also disagreed in the 2010 HAS on the question of whether local police or federal authorities should identify undocumented immigrants. A majority of African Americans (59 percent) were in favor of local police doing so, but a majority of Hispanics (59 percent) were in favor of federal authorities. Significantly more women than men, and more foreign-born than U.S.-born respondents, also favored federal identification, but responses again did not vary by income level. On another enforcement question, in 2005 the HAS found that African Americans supported fines against employers of undocumented immigrants, while a majority of Hispanics opposed the fines. A gender difference occurred in the responses, but only among U.S.-born Hispanics; U.S.-born Latina women were divided almost equally on the question.

OTHER INTERGROUP PERCEPTIONS

Beyond concerns about immigrant impact, a majority of neither African Americans nor Hispanics perceived a general sense of conflict or competition between the two groups, according to findings of the CMAS survey and the HAS. For example, when the 2010 HAS asked respondents to rate the relations between the two groups in the Houston area from 1 (very poor) to 10 (excellent), almost two-thirds of both African Americans (64 percent) and Latinos (62 percent) rated the relations between 5 and 10. Variation in the ratings by gender or income level was not significant.

A large majority of African Americans and Hispanics expressed support in the 1999 HAS for bilingual education in public schools. Among blacks, younger respondents expressed greater support, and responses did not vary significantly for gender or income differences. Questions relating to language are complicated, however. In the CMAS survey of 1996, among African American respondents 43 percent reported that the impact of the Spanish language in the Untied States was good, but 46 percent that it was bad, with differences across income and educational levels (see table 5.2). More than three-fourths of all Latino respondents reported that the impact in the Houston area was beneficial. As to speaking Spanish in the workplace, 49 percent of African Americans and large percentages of U.S.-born and foreign-born Latinos agreed that it was "okay," but 45 percent of African Americans disagreed. These questions were not asked in the HAS interviews.

Table 5.3 Frequency of Interaction Between African
          Americans and Latinos, 1996

	African American with Latinos	U.S.-Born Latino with African Americans	Foreign-Born Latino with African Americans
	(n = 600)	(n = 248)	(n = 348)
Frequently	72%	63%	34%
Sometimes	16	22	20
Almost never	6	8	25
Never	6	7	21

Source: Authors' calculation based on data from the Intergroup Relations Survey
(Center for Mexican American Studies 1996).

Blacks and Latinos in the Houston area also agreed on issues of English-speaking or American identity. Although a majority of both groups agreed slightly or strongly in the 2008 HAS that to be "truly American" a person should be able to speak English, African Americans had a larger majority (73 percent) than U.S.-born (65 percent) or foreign-born Hispanics (63 percent).

With the exception of some immigration-related issues, African Americans and Latinos in the Houston area consider that relations between the two groups are on a positive course. This perception was found in the 1996 CMAS survey and in the 2006 HAS. Moreover, information from the two surveys indicates that the perception is accompanied by behavioral conditions. In the 1996 CMAS survey, almost three-fourths of African Americans and almost two-thirds of U.S.-born Latinos reported having regular interaction (at least once a week) with one or more members of the other racial-ethnic group (see table 5.3). Among foreign-born Latinos, only about one-third reported this much interaction.

In addition, the 2006 HAS indicates that, although members in both groups reported that their closest friends were of the same ethnic group, a majority of African Americans and native-born Latinos had a close friend from the other group. Interestingly, 43 percent of foreign-born Latino respondents also said they had a close African American friend. These findings warrant a closer examination, for the literature on close black-brown friendships is nonexistent or at best scant. The workplace and neighborhood settings should be of particular interest in studying developing friendship between groups, given that the 1996 CMAS survey found that interaction between the two groups is most likely to occur in these settings. We also note, for example, the large numbers of Latinos and African Americans who work in U.S. post offices and who participate as members in the same unions.

The 2006 HAS reveals, however, that segregation in the workplace can restrict interaction. Only 11 percent of native-born Latinos said they worked with African Americans, and only 14 percent of African Americans said they worked with Hispanics. Only 3 percent of Latino immigrants said they worked with African Americans. The public schools where Latinos and African Americans attend together in large numbers are also ideal locations for observations of interactions. In the Houston Independent School District, 27 percent of all students were African American and 62 percent were Latino in the recent 2009 to 2011 school year (Houston Independent School District 2010).

DISCUSSION

The CMAS and HAS survey data indicate that intergroup perceptions of African Americans and Latinos on immigration issues are not easily predictable, and certainly not predictable from any simple notion of a zero-sum game perception operating between the two groups in which the gains of one group are viewed by the other as a loss to them. Many African Americans, and some Hispanics, have similar or the same restrictionist views as the general public on such issues as the construction of a border fence and sanctioning employers of undocumented immigrants. Blacks also share the attitudes of Hispanics on issues relating to a path for the legalization of undocumented immigrants, including one for the children of undocumented immigrants to become citizens, and promoting bilingual education in public schools. To be sure, African Americans are divided on Hispanic immigration, and thus on some issues are favorably disposed to immigrants and the impact of immigration in the Houston area.

The question remains, however, why substantial percentages, and at times majorities, of African Americans express favorable attitudes about some immigrant-related issues, or about Latinos in general, if immigration is perceived as creating economic competition or disadvantages for African Americans (Borjas 1998; Rosenfeld and Tienda 1999). In other words, why are many African Americans receptive to Latino development in their midst? One answer is that African Americans may fail to see how this development, especially immigration, threatens their interests. This answer, however, fails to appreciate the long history of African American struggles in which African Americans have developed a profound consciousness of their social situations (West 2001). To answer the question, rather than accepting that African Americans are unaware, we depart from a rigid utilitarian model of economic cost-benefit analysis and look at conditions of structure and agency in the large Houston social arena to see what may be affecting the emergence of relations between African Americans and Latinos. We continue the analysis, therefore, from the perspective that relations between African Americans and Latinos are evolving in a complex matrix of social forces that radiate from more than just the economic sphere.

From the perspective of multidimensional influences, it is important to consider the shared history of oppression of the two groups in U.S. society. Both were historically incorporated into U.S. society by force, African Americans as slaves and Mexicans as a colonized people after a war (Acuña 1981; Ture and Hamilton 1992). Furthermore, both also are racially and ethnically different from whites. Some may argue that the number of Hispanics who classify themselves as white in the census—75 percent in the Houston area in 2009 (U.S. Census Bureau 2010)—dilutes this argument. Yet the nuances of race questions may be more complex than reflected in census data. Mark Sawyer, for example, reports in chapter 6 of this volume that when a sample of Latinos in Los Angeles were asked to classify their race according to how the race question is asked in Latin America, only 19 percent chose white. A majority of Latinos in the United States are *mestizos*, that is, mixed indigenous, African, and European origin blended together during the Spanish colonization of Latin America.

As minority groups, Latinos and African Americans have life opportunities that lag considerably behind those of whites and thus have common ground on a host of issues, including inferior educational services (San Miguel 1987; Orfield 2001), lagging health care (Smedley, Stith and Nelson 2003; Gee 2008), poor housing (Shenassa, Stubbendick, and Brown 2004; Sherman 2006), high crime and incarceration rates (Smelser, Wilson, and Mitchell 2001; Mauer and King 2007), and discrimination in the labor market (Smelser, Wilson, and Mitchell 2001). These common issues have served as starting points (not only in Houston) for coalition-building dialogue between leadership sectors of the two groups.

An examination of past and recent developments reveals other key structural factors that promote positive relations between African Americans and Latinos in the Houston area. One structural development is the large numbers of Latinos and even larger numbers of African Americans in the same political party (Democratic). This united identity may shift for some elections, but endures in the long term. Highly visible and vocal local leaders of both groups often appear united in political campaigns in support of Democratic candidates and even in nonpartisan local elections. There are no indications that African Americans are lessening their Democratic identity, and Latinos are projected to swell the Democratic ranks in even larger numbers in Texas (Farrell 2008). Already the growing numbers of Latino Democrats have turned Houston and other urban areas of Texas into regions of Democratic dominance.

Politically, African Americans are more empowered than Latinos in the Houston area. African Americans hold more elected positions and are the most important group of voters not only because of size—they can constitute approximately 25 percent to 28 percent of the vote in a mayor's race—but also because they vote as a block, 90 percent of their vote going for one candidate. The white and Hispanic votes are more apt to be split among candidates. In close mayoral races, Latino voters have proved to be decisive when white and black mayoral candidates compete against each other. In one race, Latinos supported the winning white candidate, and in another the winning black candidate (Santos, Mindiola, and Salinas 2001; Mindiola, Santos, and Salinas 2003). In the only race pitting a Latino candidate against an incumbent African American, the majority of the Latino voters supported the Latino candidate, who nevertheless lost the election. These races have not led to any significant racial tensions between African Americans and Latinos.

Another arena in which blacks and Latinos are coming together in large numbers in the Houston area is education. African American and Latino students make up an overwhelming percentage of students in the Houston central public school system. As immigrant families look for low-income housing in black neighborhoods, Latino students are enrolling in sizeable numbers in traditionally African American public high schools. A variety of relations develop between African America and Latino students in these schools, from mutually supportive and friendly interaction to occasional schoolyard fights between students of both groups.

The corporate sector, meanwhile, has developed training programs specifically for African Americans, Latinos, Asians, and other minorities to experience intergroup interaction and undertake leadership roles in community agencies. One example is Project Blueprint, operated by the United Way, which recruits ethnic minority professionals for leadership training and eventual placement in volunteer positions in community boards. A significant part of the training concerns developing intergroup understanding and linkages among the diverse minority professionals in the program cycles. Project Blueprint has trained large numbers of African Americans, Latinos, and other minorities through techniques that promote lasting bonds of solidarity and common (corporate) interests (United Way of Greater Houston 2010). The Houston area has long had a capitalist class that has acted in various ways to maintain a healthy local business climate. This has included the promotion of a corporate leadership sector prepared to undertake institutional planning in the racially and ethnically diverse setting of the area (Feagin 1988). The ultimate goal of this function, according to Joe R. Feagin, is to maintain a stable social environment favorable to business growth (1988). In this pursuit, Houston continues to have no zoning ordinances.

The descriptions of institutional leaderships that promote positive understanding between African Americans and Latinos would be incomplete if they did not include the efforts of non-Hispanic whites and Asians to promote intergroup relations. One result of these efforts was the creation of the Houston Inter-Ethnic Forum in the mid-1990s, in which a racially and ethnically diverse group of Houston leaders came together to discuss issues of intergroup relations (Davila and Rodriguez 2000).

These efforts vary and include joint meetings of religious leaders from both groups, the policy of an African American police chief not to make special efforts to arrest undocumented immigrants, the decision of an African American mayor to maintain a city government office for immigrant community affairs, the actions of some African American university administrators to support the enrollment of undocumented Latino students, an African American congressional representative who highlights the need to provide legal remedies, including legalization for undocumented immigrants, and organizing by African Americans of an English training project for Latino immigrants (Davila and Rodriguez 2000; Mindiola, Niemann, and Rodriguez 2003).

In addition, as mentioned, African American and Hispanic political leaders work together to increase the strength of the Democratic Party in the Houston area. These collaborative effects are important, because research indicates that united messages from Latino and African American leaders can influence the opinion of their respective communities and that framing issues in terms of a common pursuit for justice can facilitate coalitions (see chapters 4 and 10, this volume). Given the large number of new immigrants, it is likely that Latinos have to work harder on coalition building than African Americans, who have more coalition-building experience (Kaufmann 2003).

None of these actions, by themselves or collectively, guarantee that tensions and conflict will not develop. These actions indicate, however, that institutional leaders are not allowing the course of relations to be shaped completely by market forces. A host of collaborative networks and strategies now exist that serve as resources to mobilize in times of intergroup social tensions. These resources, however, should not be oversold, because the number of people who have actually participated are small fractions of the total group populations. Given this reality, it is important to recognize the significance of the day-to-day social participation of ordinary residents of both groups.

With few exceptions, the densest concentrations of African Americans and Latinos are found in the east side, working-class neighborhoods of both groups near downtown. As the availability of housing diminishes in the east-side Mexican neighborhoods, some Latino immigrants have moved into low-rent housing in the established African American neighborhoods near downtown. The picture of daily life that emerges from the spillover of new Latino immigrants into African American wards is general peaceful coexistence with limited intergroup interaction, except in the neighborhood schools. In the established African American neighborhoods, blacks and Latinos sometimes exchange customary greetings, and occasionally chat on the front porches of homes. In nearby parks, Latino young men play soccer on the spots left available as blacks play baseball or basketball. And on surrounding streets, African American churches invite all to enter, sometimes displaying a Bienvenido sign as a special invitation.

The seepage of immigrants into established neighborhoods is still too small for any major patterns of intergroup relations to develop. One place they have started is the workforce. In an African American neighborhood bordering the southern part of the University of Houston campus, for example, Latina immigrants work side by side with African Americans in restaurants, and have been doing so for quite some time. These areas are fertile sites for studying face-to-face interaction between groups. In an upper-middle-class African American neighborhood on the west side of the university, Latinas and Latinos work in the large homes of well-to-do black families, caring for their lawns and cleaning their houses. Interactions in these circumstances involve pronounced class differences.

Yet the gradual Latino penetration into these African American areas is significant enough to make the new group visible. Given that some Latino immigrants have lived in the African American neighborhoods for as long as two decades, they are no longer strangers for many African Americans, but are still not perceived as full members of the community. The situation amounts to a transitional phase of social accommodation, allowing the two groups to recognize their common identities as working-class families struggling to survive at the margins of the urban economy. It is almost an experimental phase in day-to-day interaction in which the immature intergroup relations can become tense or continue to develop in a mostly positive manner. These scenarios will for the most part play out in African American neighborhoods where Latinos, mostly immigrants, are moving in. In the traditional, east-side Mexican American neighborhoods, African Americans are not moving in and are not found in large numbers.

Several miles away from the downtown area, in the far west side of the central city, the residential patterns of African Americans and Latinos contrast with the patterns in the east-side African American and Latino neighborhoods. In the western and southwestern sectors of the city, large numbers of African Americans and Latino residents, many of whom are new immigrants, live concentrated together in large apartment complexes, some of which have several hundred apartment units or more. In these settings, race, nationality, and ethnicity divide social spaces, and islands of social networks unite clusters of apartment units together, which sometimes or often communicate in Spanish or other languages. In contrast with the occasional intergroup interaction in old African American neighborhoods, anonymity seems to be the operating rule in the apartment neighborhoods of new immigrants and African Americans, and racially or ethically different neighbors who live only a few feet apart remain worlds apart culturally.

In the large apartment complexes in areas far from downtown, the effect of social space on intergroup relations seems less pronounced. This is because many residents are new immigrants and thus still interacting primarily through internal networks in their own languages to adapt to their new surroundings. Only youth gangs and drug-dealing groups appear to make strong territorial claims in the apartment areas. In such settings, it is difference rather than similarity that seems to shore up social identities. Yet contacts do emerge between groups. This occurs especially among immigrants who have achieved some English-language skills or between Latinos who come from Mexico and Central America and those who come from black population areas of the Caribbean. These transitional apartment settings are crucibles of intergroup relations, because the groups involved have little or no sense of social heritage in the United States. It will be their offspring, the second generation, who will give greater importance to the effects of ethnic and racial rankings in U.S. society. That is, in the transitional neighborhoods the newcomers shape new social opportunity structures that have little to do with the larger course of established racial and ethnic relations in the United States. These new dynamics of adaptation among the new immigrants portend the development of diverse and mixed relations between African Americans and Latinos that have been reported for other research settings (see, for example, chapters 11 and 12 in this volume).

PROSPECTS

Even as African Americans and Latinos expand their contact with one another across neighborhoods in the Houston area, there is no guarantee that the flow of their intergroup relations always will remain positive. This is because relations between groups everywhere arise from the underlying social structures of the immediate area and of the country as a whole, and even beyond. Changes in social structures due to economic or social-demographic shifts affect all intergroup relations, and thus African Americans and Latinos do not have full control over their interactions. Furthermore, social problems are never resolved "once and for all." Social change across time and social spaces continually recreate intergroup issues and challenges. A complex matrix of historical and contemporary dimensions frames this development—making relations between African Americans and Latinos not reducible to a zero-sum game of economic behavior.

Two groups in the Latino population appear to have special advantages for promoting positive relations between African Americans and Latinos. One consists of native-born or U.S.-reared Latinos, especially those of Mexican ancestry, because Mexicans are the largest national-origin Latino category, and stand socially between African Americans and Latino immigrants. Members of this group are more familiar with African American history and culture than immigrants are, and have, like African Americans, been heavily influenced by U.S. socialization. It is thus native-born Latinos who are more apt to have interaction with African Americans, as the CMAS survey found (see table 5.3). On the other hand, U.S.-born Latinos, such as Mexican Americans, also have much in common with Latino immigrants. The heritage, family bonds, cultural and racial affinity, and identity of U.S.-born Latinos are intertwined with Latin America and Latin Americans who migrate to the United States. Native-born Latinos are thus in a position to play a major role in explaining African Americans to immigrants and immigrants to African Americans, defusing potential conflict between the two groups.

The second group consists of Latinos with an African-origin background who emigrate from the Caribbean region. Their relationships with African Americans and other Latinos are more complex because of race. The prevailing phenotype among native-born and immigrant Latinos is mestizo, whereas among African-origin Latinos it is African. Throughout the world, African-origin peoples have endured and continue to endure more discrimination than other groups. Their status in the Spanish-speaking world therefore is not much better than that of their counterparts in the United States; but it is precisely because of this that their role in fostering better relations between African Americans and Latinos in the United States is advantageous. Do they have more value than other Latinos in the African American community because of their phenotype? Does their linguistic and cultural commonality with other Latinos overcome racial differences? These are among the questions about evolving relations between African Americans and Latinos that require further research.

NOTE

1. McVicker, Steve. "Dead, Dead, Dead." *Houston Press*, May 6, 1999, p.1.

REFERENCES

Acuña, Rodolfo. 1981. *Occupied America: A History of Chicanos*, 2nd ed. New York: Harper & Row.

African American News & Issues. 2007. "Citizens Form Group to Battle HISD Bond." October 10–16, 3.

Borjas, George J. 1998. "Do Blacks Gain or Lose from Immigration?" In *Help or Hindrance?: The Economic Implications of Immigration for African Americans*, edited by Daniel S. Hamermesh and Frank D. Bean. New York: Russell Sage Foundation.

Center for Mexican American Studies. 1996. *Intergroup Relations Survey, 1996*. Center for Mexican American Studies, University of Houston.

Davila, Rosa, and Nestor Rodriguez. 2000. "Successes and Challenges of Relations Between African Americans and Latinos in the United States at the End of the Twentieth Century." In *Beyond Racism: Embracing an Interdependent Future*, edited by Lynn Huntly. Atlanta, Ga.: Southern Education Foundation.

Farrell, Michael B. 2008. "Growing Latino Vote Turning Texas 'Blue'—Houston, Dallas Already Voting Democrat." PoliticalArticles.net, November 20. Available at: http://www.politicalarticles.net/blog/2008/11/30/grow ing-latino-vote-turning-texas-blue-houston-dallas-already-voting-demo crat (accessed May 17, 2011).

Feagin, Joe R. 1988. *Free-Enterprise City: Houston in Political-Economic Perspective.* Piscataway, N.J.: Rutgers University Press.

Gee, Gilbert C. 2008. "A Multilevel Analysis of the Relationship Between Institutional and Individual Racial Discrimination and Health Status." *American Journal of Public Health* 98(Supplement 1): 48–56.

Hagan, Jacqueline, Nestor Rodriguez, Randy Capps, and Nika Kabiri. 2003. "Effects of Immigration Reform on Immigrants' Access to Health Care." *International Migration Review* 37(2): 444–63.

Houston Independent School District. 2010. "Facts and Figures About HISD." Available at: http://www.houstonisd.org (accessed July 11, 2011).

Johnson, James H., Jr., Walter C. Farrell Jr., and Chandra Guinn. 1997. "Immigration Reform and the Browning of America: Tensions, Conflicts, and Community Instability in Metropolitan Los Angeles." *International Migration Review* 31(4): 1055–95.

Kaufmann, Karen M. 2003. "Cracks in the Rainbow: Group Commonality as a Basis for Latino and African-American Political Coalitions." *Political Research Quarterly* 56(2): 199–210.

Kinder Institute for Urban Research. 2010. *Houston Area Survey* (HAS). Houston, Tex.: Kinder Institute for Urban Research, Rice University. Available at: http://www.houstonareasurvey.org (accessed May 17, 2011).

Mauer, Marc, and Ryan S. King. 2007. "Uneven Justice: State Rates of Incarceration by Race and Ethnicity." Washington, D.C.: The Sentencing Project.

Mindiola, Tatcho, Jr., Yolanda Flores Niemann, and Nestor Rodriguez. 2003. *Black-Brown Relations and Stereotypes*. Austin: University of Texas Press.

Mindiola, Tatcho, Jr., Adolfo Santos, and Luis Salinas. 2003. "Mayor's Race in Houston: Race or Party Affiliation, November 2003 Exit Poll Results." Houston, Tex.: Center for Mexican American Studies, University of Houston.

Orfield, Gary. 2001. "Schools More Separate: Consequences of a Decade of Resegregation." Civil Rights Project. Cambridge, Mass.: Harvard University.

Rodriguez, Nestor P. 1993. "Economic Restructuring and Latino Growth in Houston." In *In the Barrios: Latinos and the Underclass Debate*, edited by Joan Moore and Raquel Pinderhughes. New York: Russell Sage Foundation.

Rodriguez, Nestor P., and Jacqueline Hagan. 1992. "Apartment Restructuring and Immigrant Tenant Struggles: A Case Study of Human Agency." *Comparative Urban and Community Research* 4:164–80.

Rosenfeld, Michael J., and Marta Tienda. 1999. "Mexican Immigration, Occupational Niches, and Labor Market Competition: Evidence from Los Angeles, Chicago, and Atlanta, 1970–1990." In *Immigration and Opportunity: Race, Ethnicity, and Employment in the United States*, edited by Frank D. Bean and Stephanie Bell-Rose. New York: Russell Sage Foundation.

San Miguel, Guadalupe. 1987. *Let Them All Take Heed*. Mexican American Monograph 11. Austin: University of Texas Press.

Santos, Adolfo, Tatcho Mindiola Jr., and Luis Salinas. 2001. "Mayoral Run Off Election December, 2001 Exit Poll Results." Houston, Tex.: Center for Mexican American Studies, University of Houston.

Shenassa, Edmond D., Amy Stubbendick, and Mary Jean Brown. 2004. "Social Disparities in Housing and Related Pediatric Injury: A Multilevel Study." *American Journal of Public Health* 94(4): 633–39.

Sherman, Arloc. 2006. "African American and Latino Families Face High Rates of Hardship." Washington, D.C.: Center for Budget and Policy Priorities.

Smedley, Brian D., Adrienne Y. Stith, and Alan R. Nelson, eds. 2003. *Unequal Treatment: Confronting Racial and Ethnic Disparities in Health Care*. Washington, D.C.: National Academies Press.

Smelser, Neil J., William Julius Wilson, and Faith Mitchell, eds. 2001. *America Becoming: Racial Trends and Their Consequences* Vol. 2. Washington, D.C.: National Academies Press.

Ture, Kwame, and Charles V. Hamilton. 1992. *Black Power: The Politics of Liberation in America*. New York: Vintage Books.

United Way of Greater Houston. 2010. "Project Blueprint." Available at:

http://www.unitedwayhouston.org/leadership/pblueprint.html (accessed July 12, 2010).

U.S. Census Bureau. 2010. *2009 American Community Survey, 1-Year Estimates*. Available at: http://www.data.gov/raw/4309 (accessed June 30, 2010).

West, Cornel. 2001. *Race Matters*. Boston, Mass.: Beacon Press.

CHAPTER 6

Politics in Los Angeles

Mark Q. Sawyer

African Americans and Latinos in Los Angeles are increasingly occupying the same space. Traditionally African American, South Los Angeles has in recent years become a majority Latino area. As a result, school populations are changing and African Americans and Latinos are interacting everywhere else as well, from churches to prisons (Dzidzienyo and Oboler 2005). When considering how collective action might change attitudes among African Americans and Latinos beyond the context of economic competition, the political realm cannot be neglected (Waldinger and Bozorgmehr 1996). Although much research has been done on black-white ethnic relations in neighborhoods, relations between African Americans and Latinos are becoming increasingly important. Incidents in the streets as well as past and current election cycles have yielded different schools of thought. Some have argued that coalition politics are inevitable, and others that intergroup conflict, or at least distance, is the most likely outcome (Vaca 2004; Hutchinson 2007).

Events on the ground have not resolved any issues, however. Mexican American Antonio Villaraigosa was first elected mayor in 2005 with an overwhelming majority of the black vote. This was exciting, but it came only after an equally overwhelming majority of black voters had helped elect Villaraigosa's white opponent in 2001. Latinos have been just as ambivalent in both national and local races. Although nearly two-thirds of Latinos exit-polled in the 2008 presidential election reported that they cast their vote for Obama, most Latinos still express considerable antiblack prejudice. Substantial violence against African Americans also persists within Los Angeles neighborhoods.[1] Additionally, a nontrivial number of African Americans have joined with anti-immigrant groups in California both in the past and currently, explicitly stating positions against Latinos and their interests (Hutchinson 2007). The issues are thus complex and, even in the context of Los Angeles, where some issues present serious problems, Latinos and African Americans nonetheless converge on some issues and feelings.

One central question that lingers is whether the basic interaction between blacks and whites serves as a blueprint for understanding the interaction between blacks and Latinos. Some suggest that Latinos are ethnics on their way to assimilating toward whiteness. Others argue that currently and historically Latinos have been racialized in the United States. In no place in America are those dynamics more on display than in Los Angeles—which is both a receiving destination and home to a well-established, multigenerational, and politically powerful Latino population that interacts with a large and equally well-established African American populace.

Los Angeles has a unique past. Once a part of Mexico, until the defeat of Mexico in the Mexican-American War, it has a racial history set simultaneously in the norms of Latin America and those of the United States (Menchaca 2001). This framework has evolved into a contemporary Los Angeles with a history of political coalitions between African Americans and Latinos and some conflict. Tom Bradley, the first African American mayor of the city, was in part elected with the help of the Latino population. Antonio Villaraigosa, the city's first Latino mayor, was defeated in his first run by Kenneth Hahn, largely with the support of black voters. In his second campaign, however, exit polls report that Villaraigosa received a solid majority of black votes. This shift in African American support came after the racially charged Proposition 187, which sought to deny basic services to undocumented immigrants, passed with only a slim majority of African American support but overwhelming support from whites.

Los Angeles has seen both cooperation and conflict between the racial and ethnic groups living there. In California more generally, black and Latino prisoners are segregated in prisons because of a history of heated conflicts, some of which spill out into the streets of Los Angeles and lead to killings. One such incident was the result of some black residents' being targeted by Latino gangs. After a high school football star was murdered, anti-immigrant groups attempted to use the African American community to launch a repeal of Order 40, which prevents the Los Angles Police Department (LAPD) from cooperating with immigration officials. The effort failed, but it underscored the reality that some African American residents see Latinos as a threat. Moreover, the Latino population is growing most rapidly in what were once African American neighborhoods (Hunt and

Ramón 2010). Looking more closely at the relationship between the groups is thus merited.

This chapter relies on the 2007 Los Angeles County Social Survey (LACSS), which was conducted by the University of California–Los Angeles (UCLA) Center for the Study of Race, Ethnicity, and Politics to assess opinions, attitudes, and behaviors related to coalitional politics in Los Angeles County. The study respondents included 275 African Americans, 275 Latinos (71 percent Mexican, 53 percent of interviews conducted in Spanish), 260 whites, and 276 Asian Americans. The survey provides a unique look into intergroup relations in Los Angeles County and included modules designed to reveal the nature of intergroup relations not only between blacks and whites but also among minority groups.

This chapter explores a series of dimensions to examine the possibility for social and political cooperation between African Americans and Latinos in the Los Angeles area. Its central argument is that a series of uneven patterns across these dimensions point to both problems and possibilities in relations between African Americans and Latinos in Los Angeles.

IDENTITY

One question inevitably raised when African American and Latino coalitions are discussed is whether Latinos identify as whites (see chapter 7, this volume). In the 2001 census, half of all Latinos identify as whites, the other half as Other. It is not clear whether those who identify as white are identifying with the ideas and attitudes of white Americans or merely describing their skin color. Evidence is substantial that even those who do identify as white do not see their identities as indistinguishable from those of white Americans. Latin America has its own legacy of race, which has included antiblack prejudice and discrimination, albeit distinct from that in the United States. Similarly, U.S.-born Latinos within all groups frequently experience racial prejudice, and some nontrivial percentage within the United States consider themselves black or indigenous. However, although indigenous identity is a significant part of Latino identity in Los Angeles, the Latino groups who most identify as black in the United States are Dominicans and Puerto Ricans, very few of whom live in Los Angeles County. Most Latinos living in Los Angeles County are of Mexican or Central American origin. This means that they come from places where—despite a history of slavery and the existence of small pockets of people of African descent—blackness has been erased within national racial discourse. Thus, many Mexicans and Central Americans see blackness as "foreign." Similarly, many African Americans, especially in the United States, have little knowledge of the substantial presence of people of African descent in Latin America or the history of Mexico's role in providing safe passage and protection for citizens of African descent and African Americans fleeing slavery in the United States.

Although racial identity for blacks and Asians is perceived in the United States to be a stable phenomenon, literature on Latinos and the question of race is substantial (Hattam 2007). Much of this literature seeks to answer the major question of how we assess Latino identity: are they whites in waiting, in terms of how they see themselves? Much of the orthodox literature on immigration posits Latinos as ethnics in the same vein as ethnic white migrants of the early twentieth century (Hayes-Bautista and Rodríguez 1994; Alba and Nee 2003; Hayes-Bautista 2004). However, a growing literature citing the experiences of Latino groups like Puerto Ricans, Mexicans, and Dominicans, who are perceived to be phenotypically distinct from whites or indistinct from blacks, has suggested that Latinos are becoming racialized in ways similar to African Americans despite the vast variation in terms of phenotype and location of national origin (Alcoff 2000; Telles and Ortiz 2008). Still another group sees the diversity of Latinos as being somehow outside race, arguing that Latinos, given their so-called mixed-race identity and the history of mestizaje, will destabilize notions of race in the United States (Rodriguez 2007). The tendency of Latinos and, in particular, Mexicans in the United States to choose either Other, white, or multiple categories on the census has contributed greatly to this debate (Bean and Tienda 1988; Rodriguez 2000). Adjudicating between these points of view is difficult to do here, but we can gain some purchase in terms of whether Latinos think of themselves as an ethnic group or a racialized minority.

One approach I took was to offer Latinos familiar categories from Latin America rather than the traditional census categories presented to them in the United States. In figure 6.1, we see how Latinos chose to identify when offered a range of categories used throughout Latin America. Thirty percent selected Other. However, this is far fewer than the number who select Other on the census (Rodriguez 2000).

Table 6.1 Latino American Racial Self-Descriptions

Denomination	Percentage
Blanco	19
Moreno	17
Mestizo	15
Trigueño	11
Indio	7
Negro	1
Mulato	1
None of these	30

Question: Now, I want to ask you about some other ways that Latino Americans describe themselves racially. Are you . . . [denominations]?

Source: Author's compilation based on his own research, the 2007 Los Angeles County Social Survey.

Similarly, the choice of white goes down substantially as well. Only 19 percent of Latinos think of themselves as white in the context of the survey when presented with the other categories. Latin American categories absorb the majority of responses. When we look at U.S. born versus foreign born we see an even more stark difference. We can see this dynamic in table 6.1.

When we examine foreign-born Latinos, the prevailing category shifts dramatically. Table 6.2 demonstrates this shift in racial identification between U.S.- and foreign-born Latinos. Fifty-five percent of foreign-born Latinos choose the category Moreno (dark-skinned), whereas almost 24 percent of their U.S.-born counterparts choose the category None of These. For the foreign born, the spread of the distribution of choices was much more scattered, showing that over time second-generation Latinos transition from thinking of themselves in the polychromatic terms more consistent with Latin America. That said, it is clear that though Latinos might not think of themselves as ethnic whites, they have a different conception of race that is not entirely compatible with the stable categories defined by the black-white paradigm. What is unclear is how those who identify as None of These or Moreno think of themselves with respect to African Americans or other minorities. What is clear is that whiteness is not how they see themselves. This presents some opportunity for coalition building but also presents challenges.

Latino immigrants and U.S.-born Latinos seemingly approach racial categorization in a very different way from African Americans.

Table 6.2 Latino American Racial Self-Descriptions

Denomination	Foreign Born	U.S. Born
Blanco	15.7%	20.1%
Moreno	3.7	24.1
Mestizo	12.0	16.1
Trigueño	1.9	16.1
Indio	6.5	7.5
Negro	1.9	0.6
Mulato	0.9	0.6
None of these	54.6	14.4

Source: Author's compilation based on his own research, the 2007 Los Angeles County Social Survey.

However, black identity has become thought of as more complex but is considered more of an on-off phenomenon; fewer African Americans choose mixed race despite the legacy of racial mixture and the general public thinking of people as either black or not black (Torres-Saillant 1998; Cohen 1999; Waters 1999; Cordero-Guzmán, Smith, and Grosfoguel 2001; Dawson 2001). It is possible that in contexts where African Americans and Latinos in Los Angeles are discussing race, they may be thinking of very different phenomena. Latinos may be seeing themselves in terms of either other or chromatic categories, and African Americans as either on one side of the color line or another. However, Latinos in the second generation tend to choose the category Other, whereas a plurality of recent immigrants select Moreno, a category that denotes darker skin. This suggests that, at a minimum, though not exactly compatible, African American and Latino identities in Los Angeles are not opposed to each other.

ISSUE SALIENCE

In terms of assessing the essential issues that define African American–Latino relations, we need to get an idea of what issues each group sees as central to their current concerns. This section explores both the most important issues for each group, and the degree to which those issues offer potential for cooperation or conflict.

One important foundation for coalition formation is whether groups consider the same issues important. In figure 6.1, we see their views on Los Angeles in general, but also the issues specific groups consider most important. Immigration, crime, and traffic were the

Figure 6.1 Most Important Problem Facing Los Angeles

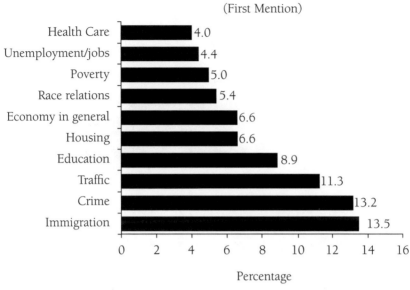

(First Mention)

Health Care	4.0
Unemployment/jobs	4.4
Poverty	5.0
Race relations	5.4
Economy in general	6.6
Housing	6.6
Education	8.9
Traffic	11.3
Crime	13.2
Immigration	13.5

0   2   4   6   8   10   12   14   16

Percentage

Source: Author's calculations based on his own research, the 2007 Los Angeles County Social Survey.

issues mentioned first in an open-ended question that Angelenos chose, with an almost even split between those who thought there were too many illegal immigrants and those who thought immigrants did not have enough rights. However, when we turn to what issues the group faces, we get very different answers.

African Americans see unemployment, education, and racial discrimination as the central issues facing the black community. To the extent that some may attribute unemployment to undocumented immigrants, building coalitions on the issue may be difficult. However, the issue of immigration does not appear on the list of African American issues. Thus, immigration per se is not a problem for African Americans but may be one only inasmuch as they perceive it to negatively affect their employment prospects (see figure 6.2).

For Latinos, the picture is slightly different. Latinos see immigration, education, and racial discrimination as their main problems, and the overwhelming majority believe that immigrants do not have enough rights. Again, as with African Americans, the portrait is mixed. The Latino focus on the issue of immigration may trigger African

Figure 6.2 Most Important Problem Facing African Americans

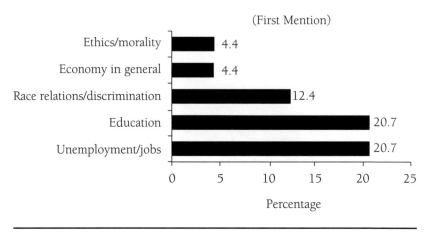

(First Mention)

Ethics/morality	4.4
Economy in general	4.4
Race relations/discrimination	12.4
Education	20.7
Unemployment/jobs	20.7

Percentage

Source: Author's calculations based on his own research, the 2007 Los Angeles County Social Survey.

American concerns about jobs. However, both groups share concerns related to racial discrimination, Latinos perhaps seeing the issue largely through the lens of nativism and immigration and African Americans through the question of unemployment and jobs. Education and inequality may perhaps be the first and most fruitful area for coalitions. It scores high for both groups, and connects to the joint concern of racial discrimination and inequality. However, if activists in early moments of coalition-building trigger a debate that centers around African American unemployment versus Mexican immigrant rights, the coalition will likely be derailed. It is important to steer African Americans from seeing problems of unemployment as caused by immigration and pushing Latinos toward connecting their concerns about immigration as part of a broader narrative of racial discrimination that equally affects African Americans. We can see this point of tangency in figure 6.3.

IMMIGRATION

Immigration has been an issue of accelerated importance on the national stage and in California for some time. The passage of Proposition 187 with majority black support is one area that speaks to potential conflicts. Since the turn of the century, when European im-

Figure 6.3 Most Important Problem Facing Latinos

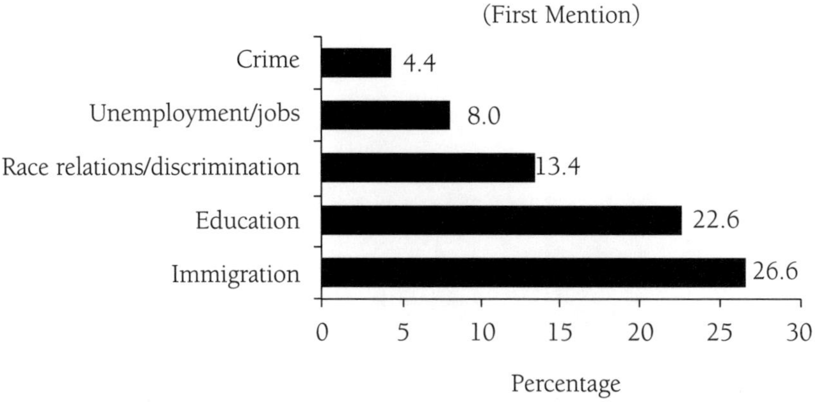

(First Mention)

Problem	Percentage
Crime	4.4
Unemployment/jobs	8.0
Race relations/discrimination	13.4
Education	22.6
Immigration	26.6

Percentage

Source: Author's calculations based on his own research, the 2007 Los Angeles County Social Survey.

migrants, in particular, made the transition from their original ethnic identity to whiteness and frequently adopted virulent forms of anti-black racism in their quest for whiteness, African Americans have been ambivalent about immigration. Groups have tended to racially distance themselves from African Americans and have embraced antiblack racism (Roediger 2005). The long-standing issue has been that African Americans, in the past and present, widely believe that immigration harms their employment prospects. African Americans, more than any other group, feel that undocumented immigrants hurt the economy in Los Angeles. Meanwhile, Latinos are the group most likely to say that undocumented immigrants help the economy. This juxtaposition of beliefs presents a challenge for those trying to forge political coalitions around workforce issues. Figure 6.4 highlights attitudes about whether immigrants help or hinder the economy.

When asked which of the current immigration proposals they supported, African Americans, like most non-Latinos, demonstrated a plurality of support for allowing undocumented immigrants to remain if they meet certain conditions, such as paying a fine (see table 6.3). Only Latinos overwhelmingly support immediate amnesty, and African Americans were the least likely to support it. The good news is the emerging consensus on undocumented immigration, that in general the undocumented should be allowed to stay if they meet certain conditions. This falls short of amnesty, but it is clear that,

Figure 6.4 Do Illegal Immigrants Hurt or Help the Economy?

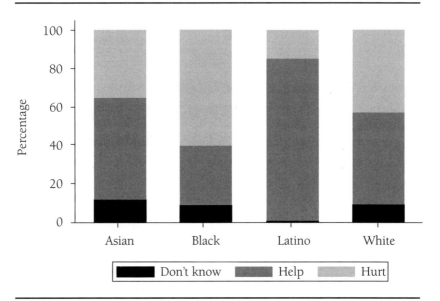

Source: Author's calculations based on his own research, the 2007 Los Angeles County Social Survey.

Figure 6.5 A Lot of Political Commonality

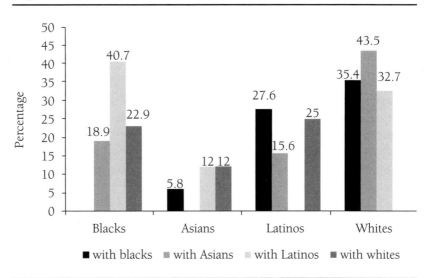

Source: Author's calculations based on his own research, the 2007 Los Angeles County Social Survey.

Table 6.3 Support for Immigration Policy Alternatives

Race	Policy Alternative	Percentage
Black	Make illegal	20.7
	Guestworker	17.8
	Allow to remain	42.9
	Grant amnesty	8.4
Asian	Make illegal	11.6
	Guestworker	27.5
	Allow to remain	46.7
	Grant amnesty	10.9
Latino	Make illegal	3.3
	Guestworker	6.3
	Allow to remain	43.6
	Grant amnesty	46.6
White	Make illegal	13.9
	Guestworker	19.6
	Allow to remain	48.1
	Grant amnesty	12.3

Question: Which of the following comes closest to your view about what government policy should be toward illegal immigrants currently residing in the United States? Should the government . . . [alternatives]?

Source: Author's compilation based on his own research, the 2007 Los Angeles County Social Survey.

even among African Americans, support for massive deportations is not widespread. However, it is also clear that more and better information on the positive and negative effects of immigration on employment opportunities for African Americans is needed. Also, the civil- and human-rights dimensions of immigration as an issue might be a central area of focus, rather than the economic justice dimension. The building blocks of a coalition depend on whether groups perceive themselves to share interests. Blacks and Latinos are more likely to feel they have political commonality with one another than any other groups. However, almost a majority of African Americans feel they have strong political commonality with Latinos, whereas slightly less than 30 percent of Latinos reciprocate the belief. The challenge in this area, then, is to raise the feeling of political commonality with blacks among Latinos, where they will find a willing coalition partner. Figure 6.5 shows the feelings of commonality among African Americans and Latinos with one another and with other groups.

RACIAL ATTITUDES

One central question that has surrounded the study of minority relations has been the degree to which negative stereotypes exist and, secondarily, the degree to which those attitudes determine policy preferences about the target group. Among whites and African Americans and Latinos, those connections are clear. Negative racial attitudes among whites are predictors of policy positions that are harmful to the interests of the target group. This section explores these dimensions with regard to African Americans and Latinos in Los Angeles.

STEREOTYPES

One major issue in terms of intergroup relations is the degree to which groups support stereotypes about one another. Here we examine a range of stereotypes by groups to understand the degree to which groups perceive one another according to prevalent stereotypes. In this analysis, we examine the degree to which respondents felt that members of a group prefer welfare to work, speak English well, and are involved in gangs and drugs. For whites, traditionally these stereotypes have had high salience. This means they predict support for various crime policies, affirmative action, immigration policies, welfare, party identification, and a host of other variables. Although these issues do not seem to have the same salience for African Americans and Latinos, they are important nonetheless in that even if a group thinks the stereotype applies to them, members of the group do not like to hear others use that stereotype.

In terms of the welfare stereotype, Latinos perceive African Americans as preferring welfare to working for a living. African Americans, though, see no difference between Latinos and themselves in terms of welfare prevalence. Asians, meanwhile, see both Latinos and blacks as having very high preferences for welfare. Table 6.4 demonstrates the prevalence of these stereotypes among the groups.

We asked another question: "Do these groups speak English well or poorly?" Blacks see Latinos and Asians as speaking English poorly but especially single out Latinos relative to Asians (table 6.5). At the

Table 6.4 Welfare Stereotype Prevalence*

Race of Respondent	Race of Target Group	Stereotype Prevalence **
Black	White	18%
	Black	31
	Latino	30
	Asian	13
Asian	White	10
	Black	69
	Latino	61
	Asian	13
Latino	White	24
	Black	55
	Latino	23
	Asian	19
White	White	15
	Black	27
	Latino	22
	Asian	11
Full sample	White	18
	Black	45
	Latino	34
	Asian	15

Source: Author's compilation based on his own research, the 2007 Los Angeles County Social Survey.
* Welfare stereotype prevalence scale ranges from 1 to 7, where 1 means that people in that category prefer to be self-supporting and 7 that people prefer welfare.
** Stereotype prevalence measures the percent of individuals who reported scale values between 5 and 7 (top scores) about the target group's welfare prevalence. Rounded values.

same time, 23 percent of the Latinos surveyed think that blacks speak English poorly, even though the overwhelming majority of African Americans have English as their first and only language. Stereotypes about English-language proficiency are problems for Asian Americans and Latinos, both of whom are perceived to be foreign. African Americans face some stereotype around English proficiency from Latinos that dovetails with those about intelligence.

Criminality is a common racial stereotype that dogs ethnic and racial minorities, African Americans and Latinos in particular. Despite relatively similar rates of illegal drug use and abuse across all racial and ethnic groups, African Americans and Latinos are dispro-

Table 6.5 Language Stereotype Prevalence*

Race of Respondent	Race of Target Group	Stereotype Prevalence**
Black	White	15%
	Black	21
	Latino	49
	Asian	34
Asian	White	2
	Black	6
	Latino	38
	Asian	33
Latino	White	8
	Black	23
	Latino	31
	Asian	35
White	White	12
	Black	18
	Latino	49
	Asian	21
Full sample	White	9
	Black	18
	Latino	49
	Asian	31

Source: Author's compilation based on his own research, the 2007 Los Angeles County Social Survey.
* Language stereotype prevalence scale ranges from 1 to 7, where 1 means that people in that category tend to speak English poorly and 7 means that people in that category tend to speak English well.
** Stereotype prevalence measures the percent of individuals who reported scale values between 1 and 3 (low scores) about the target group's language prevalence. Rounded values.

portionally incarcerated for drugs at increasing rates. Gang crime is also experienced across racial groups. However, it is clear that this stereotype is disproportionately applied to African Americans and Latinos. In many cases, even African Americans and Latinos do not protest this stereotype. They also both see the other group as heavily involved in gangs and drugs. However, although African Americans see African American and Latino involvement about equally, Latinos place African American involvement in gangs and drugs at even higher levels than their own. Thus, although Latinos believe the stereotype about themselves, they believe that it applies even more with

Table 6.6 Drugs and Gangs Stereotype Prevalence*

Race of Respondent	Race of Target Group	Stereotype Prevalence**
Black	White	35%
	Black	59
	Latino	60
	Asian	35
Asian	White	18
	Black	66
	Latino	51
	Asian	15
Latino	White	38
	Black	71
	Latino	56
	Asian	30
White	White	15
	Black	39
	Latino	40
	Asian	15
Full sample	White	17
	Black	59
	Latino	52
	Asian	23

Source: Author's compilation based on his own research, the 2007 Los Angeles County Social Survey.

* Drugs and gangs stereotype prevalence scale ranges from 1 to 7, where 1 means that people in that category tend not to be involved with drugs and gangs and 7 means that people in that category tend to be involved in drugs and gangs.

** Stereotype prevalence measures the percent of individuals who reported scale values between 5 and 7 (high scores) about the target group's drugs and gangs prevalence. Rounded values.

respect to African Americans. These stereotypes can be seen in table 6.6.

SYMBOLIC RACISM

The American public has largely rejected biological notions of racism. In its place is symbolic racism (Kinder and Sanders 1996; Sears 1993). Symbolic racism measures the degree to which individuals blame racial minorities for inequality, rather than discrimination or structural racism. For whites, measures of symbolic racism have proved useful in predicting support for affirmative action and other issues, such as

Figure 6.6 Symbolic Racism by Race

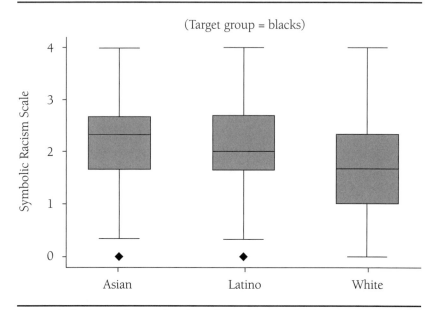

(Target group = blacks)

Source: Author's calculations based on his own research, the 2007 Los Angeles County Social Survey.

support for black candidates among whites. In general, whites who score high on levels of symbolic racism oppose affirmative action and a range of other redistributive policies seen as benefiting blacks. Figure 6.6 presents mean levels of symbolic racism.

We see in figure 6.6 that Latinos score slightly higher than whites on the mean scale but significantly lower than Asians. These differences are largely produced by the large number of foreign-born respondents taking the survey in their native language. There is some evidence that even symbolic racism in the United States is subject to some level of political correctness, and that immigrants—especially from Asia, Mexico, and Latin America—have generally underdeveloped notions of racism (Sawyer 2005). However, we will later see beyond the mean levels of symbolic racism what effect the concept has on structuring policy preferences.

MULTIVARIATE ANALYSIS

Beyond the overall mean differences, we can assess whether stereotypes, symbolic racism, and other factors structure African American

Table 6.7 OLS Regressions; Support for Affirmative
          Action at UCLA

	Model 1 (Latinos)	Model 2 (Whites)
Education (1–10)	−.025	.018
	(.036)	(.05)
Income group (1–12)	−.034	−.093***
	(.037)	(.029)
Gender (0–1; 1 = male)	−.092	.1
	(.175)	(.176)
Age group (1–6)	.022	−.028
	(.056)	(.063)
Ideology (1–3; 3 = conservative)	−.059	−.352***
	(.117)	(.127)
Symbolic racism (1–5)	−.343***	−.538***
	(.112)	(.096)
Stereotype-blacks (1–7)	−.117	.013
	(.075)	(.076)
Immigrant (0–1; 1 = immigrant)	−.178	
	(.201)	
Constant	5.43***	5.47***
	(.569)	(.622)
R-square	.07	.24
N	262	246

Source: Author's compilation based on his own research, the 2007 Los Angeles County Social Survey.
* $p < .1$, ** $p < .05$, *** $p < .01$

and Latino attitudes about immigration policy and affirmative action. We can also assess the effects of these variables relative to how they structure white opinions on these topics. The relatively similar sample size of all groups allows for this analysis and provides an interesting look into what motivates these outcomes for each group.

The first model examines the effects of stereotypes and symbolic racism on attitudes about affirmative action. In particular, it examines whether symbolic racism on the part of whites and Latinos affects willingness to support affirmative action in order to remedy the fact that African Americans make up less than 1 percent of the entering UCLA freshman class.

We find that symbolic racism predicts opposition to affirmative action for both whites and Latinos. Stereoytpes play a role in either case. However, the effect of symbolic racism is much stronger for whites

Figure 6.7 Support for Affirmative Action and Symbolic Racism

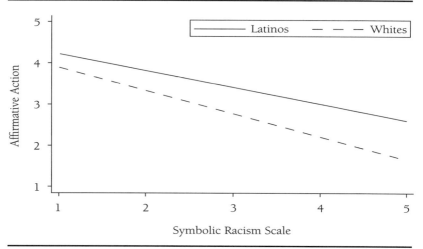

Source: Author's calculations based on his own research, the 2007 Los Angeles County Social Survey.
Note: Affirmative Action are fitted values of the regressions; other regressors set at their mean.

Table 6.8 Logistic Regressions, Support for Anti-Immigrant Policy

	Model 1	Model 2
	(Blacks)	(Whites)
Education (1 – 10)	−.097	.001
	(.081)	(.104)
Income group (1 – 12)	.128**	.004
	(.061)	(.066)
Gender (0–1; 1 = male)	−.157	−.123
	(.337)	(.398)
Age group (1–6)	.147	−.011
	(.1)	(.143)
Ideology (1–3; 3 = conservative)	−.078	.308
	(.24)	(.277)
Stereotype Latinos (1–7)	.344***	.562***
	(.125)	(.166)
Constant	−3.3***	−4.74***
	(1.05)	(1.4)
Log likelihood	−133.5	−94.8
N	275	260

Source: Author's compilation based on his own research, the 2007 Los Angeles County Social Survey.
$* p < .1, ** p < .05, *** p < .01$

Figure 6.8 Support for Anti-Immigrant Policy and Stereotypes of Latinos Among Blacks and Whites

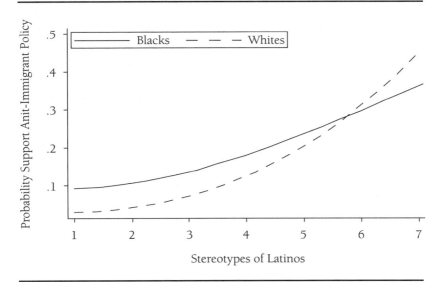

Source: Author's calculations based on his own research, the 2007 Los Angeles County Social Survey..
Note: Probabilities are fitted values of the regressions; other regressors set at their mean

than it is for Latinos, demonstrating that the set of beliefs, though salient, has a muted effect among Latinos. For whites, the model is much more predictable, lower income and conservative ideology contributing to a negative view of using affirmative action to remedy UCLA's enrollment imbalance. For Latinos, these measures play little role. The results of the effects of symbolic racism on attitudes about affirmative action at UCLA can be seen in table 6.7 and figure 6.7.

A similar model emerges with immigration policy (see table 6.8 and figure 6.8). Support for massive deportation of immigrants among blacks and whites is in part driven by stereotypes about Latinos, but those stereotypes operate more strongly for whites than for blacks. In cases of affirmative action and immigration policy, support by both blacks and Latinos is driven by similar forms of bias against the other group. However, that bias has less of an effect among minorities than it does with whites. These differences are not driven by sample size in some surveys, because sample sizes are similar across groups. We see in this area that though stereotypes and symbolic racism play a key role in structuring attitudes for all groups, measures tend to be more powerful for whites than for African Americans or Latinos. We therefore must attempt to deal with those issues within African American and Latino communities.

CONCLUSION

The Los Angeles County Social Survey demonstrates both the clear possibilities and the substantial challenges for building coalitions among Latinos and African Americans in Los Angeles. The election of Mayor Antonio Villaraigosa with majority African American support in 2005 demonstrates that this form of coalitional work has worked but that it can also be episodic and easily interrupted by events. Stuctural issues are also a factor. Lingering stereotypes among the groups and the perception by African Americans that immigration negatively affects African American employment opportunities presents a clear challenge. Much of the Latino organizational infrastructure in Los Angeles is organized around the issue of immigration. However, a greater focus on education, health, opportunity, and racial justice might help build common ground and open opportunities to develop a more consensual understanding of immigration and its economic impact.

Like Matt Barreto and Gabriel Sanchez (2008), as well as the authors of chapters 2, 4, and 9 in this volume, I find that although coalitions among African Americans are neither inevitable nor impossible, both promise and problems are substantial. As Kevin Wallsten and Tatishe Nteta demonstrate in chapter 4 of this volume, framing on the part of elites and at the grassroots level will be critical in building bridges on issues, identities, and education about various misconceptions, such as stereotypes.

Los Angeles is a complicated landscape and though the problems are substantial on key issues related to workforce development, critical opportunities for shared work and interests across these groups that have been so disadvantaged over time are available. The data demonstrate substantial openings that must be supported by critical mobilization of resources. However, to reach and capture the imagination of a mass audience these resources must be carefully calibrated so as to build bridges and not pour salt into existing wounds.

NOTES

1. "Black-Hispanic Gang Rivalries Plague Los Angeles," *Fox News*, August 12, 2006 (available at: http://www.foxnews.com/story/0,2933,208083,00. html); V. Kim "Two Gang Members Convicted of Hate-Crime Murders," *Los Angeles Times*, September 10, 2010 (available at: http://articles.latimes.com/2010/sep/10/local/la-me-0910-harborgateway-20100910); Hutchinson 2005.

REFERENCES

Alba, Richard, and Victor Nee. 2003. *Remaking the American Mainstream: Assimilation and Contemporary Immigration*. Cambridge, Mass.: Harvard University Press

Alcoff, Linda Martin. 2000. "Is Latina-o Identity a Racial Identity?" In *Hispanics-Latinos in the United States*, edited by Jorge J. E. Gracia and Pablo De Greiff. New York: Routledge.

Barreto, Matt, and Gabriel Sanchez. 2008. "Social and Political Competition Between Latinos and Blacks: Exposing Myths, Uncovering New Realities." Paper presented at the Latino National Survey Conference. Cornell University (November 12, 2008).

Bean, Frank D., and Marta Tienda, eds. 1988. *The Hispanic Population of the United States*. New York: Russell Sage Foundation.

Cohen, Cathy J. 1999. *The Boundaries of Blackness: AIDs and the Breakdown of Black Politics*. Chicago: University of Chicago Press.

Cordero-Guzmán, Hector R., Robert C. Smith, and Ramon Grosfoguel. 2001. *Migration, Transnationalization, and Race in a Changing New York*. Philadelphia, Pa.: Temple University Press.

Dawson, Michael C. 2001. *Black Visions: The Roots of Contemporary African-American Political Ideologies*. Chicago: University of Chicago Press.

Dzidzienyo, Anani, and Suzanne Oboler 2005. *Neither Enemies nor Friends: Latinos, Blacks, Afro-Latinos*. New York: Palgrave Macmillan.

Hattam, Victoria C. 2007. *In the Shadow of Race: Jews, Latinos, and Immigrant Politics in the United States*. Chicago: University of Chicago Press.

Hayes-Bautista, David E. 2004. *La Nueva California: Latinos in the Golden State*. Berkeley: University of California Press.

Hayes-Bautista, David E., and Gregory Rodríguez. 1994. *Latino South Central*. Los Angeles: Alta California Policy Research Center.

Hunt, Darnell M., and Ana-Christina Ramón. 2010. *Black Los Angeles: American Dreams and Racial Realities*. New York: New York University Press.

Hutchinson, Earl O. 2005. "Los Angeles School Brawls Expose Black-Latino

Tension." *New America Media*, April 25, 2005. Available at: http://news
.ncmonlinecom/news/view_article.html?article_id=00c83b0739520c4f38
0469df2c520743 (accessed July 20, 2011).

————. 2007. *The Latino Challenge to Black America*. Los Angeles, Calif.:
Middle Passage Press.

Kinder, Donald R., and Lynn M. Sanders. 1996. *Divided by Color: Racial
Politics and Democratic Ideals*. Chicago: University of Chicago Press.

Menchaca, Martha 2001. *Recovering History, Constructing Race: The Indian,
Black, and White Roots of Mexican Americans*. Austin: University of Texas
Press.

Rodriguez, Clara E. 2000. *Changing Race: Latinos, the Census, and the History
of Ethnicity in the United States*. New York: New York University Press.

Rodriguez, Gregory 2007. *Mongrels, Bastards, Orphans, and Vagabonds: Mexican Immigration and the Future of Race in America*. New York: Pantheon
Books.

Roediger, David R. 2005. *Working Toward Whiteness: How America's Immigrants Became White*. New York, Basic Books.

Sawyer, Mark Q. 2005. *Racial Politics in Post-Revolutionary Cuba*. New York:
Cambridge University Press.

Sears, David O. 1993. "Symbolic Politics: A Socio-Psychological Theory." In
Explorations in Political Psychology, edited by Shanto Iyengar and William
J. McGuire. Durham, N.C.: Duke University Press.

Telles, Edward, and Vilma Ortiz. 2008. *Generations of Exclusion: Mexican
Americans, Assimilation, and Race*. New York: Russell Sage Foundation.

Torres-Saillant, Silvio. 1998. "Visions of Dominicanness in the United
States." In *Borderless Borders: U.S. Latinos, Latin Americans, and the Paradox of Interdependence*, edited by Frank Bonilla, Edwin Melendez, Rebecca
Morales, and Maria de los Angeles Torres. Philadelphia, Pa.: Temple University Press.

Vaca, Nicholás C. 2004. *The Presumed Alliance: The Unspoken Conflict Between Latinos and Blacks and What It Means for America*. New York: HarperCollins.

Waldinger, Roger D., and Mehdi Bozorgmehr, eds. 1996. *Ethnic Los Angeles*.
New York: Russell Sage Foundation.

Waters, Mary C. 1999. "Explaining the Comfort Factor: West Indian Immi-
grants Confront American Race Relations." In *The Cultural Territories of
Race: Black and White Boundaries*, edited by Michèle Lamont. Chicago:
University of Chicago Press.

PART IV

New Relations in
New Destinations

CHAPTER 7

Intergroup Relations in Three Southern Cities

Paula D. McClain, Gerald F. Lackey, Efrén O. Pérez,
Niambi M. Carter, Jessica Johnson Carew,
Eugene Walton Jr., Candis Watts Smith,
Monique L. Lyle, and Shayla C. Nunnally

Immigration to the United States soared between the 1990 and 2000 censuses and continued at high rates between 2000 and 2007, resulting in significant demographic shifts in some regions of the country. Most of this increase is Latino, and the region most affected is the South. A number of southern states—North Carolina, Alabama, and Georgia—reported substantial increases in their Latino populations from 1990 to 2000 (U.S. Bureau of the Census 2000a). Many saw even greater growth between 2000 and 2007. North Carolina, for example, experienced a 68.8 percent increase, from 377,084 in 2000 to 636,442 in 2007, and Arkansas 77.8 percent, from 85,303 in 2000 to 145,918 in 2007 (Pew Hispanic Center 2007). Moreover, the top five states with the largest growth in Latino population between 2000 and 2006 were in the South—Arkansas, Georgia, South Carolina, Tennessee, and North Carolina (U.S. Bureau of the Census 2008). The South in fact has the second-largest concentration of Latinos, 14.5 percent, after the West, 26.6 percent (U.S. Bureau of the Census 2008).

No other region of the country has been as defined by race as the South. These new immigrants are moving into a region where race and race relations between blacks and whites have influenced virtually every important outcome, for example, life chances, educational opportunities, legal rights, and violent treatment, among other things. Given how recent this Latino immigration has been, it is not surprising that little scholarly attention has yet been paid. Some economists have begun to examine labor force effects of and the types of jobs Latino immigrants take in the South (Ciscel, Smith, and Mendoza 2003; Griffith 1993; Kandel and Parrado 2004; Mohl

2003; Murphy, Blanchard, and Hill 2001; Torres 2000), and several social scientists have done or are doing ethnographic studies in selected southern communities (see, for example, Henken 2005; Hernández-León and Zúñiga 2000, 2001, 2002, 2003, 2005; Marrow 2008; Winders 2008).

The changes in the racial dynamic of the South raise many questions that need to be addressed. For example, how are native-born black and white Americans reacting to the presence of a third population with little or no history in the region? How do these new immigrants perceive relations with their new black and white neighbors? Research in the area of the effects of Latino immigration on intergroup relations in the South is, as just noted, recent and not extensive (McClain et al. 2006, 2007; Marrow 2008). This chapter provides a glimpse at the context in which racial intergroup relations will be developed in three southern locations that represent three distinct southern environments: majority black (Memphis, Tennessee), more or less equal black and white populations (Durham, North Carolina), and minority black (Little Rock, Arkansas).

WHITE ATTITUDES TOWARD IMMIGRATION

Research in political science on white attitudes toward immigration has run along four parallel lines of inquiry—number and type of immigrants, economic perceptions, cultural concerns, and prejudice.[1] Research in the first area, number and type of immigrants, examines the extent to which opposition to foreigners is influenced by the demographic balance between immigrants and native-born populations. Caroline Tolbert and Rodney Hero (1996), in an examination of county support for Proposition 187, California's 1994 anti-immigrant ballot measure, find that net of party affiliation and economic conditions, the proportion of Latinos within a given county had a significant and positive effect on county support for the ballot initiative. This relationship, however, is qualified by the racial-ethnic balance of counties. Counties where Anglos and Latinos make up the bulk of the population strongly supported Proposition 187, whereas counties with a more heterogeneous racial-ethnic composition manifested weaker support for the anti-immigrant measure. Additionally, M. W. Hood and Irwin Morris (1998) found that individual support for increased levels of immigration decreased as proximity to large populations of undocumented immigrants increased. Other studies, however, failed to find any relationship between anti-immigrant opinion and proximity to large populations of foreigners (Hood and Morris 1997, 2000; Stein, Post, and Rinden 2000).

Other scholars have paid special attention to the role economic factors play in generating white opposition to immigration. Although research has shown that one's personal economic situation is a poor predictor of one's position on immigration policy, one's view about national economic health, as well as one's concern with the negative effect of immigrants on job opportunities and taxes, strongly predict individual opposition to higher levels of immigration (Alvarez and Butterfield 2000; Citrin et al. 1997; Espenshade and Hempstead 1996; Harwood 1983; Kessler 2001).

The third approach to examining white attitudes toward immigration is to investigate the role of a perceived threat to the national culture (Fetzer 2000). Indeed, a series of studies document that an individual's perception that immigrants endanger national cultural identity is a key predictor of opposition to immigration (Sniderman et al. 2000; Citrin et al. 1997; Citrin, Reingold, and Green 1990; Hood and Morris 1997; Hood, Morris, and Shirkey 1997). According to these analyses, immigrants are considered a threat because they imperil the integrity of national identity by introducing foreign customs, languages, values, and traditions to the destination country.

Finally, some researchers have focused on the role of prejudice in activating opposition to immigration. This line of inquiry finds that bigotry toward immigrants is a powerful predictor of white opposition to immigration (Citrin et al. 1997; Burns and Gimpel 2000). Efrén Pérez (2008) refines these results by suggesting that prejudice toward immigrants comes in explicit and implicit manifestations. The former concerns the type of prejudice individuals are willing and able to report, and the latter involves a manifestation of prejudice that is automatic and often beyond an individual's introspection. Pérez finds that though explicit prejudice influences subjects' views of Latino and non-Latino immigrants, implicit prejudice is honed in on a specific target, namely, Latino immigrants. Moreover, although people can suppress the influence of explicit prejudice on their judgments, they find it difficult to control the influence of implicit biases.

BLACK ATTITUDES TOWARD IMMIGRATION

A good deal of research has focused on white attitudes toward immigration, but substantially less attention has been paid to the attitudes of blacks. Yet historically blacks have expressed their opinions during each wave of immigration to the United States. European immigration in the nineteenth and twentieth centuries was particularly troublesome for blacks, who were routinely excluded from employment opportunities in favor of white immigrants (Berthoff 1951; Parker 1948; Roediger 1999; Hellwig 1981; Higham 1975; Rubin 1978). Furthermore, the ease with which European immigrants adopted antiblack racism and engaged in antiblack violence created among blacks a sense of threat—physical, economic, and political—from immigration and immigrants (Ignatiev 1997; Jacobson 2001; Roediger 1999). Nevertheless, this sense did not manifest into anti-immigrant sentiments, but instead created a sense of ambivalence toward immigration (Diamond 1998; Hellwig 1981; Rubin 1978).

Black opinion and concern, however, were scarcely limited to European immigrants, and extended during the twentieth century to Asian and West Indian immigration. The principle concern was whether these groups would be viewed more positively and possibly leapfrog over the native-born black population. To a certain extent, these fears were confirmed as whites perceived West Indian immigrants as different from, and perhaps better than, African Americans. Likewise, despite considering Asians as foreign, whites deemed them superior to native-born blacks. Given the urban nature of settlement patterns, many new immigrants were moving into predominately black areas. Many blacks thus found themselves living in an increasingly heterogeneous racial context.

The limited literature on attitudes of blacks toward immigration in general presents a mixed picture of black attitudes. Thomas Espenshade and Katherine Hempstead suggest that blacks, along with Hispanics and Asians, are more likely to express pro-immigration views than non-Hispanic whites are (1996), yet these findings run counter to earlier findings (Espenshade and Calhoun 1993). Scott Cummings and Thomas Lambert, in a comparison of Anglo and black attitudes toward Hispanic and Asian American communities, found that blacks harbored no more negative sentiment toward Asian and Hispanic communities than their white counterparts (1997). Moreover, the authors discovered that the issues that move black opinion are not the same as those that affect white opinion, suggesting that the factors that shape black opinion on immigration may differ from those that shape white opinion.

Jeff Diamond (1998) found much the same result—blacks held somewhat milder attitudes than whites with respect to immigration, albeit with some caveats. Although a majority of whites supported a moratorium on immigration, a majority of blacks opposed it. Yet a majority of blacks favored a reduction in the level of immigration, and when the questions addressed economic costs associated with immigration, blacks were more likely to be in favor of restricting immigration than whites were. Yet, when public officials and the media begin to use race as a frame for immigrants and immigration, then blacks tend to modify their opinions and become less supportive of efforts to restrict immigration.

James Johnson, Walter Farrell, and Chandra Guinn, analyzing data from the 1994 Los Angeles County Social Survey, found that about half of non-Latino and black respondents believed that they would have less or a lot less political and economic influence than they currently have if immigration continued at the present rate (1997). On the other hand, Jack Citrin and colleagues found that concern about financial stress from immigration was not more significant in influencing attitudes about immigration among blacks than among whites (1997).

Michael Thornton and Yuko Mizuno (1999) found that concerns about economic health might influence black opinion on immigration and immigrant groups. Using data from 1984, the authors discovered that blacks generally held more positive attitudes toward immigrants. Additionally, black men were more likely than black women to feel closer to all groups involved. Yet feelings of economic insecurity did not appear to make blacks feel more negatively toward West Indian and Hispanic immigrants. Although Thornton and Mizuno hypothesized that more economic insecurity would dampen black attitudes toward immigrants, they did not find consistent evidence to support this claim.

Niambi Carter (2007) examined the relationship between blacks' perceptions of their place in American society and the relationship to attitudes toward immigration. She found some support for the idea that black attitudes are mediated by their perceptions of white discrimination. In particular, those blacks who felt that the promise of political inclusion secured during the civil rights movement had yet to be realized were ambivalent about immigration. As a result, immigration for blacks became a vehicle for airing their grievances for this unfulfilled promise of American citizenship. Although blacks were fearful that continuing immigration could be harmful to their community, they were not in favor of a complete restriction on immigration.

In a study examining the attitudes toward Latino immigrants by native-born blacks in a southern city, Paula McClain and her colleagues found that blacks perceived more of an economic threat, especially in the belief that they were losing jobs to Latinos, from Latino immigration than did whites (2007). Yet, although not to the degree that blacks were, a good portion of whites were also concerned about continued Latino immigration.

Marylee Taylor and Matthew Schroeder (2010) found that blacks' attitudes toward Latinos were cooler when there had been dramatic growth in the Latino population in recent years. They noticed that the places these cooler feelings existed were localities without established Latino communities, where Latinos represented a new population. Most southern locations in the country would fall into this category.

What remains constant across these studies is that blacks have an uneasy relationship with immigration. On the one hand, they are generally lukewarm in their support for immigration because of the losses, real or perceived, incurred by their community (Scott 1999). On the other, they are opposed to supporting what they see as racist efforts to harm other communities of color (Carter 2007; Diamond 1998). At present, black concerns about racial progress remain a vital lens through which they view the issue of immigration (Carter 2007).

RESEARCH SETTINGS

We use three southern cities—Durham, North Carolina; Memphis, Tennessee; and Little Rock, Arkansas—to examine questions of the attitudes about immigration and intergroup relations among blacks, whites, and Latinos. Each of these locations represents a different southern environment. Memphis has a black majority. Durham has roughly equal populations of blacks and whites. Little Rock has a black minority.

DURHAM, NORTH CAROLINA

The city of Durham, like many southern locations, is undergoing demographic change. In 1990, Latinos were slightly more than 1 percent of the population, but by 2000, 8.6 percent. For decades, whites were the majority in Durham, with 51.6 percent in 1990, but the increasing Latino population, along with a smaller increase in the Asian population, has reduced the white proportion to the point where in 2000 whites were 45.5 percent and blacks 43.8 percent.[2] By 2008, both the white and black populations had declined, but were still virtually equal in proportion—whites 40.9 percent and blacks 39.6 percent. The Latino proportion rose from 8.6 percent in 2000 to 12.3 percent in 2008 (see table 7.1).

As southern cities go, Durham is relatively new (postbellum), incorporated in 1869. As white Durham developed, a parallel black community, Hayti, was developing just outside of Durham proper (Anderson 1990; Boyd 1925). Land in the Hayti district was recorded as being sold to blacks around 1877. William Boyd (1925, 284) estimates that the value of black property in Durham exceeded $4 million in 1923. Jean Anderson (1990) suggests that the strong black leadership in Durham and its connections to some of the city's major white leaders were important for maintaining peaceful relations between blacks and whites (see also Greene 1996; Brown 1997; Houck 1941).

Despite a history of racial segregation extending back to the 1870s, Durham has historically had a very prosperous upper- and upper-middle-class black community. One of the great ironies of segregation, in fact, was that it allowed many black businesses to flourish and prosper, as was the case in Durham. The largest black-owned insurance company in the United States, North Carolina Mutual, was founded in Durham and is still headquartered there. In addition, Durham supports a number of black banks, libraries, hospitals, educational institutions, and numerous other businesses. Much of this black middle class is present and active in everyday Durham today. For example, the median black family income in Durham in 2000 was $38,043. Slightly more than three in four, 78 percent, of the Durham black population age twenty-five and older have finished high school. By the same token, black poverty is significant. Almost one in five, or 18.9 percent, lived below the poverty level in 2000 (U.S. Bureau of Census 2000b).

Table 7.1 Population Characteristics, 2008

	Raw Total	Percentage of City
Durham, N.C.		
City population	212,789	100%
Non-Hispanic whites	87,078	40.90
African Americans	84,351	39.60
Hispanics-Latinos	26,237	12.30
Mexican	17,020	8.80
Puerto Rican	1,555	0.70
Cuban	168	0.10
Other Latino	7,494	3.50
Asians	9,740	4.60
Male	102,669	48.20
Female	110,120	51.80
Memphis, Tenn.		
City population	643,329	100%
Non-Hispanic whites	189,952	29.50
African Americans	401,401	62.40
Hispanics-Latinos	32,371	5.00
Mexican	24,803	3.90
Puerto Rican	1,159	0.20
Cuban	703	0.10
Other Latino	5,706	0.90
Asians	10,672	1.70
Male	304,909	47.40
Female	338,420	52.60
Little Rock, Ark.		
City Population	188,704	100%
Non-Hispanic whites	91,966	48.70
Non-Hispanic African Americans	78,503	41.60
Hispanics-Latinos	10,142	5.40
Mexican	7,882	4.20
Puerto Rican	176	0.10
Cuban	22	0.00
Other Latino	2,062	1.10
Asians	4,702	2.40
Male	90,570	48.00
Female	98,134	52.00

Source: Authors' compilation of data from the 2006–2008 American Community Surveys (U.S. Bureau of the Census 2008).
Note: Hispanics/Latinos can be of any race.

Given the strength of this elite group, black political power in Durham is in the hands of highly educated, oftentimes very wealthy, black citizens, and they have been very successful in achieving their objectives, primarily through their political organization. Given blacks' political success and access to the ballot, Durham County was not one of the forty North Carolina counties covered by Section 5 of the Voting Rights Act of 1965.

Although black elites were the face of civil rights in Durham, the movement would not have thrived without significant contributions from the black poor and working class (Davidson 2007). The exigencies of racism made the coalition between poor and wealthy blacks necessary, but tensions between these communities were significant (Davidson 2007). Despite their alliance, wealthier blacks were much more economically secure, primarily because of the strong business sector, than poor blacks, many of whom risked being fired by white employers for their activism (Davidson 2007). Moreover, in many poor black communities black elites owned and operated the services and housing, and poor blacks found that racial solidarity did not prevent wealthier blacks from exploiting them.

Durham's Latino population is from economically depressed countries, such as Mexico, and Central America, and the majority of immigrants come from Mexico.[3] As such, many of the immigrants have little education and are mostly unskilled workers. Only 36.4 percent of Latinos age twenty-five and older in Durham have finished high school. Their low levels of education and skills means that many Latinos in Durham hold low-paying, unskilled jobs. Latino immigrants and low-skilled blacks most likely compete for the same jobs and social services.[4]

MEMPHIS, TENNESSEE

Memphis is a much larger city than either Durham or Little Rock, and had in 2008 a population of 643,329. Memphis also has a black majority, 62.4 percent, non-Hispanic whites making up 29.5 percent and Latinos, 5 percent. In 1990, only 4,455 Latinos lived in Memphis, but by 2008 that number had risen to 32,371. The numbers continue to increase. Most are of Mexican heritage, specifically, interviews reveal, from the west-central Mexican states of Jalisco, Michoacan, Guanajuato, and San Luis Potosi (Burrell et al. 2001).[5]

Memphis has always been a city of commerce. Given its location on the Mississippi River, it has served as a hub for trade, manufacturing, and distribution since the early 1800s. A mainstay of southern industry, the city has also consistently attracted immigrants. Irish, German, and Jewish newcomers made Memphis their home from the 1820s through the beginning of the 1900s. Indeed, by 1860, the foreign-born population of Memphis made up nearly 31 percent of the city total (Biles 1988). This immigrant heritage thus distinguishes Memphis from other southern cities, particularly the other two in our study. Immigrants have left their mark on the city's social, economic, and political structure. Altina Waller (1984), for instance, explains how the Irish immigrants of the 1820s eventually filled the ranks of police officers in Memphis by mid-century.

Memphis also stands apart from other southern municipalities in that its black residents do not predate the Civil War; rather, African Americans began settling in the city in large numbers only in the wake of the war. Former black slaves from the surrounding environs, freed by Union soldiers, flocked to the city and settled in neighborhoods traditionally inhabited by Irish, Italians, and German immigrants (Lewis 1998). Tensions ensued as the perception of competition over jobs and housing gripped the mostly Irish denizens of these neighborhoods (Waller 1984; Lewis 1998; Biles 1988). Thus, in an ironic twist of roles, Memphis's early foreign-born residents looked down on native-born blacks as both outsiders and competitors.

In some ways, however, Memphis is similar to Durham, in that, although Jim Crow laws dictated the parameters of black and white public interactions, leaving blacks disenfranchised at the state and national level, African Americans enjoyed the right to vote in municipal elections—a pattern incongruent with most other southern cities at the time. This modicum of political muscle had its limitations, however. Black votes in Memphis city politics counted only to the extent that they were cast in favor of the Republican political machine spearheaded by Edward Crump, which dominated local politics from the early 1900s through the early 1950s (Dowdy 2006).

Political power did not come easily to black Memphians. The Crump machine refused to run black candidates. This extended exclusion from elective office made it extremely difficult for blacks to gain a foothold politically (Wright 2000). The Memphis civil rights movement and events such as the assassination of Martin Luther King Jr. in 1968 substantially increased tension between blacks and whites. The first black candidate ran for mayor in 1967, but though the black population was growing in size, the city's white voting-age population was larger, and whites controlled the electoral process through at-large elections for a portion of the seats on city council (Wright 2000, 85). Blacks were not successful in electing a black mayor until 1991, and then only in a racially divisive and polarizing campaign (Wright 2000, 123–72).

Despite the racial tensions, segregation, and political polarization, black Memphis developed the full range of black class structures similar to those of Durham. Blacks owned businesses, newspapers, banks and savings and loans, an amusement park, and numerous other businesses (Wright 2000, 35). Memphis thus resembles Durham in class structure, but differs in its level of cooperative race relations.

LITTLE ROCK, ARKANSAS

For most Americans of a certain age cohort, Little Rock is seared in memory as the site of the integration of Central High School in 1957. The city has a tortured civil rights history, one that appears to still affect the attitudes of its residents. Non-Latino whites remain the majority, 48.7 percent, though their proportion is not as great as it was. Blacks make up about two-fifths of the population, 41.6 percent. Latinos constitute 5.4 percent, and among them Mexicans, at 77.7 percent, are the dominant group. In 2005, 67 percent of Arkansas's immigrant population came from Mexico as well as other Latin and Central American countries (Capps et al. 2007), but many Latinos in the state are also coming from traditional immigration destinations, including California, New Mexico, and Arizona (*The Economist* 2007)

Latino immigrants began to put down roots in Arkansas beginning in the 1980s, although there have been transient communities of Latinos in the state due to seasonal agricultural work since the 1890s (Leidermann 2007; Capps et al. 2007). As the poultry industry in the northwestern and southeastern regions of Arkansas grew, demand for unskilled, cheap labor increased. These jobs are largely filled by Latino immigrants.

Arkansas did not initially institute universal segregation, which partially contributed to the upward economic and social mobility of some blacks, specifically in cities like Little Rock. As the status of whites declined, however, in the face of this black mobility—particularly beginning at the end of the nineteenth century—whites increasingly called for increased white solidarity and more strident racial segregation (Graves 1989, 436). Little Rock has a history of both relative integration, from the 1870s to 1890s and 1900s, and fierce segregation, particularly from the beginning of the twentieth century on. Public schools were widely segregated almost immediately after the end of the Civil War, though there had been some peaceful integration before 1957, as seen with the state university, some medical and law schools, as well as a few small colleges. Public transportation was segregated under Jim Crow laws, though the bus system was integrated before 1957. Some of the race relations problems in Little Rock came out of the relative independence of the city's black community. This independence allowed for some black economic mobility, which was not acceptable to many whites, especially lower-class whites (Graves 1989).

Black independence also created increased tensions between blacks and whites. These tensions came to a head with the forced integration of Central High School in September 1957. The struggle between Governor Orval Faubus and President Eisenhower over the use of federal troops created more tensions as the state National Guard was used to keep the nine black students out on one day and ordered to support and protect their integration the next. Although federal troops were eventually mobilized to enforce the integration, their failure to protect black students from attacks by some white students served to encourage more anti-integration behavior. Additionally, once the troops left, the black students faced even more violent and nonviolent backlash from white students, and the black students generally received harsher disciplinary action for the incidents they were involved in (Kirk 2002).

Given these histories, we want to explore the attitudes of blacks, whites, and, in some cases, Latinos on continued immigration, the perceived economic effects of continued Latino immigration, and the perceptions of the political effects of immigration for each group. We posit no specific hypotheses for this chapter, and no attempt is made to provide multivariate explanations for the attitudes that are identified. Our intent is to highlight the changing patterns of relationships and suggest potential points of tension or conflict, and also possible areas for cooperation. We do, however, test for statistically significant differences in attitudes on several measures.

DATA

The analyses in this chapter are based on two surveys—the 2003 Durham Survey of Intergroup Relations (DSIR) (n = 500) and the 2007 Three City Survey of Intergroup Relations (TCSIR). The cities surveyed in the 2007 data are a resurvey of Durham with the addition of Little Rock and Memphis. Both surveys were conducted specifically for our project by the Center for Survey Research (CSR) of the University of Virginia using a computer-aided telephone interviewing (CATI) system, employing random-digit dialing (RDD) and dialing of directory-assisted Hispanic surname sample.[6] The 2003 survey was conducted from May 4 through June 22, 2003, and interviews were conducted in both English and Spanish (32 percent in Spanish, which translates to 95.8 percent of the Latino sample).[7] A race-ethnicity quota was implemented to achieve a minimum of 150 whites, 150 blacks, and 150 Latinos; the remaining fifty respondents were not under this quota restriction and represent a number of racial-ethnic backgrounds. Interviews were completed with 500 residents of the city of Durham for an overall response rate of 21.6 percent.[8] The sample of 500 consists of 160 whites (32 percent), 151 blacks (30 percent), 167 Latinos (34 percent), 6 Asians (1.2 percent), 12 who self-designated as Other (2.4 percent), and 1 who did not indicate a racial category (.2 percent).[9]

The 2007 surveys were conducted from April 6 to October 27, 2007, and interviews were conducted in both English and Spanish. More than 90 percent of the Latino sample in all three cities opted to be interviewed in Spanish. Again, a race-ethnicity quota was implemented to achieve a minimum of 300 whites, 300 blacks, and 300 Latinos in each city, with the ability to pick up other respondents not under this quota in the random-digit dialing process. Interviews were completed with 977 residents of Durham, 825 residents of Little Rock, and 978 residents of Memphis.[10]

In Durham, the sample of 977 consists of 317 whites (32.4 percent), 318 blacks (32.5 percent), 316 Latinos (32.3 percent), 23 Asians (2.4 percent), and 21 who self-designated as Other (2.1 percent). In Little Rock, the sample of 825 consists of 348 whites (42.2 percent), 315 blacks (38.2 percent), 127 Latinos (16.6 percent), 13 Asians (1.6 percent), 13 who self-designated as Other (1.6 percent), and 2 who did not indicate a racial category (.2 percent). In Memphis, the sample of 978 consists of 327 whites (33.4 percent), 338 blacks (34.6), 312 Latinos (31.9 percent), 4 Asians (.4 percent), and 13 who self-designated as Other (1.3 percent).[11]

CONCERN ABOUT CONTINUED LATINO IMMIGRATION

The distribution of responses on questions about possible effects of continued Latino immigration is presented in table 7.2.[12] The top portion of the table displays the responses to the question of how concerned respondents are about the growing Latino population in the United States in general for Durham in 2003 and 2007, and the bottom portions show the responses for Memphis and Little Rock for 2007. Blacks in Durham appear to be the most concerned (combined categories of somewhat and a great deal), slightly more than 61 percent expressing some level of concern in both 2003 and 2007.[13] Whites in Durham appeared to be the least concerned in 2003, 36.9 percent indicating no concern, and another 21.7 percent indicating a little concern. But by 2007, more than three-fifths, 61.1 percent, were somewhat concerned or concerned a great deal about the growing Latino populations.

Of particular interest is that Durham Latinos also appear concerned about the growing Latino population—more than a majority, 58.3 percent in 2003, and 55.4 percent in 2007, expressing either some or a great deal of concern. On the surface, this finding seems counterintuitive; yet it is possible that Latino immigrants believe that increased Latino immigration might not be the best situation for immigrants already here. As shown in table 7.2, the differences between 2003 and 2007 for the responses of all three groups are statistically significant.

Unlike their counterparts in Durham in both 2003 and 2007, whites in Memphis appear to be more concerned, 53.8 percent, about continued Latino immigration than blacks are, 48.7 percent. But neither of these levels is as high as in Durham. Again of interest is the extremely large proportion of Latinos either somewhat or a great deal concerned about continued Latino immigration, 65.2 percent, more than either blacks or whites in Memphis. These differences among groups are statistically significant.

Whites in Little Rock appear to be more like their counterparts in Memphis, a slightly higher proportion, 56.6 percent, expressing con-

Table 7.2 Concern About Growing Latino Population

	Whites		Blacks		Latinos	
	2003	2007	2003	2007	2003	2007
Durham						
Not at all	36.90%	21.60%	28.80%	24.00%	33.50%	33.20%
	(58)	(65)	(43)	(72)	(57)	(102)
A little	21.70	17.30	10.1	14.30	8.20	11.40
	(34)	(52)	(15)	(43)	(14)	(35)
Somewhat	24.20	28.80	30.20	31.00	25.90	17.90
	(38)	(87)	(45)	(93)	(44)	(55)
A great deal	17.20	32.20	30.90	30.70	32.40	37.50
	(27)	(97)	`(46)	(92)	(55)	(115)
Total	100%	100%	100%	100%	100%	100%
	(n = 157)	(n = 301)	(n = 149)	(n = 300)	(n = 170)	(n = 307)
	X^2 sig.	$p < .001$	X^2 sig.	$p < .001$	X^2 sig.	$p < .001$
Memphis						
Not at all		25.30%		32.30%		25.90%
		(79)		(100)		(79)
A little		21.20		19.00		8.90
		(66)		(59)		(27)
Somewhat		26.90		23.50		19.00
		(83)		(73)		(58)
A great deal		26.90		25.20		46.20
		(84)		(78)		(141)
Total		100%		100%		100%
		(n = 312)		(n = 310)		(n = 305)
		X^2 sig.		$p < .001$		
Little Rock						
Not at all		25.6%		30.50%		32.20%
		(85)		(91)		(39)
A little		17.00		16.10		11.60
		(59)		(48)		(14)
Somewhat		30.70		28.90		25.60
		(102)		(86)		(31)
A great deal		25.90		24.50		30.60
		(86)		(73)		(37)
Total		100%		100%		100%
		(n = 332)		(n = 298)		(n = 121)
		X^2 sig.		$p < .001$		

Source: Authors' compilation of data collected for this project (McClain 2003, 2007).
Note: Standard errors in parentheses.

cern about continued Latino immigration than blacks, 53.4 percent. But, again, the levels for both groups are not as high as for blacks and whites in Durham. The differences among the groups in both Memphis and Little Rock are also statistically significant.

In chapter 8 in this volume, Monica McDermott identifies class-based dynamics among blacks in Greenville, South Carolina, in their attitudes toward Latinos. Although our questions do not parallel McDermott's and our data are survey rather than ethnographic, we ran analyses (results not shown) to see whether differences among blacks on concern about the growing Latino population in our three cities were class based. Using income as a proxy for class, we find no statistically significant differences among blacks in any of our three cities. This means that blacks making $15,000 or less are just as likely to be concerned a great deal about the growing Latino population as those making $100,000 and more. The reverse, of course, is also true. Our findings do not negate McDermott's finding of class-based differences in attitudes; it simply highlights the ability of McDermott to observe nuances of body language and speech intonation in her ethnographic research that cannot be captured by our survey research.

ECONOMIC EFFECTS OF CONTINUED LATINO IMMIGRATION

As we identify in table 7.2, Latino immigrants also appear to be concerned about the growing Latino population. Our speculation that Latino immigrants might perceive increased immigration as not being in the best interests of immigrants already in the area might be reinforced with responses on the continued effects that Latino immigration will have on the economic opportunities of the various racial groups.[14] Almost half, 47.6 percent, of Latino immigrants in Durham surveyed in 2003 feel that continued Latino immigration will reduce economic opportunities for Latinos (see table 7.3). Yet, by 2007, there appeared to be a slight shift. Only 34 percent believed that continued Latino immigration would reduce economic opportunities for Latinos; 42.5 percent believed that it would lead to increased economic opportunity. The reasons for this shift are unknown at the moment, but it might suggest that the increased numbers of Latinos in Durham might have led to a comfort level that was not present in 2003.

The group that feels they have the most to lose economically is native-born blacks in Durham. In 2003, 61 percent believed that their economic opportunity would be a lot less or some less as a result of Latino immigration. By 2007, that number had decreased only slightly, to 55.60 percent. Whites in Durham, however, believe that their economic opportunities will not be affected by continued Latino immigration—55 percent in 2003 and 56.6 percent in 2007.

The group that feels they have the most to lose economically is native-born blacks in Memphis, as in Durham: a slight majority, 50.9 percent, believe their economic opportunity will be a lot less or somewhat less as a result of Latino immigration. Whites in Memphis believe that their economic opportunities will not be affected by continued Latino immigration, almost a majority, 49.10 percent. Thus whites for the most part appear not to perceive an economic threat from Latino immigration. Although almost two-thirds of Latinos are concerned about continuing Latino immigration, only two-fifths—41 percent—feel that continued Latino immigration will reduce economic opportunities for Latinos, and a little more than one-third—35 percent—believe that they will have some more or probably more economic opportunity if Latino immigration continues. This suggests, although marginally, that Latinos in Memphis might be more concerned about their economic opportunities with continued immigration than their counterparts in Durham.

Again of interest is the extremely large proportion of Latinos in Little Rock who are concerned about continued Latino immigration, 56.2 percent, on par with those of blacks and whites. Those who feel they have the most to lose economically are native-born blacks in Little Rock, as in Durham and Memphis—a majority, 54.7 percent. As in Memphis, whites in Little Rock believe their economic opportunities will not be affected by continued Latino immigration, almost a majority, 53.4 percent.

Although a majority of Latinos are concerned about continuing Latino immigration, only a little more than one-quarter, 29.2 percent, feel that it will reduce economic opportunities for them. Close to half, 45 percent, believe they will have some more or probably more economic opportunity if the immigration continues. It appears from this simple analysis that Latinos in Memphis and Little Rock see positive economic gains for their group. All of the differences among the groups are statistically significant.

To further complicate our analysis, we check to see whether class-based differences exist among blacks about the loss of economic op-

Table 7.3 Immigration Continues: How Much Economic Opportunity Will Your Racial Group Have

	Whites		Blacks		Latinos	
	2003	2007	2003	2007	2003	2007
Durham						
A lot less than now	7.90%	9.10%	22.70%	16.60%	13.00%	7.10%
	(12)	(27)	(32)	(54)	(21)	(21)
Some less than now	24.50	24.90	38.30	39.00	34.60	26.90
	(37)	(74)	(54)	(113)	(56)	(79)
No more than now	55.00	56.60	24.80	26.60	21.60	23.50
	(83)	(168)	(35)	(77)	(35)	(69)
Some more than now	11.90	7.10	12.10	14.10	24.10	31.30
	(18)	(21)	(17)	(41)	(39)	(92)
Probably more than now	.70	2.40	2.10	1.70	6.80	11.20
	(1)	(7)	(3)	(5)	(11)	(33)
Total	100%	100%	100%	100%	100%	100%
	(n = 151)	(n = 297)	(n = 141)	(n = 290)	(n = 162)	(n = 294)
	X^2 sig.	$p < .001$	X^2 sig.	$p < .001$	X^2 sig.	$p < .001$
Memphis						
A lot less than now		7.70%		17.20%		11.00%
		(23)		(51)		(33)
Some less than now		31.10		33.70		30.00
		(93)		(100)		(90)

No more than now	49.10	31.30	24.00
	(147)	(93)	(72)
Some more than now	10.40	14.10	26.00
	(31)	(42)	(78)
Probably more than now	1.50	3.70	9.00
	(5)	(11)	(27)
Total	100%	100%	100%
	(n = 299)	(n = 297)	(n = 300)
	X^2 sig.	$p < .001$	
Little Rock			
A lot less than now	5.80%	17.10%	10.00%
	(19)	(49)	(12)
Some less than now	30.40	37.60	19.20
	(99)	(108)	(23)
No more than now	53.40	30.70	25.80
	(174)	(88)	(31)
Some more than now	8.90	12.90	31.70
	(29)	(37)	(38)
Probably more than now	1.50	1.70	13.30
	(5)	(5)	(16)
Total	100%	100%	100%
	(n = 326)	(n = 287)	(n = 120)
	X^2 sig.	$p < .001$	

Source: Authors' compilation of data collected for this project (McClain 2003, 2007).
Note: Standard errors in parentheses.

portunity from Latino immigration; differences are statistically significant in Memphis only. Blacks making $35,000 and less are more
likely than those making $75,000 or more to feel that blacks will
have somewhat less or a lot less economic opportunity from Latino
immigration ($X^2 = 47.65$, $p < .05$) (results not shown). The finding of
more concern among working- and lower-class blacks on this question is similar to McDermott's findings of working-class blacks being
more negative about Latinos, but is not consistent with her findings
of negative attitudes among upper-middle-class blacks.

Also of significance is the similarity of our results on blacks in
Memphis, Little Rock, and Durham being the most concerned about
a loss of economic opportunity from Latino immigration to those of
chapter 6 in this volume on Los Angeles. Although not addressing
black economic opportunities specifically, Sawyer finds that blacks
are far more likely than Asian Americans and whites to say that illegal
immigrants hurt the economy in Los Angeles.

Chapter 1 in this volume suggests that there is no observable effect
on the job earnings of low-skilled native-born blacks from Latino immigrants, specifically Mexican immigrants, based on census data. Yet
our data are survey data that measure respondents' attitudes and beliefs, which may or may not conform to the objective reality of a situation. Census data might not show an effect on job earnings of blacks
from Latino immigrants, but Rebecca Powers, using interview data
with 292 employers in Pitt County, North Carolina, found that employers preferred to hire Latinos over blacks (2005). It is possible
that this pattern might be present in other parts of the South, which
might lead people to nevertheless perceive an economic threat from
Latino immigration, regardless of whether one exists empirically.

POLITICAL EFFECTS OF
CONTINUED IMMIGRATION

In some cities, blacks and whites viewed the economic effects of
continued Latino immigration differently, but the picture changed
when respondents were asked about their perceptions of the effect
of continued immigration on their racial group's political influence
(see table 7.4).[15] Whereas whites in Durham did not feel an economic threat from Latino immigration, they did perceive a political
threat: exactly half, 50 percent, in 2003 and a solid majority, 56.5
percent, in 2007 felt that whites would lose either a lot or some

political influence. On the other hand, in 2003, only about one-fifth of blacks, 20 percent, believed that they would lose a lot of power, which rose to 49 percent when combined with those who felt that they would lose some power. The same pattern appeared in 2007, when 48.3 percent of blacks felt that continued Latino immigration would result in a lot or somewhat less political power. Blacks in Durham feel Latino immigration threatens both their economic and political positions, whereas their white counterparts believe the threat is a political one only.

As one would expect, Latino attitudes differ substantially from those of blacks and whites in Durham. Almost three-quarters of Latino immigrants, 71.2 percent, in 2003 felt that they would gain political influence (combined some more and probably more) from the continuation of Latino immigration; this figure rose to 77.2 percent in 2007. Of course, in terms of electoral power, Latino immigrants will have to become U.S. citizens to exert real electoral power, but even in the absence of citizenship blacks and whites perceive a loss of political power and Latino immigrants perceive a gain.

Yet again, with the question of the loss of political influence as a result of continued Latino immigration, whites in Memphis are only slightly more concerned about the loss of political influence, 55 percent, than blacks, 50 percent. As in Durham, and as expected, almost three-fourths of Latinos, 71.2 percent, believe that continued Latino immigration will give them some or probably more political influence. Thus it appears blacks in Memphis perceive both an economic and political threat, and whites more of a political threat. Given that Memphis is a majority-black city, whites might now perceive a threat on both fronts, from Latinos and from blacks.

Like their counterparts in Durham and Memphis, whites in Little Rock are also concerned about a loss of political influence, 56.4 percent, because of immigration. Blacks are also concerned, a solid 54.6 percent majority. Again as in Durham and Memphis, three-fourths of Latinos, 75.2 percent, believe that continued Latino immigration will give them some or probably more political influence. Whites in Little Rock thus appear to not be concerned about economic losses but to definitely be concerned about losing political influence. Blacks, as in Durham and Memphis, are concerned about a loss of both. Again, all of the differences are statistically significant. There were also no statistically significant class differences among blacks in all three cities on this question.

Table 7.4 Immigration Continues: How Much Political Influence Will Your Racial Group Have

	Whites		Blacks		Latinos	
	2003	2007	2003	2007	2003	2007
Durham						
A lot less than now	3.90%	13.60%	19.30%	16.80%	3.70%	.70%
	(6)	(40)	(28)	(48)	(6)	(2)
Some less than now	46.10	42.90	29.70	31.50	8.00	5.90
	(70)	(126)	(43)	(90)	(13)	(17)
No more than now	41.40	36.40	29.70	30.80	17.20	16.30
	(63)	(107)	(43)	(88)	(28)	(47)
Some more than now	6.60	4.80	20.00	17.50	36.80	54.00
	(10)	(14)	(29)	(50)	(60)	(156)
Probably more than now	2.00	2.40	1.40	3.50	34.40	23.20
	(3)	(7)	(2)	(10)	(56)	(67)
Total	100%	100%	100%	100%	100%	100%
	(n = 152)	(n = 294)	(n = 145)	(n = 286)	(n = 163)	(n = 289)
	X^2 sig.	$p < .001$	X^2 sig.	$p < .001$	X^2 sig.	$p < .001$
Memphis						
A lot less than now		12.70%		17.20%		3.20%
		(38)		(51)		(9)
Some less than now		42.30		33.70		11.40
		(127)		(100)		(32)

No more than now	35.70	31.30	14.20
	(107)	(93)	(40)
Some more than now	7.70	14.10	52.70
	(23)	(42)	(148)
Probably more than now	1.70	3.70	18.50
	(5)	(11)	(52)
Total	100%	100%	100%
	(n = 300)	(n = 297)	(n = 281)
	X^2 sig.	$p < .001$	
Little Rock			
A lot less than now	10.10%	17.10%	2.50%
	(33)	(49)	(3)
Some less than now	46.30	37.60	6.60
	(151)	(108)	(8)
No more than now	37.40	30.70	15.70
	(122)	(88)	(19)
Some more than now	4.30	12.90	42.10
	(14)	(37)	(51)
Probably more than now	1.8	1.70	33.10
	(6)	(5)	(40)
Total	100%	100%	100%
	(n = 326)	(n = 287)	(n = 121)
	X^2 sig.	$p < .001$	

Source: Authors' compilation of data collected for this project (McClain 2003, 2007).
Note: Standard errors in parentheses.

PERCEPTION OF RACE
RELATIONS GENERALLY

The frequencies for the question on the state of race relations in the cities of Durham, Memphis, and Little Rock are presented in table 7.5.[16] With regards to race relations in general, blacks and Latinos have far more favorable views of the state of race relations—somewhat positive and very positive—in Durham, 50.6 and 50.9 percent respectively in 2003 and 53.3 percent and 71.2 percent in 2007. Whites were split, 41.9 percent believing that relations were either somewhat positive or very positive, or somewhat negative or very negative, in 2003, and much the same in 2007, 45 percent somewhat or very positive and 39.4 percent very negative or somewhat negative. The reasons for this white ambivalence are unclear, given more positive responses on a number of other dimensions.

There appears to be a real disconnect, however, between whites and blacks and Latinos when questioned about race relations in Memphis in general (see table 7.5). An overwhelming majority of whites, 62.6 percent, believe that relations are very or somewhat negative, versus only 28.2 percent of blacks and 27.1 percent of Latinos. Despite differences in their perception of the effects of Latino immigration, blacks and whites in Little Rock believe that race relations in general are good, 54.7 and 56.9 percent respectively, as do Latinos, 47.6 percent.

RELATIONS BETWEEN BLACKS
AND WHITES

In Durham, nearly half of whites, 46.3 percent, believed that relations between whites and blacks in general are either somewhat positive or very positive in 2003 and slightly more than half, 53 percent, did so in 2007 (see table 7.6).[17] Only about one-quarter, 26 percent, in 2003 and only 20 percent in 2007 felt that relations were either somewhat negative or very negative.

Blacks appear to view their relations with whites more positively than whites view theirs with blacks, but only slightly so. In 2003, a majority of blacks, 54.2 percent, believed that relations with whites were somewhat or very positive, and approximately 26 percent felt that they were somewhat or very negative. By 2007, the positive majority had increased to 63.7 percent.

This pattern of white opinion continues in Memphis. A majority of whites, 57.5 percent, feel relations between blacks and whites is very or somewhat negative, whereas only 33.9 percent of blacks feel this way. Maybe the dynamic of being a minority in the city creates a dynamic among whites. Despite a tortured racial history, or perhaps because of it, blacks and whites in Little Rock believe that relations between the two groups are somewhat or very positive, 60.4 and 56.9 percent respectively. All of the differences are statistically significant.

RELATIONS BETWEEN WHITES AND LATINOS

On the other hand, when whites are asked about relations between whites and Latinos in general in Durham, a slightly different picture emerges.[18] Whites are more conflicted about their relations with Latinos than they are about those with blacks. Equal percentages in 2003, 40.1 percent, believed relations between whites and Latinos were either very negative or somewhat negative or very or somewhat positive. By 2007, almost half, 49.5 percent, felt that relations between Latinos and whites were very or somewhat positive, but the number of whites who were not sure increased from 19.7 percent in 2003 to 28.6 percent in 2007 (see table 7.7).

Latinos are slightly more positive about their relations with whites than whites are about Latinos. Only about one-third, 33.8 percent, feel relations between Latinos and whites are very negative or somewhat negative, whereas a slight majority, 51.3 percent, feel very or somewhat positive. On the other hand, in Memphis, both whites and Latinos believe that relations between the two groups are somewhat or very positive, 49.6 and 59.2 percent respectively, in contrast to their view of their relations with blacks. In Little Rock, both whites and Latinos believe relations between the two groups are somewhat or very positive, 58.4 and 55.9 percent respectively. All of the differences are statistically significant.

RELATIONS BETWEEN BLACKS AND LATINOS

With respect to Latinos in Durham, in 2003 blacks believed relations were better than those with whites, 59.4 percent feeling somewhat or very positive (see table 7.8).[19] The same year, less than a quarter, 23.2

Table 7.5 Attitudes About Race Relations in General

	Whites		Blacks		Latinos	
	2003	2007	2003	2007	2003	2007
Durham						
Very negative	4.50%	5.30%	3.30%	3.60%	6.30%	2.00%
	(7)	(16)	(5)	(11)	(10)	(6)
Somewhat negative	36.40	34.10	28.00	28.10	24.50	11.40
	(56)	(103)	(42)	(85)	(39)	(35)
Not positive or negative	18.20	15.60	18	14.90	18.20	15.40
	(28)	(47)	(27)	(45)	(29)	(47)
Somewhat positive	37.30	42.10	47.30	47.00	46.50	69.60
	(58)	(127)	(71)	(142)	(74)	(213)
Very positive	3.20	3.00	3.30	6.30	4.40	1.60
	(5)	(9)	(5)	(19)	(7)	(5)
Total	100%	100%	100%	100%	100%	100%
	(n = 154)	(n = 302)	(n = 150)	(n = 302)	(n = 159)	(n = 306)
	X^2 sig.	$p < .001$	X^2 sig.	$p < .001$	X^2 sig.	$p < .001$
Memphis						
Very negative		21.60%		1.90%		4.10%
		(68)		(34)		(12)
Somewhat negative		41.00		26.30		23.00
		(129)		(82)		(68)

Not positive or negative	13.30	17.90	40.50
	(42)	(56)	(120)
Somewhat positive	22.20	38.10	30.40
	(70)	(119)	(90)
Very positive	1.90	6.70	2.00
	(6)	(21)	(6)
Total	100%	100%	100%
	(n = 315)	(n = 312)	(n = 296)
	X^2 sig.	$p < .001$	
Little Rock			
Very negative	4.80%	5.00%	4.00%
	(16)	(15)	(5)
Somewhat negative	17.20	22.50	24.20
	(57)	(68)	(30)
Not positive or negative	21.10	17.90	24.20
	(70)	(54)	(30)
Somewhat positive	52.40	47.40	40.30
	(174)	(143)	(50)
Very positive	4.50	7.30	7.30
	(15)	(22)	(9)
Total	100%	100%	100%
	(n = 332)		(n = 124)
	X^2 sig.	$p < .001$	

Source: Authors' compilation of data collected for this project (McClain 2003, 2007).
Note: Standard errors in parentheses.

Table 7.6 Relations Between Whites and Blacks

	White		Black	
	2003	2007	2003	2007
Durham				
Very negative	4.40%	4.30%	4.60%	2.00%
	(6)	(13)	(6)	(6)
Somewhat negative	30.10	26.70	21.40	18.00
	(41)	(80)	(28)	(57)
Not positive or	19.10	16.00	19.80	15.50
negative	(26)	(48)	(26)	(47)
Somewhat positive	41.20	48.30	49.60	59.10
	(56)	(145)	(65)	(179)
Very positive	5.10	4.70	4.60	4.60
	(7)	(14)	(6)	(14)
Total	100%	100%	100%	100%
	(n = 136)	(n = 300)	(n = 131)	(n = 303)
	X^2 sig.	$p < .001$	X^2 sig.	$p < .001$
Memphis				
Very negative		16.50%		9.50%
		(52)		(30)
Somewhat negative		41.00		24.40
		(129)		(77)
Not positive or		12.70		11.40
negative		(40)		(36)
Somewhat positive		27.60		50.50
		(87)		(159)
Very positive		2.20		4.10
		(7)		(13)
Total		100%		100%
		(n = 315)		(n = 315)
		X^2 sig.		$p < .001$
Little Rock				
Very negative		2.70%		5.60%
		(9)		(17)
Somewhat negative		20.40		21.80
		(68)		(66)
Not positive or		20.10		12.20
negative		(67)		(37)
Somewhat positive		52.30		53.50
		(174)		(162)

Table 7.6 (*Cont.*)

	White		Black	
	2003	2007	2003	2007
Very positive		4.50		6.90
		(15)		(21)
Total		100%		100%
		(n = 333)		(n = 303)
		X^2 sig.		$p < .001$

Source: Authors' compilation of data collected for this project (McClain 2003, 2007).
Note: Standard errors in parentheses.

Table 7.7 Relations between Whites and Latinos in General

	White		Latino	
	2003	2007	2003	2007
Durham				
Very negative	8%	1.7%	6.5%	1.00%
	(11)	(5)	(10)	(3)
Somewhat negative	32.1	20.2	27.3	9.80
	(44)	(58)	(42)	(29)
Not positive or	19.7	28.6	14.9	31.30
negative	(27)	(82)	(23)	(93)
Somewhat positive	35	42.9	46.1	53.90
	(48)	(123)	(71)	(160)
Very positive	5.1	6.6	5.2	4.00%
	(7)	(19)	(8)	(12)
Total	100%	100%	100%	100%
	(n = 137)	(n = 287)	(n = 154)	(n = 297)
	X^2 sig.	$p < .001$	X^2 sig.	$p < .001$
Memphis				
Very negative		2.2%		1%
		(6)		(3)
Somewhat negative		17.9		9.7
		(49)		(29)
Not positive or		30.3		30.1
negative		(83)		(90)
Somewhat positive		43.8		53.8
		(120)		(161)
Very positive		5.8		5.4
		(16)		(16)
Total		100%		100%
		(n = 274)		(n = 299)
		X^2 sig.		$p < .001$

(*Table continues on p. 230.*)

Table 7.7 *(Cont.)*

	White		Latino	
	2003	2007	2003	2007
Little Rock				
Very negative		17%		7.1%
		(5)		(9)
Somewhat negative		19.9		14.2
		(58)		(18)
Not positive or		19.9		14.2
negative		(58)		(29)
Somewhat positive		51.9		45.7
		(151)		(58)
Very positive		6.5		10.2
		(19)		(13)
Total		100%		100%
		(n = 291)		(n = 127)
		X^2 sig.		$p < .001$

Source: Authors' compilation of data collected for this project (McClain 2003, 2007).
Note: Standard errors in parentheses.

percent, considered relations to be very or somewhat negative, which figure increased to 26.6 percent in 2007. Latinos, however, consider relations with blacks to be more negative than blacks perceive of Latinos. In 2003, almost a third of Latinos, 31.5 percent, saw relations as very or somewhat negative, but 45.3 percent did so in 2007. Similarly, 50.9 percent thought that relations were either somewhat or very positive in 2003, whereas only 23 percent did so in 2007. Something soured Latinos on their perceptions of their relations with blacks. Only the differences identified in 2007 are statistically significant.

Opinion appears to diverge on the part of blacks and Latinos about their relations in Memphis. More than three-fifths of Latinos, 62.1 percent, feel that their relations with blacks in Memphis are very or somewhat negative, yet only 28.8 percent of blacks perceive relations this way. Again, maybe it is the situation of being a small minority in a majority-black city that creates this perception. But it might also be that because blacks are in the majority, they are not as aware of the nature of relations with whites and Latinos, who are minorities. This is an interesting question that needs to be explored in more detail.

The same differences are also present in Little Rock. A solid ma-

Table 7.8 Relations Between Blacks and Latinos in General

	Black		Latino	
	2003	2007	2003	2007
Durham				
Very negative	8.7%	2.5%	5.7%	12.0%
	(12)	(8)	(9)	(36)
Somewhat negative	14.49	24.1	25.8	33.3
	(20)	(68)	(41)	(100)
Not positive or	17.39	26.6	17.6	31.7
negative	(24)	(75)	(28)	(95)
Somewhat positive	54.35	41.8	47.8	22.0
	(75)	(118)	(76)	(66)
Very positive	5.07	4.6	3.1	1.0
	(7)	(13)	(5)	(3)
Total	100%	100%	100%	100%
	(n = 138)	(n = 282)	(n = 159)	(n = 300)
	*X^2 sig.	$p < .001$	*X^2 sig.	$p < .001$
Memphis				
Very negative		6.3%		20.9%
		(18)		(64)
Somewhat negative		22.5		41.2
		(64)		(126)
Not positive or		20.7		22.9
negative				
		(59)		(70)
Somewhat positive		42.1		15.0
		(120)		(46)
Very positive		8.4		0
		(24)		(0)
Total		100%		100%
		(n = 285)		(n = 306)
		X^2 sig		$p < .001$
Little Rock				
Very negative		3.8%		7.9%
		(10)		(10)
Somewhat negative		16.5		31.7
		(43)		(40)
Not positive or		24.1		26.2
negative		(63)		(33)
Very positive		6.1		3.2
		(16)		(4)

(*Table continues on p. 232.*)

Table 7.8 (*Cont.*)

	Black	Latino
Total	100%	100%
	(n = 261)	(n = 126)
	X^2 sig.	$p < .001$

Source: Authors' compilation of data collected for this project (McClain 2003, 2007).
Note: Standard errors in parentheses.

jority of blacks, 55.5 percent, feel that their relations with Latinos are somewhat or very positive, whereas almost two-fifths of Latinos, 39.6 percent, feel that relations are either somewhat or very negative. A pattern that emerges in all three cities is that blacks perceive more positive relations with Latinos than Latinos perceive with blacks. There are also no statistically significant class-based differences among blacks on the nature of relations with Latinos in all three cities.

Although not examining the same question, chapter 2 of this volume identifies patterns that might underscore our results about Latinos' perceiving more negative relations with blacks. Using the 2006 Latino National Survey, Michael Jones-Correa finds, in general, that foreign-born Latinos are less likely to perceive commonalities with black Americans. Although he examines differences between traditional immigrant-receiving states and new immigrant destinations, that is, the South, he does not find state-specific differences on some of his attitude questions.

DISCUSSION

Our objective was to determine what effect Latino immigration into three southern cities had on intergroup relations. Additionally, we wanted to learn whether city context made a difference on the perceptions of intergroup relations. What our analyses show is that, in some instances, city context does make a difference, but in other instances the effects are more generalized.

In Durham, blacks and whites make up similar proportions of the population, and both groups are more concerned about the growing Latino population than their counterparts in other cities are. Yet in 2003 whites in Durham were not concerned, but by 2007 they were.

Reasons for the shift are speculative, but several things occurred in the interim that might provide an explanation. North Carolina has experienced rising and increasingly anti-Latino immigrant rhetoric, from both organized anti-immigration groups and elected officials (McClain 2006). Moreover, the immigrant rallies in 2006 played out in North Carolina against this backdrop of rising anti-Latino immigrant feelings.

Although both blacks and whites in Durham are concerned about increases in Latino immigration, in Memphis, a majority-black city, whites are more concerned than blacks are. The situation is the same in Little Rock, where whites are in the majority but are still more concerned than blacks. Thus, at least on this issue, it might not matter if whites live in a city in equal proportion, minority proportion, or a majority proportion: concerns about Latino immigration might be more generalized among southern whites regardless of demographics. Moreover, regardless of city context, whites do not feel threatened economically.

What is clear across all cities is that blacks perceive that they have the most to lose economically from the increasing Latino population in their cities, but also feel threatened politically, though slightly less than whites. That blacks in Memphis, a majority-black city, also feel this threat suggests that they might perceive their hold on political power as tenuous. Yet, whites in Memphis also feel threatened politically. Thus, city population demographics appear to matter for whites with respect to declining political influence as a result of Latino immigration.

What is different, however, is that whites in Memphis, our majority-black city, overwhelmingly believe race relations are negative, unlike both blacks and Latinos. But whites and Latinos converge on their perceptions of their relations with blacks—both see them as negative. Blacks, on the other hand, believe that they have positive relations with both groups. That both whites and Latinos are a minority might account for their view that their relations with blacks are negative.

On the other hand, blacks and whites in Little Rock, where whites are a plurality, believe that relations between the two groups are basically positive. Although blacks do not manifest the angst against whites that whites do against blacks in Memphis, they are concerned about a loss of political power from continued Latino immigration.

CONCLUSION

This analysis provides a window into the relations that might develop among black, white, and Latino immigrants in southern locations. Understanding the nature of these relations is significant given that the South is fast becoming a tripartite region, however mired in the historical black-white dynamic that frames relations among groups and continues to structure its politics.

The 2003 survey reported in this paper was funded by a grant from The Ford Foundation (St. Benedict the Black meets the Virgin of Guadalupe Project, Grant #1025–1445). The 2007 survey was funded by a grant from the Russell Sage Foundation ("What's New about the New South: Race, Latino Immigration, and Inter-group Relations?," Grant # 88–06–11).

NOTES

1. This section borrows heavily from Efrén Pérez (2008).
2. Both of these groups gained in absolute numbers of people, but lost as a proportion of the population from 1990 to 2000, and in the 2000 to 2006 time interval.
3. The *News and Observer* (Raleigh) identified that many of the Mexican immigrants into North Carolina come primarily from rural towns in the state of Puebla (November 29, 30, 1998). For the most part, these immigrants are unskilled and poorly educated.
4. In a series of articles throughout 2002 chronicling the lives of area residents living in poverty, the *Herald Sun* (Durham) provided a picture of life for Latinos in Durham. Fully 26 percent of the more than 16,000 Latinos in Durham at the time lived below the federal poverty level, and, to make a good living, they must work more than one job (Claudia Assis and Julian Pecquet "Hispanics' search for a Better Life Pushes Durham into Poverty," September 25, 2002, A12).
5. This is based on interviews with local immigrants (Burrell et al. 2001). Anecdotal evidence comports with this more systematic evidence. For instance, several buses offer direct trips from Memphis to various cities in the noted Mexican states.
6. We recognize the problems associated with drawing a sample from a listing of Hispanic surnames, for example, missing Hispanics with non-His-

panic last names, and those married to non-Hispanics. We also acknowledge that some Latino immigrants might not have phones in their homes. Given the recency of the Hispanic population in Durham and the high proportion of immigrants, however, we chose the sampling frame that would give us the highest probabilities of reaching a Latino respondent.

7. We had the questionnaire translated by a Spanish-language organization in Chapel Hill, North Carolina. To check the translation and to ensure that it tracked the English-language version, the survey organization drew a small sample of Latinos in Durham for the sole purpose of checking the translation. As a result, changes were made to the translation. The revised Spanish-language version was then pretested on another small sample of Latinos in Durham.

8. A total of 4,208 telephone numbers were attempted in the course of the survey and a total of 14,014 call attempts were made. The American Association for Public Opinion Research (AAPOR) rate was calculated using the full call history of each number, which was recorded automatically by the CATI software. The response rate was calculated according to AAPOR suggested formula RR3, with $e1 = .50$ and $e2 = .78$. We estimated $e1$ and $e2$ based on an analysis of residency rates and the occurrence of out-of-area households in our sample. Partial interviews are not counted in the numerator of the RR3 formula.

9. Because of the use of the Hispanic surname sample and racial-ethnic quotas, sampling error is more difficult to calculate. The sample may be viewed as part of two separate populations. Within the RDD sample, the source of 276 completions, the probability of selection is known and the margin of error is 5.9 percent. Within the surname oversample, providing 244 completed interviews, all households listed under a resident with a Hispanic surname were attempted; however, Hispanics were included in RDD calling and non-Hispanics were included in the oversample. Non-Hispanics with Hispanic surnames had a greater chance of selection than non-Hispanics in the RDD sample who do not have Hispanic surnames. If we assume this to be a more or less random occurrence, then the margin of error for each of the three racial-ethnic groups is roughly 8 percent.

10. Interviewing in Little Rock proved particularly problematic because it was difficult to persuade blacks and Latinos to participate in the survey. The CSR was successful in getting the full quota of blacks, but was not successful in filling the quota on Latinos. Thus, the size of the Latino sample in Little Rock is less than in the other two cities.

11. A total of 28,209 telephone numbers were attempted in the course of the survey in the three cities and a total of 150,444 call attempts were made. The American Association for Public Opinion Research rate was calculated using the full call history of each number that was recorded

automatically by the CATI software. The response rate was calculated according to AAPOR suggested formula RR4, with e1 = .189 and e2 = .945. We estimated e1 and e2 based on an analysis of residency rates and the occurrence of out-of-area households in our sample. Partial interviews are not counted in the numerator of the RR4 formula.

12. Question wording: The Latino population is rapidly growing in the United States. How do you feel about this shift, does it concern you (1) a great deal; (2) somewhat; (3) a little; or (4) not at all?

13. For presentational purposes, we describe our results by collapsing some categories within a survey question. The substantive conclusions of our findings, however, remain unchanged if we make comparisons using the original categories for each question (see tables 7.2 to 7.8 for the relevant chi-square tests).

14. Question wording: What about economic opportunity? If immigration to this country continues at the present rate, do you believe [respondent's racial group] people will have more or less economic opportunity? Would you say (1) probably would have a lot more economic opportunity than now; (2) some more opportunity than now; (3) no more or less opportunity than now; (4) some less opportunity than now, or (5) a lot less opportunity than now?

15. Question wording: If immigration to this country continues at the present rate, how much political influence do you believe [insert R's race group] people will have? Would you say 1) probably a lot more political influence than now; 2) some more political influence than now; 3) no more influence than now; 4) some less influence than now; 5) a lot less influence than now?

16. Question wording: In your opinion, racial relationships in (Durham/Memphis/Little Rock) are (1) very positive; (2) somewhat positive; (3) neither positive or negative; (4) Somewhat negative; 5) very negative.

17. Question wording: The relationship between blacks and whites: Are they (1) very positive; (2) Somewhat positive; (3) neither positive nor negative; (4) somewhat negative; (5) very negative.

18. Question wording: The relationship between whites and Latinos in general: Are they (1) very positive; (2) somewhat positive; (3) neither positive nor negative; (4) somewhat negative; (5) very negative.

19. Question wording: The relationship between blacks and Latinos in general: Are they (1) very positive; (2) somewhat positive; (3) neither positive nor negative; (4) somewhat negative; (5) very negative.

REFERENCES

Alvarez, R. Michael, and Tara L. Butterfield. 2000. "The Resurgence of Nativism in California? The Case of Proposition 187 and Illegal Immigration." *Social Science Quarterly* 81(1): 167–80.

Anderson, Jean Bradley. 1990. *Durham County: A History of Durham County.* Durham, N.C.: Duke University Press.

Berthoff, Rowland T. 1951. "Southern Attitudes Toward Immigration, 1865–1914." *Journal of Southern History* 17(3): 328–60.

Biles, Roger. 1988. "Cotton Fields or Skyscrapers? The Case of Memphis, Tennessee." *Historian* 50(2): 210–33.

Boyd, William Kenneth. 1925. *History of Durham: City of the New South.* Durham, N.C.: Duke University Press.

Brown, Leslie. 1997. "Common Spaces, Separate Lives: Gender and Racial Conflict in the 'Capital of the Black Middle Class.'" Ph.D. diss., Duke University.

Burns, Peter, and James G. Gimpel. 2000. "Economic Insecurity, Prejudicial Stereotypes, and Public Opinion on Immigration Policy." *Political Science Quarterly* 115(2): 201–25.

Burrell, Luchy S., Steve Redding, Sonya Schenk, and Marcela Mendoza. 2001. "New 2000 Estimates of the Hispanic Population for Shelby County, Tennessee." Memphis, Tenn.: Regional Economic Development Center, University of Memphis.

Capps, Randolph, Everett Henderson, John D. Kasarda, James H. Johnson, Stephen J. Appold, Derrek L. Croney, Donald J. Hernandez, and Michael E. Fix. 2007. "A Profile of Immigrants in Arkansas." Washington, D.C.: Urban Institute.

Carter, Niambi M. 2007. "The Black/White Paradigm Revisited: African Americans, Immigration, Race, and Nation in Durham, N.C." Ph.D. diss., Duke University.

Ciscel, David H., Barbara Ellen Smith, and Marcela Mendoza. 2003. "Ghosts in the Global Machine: New Immigrants and the Redefinition of Work." *Journal of Economic Issues* 37(June): 333–41.

Citrin, Jack, Donald P. Green, Christopher Music, and Cara Wong. 1997. "Public Opinion Toward Immigration Reform: The Role of Economic Motivations." *Journal of Politics* 59(August): 858–81.

Citrin, Jack, Beth Reingold, and Donald P. Green. 1990. "American Identity and the Politics of Ethnic Change." *Journal of Politics* 52(4): 1124–54.

Cummings, Scott, and Thomas Lambert. 1997. "Anti-Hispanic and Anti-Asian Sentiments among African Americans." *Social Science Quarterly* 78(2): 338–53.

Davidson, Osha Gray. 2007. *The Best of Enemies: Race and Redemption in the New South.* Chapel Hill: University of North Carolina Press.

Diamond, Jeff. 1998. "African-American Attitudes Towards United States Immigration Policy." *International Migration Review* 32(Summer): 451–70.

Dowdy, G. Wayne. 2006. *Mayor Crump Don't Like It: Machine Politics in Memphis.* Jackson: University Press of Mississippi.

The Economist. 1998. "El Barrio de Fayetteville." *The Economist,* September 19, 1998, p. 39.

Espenshade, Thomas J., and Charles A. Calhoun. 1993. "An Analysis of Public Opinion toward Undocumented Immigration." *Population Research and Policy Review* 13(3): 189–224.

Espenshade, Thomas J., and Katherine Hempstead. 1996. "Contemporary American Attitudes Toward U.S. Immigration." *International Migration Review* 30(Summer): 535–70.

Fetzer, Joel S. 2000. *Public Attitudes toward Immigration in the United States, France, and Germany.* Cambridge: Cambridge University Press.

Graves, John William. 1989. "Jim Crow in Arkansas: A Reconsideration of Urban Race Relations in the Post-Reconstruction South." *Journal of Southern History* 55(3): 421–48.

Greene, Christina. 1996. "Our Separate Ways: Women and the Black Freedom Movement in Durham, N.C., 1940s–1970s." Ph.D. diss., Duke University.

Griffith, David. 1993. *Jones's Minimal: Low-Wage Labor in the United States.* Albany: State University of New York Press.

Harwood, Edwin. 1983. "Alienation: American Attitudes toward Immigration." *Public Opinion* 6(3): 49–51.

Hellwig, David J. 1981. "Black Leaders and United States Immigration Policy, 1917–1929." *Journal of Negro History* 66(2): 110–27.

Henken, Ted. 2005. "Undocumented in Dixie: Mexican-Indian Immigration in Rural, 'New South' Alabama." Paper prepared for presentation at the Russell Sage Foundation conference, Immigration to the United States: New Sources and Destinations. New York (February 3–4, 2005).

Hernández-León, Rubén, and Victor Zúñiga. 2000. "'Making Carpet by the Mile': The Emergence of a Mexican Immigrant Community in an Industrial Region of the U.S. Historic South." *Social Science Quarterly* 81 (March): 49–66.

———. 2001. "A New Destination for an Old Migration: Origins, Trajectories, and Labor Market Incorporation of Latinos in Dalton, Georgia." In *Latino Workers in the Contemporary South,* edited by Arthur D. Murphy, Colleen Blanchard, and Jennifer A. Hill. Athens: University of Georgia Press.

———. 2002. "Social Capital of Mexican Communities in the South." *Southern Perspectives* 6(1): 1, 3, 4.

———. 2003. "Mexican Immigrant Communities in the South and Social Capital: The Case of Dalton, Georgia." *Southern Rural Sociology* 19(1): 20–45.

———. 2005. "Appalachia Meets Aztlán: Mexican Immigration and Intergroup Relations in Dalton, Georgia." In *New Destinations: Mexican Immigration in the United States,* edited by Rubén Hernández-León and Victor Zúñiga. New York: Russell Sage Foundation.

Higham, John. 1975. *Send These to Me: Jews and Other Immigrants in Urban America*. New York: Atheneum.

Hood, M. V., III, and Irwin L. Morris. 1997. "Amigo o Enemigo? Context, Attitudes, and Anglo Public Opinion Toward Immigration." *Social Science Quarterly* 78(2): 309–23.

———. 1998. "Give Us Your Tired, Your Poor, . . . But Make Sure They Have a Green Card: The Effects of Documented and Undocumented Migrant Context on Anglo Opinion toward Immigration." *Political Behavior* 20(1): 1–15.

———. 2000. "Brother, Can You Spare a Dime? Racial/Ethnic Context and the Anglo Vote on Proposition 187." *Social Science Quarterly* 81(1): 194–210.

Hood, M. V., III, Irwin L. Morris, and Kurt A. Shirkey. 1997. "Quedate o Vente: Uncovering the Determinants of Hispanic Public Opinion Toward Immigration." *Political Research Quarterly* 50(3): 627–47.

Houck, Thomas H. 1941. "A Newspaper History of Race Relations in Durham, North Carolina, 1910–1940." Masters' thesis, Duke University.

Ignatiev, Noel. 1997. *How the Irish Became White*. New York: Routledge.

Jacobson, Matthew Frye. 2001. *Whiteness of a Different Color: European Immigrants and the Alchemy of Race*. Cambridge, Mass.: Harvard University Press.

Johnson, James H., Walter C. Farrell, and Chandra Guinn. 1997. "Immigration Reform and the Browning of America: Tensions, Conflicts, and Community Instability in Metropolitan Los Angeles." *International Migration Review* 31(Winter): 1055–95.

Kandel, William, and Emilio A. Parrado. 2004. "Hispanics in the American South and the Transformation of the Poultry Industry." In *Hispanic Spaces, Latino Places: Community and Cultural Diversity in Contemporary America*, edited by Daniel D. Arreola. Austin: University of Texas Press.

Kessler, Alan J. 2001. "Immigration, Economic Insecurity, and the 'Ambivalent' American Public." Working Paper 41. San Diego, Calif.: Center for Comparative Immigration Studies.

Kirk, John A. 2002. *Redefining the Color Line: Black Activism in Little Rock, Arkansas, 1940–1970*. Gainesville: University Press of Florida.

Leidermann, Michel. 2007. "Latinos." In *The Encyclopedia of Arkansas History and Culture*. Little Rock: Central Arkansas Library System. Available at: http://www.encyclopediaofarkansas.net.

Lewis, Selma S. 1998. *A Biblical People in the Bible Belt: The Jewish Community of Memphis, Tennessee, 1840s–1960s*. Macon, Ga.: Mercer University Press.

Marrow, Helen B. 2008. "Hispanic Immigration, Black Population Size, and Intergroup Relations in the Rural and Small-Town South." In *New Faces in New Places: The Changing Geography of American Immigration*, edited by Douglas S. Massey. New York: Russell Sage Foundation.

McClain, Paula D. 2003. *Durham Study of Intergroup Relations (DSIR)*. Principal Investigator: Paula D. McClain (Ford Foundation Grant #1025-1445); not publically available.

———. 2006. "North Carolina's Response to Latino Immigrants and Immigration." In *Immigration's New Frontiers: Experiences from the Emerging Gateway States*, edited by Greg Anrig Jr. and Tova Andrea Wong. New York: Century Foundation Press.

———. 2007. *Three City Survey of Intergroup Relations (TCSIR)*. Principal Investigator: Paula D. McClain (Russell Sage Foundation Grant #88-06-11); not publically available.

McClain, Paula D., Niambi M. Carter, Victoria M. DeFrancesco Soto, Monique L. Lyle, Jeffrey D. Grynaviski, Shayla C. Nunnally, Thomas J. Scotto, J. Alan Kendrick, Gerald F. Lackey, and Kendra Davenport Cotton. 2006. "Racial Distancing in a Southern City: Latino Immigrants' Views of Black Americans." *Journal of Politics* 68(3): 571–84.

McClain, Paula D., Monique L. Lyle, Niambi M. Carter, Victoria M. DeFrancesco Soto, Gerald F. Lackey, Kendra Davenport Cotton, Shayla C. Nunnally, Thomas J. Scotto, Jeffrey D. Grynaviski, and J. Alan Kendrick. 2007. "Black Americans and Latino Immigrants in a Southern City: Friendly Neighbors or Economic Competitors?" *Du Bois Review* 4(1): 97–117.

Mohl, Raymond A. 2003. "Globalization, Latinization, and the Nuevo New South." *Journal of American Ethnic History* 22(Summer): 31–66.

Murphy, Arthur D., Colleen Blanchard, and Jennifer A. Hill. 2001. *Latino Workers in the Contemporary South*. Athens: University of Georgia Press.

Parker, Frederick B. 1948. "The Status of the Foreign Stock in the Southeast: A Region-Nation Comparison." *Social Forces* 27(2): 136–43.

Pérez, Efrén O. 2008. "No Way José: The Nature and Sequence of U.S. Anti-Immigrant Opinion." Ph.D. diss., Duke University.

Pew Hispanic Center. 2007. "Statistical Portrait of Hispanics in the United States, 2007." Table 12, Hispanic Population by State, 2007. Washington, D.C.: Pew Research Center. Available at: http://www.pewhispanic.org/files/factsheets/hispanics2007/Table-12.pdf (accessed May 11, 2010).

Powers, Rebecca S. 2005. "Working It Out in North Carolina: Employers and Hispanic/Latino Immigrants." *Sociation Today* 3(2). Available at: www.ncsociology.org/sociationtoday/v32/powers.htm (accessed May 11, 2010).

Roediger, David R. 1999. *The Wages of Whiteness: Race and the Making of the American Working Class*. Rev. ed. New York: Verso.

Rubin, Jay. 1978. "Black Nativism: The European Immigrant in Negro Thought, 1830–1960." *Phylon* 39(3): 193–202.

Scott, Daryl. 1999. "'Immigrant Indigestion': A. Philip Randolph: Radical and Restrictionist." Washington, D.C.: Center for Immigration Studies.

Sniderman, Paul M., Pierangelo Peri, Rui J. De Figueiredo Jr., and Thomas Piazza. 2000. *The Outsider: Prejudice and Politics in Italy*. Princeton, N.J.: Princeton University Press.

Stein, Robert M., Stephanie Shirley Post, and Allison L. Rinden. 2000. "Reconciling Context and Contact Effects on Racial Attitudes." *Political Research Quarterly* 53(2): 285–303.

Taylor, Marylee C., and Matthew B. Schroeder. 2010. "The Impact of Hispanic Population Growth on the Outlook of African Americans." *Social Science Research* 39(3): 491–505.

Thornton, Michael C., and Yuko Mizuno. 1999. "Economic Well-Being and Black Adult Feelings Toward Immigrants and Whites, 1984." *Journal of Black Studies* 30(1): 15–44.

Tolbert, Caroline J., and Rodney E. Hero. 1996. "Race/Ethnicity and Direct Democracy: An Analysis of California's Illegal Immigration Initiative." *Journal of Politics* 58(3): 806–18.

Torres, Cruz C. 2000. "Emerging Latino Communities: A New Challenge for the Rural South." *Southern Rural Development Center* 12(August): 1–8.

U.S. Bureau of the Census. 2000a. *Census of Population*. Available at: http://factfinder.census.gov (accessed May 11, 2011).

———. 2000b. *2000 Redistricting File*. Available at: http://censtats.census.gov/ (accessed May 11, 2011).

———. 2008. *2006–2008 American Community Survey 3-Year Estimates*. Available at: http://www.census.gov/acs (accessed May 11, 2011).

Waller, Altina L. 1984. "Community, Class, and Race in the Memphis Riot of 1866." *Journal of Social History* 18(2): 233–46.

Winders, Jamie. 2008. "Nashville's New *Sonido:* Latino Migration and the Changing Politics of Race." In *New Faces in New Places: The Changing Geography of American Immigration*, edited by Douglas S. Massey. New York: Russell Sage Foundation.

Wright, Sharon D. 2000. *Race, Power, and Political Emergence in Memphis*. New York: Garland Publishing.

CHAPTER 8

Black Attitudes and Hispanic Immigrants in South Carolina

Monica McDermott

Blacks and Latinos have developed a complicated set of relationships in a variety of arenas in urban areas scattered across the
Northeast, Midwest, and Southwest. However, the arrival of a large
Latino (or Hispanic, as it is locally termed) population in the Southeast is causing such interracial relationships to be largely negotiated
anew. As one might imagine, the process is far from simple—in a region long dominated by the black-white color line, the presence of a
new group can destabilize ethnic relations, though not necessarily
Latino attitudes toward the native born (see chapter 2, this volume).
Consequently, different segments of the black community respond
differently to the Hispanic presence.

Between August 2005 and September 2006, I conducted ethnographic fieldwork in and around Greenville, South Carolina, to better
understand the impact that Hispanic immigration was having on the
native-born population (see table 8.1 for a population breakdown of
Greenville County). Greenville lies midway between Atlanta and
Charlotte—both of which are also new destinations (Singer, Hardwick, and Brettell 2008). I lived and worked alongside both black and
white southerners to capture the degrees to which the Hispanic presence had had an impact on their lives—if at all. I also conducted a
number of interviews with black and white respondents of varied
class backgrounds. In September 2009, I returned to the field to conduct additional interviews, primarily with black and white working-
class and poor residents, to assess their views about immigration in
the midst of an economic recession. In this chapter, I focus specifically on the main pattern of results among the black community in
the Greenville area, which is the nonmonotonic class effect for attitudes toward Hispanics. Working-class and upper-middle-class

Table 8.1 Greenville County Population

	1990	2000	2005
White	80.9%	77.5%	75.6%
Black	18%	18.3%	18.8%
Hispanic	0.9%	3.8%	5.8%

Source: Author's compilation based on data from U.S. Census STF-1 files (U.S. Bureau of the Census 1990, 2000) and American Community Survey 2005 (U.S. Bureau of the Census 2005).

blacks are largely negatively disposed toward Hispanics, and lower-middle-class blacks are largely positively disposed.

The source of these attitudes is likely found in a type of group threat for each class, albeit a different type for each group. The working-class case is the most straightforward, this group being the most likely to lose jobs to Hispanic laborers. Many of the middle-class blacks who expressed animosity toward the Hispanic presence felt that their community rather than they themselves personally were losing out at the expense of Hispanics. The black lower middle class, because they were often supervisors and thus thought that they could secure raises or job security by learning Spanish or befriending Hispanic workers, saw Hispanics as an opportunity to get ahead on the job.

While this research echoes findings from survey data on black attitudes, it also suggests that researchers begin looking for curvilinear patterns in black attitude data. The black lower middle class could potentially be an important basis for the building of black-Hispanic coalitions, especially in lower-income communities or communities in new destinations.

PREVIOUS RESEARCH

Although the literature on immigrant incorporation and on the impact of immigration on local race relations is extensive (for a recent review, see Waters and Jiménez 2005), that on the effects of immigration on race relations in the Southeast and Midwest is notably less, no doubt because of the recentness of this phenomenon. Nonetheless, several demographic and ethnographic studies of immigration to nontraditional receiving communities or new destinations have detailed the processes of immigrant incorporation and, to a lesser extent, the impact on local, native-born populations (Zúñiga and Hernández-León 2005; Marrow 2009).

The passage of the Immigration Reform and Control Act of 1986 (IRCA) is a major reason that so many Mexican immigrants have settled in new destinations, given that the amnesty-granting provisions of this law granted an unprecedented degree of geographic mobility to formerly undocumented immigrants (Durand, Massey, and Parrado 1999). Because many of the arrivals to new destinations are secondary migrants, often pushed out of their primary destinations, such as Los Angeles (see Light 2006), they are able to draw on social capital accumulated in traditional gateways to ease the transition to social life in their new homes (Zúñiga and Hernández-León 2004). As a partial consequence, many of these newcomers are likely to become long-term residents and settle their entire families into community life (Hernández-León and Zúñiga 2000).

Immigrants to new destinations such as the rural Midwest and the Southeast have been met with both hostility and open arms (Grey and Woodrick 2005; Rich and Miranda 2005). Hostility between blacks and Hispanics has been especially salient in the Southeast (Mohl 2005). Social class is especially important in determining the reception of immigrants by native-born whites and blacks (Hernández-León and Zúñiga 2005; Rich and Miranda 2005). In the state of Georgia, specifically, length of residence in the state is an important predictor of immigrant hostility, as is perception of economic threat (Neal and Bohon 2003).

According to standard social distance measures, blacks in rural North Carolina prefer to be closer to whites than to those they refer to as Mexicans (Randall and Delbridge 2005), a finding mirrored among whites, although by a smaller margin. Mexicans in this study also prefer closeness to whites over blacks, a finding reflected in a survey of Latinos in the Raleigh-Durham area (McClain et al. 2006). Mariel Rose (2007) observed even greater social distance between Hispanics and blacks than between Hispanics and whites or Indians in western North Carolina. Economic competition is a major factor driving black attitudes toward Latinos, such that the larger the relatively economically advantaged Latino population, the greater the negative black sentiment (Gay 2006). Perceptions that Hispanics take black manual jobs can inflame tensions between the two communities in the South (Mantero 2008). Competition can also play out in fights over community resources, even those as seemingly paltry as welfare payments (Mindiola, Niemann, and Rodriguez 2003). However, Hispanics still pose a minimal political threat in the South, because their voter registration rates in the Carolinas and Georgia are well behind their rates in the general population (Bullock and Hood 2006).

Class differences have long been significant among the black community (see, for example, Frazier 1957), and the black middle class is especially vulnerable (Patillo 2005; Prince 2007) because of structural factors as well as everyday acts of racism (Feagin and Sikes 1995). For example, blacks with a high socioeconomic status are more likely to be segregated from whites than high SES Hispanics or Asians are, although the effect of socioeconomic status on reducing segregation has been decreasing since 1990 (Iceland and Wilkes 2006). This vulnerability coupled with relative advantage has resulted in a much more liberal set of political attitudes among middle-class blacks than among their working-class counterparts (Hochschild 1996; McDermott 1994).

DATA AND METHODS

The primary method used in this research is targeted participant observation. This involves living and working alongside the community of interest, much like a traditional workplace ethnography, a central feature of which is the integration of oneself into the community by working alongside its members. Unlike traditional workplace ethnographies, however, the analytical focus is not the labor process or labor-management relations. Instead, the trust and rapport generated in the workplace are used to facilitate observations about the area of interest, for example, how blacks talk about race and interact with Hispanics in their daily lives. The analytical focus rather than convenience determines site selection, as well.

In addition, I conducted a dozen or so in-depth interviews with black and white residents of the Greenville metropolitan statistical area (MSA) in public settings such as laundromats, public parks, restaurants, and occasionally on the front porches of homes. Neighborhoods that bordered large Hispanic communities were targeted. Middle-class whites as well as poor blacks and whites were interviewed, interviews lasting approximately forty-five minutes to one hour and recorded when the respondent granted permission. The interview schedule consisted of a number of questions about neighborhood problems, crime, changes in the community, and so on (see online appendix 8.A1, available at http://www.russellsage.org/telles_sawyer_on line_appendix.pdf), but never mentioned Hispanics or immigration with the intention of eliciting mentions of Hispanics with reference to these issues. As expected, all but one respondent commented on the Hispanic population in response to the questions about neighborhood change and problems. I was initially concerned about substantial race of interviewer effects, because I am a white woman, but most black respondents expressed negative attitudes toward Hispanics—the opposite of the socially desirable response. Nonetheless, the majority of data I rely on are from the ethnographic component of the study; evidence provided from interviews is specified as such.

SITE SELECTION

South Carolina ranked sixth in the country in Hispanic population growth between 1990 and 2000 (Rose 2007) and seventh in the percentage of those who speak English either not well or at all (Schmid 2002). The Greenville MSA, specifically, is one of several hyper-growth Latino destinations identified by Roberto Suro and Audrey Singer (2002), or areas that experienced at least a 300 percent growth in the Latino population between 1980 and 2000. After narrowing the list of hypergrowth destinations to those metro areas that were new destinations with substantial black populations, I used personal networks to get a job as a traveling sales vendor in the Greenville area. Because the research employed an element of deception, I granted the company the right to vet any manuscripts resulting from the research to ensure that the company's identity is protected.

The massive influx of immigration to Greenville was occurring at the same time that a major employer, the textile industry, was leaving (see table 8.2), sending the unemployment rate up toward 7 percent. As a result, competition for low-wage, non-service-sector jobs was keen. Employment in the construction industry, after years of stability, increased slightly between 1990 and 2000, and this workforce shifted from a mix of black and white male employees to a significantly Hispanic labor force. Construction has been a major draw for Hispanic immigrants throughout the South, such as the case with Atlanta (Amado 2006). The Hispanic immigration, with the exception of a small Colombian stream, had little impact on professional and managerial jobs.

Table 8.2 Percentage of Workers in Greenville, S.C. MSA

Industry	1950	1970	1980	1990
Agriculture	8.1	2.1	1.4	1
Construction	7.6	7	7.6	7.6
Yarn, Thread and Fabric[a]	27	15.6	12.3	6.2
Eating and Drinking	2	2.9	4	5.4
Private Households	5.5	2.7	1.2	0.9
Educational Services	3.5	9.6	7.9	7.8

Source: Author's compilation based on data from Integrated Public-Use Microdata Series (Ruggles et al. 2010).
[a]Includes industries employing 5 percent or more workers.

The black community is largely concentrated in Greenville's urban center and a crescent-shaped series of suburban neighborhoods, some of which are quite poverty stricken. While I was conducting my fieldwork in 2005 and 2006, Greenville became the final county in the United States to vote to celebrate Martin Luther King Day—it passed with a vote of 7 to 5 after opponents argued the cost of continuing to ignore the holiday would be too great. Native son Jesse Jackson, who was raised by his grandmother in downtown Greenville, helped organize to have the holiday recognized and joined the community to celebrate when the day finally arrived.

EMPLOYMENT

I secured a job as a sales vendor with the intent of surreptitiously observing mixed-race groups of adults going about their daily business to evaluate the degree to which race and ethnicity structured their speech and practices. I worked for a company that stocked DVDs and CDs in discount stores and drug stores throughout the Southeast. My job consisted of spending several hours each week in a particular store filling accounts with the store manager, cleaning and stocking the product racks, and removing outdated merchandise. The entire process provided ample time to observe what was occurring in the stores, and the clipboard that I carried to keep track of the accounts provided cover for the field notes I collected. After the job was completed, I made a point of hanging out with the cashiers and, on occasion, the manager afterward. In most cases, the racial composition of the staff mirrored that of the neighborhood with one glaring exception—no Hispanics were employed in any of the discount or drug stores.

The sales route I traveled regularly was centered in the urban areas of Greenville and Spartanburg in a mix of race- and class-based neighborhoods: some of these had a large Hispanic presence, others did not. A number of offshoots from the route went through rural areas, some almost entirely white, others with a significant black presence. In the rural areas, too, the size of the Hispanic population varied.

After nine months of working for the DVD company, the parent corporation filed for bankruptcy and the workers were summarily informed by email that we had been relieved of our jobs. With four months left in the field, I decided to apply to discount stores I had serviced while working for the DVD company. I eventually secured employment as a stockperson at a store in a rural, predominantly white area with one black female employee and the remainder white female employees. The customers were a mix of whites, blacks, and Hispanics, primarily with poor and working-class backgrounds. Although the job stocking shelves did not provide as much opportunity to observe a wide range of customers, given that much of my time was spent in concentrated activity or in the back of the store, it did provide a chance to get to know the other workers very well.

RESIDENCE

I rented a home in a working-class neighborhood in Greenville County that was approximately 50 percent Hispanic, 30 percent white, and 20 percent black. The subdivision was located in one of three sections of Greenville that had a heavy concentration of Hispanics; in this case, the homes were all quite new, the oldest having been completed in 2002. In some cases, Hispanic construction workers moved into the houses they had just finished building as part of construction crews. Perhaps because the neighborhood was less established and the surrounding area was racially mixed, the subdivision was, after Hispanics, roughly even in the number of blacks and whites.

The homes were detached and had separate yards, but were located close together, resulting in considerable opportunity for interactions with immediate neighbors. In addition, I was on the newsletter committee for the fairly active homeowners' association, which kept me abreast of the key issues facing the community and introduced me to neighbors I might not otherwise meet (the newsletter was translated into Spanish on the reverse, so coordination with a middle-aged female Hispanic neighbor was required). I also made a point of walking my small dog through the subdivision, which apparently led me to seem approachable and friendly, as it was the starting point of many conversations.

SHOPPING, DINING

While I worked for the DVD company, I made a point of shopping, dining, and engaging in leisure activities in the immediate vicinity of the store I was servicing. In some cases, this meant eating at an all-white diner (in terms of customers and wait staff) in an almost entirely black neighborhood near a discount store with a mainly black staff and a mix of black and white customers. In other cases, I sipped expensive gin martinis in order to overhear how a middle-aged, affluent white man would react to the presence of a young black woman sitting next to him at an exclusive bar (he made a point of slowly explaining the merits of different types of drinks to her). The one type of restaurant that reliably provided a mixed black-Hispanic customer base was the all-you-can-eat buffet. Long a staple of southern cuisine, Hispanics preferred this option because no language skills were required to obtain food.

CHURCHES

For many in the Greenville MSA, social life revolved around religion. An early question asked in the process of getting to know people is where they go to church. I tried to attend the weekly services and, occasionally, other social events held by area churches. Although southern churches are still quite segregated, there is more integration, especially among evangelical churches, than there was.

One of the churches I attended most frequently was a majority-white, evangelical, and charismatic church with a few blacks and Hispanics. It offered frequent social events and was very involved in outreach. I also attended an entirely white mainstream church that was very difficult to penetrate—performances would be put on for the public, but socializing was conducted primarily among members of the congregation. Likewise, I sometime attended an entirely black congregation that was one of the elite churches in the community. I would often be the only white person in the church aside from the sound and video crew, who were always white. I generally tried to hide in a corner of the massive church and observe, hoping to be as inconspicuous as possible. Finally, I attended a multiracial mega-church with a congregation that was about 60 percent black and 40 percent white. Black-white interaction was encouraged by the minister, a white man who spoke with a black English accent. Unfortunately, and perhaps tellingly, I could not find a church that had a significant mix of black and Hispanic parishioners.

MAIN POINTS OF CONTACT WITH BLACKS

Seven places in particular were my main contact points with black respondents: the Black History Museum, the black church, survival Spanish class, my neighborhood, stores I visited while on the job, the hairdresser, and in-depth interviews.

After seeing an advertisement in the local newspaper for an exhibit on segregated schools at a local museum, I drove to the Black History Museum during the four hours it was open. Although all of the doors were locked, I heard rustling inside and a light-skinned, middle-aged black woman opened the door and asked me whether she could help me. When I mentioned the exhibit, she opened the door further and let me into the building, which was a converted Victorian home. The exhibit turned out to be nothing more than a few pieces of poster board with a few old photos taped to them; five or six black women sat at a table in the back of the room talking, laughing, and working on a crafts project. When I mentioned to a woman nearby that I went to school with the son of one of the men who was prominently featured in the exhibit, she became much more interested in me, striking up a conversation about where I had grown up and which schools I had attended. Three hours of conversation later, I was a volunteer docent for the museum.

In addition to the Black History Museum, the other major point of contact I had with affluent blacks was the black church. Located in a mixed-race, middle-class suburb of Greenville, the church regularly attracted notable guest speakers of national renown, as well as a who's who of Greenville's black elite. I had few conversations with blacks at this church because I was not typically included in social events, but I did try to attend services and larger events to record observations.

The most extended, in-depth contact that I had with members of the black lower middle class was in my Spanish class. The class was advertised as being for those who needed to learn Spanish "NOW," with advertisements posted in public places as well as in newspaper advertisements. The first class in which I enrolled, held in a library not far from my neighborhood, was about half black and half white, and had a Colombian-American teacher. The black participants were all middle class, and included a construction foreman, several nurses, a teacher, and a social worker. In all of their cases, the desire to learn Spanish stemmed from a desire to get ahead at work. In contrast, whites in the class expressed a variety of reasons for taking the course, including wanting to better enjoy a Caribbean vacation, wanting to homeschool a child in Spanish, and wanting to communicate with a Spanish-speaking spouse.

My neighborhood was an additional point of contact given that about 20 percent of the subdivision I lived in was black. My neighbor directly across the street was black, as was the family who lived three houses down, and one black resident was very active in community affairs. Although much interaction was within racial groups, considerably more cross-racial interaction occurred between whites and blacks than between Hispanics and blacks.

Perhaps the greatest source of contact with blacks was in the stores I worked in as a sales vendor and as a stockperson. Especially in the majority-black neighborhoods in central city Greenville and Spartanburg (a neighboring city in the MSA), opportunity to observe customer interactions was frequent and to interact with the mostly black workforce was considerable. When I switched jobs to become a stocker, one of the employees was black, and I came to know her quite well.

A final point of contact with the black population was through the black hairdresser I regularly visited. She initially was unsure as to whether she could cut my "white" hair, but experimented and agreed, after which point I gained entry into one of three majority-black environments I observed during my fieldwork, the others being the black church and the Black History Museum. This environment was much friendlier, however, and I was able to listen to animated conversations after a short period of small talk every month or so.

Finally, I conducted in-depth interviews with nine black respondents. As mentioned earlier, given the sensitivity of discussions of matters of race and ethnicity, I am concerned about social desirability effects in the case of these interviews, especially because they were not men and women I had built up a relationship with over a long period. Nonetheless, some useful insights may be drawn if the results are interpreted in context.

FINDINGS

In general, the black community exhibited a quiet hostility toward the Hispanic community. Interactions were few, despite near constant opportunities for such in stores, government offices, and other public spaces. Active avoidance was sometimes practiced, as when a middle-aged black woman sat in her car outside a laundromat to wait for her laundry to finish rather than share the waiting room with three Hispanic customers.[1] Interactions are a two-way street, of course, and the Hispanic community appeared equally distant from the black community in day-to-day life (see, for example, chapter 12 in this volume). Nonetheless, a number of opportunities arose in which blacks had occasion to express their opinions toward the Hispanic population, often during the ethnographic phase of the research, when they did not realize they were being studied, as well as at other times during interviews, when the objectives of the research were more clear.[2]

WORKING-CLASS BLACKS

The mildest form of approbation toward Hispanics can perhaps be appreciated only when compared with blacks' public interactions with whites. During my thirteen months in the field, I cannot recall a black woman scolding a white child she did not know; however, both black and white women would scold Hispanic children who misbehaved with relative frequency. For example, a heavily tattooed Hispanic man wearing a muscle-tee was standing in the back of the post office in my mixed-race neighborhood. He was speaking in Spanish into a cellphone and waiting for a woman and a young girl at the front of the line. The young girl began to rip apart the paper backing for a $10 phone card, rendering the card unusable, when a black woman in line exclaimed loudly, "Where did the father go?" An older white woman responded, "He's right over there." The black woman called out to the presumed father, "Sir, she just ripped up something that was $10." The man, still talking on the phone, started to walk toward the girl. The woman with the girl, presumably the mother, who had been buying a money order at the counter, realized what the girl had been doing and pulled her aside, taking the shredded paper and card from her hand and placing it behind the display rack of cards. The black woman and two white women standing near her in line scoffed and shook their heads.

Other expressions of Hispanic resentment took the form of sarcasm, such as when a middle-aged black woman entered a Frank's store in a rural, majority-white area, where I was working near the Christmas holidays. A black musical Santa Claus had been displayed at the front of the store, and the black woman entered the store and loudly asked where the white and Spanish Santas were. The white female manager said that the white Santa Claus was in the back. The black woman demanded to know where the Spanish Santas were. A white female cashier responded, "You'll have to ask the company that makes them." The manager yelled, "We don't have a Spanish Santa." The black woman responded that they should have all three lined up at the front of the store. "People are speaking all kinds of languages. You've got to have the Spanish Santa." As the black woman was out of earshot, the white manager hissed, "She's ignorant."

Although it is possible that the black woman's wish for Spanish Santa reflected an honest desire to see the new diversity of the area reflected in holiday decorations, it is far more likely, especially given the woman's tone of voice, that her request was sarcastic. The white manager's response is also instructive—"Ignorant!" she spits out, clearly taking the black woman's request for Spanish Santa at face value. To request a Spanish Santa on par with a black and a white Santa is the height of ignorance in many parts of the rural white South still operating under the black-white color line.

Although there were few opportunities to watch black employees interact with Hispanic supervisors at the jobs I held, because all of the employees were either black or white, some jobs in the community had Hispanic supervisors. At a fast food restaurant in Anderson (one of the three cities within the Greenville MSA), for example, a middle-aged Hispanic manager was giving commands to a black male worker in front of two white workers and three white customers, myself among them. The black male leaned against a booth, smiling lazily, saying nothing. In response to the manager's increasing anger, he responded, "You should have told me last night." She had been asking him to sweep the floor, and was not smiling in response to his refusal, which was a clear lack of respect for her authority.

Conversely, black women taking an assertive role with Hispanics, both male and female, was much more common. For example, a working-class black female shopper leaving one of the discount stores became incensed with a group of Hispanic men for making too much noise and yelled at them to "stop making all of that racket." Never mind that the men were part of a construction crew contracted to repair the sidewalk in front of the store. For their part, the men left laughing and speaking loudly to one another in Spanish, and the black woman remained furious that she had been disturbed by a lower-status group engaged in a, frankly, ordinary event.

As mentioned earlier, however, intergroup trust and generosity is a two-way street. Three young girls lived near my house, two Hispanics and one black; the Hispanic girls typically did not play with the black girl, but on this one occasion they all played together under the watchful eye of the Hispanic girl's father. As I rounded the corner with my dog that I was walking, one of the Hispanic girls asked the black girl, "What's that?" "That's a dog!" She exclaimed, at which point the mother and grandmother of the black girl brought out ice cream cones for all three girls. Throughout the exchange, the father of the Hispanic girls sat and stared impassively, making no move to approach the scene nor to thank the women for the ice cream. However, when I nodded to him as I walked by with my dog, he smiled broadly and said hello, presumably because I am white.

An interview with a black respondent who did not mention Hispanics at all was with a poor man living in a recently constructed home as part of a program to resettle residents out of public housing. Even without mentioning Hispanics directly, several of the comments that he makes are instructive. One of his main concerns throughout the interview is the loss of black businesses, especially the black business district that has long stood in downtown Greenville. He grew up during the era of segregated schools and regretted having to watch his children integrate in local high schools, believing that they would have been better off in the same segregated schools he attended, primarily because of what he called the different culture. He felt that crime was not necessarily a significant problem because "we can't know what is on a person's mind," or what compels them to commit the crime; for instance, the person might be trying to feed his family or have no other job prospects. The biggest problem, he felt, is instead that the United States is a "communist country," with land grabs of black-owned property as well as a restriction of free-speech rights. Although he was correct that large, government-financed interests were buying black-owned businesses downtown, many other black-owned businesses in the part of Greenville where he lives were being bought and rented by Hispanic entrepreneurs. It would be only one small step from anticommunism to anti-immigrant sentiment should this connection be made.

I interviewed a middle-aged black female high school dropout in a laundromat who was quite serious throughout the interview, speaking of drug abuse in her family, the history of racial conflict and present tensions in Greenville, and so on. After each interview, I administered a short demographic questionnaire that included a question about racial identification. When I asked her if she were Hispanic, she began snorting with laughter, looking around and gesturing at the Hispanic women in the laundromat, and shook her head. There was clearly a safe and comfortable degree of social distance in terms of identity in this case.

Finally, in an exception that may prove the rule, a middle-aged black man, who had been unemployed for decades and was living in a public housing project on the verge of being demolished, was positively disposed toward new immigrants. Presumably because there was no competition in the labor market there was no source for negative attitudes. When asked how the neighborhood had changed during the previous twenty years, he responded that there were now "Hispanics and Puerto Ricans. . . . [I got] no grudge against anybody. I treat everyone like they want to be treated." The rest of his interview was not without criticism. He heaped it quite liberally on the police, for example, but Hispanics did not seem to be a factor for him.

Upper-Middle-Class Blacks

Although ethnographic studies necessarily select only a small slice of social life, the information on upper-middle-class blacks comes from an especially restricted set of sources. The small size and exclusivity of the community is difficult to access for a researcher in the guise of a working-class white woman. However, I was able to connect with a group of older affluent black women at the Black History Museum; many of the rest of my observations come from the elite black church in suburban Greenville.

My first day at the Black History Museum, I spent well over an hour talking with Rose, a black woman in her late sixties who had worked as a schoolteacher in the public school system for more than thirty years. After spearheading the establishment of the museum, she had become a noted figure in the community, appearing in several newspaper articles while I was living there, and she was clearly looked up to by the other volunteers. After I explained that I was in town visiting from California but had grown up in the area, she described the difficulty of making the transition from segregated to integrated schools during the early 1970s, and we compared notes on families we both knew. As I was getting ready to leave, both of us laughing over a joke, she asked me what sort of project I was working on (I had told her that I was a sociology professor); when I responded that I was studying Latino immigration to the Southeast, the laughter immediately stopped, her face froze, and she pursed her lips. "What?" she asked. "Mexican immigration to Greenville," I replied. She laughed scornfully, looked away, and that was clearly the end of our conversation. Another woman, Honey, had watched the scene unfold and seemingly took pity on me. She asked me if I spoke Spanish, to which I responded, *un poquito*. She said okay and nodded, staring. Feeling somewhat desperate, I tried to explain the project further, detailing its aims to explore the impact of immigration on the native born—she just silently nodded in return, and I left for the day.

In this case, the mere mention of the Latino community caused disapproval, if not outrage, among community members who were working so hard to bring attention to the intense hardships enduring by the local black community. The museum itself, which contained spare yet shocking exhibits on the days of segregated schooling in the county, was barely staying afloat, patronized almost exclusively by the black community and school groups. A collective shift in focus, with a corresponding shift in funding and patronage, to the hardships of another nonwhite group might seem like the final and insurmountable straw. This outlook fit with conversations I was to later have with some of the women at the museum about issues such as community policing. After a series of muggings had plagued a majority-Hispanic apartment complex, the Hispanic community had demanded meetings with the Greenville Police Department. The police promptly responded—a response that occasioned anger and resentment among black community leaders, many of whom had, in their words, been trying for decades to arrange just such meetings to no avail.

An expression of this pent-up resentment may have reached its height during a church service at the black church during a special sermon led by a nationally famous pastor who has also been very politically active. The sermon had been advertised in mainstream newspapers that reached a large white audience, so about 1 percent—six to seven—of the attendees were white; no attendees appeared to be Hispanic. As the structured portion of the service gave way to the sermon, the preacher made repeated reference to being in "our house" where we can talk about the issues facing "our community," by which it was increasingly clear he meant the black community—speaking of high drop out rates, high unemployment rates, high out-of-wedlock births, and so on. At one point, the speaker launched into a critique of those with power in the county; he referred to it as what was "behind the curtain." One of the occurrences behind the curtain is that "Greenville opens its arms to newcomers while we lose promotions and jobs." Much applause and cheering followed; from some people, especially men, he received a standing ovation.

LOWER-MIDDLE-CLASS BLACKS

In marked contrast to the negative or avoidant attitudes reported above, lower-middle-class blacks were often enthusiastic about befriending Hispanics, learning more about Hispanic culture and language, and in some cases actively standing up for them. In almost all cases, the pro-Hispanic blacks held jobs in social services, nursing, or construction or factory work, where they directly supervised a primarily Hispanic labor force. Most of their contact with Hispanics came from the job, but occasionally extended to the neighborhood. Although a selection effect is no doubt at work for the blacks I observed in Spanish class, I also noticed positive attitudes by the lower middle class toward Hispanics at work and in my neighborhood.

Several of the blacks in my Spanish class explicitly remarked on the delight they were experiencing at learning to speak a few words of Spanish with employees or clients. Terry said of her friend Norman, a foreman for a construction company, that his workers "think he's the best thing in the world" when he speaks Spanish with them (according to what I heard in class, Norman could speak virtually no Spanish, but made tremendous effort to do so). In response to Terry's comment, Norman looked down and chuckled, seemingly embarrassed yet pleased by the attention.

At other times, potentially difficult interactions were handled with respect in the class, such as the occasion when the teacher spoke for quite some time about the use of *Negro* as a term for blacks. Claiming that there is nothing wrong with the term and what should be used in Spanish, two of the black students began chuckling quietly. In response, the teacher described her "very, very dark-skinned friend" Tony, whom everyone just called *Negro* instead of Tony. This prompted even louder laughter, although most of the white students were looking down at their notebooks. The teacher gave up at this point and moved on to the next lesson.

At the annual homeowners' association meeting for my neighborhood, an interesting and heated conversation emerged about the supposed absence of Hispanic homeowners from the meeting.[3] A white woman in her sixties who had relocated to Greenville from New York was the most vocally anti-Hispanic, and a middle-aged black female nurse was the most supportive. The white New Yorker said, "They understand things they want to understand" in reaction to someone defending the Hispanic neighbors, stating they might not have known about the meeting or the importance of attending. The black woman firmly and angrily stated, "I disagree with that statement." Someone else responded, "There are a lot of cultural differences," to which the black woman said, "There is a lot of intimidation for some people." The New Yorker scornfully replied, "Oh, I don't buy that." The black woman turned to her and said, "We've got to do more to get to know our neighbors." She ultimately suggested that the association establish a human relations committee.

In this exchange, it is clear that the black woman had both more knowledge of the challenges facing the Hispanic community and more sympathy for their difficulties than her white counterparts did. In all likelihood, this knowledge comes from her work as a nurse, one of the few jobs in the county that would almost certainly have put her into frequent contact with the Hispanic population. This, coupled with, in her case, living in a neighborhood that is approximately half Hispanic, indicates that her exposure to this population will be frequent, and usually with her as the higher-status party. The last point is key—sympathy and concern are much easier for any group to bestow on a lower-status party than on a higher-status one.

CONCLUSION

In contrast to the linear class (as measured by education) patterning of attitudes toward Hispanics in the white community (Chandler and Tsai 2001), with upper-class whites most likely to have positive attitudes, the class effect among blacks is nonmonotic. Lower-middle-class blacks are the most positively disposed toward Hispanics, not just in opinion but also in the desire to be close to and to learn about the community. Working-class and upper-middle-class blacks typically had negative attitudes.

The negative attitudes of working-class blacks are most likely rooted in a sense of economic competition; many people I interviewed during the return trip to Greenville in 2009 were explicit about this. In chapter 7 of this volume, Paula McClain and her colleagues find that blacks, in general, are the most likely to perceive economic competition from Latinos, even though they actually perceive race relations to be quite positive. The degree to which this economic competition is real or perceived is an open question at the level of the Greenville MSA. The research of Frank Bean and his colleagues (see chapter 2 in this volume) suggests that perception trumps reality. Rumors, anecdotes, and the placement of Latinos in visible jobs, in tandem with high black unemployment, can feed these perceptions.

IMPLICATIONS

Although the findings presented here are obviously based on only a few cases, it would be useful to test the generalizability of these patterns by looking for curvilinearity in black responses to nationally representative survey data. Typically, class controls such as income and education are measured linearly and thus would not capture the patterns described here. An especially liberal or positive lower middle class on the dimension of Hispanic attitudes could extend to an especially positive or liberal group on other issues, especially in cases where group position theory is the optimal explanation.

It is possible that class distinctions made within the black community are driving some of the attitudes reported here. Although I did not hear any black residents comment on the class background of other blacks, with the exception of some upper-middle-class blacks expressing the need for the community to "take care of ourselves" or "stick together," I have encountered the denigration of poor, or ghetto, blacks by their more affluent counterparts in earlier work (McDermott 2006). However, I think that it is the presence of immigrants that is driving attitudes, in that the interviews never asked specifically about Hispanics or immigration, yet the vast majority of respondents brought the issue up voluntarily.

Outside academia, much has been made of attempts to forge inter-racial coalitions, and the difficulties inherent in doing so, especially in new destinations, where the color line remains so rigid. This research suggests that social class be taken into account in a very particular way—that attempts to forge movements and alliances between lower-middle-class blacks and working-class Hispanics are the most likely to meet with success. Other coalitions are more likely to be rife with stereotypes and unstable power dynamics. On a related note, outreach efforts directed at reducing negative Hispanic affect among the black community should be targeted at the black lower middle class first, which is by far the most receptive population, then allowed to move out through network contacts from there. The black lower middle class has a reputation as, by and large, solid hard workers, and their words and actions carry considerable weight.

Limitations and Future Research

One of the central limitations of the research is the relatively small area in which it was conducted. Even though the job was designed to allow for travel in urban and rural areas as well as areas with and without large numbers of immigrants, the locations were still within a hundred miles of the same metropolitan area. The area was one of the new destinations, important and interesting as such, yet likely to have limited applicability to established gateway communities such as New York or Los Angeles. The nature of an ethnographic field project means that the observations will be nonrandom; this is especially true when the project is designed to maximize observations of native-born interactions with Hispanics. Nonetheless, ethnography's flaws can also be its blessings, in that sustained observations of the behaviors and groups of interest are often the only way to uncover new social processes.

Aside from a renewed focus on nonlinear class effects among blacks in public opinion data, another research topic suggested by the findings presented here is an exploration of the black supervisory experience, especially with regard to Hispanic employees. Does black experience of having relative power and status in the workplace mitigate negative or competitive feelings often identified elsewhere in the literature? What about the experience from the Latino perspective? Is resentment heightened or are stereotypes upended? One can imagine the possibility of either scenario.

Regardless of which scenario dominates, Hispanic immigrants have complex meanings for native-born blacks in the Greenville MSA. Although some in the community are clearly energized and excited by the presence of new coworkers representing new cultures, many others are unhappy with the changes, especially with the loss of some traditionally black businesses. In addition, the racial identity of the newcomers and the ways in which they fit into a dichotomous racial hierarchy initially caused confusion and uncertainty. Unfortunately, this confusion had solidified into resentment by 2009, after the polarizing effect of the 2006 immigration marches and the effects of a serious economic recession.

NOTES

1. I had spent some time observing and conducting interviews in this laundromat, and found it very unusual not to wait in the waiting room unless standing outside to smoke a cigarette.
2. Quotations from each type of data collection are clearly distinguished throughout the chapter.
3. In fact, a Hispanic graduate student working with me was at the meeting silently taking notes, unnoticed by the rest of the attendees.

REFERENCES

Amado, Maria Luisa. 2006. *Mexican Immigrants in the Labor Market: The Strength of Strong Ties*. New York: LFB Scholarly Publishing.

Bullock, Charles S., III, and M. V. Hood III. 2006. "A Mile-Wide Gap: The Evolution of Hispanic Political Emergence in the Deep South." *Social Science Quarterly* 87(5): 1117–35.

Chandler, Charles R., and Yung-mei Tsai. 2001. "Social Factors Influencing Immigration Attitudes: An Analysis of Data from the General Social Survey." *Social Science Journal* 38(2): 177–88.

Durand, Jorge, Douglas S. Massey, and Emilio A. Parrado. 1999. "The New Era of Mexican Migration to the United States." *Journal of American History* 86(2): 518–36.

Feagin, Joe, and Melvin P. Sikes. 1995. *Living with Racism: The Black Middle-Class Experience*. Boston, Mass.: Beacon Press.

Frazier, E. Franklin. 1957. *Black Bourgeoisie*. New York: The Free Press.

Gay, Claudine. 2006. "Seeing Difference: The Effect of Economic Disparity on Black Attitudes toward Latinos." *American Journal of Political Science* 50(4): 982–97.

Grey, Mark A., and Anne C. Woodrick. 2005. "'Latinos Have Revitalized Our

Community': Mexican Migration and Anglo Responses in Marshalltown, Iowa." In *New Destinations: Mexican Immigration in the United States*, edited by Victor Zúñiga and Rubén Hernández-León. New York: Russell Sage Foundation.

Hernández-León, Rubén, and Victor Zúñiga. 2000. "'Making Carpet by the Mile': The Emergence of a Mexican Immigrant Community in an Industrial Region of the U.S. Historic South." *Social Science Quarterly* 81(1): 49–66.

———. 2005. "Appalachia Meets Aztlán: Mexican Immigration and Intergroup Relations in Dalton, Georgia." In *New Destinations: Mexican Immigration in the United States*, edited by Victor Zúñiga and Rubén Hernández-León. New York: Russell Sage Foundation.

Hochschild, Jennifer L. 1996. *Facing Up to the American Dream: Race, Class and the Soul of the Nation*. Princeton, N.J.: Princeton University Press.

Iceland, John, and Rima Wilkes. 2006. "Does Socioeconomic Status Matter? Race, Class, and Residential Segregation." *Social Problems* 53(2): 248–73.

Light, Ivan. 2006. *Deflecting Immigration: Networks, Markets, and Regulation in Los Angeles*. New York: Russell Sage Foundation.

Mantero, Jose Maria. 2008. *Latinos and the U.S. South*. Westport, Conn.: Praeger.

Marrow, Helen. 2009. "Immigrant Bureaucratic Incorporation: The Dual Roles of Professional Missions and Government Policies." *American Sociological Review* 74(5): 756–76.

McClain, Paula D., Niambi M. Carter, Victoria M. DeFrancesco Soto, Monique L. Lyle, Jeffrey D. Grynaviski, Shayla C. Nunnally, Thomas J. Scotto, J. Alan Kendrick, Gerald F. Lackey, and Kendra Davenport Cotton. 2006. "Racial Distancing in a Southern City: Latino Immigrants' Views of Black Americans." *Journal of Politics* 68(3): 571–84.

McDermott, Monica. 1994. "Race-Class Interactions in the Formation of Political Ideology." *Sociological Quarterly* 35(2): 347–66.

———. 2006. *Working-Class White: The Making and Unmaking of Race Relations*. Berkeley: University of California Press.

Mindiola, Tatcho, Jr., Yolanda Flores Niemann, and Nestor Rodriguez. 2003. *Black-Brown Relations and Stereotypes*. Austin: University of Texas Press.

Mohl, Raymond A. 2005. "Globalization, Latinization, and the *Nuevo* New South." In *Globalization and the American South*, edited by James C. Cobb and William Stueck. Athens: University of Georgia Press.

Neal, Micki, and Stephanie A. Bohon. 2003. "The Dixie Diaspora: Attitudes towards Immigrants in Georgia." *Sociological Spectrum* 23(2): 181–212.

Pattillo, Mary. 2005. "Black Middle-Class Neighborhoods." *Annual Review of Sociology* 31: 305–29.

Prince, Sabiyha. 2007. "Will the Real Black Middle Class Please Stand Up?"

In *More Unequal: Aspects of Class in the United States*, edited by Michael D. Yates. New York: Monthly Review Press.

Randall, Nancy Horak, and Randall Delbridge. 2005. "Perceptions of Social Distance in an Ethnically Fluid Community." *Sociological Spectrum* 25(1): 103–22.

Rich, Brian L., and Marta Miranda. 2005. "The Sociopolitical Dynamics of Mexican Immigration in Lexington, Kentucky, 1997–2002: An Ambivalent Community Responds." In *New Destinations: Mexican Immigration in the United States*, edited by Victor Zúñiga and Rubén Hernández-León. New York: Russell Sage Foundation.

Rose, Mariel. 2007. "Appalachian *Mestizaje*." In *Constructing Borders/Crossing Boundaries: Race, Ethnicity, and Immigration*, edited by Caroline B. Brettell. Lanham, Md.: Lexington Books.

Ruggles, Steven, J. Trent Alexander, Katie Genadek, Ronald Goeken, Matthew B. Schroeder, and Matthew Sobek. 2010. *Integrated Public Use Microdata Series: Version 5.0* [Machine-readable database]. Minneapolis, MN: Minnesota Population Center [producer and distributor].

Schmid, Carol. 2002. "Immigration and Asian and Hispanic Minorities in the New South." *Sociological Spectrum* 23(2): 129–57.

Singer, Audrey, Susan W. Hardwick, and Caroline B. Brettell. 2008. *Twenty-First-Century Gateways: Immigrant Incorporation in Suburban America*. Washington, D.C.: Brookings Institution Press.

Suro, Roberto, and Audrey Singer. 2002. "Latino Growth in Metropolitan America: Changing Patterns, New Locations." Washington, D.C.: Brookings Institution Press.

U.S. Bureau of the Census. 1990. *Census of Population and Housing: 1990*, Summary Tape File 1. Washington: U.S. Bureau of the Census.

———. 2000. *Census of Population and Housing: 2000*, Summary File 1. Washington: U.S. Bureau of the Census.

———. 2005. *American Community Survey, 2005 Summary Tables*. Washington: U.S. Bureau of the Census.

Waters, Mary C., and Tomás Jiménez. 2005. "Assessing Immigrant Assimilation: New Empirical and Theoretical Challenges." *Annual Review of Sociology* 31: 105–25.

Zúñiga, Victor, and Rubén Hernández-León. 2004. "Mexican Immigrant Communities in the South and Social Capital: The Case of Dalton, Georgia." *Southern Rural Sociology* 19(1): 20–45.

———, eds. 2005. *New Destinations: Mexican Immigration in the United States*. New York: Russell Sage Foundation.

PART V

Coalition Building

CHAPTER 9

Black, Brown, Young, and Together

Regina M. Freer and Claudia Sandoval Lopez

A s blacks and Latinos[1] increasingly interact in social, economic, and political contexts across the country, many ponder the circumstances required for these two groups, often tied so closely by objective conditions, to work together to improve their lives. What are the circumstances that increase the likelihood they will cooperate and coalesce rather than engage in conflict? This chapter tackles the question by examining relationships between black and Latino youth, specifically querying whether any connection exists between how youth feel and think about their own racial-ethnic group and their willingness to form alliances across racial-ethnic group lines.

If formation of cooperative relationships between blacks and Latinos is a goal, should their respective, distinct identities be emphasized or deemphasized? Put differently, does the expression of blackness and Latino-ness make cooperation between the two more or less likely to occur? We join scholars who are interested in the question of what the relationship is between intragroup affinity-solidarity and intergroup affinity-solidarity. Assumptions about how to answer this question run in opposite directions. On the one hand, it can be argued that intergroup relations will be constrained by intragroup allegiance that is too strong. According to such a view, individuals with strong racial-ethnic group consciousness will tend to see the world in us-versus-them terms, seeking to strengthen the cohesion of the ingroup by emphasizing the boundaries between the in- and the outgroups. Stated another way, the more nationalist individuals are and the more they feel proud of and celebrate their unique and distinctive culture and history as a group, the less likely they will be to want to engage with those who don't share the characteristics that define their uniqueness. For some, concerns along these lines lead to calls for a color-blind or identity-blind approach to relation building, whereas for others, the concern suggests a need to deemphasize difference and focus instead strictly on what is held in common, such as circumstances or issue positions (for reviews of liberal and conservative arguments in favor of identity-neutral approaches, see Guinier and Torres 2002; Brown et al. 2005).

On the other hand, some argue that intragroup solidarity sets the stage for intergroup relations, making them more likely to occur. This potentially works on two levels. First, the fomentation of intragroup solidarity offers a base of secure identity that is perceived as being less likely to be manipulated or threatened by engagement with other groups (Ture and Hamilton 1967). Second, the development of intragroup solidarity primes individuals for collective thinking and action necessary for intergroup relationships to develop. The leap from identity as an individual to a black-Latino coalition-based group identity is an iterated one, with development or reinforcement of black or Latino identity as a way station. This perspective does not assume that an us-them divide necessarily results from recognizing difference. Instead it posits recognition and perhaps even celebration of difference as an important component in the process of building interracial and interethnic solidarity.

We want to engage this debate over the role of ethnic and racial identity in relations between blacks and Latinos. Examining young people in particular, we explore the relationship between intragroup and intergroup affinity, solidarity, and coalition building.

As evidenced by Regina Freer (1999) and other authors in this volume, relations between blacks and Latinos can be understood as falling along a continuum of types of interaction, with active and intentional conflict at one end of the spectrum, and active and intentional cooperation at the opposite end. Between these two we find coexistence that is nuanced and can trigger different forms of conflict or cooperation. In chapter 12, Cid Martinez and Victor Rios in particular illuminate a form of relations they call avoidance, which is essentially a bargain struck between gang members to avoid active conflict. We describe this as intentional coexistence. Such interactions might collapse into conflict should the avoidance bargain fall apart or be violated, but it might also be the foundation for more active cooperation between gangs. Such intentional coexistence is distinct from what is likely the most common state of relations between blacks and Latinos: unintentional, day-to-day coexistence whereby neighbors or residents pay little or no attention to one another. Because such unintentional coexistence is a nonevent, it is difficult to study. Conflict, which is arguably easier to study, has garnered the most scholarly attention. From studies of labor market competition (Johnson and Oliver 1989; McClain 1993; Gay 2006; chapter 2 in this volume) to those exploring electoral competition (Falcon 1988; Kaufmann 2003b) to those examining divergence on public policy issues like immigration (Johnson, Farrell, and Guinn 1997; Kamasaki and Yzaguirre 1991), scholarship on conflict is relatively robust. Although much effort has gone into empirical study of when and why blacks and Latinos engage in or see themselves as being in conflict, questions of when and why the two get along and actively cooperate are less often explored. Examining their intentional cooperation is therefore warranted.

When cooperative relations are examined, scholars tend to concentrate on black-white relations and environs and they more often than not focus on the context of electoral and governing coalitions in the formal political arena. Raphael Sonenshein's (1993) work on biracial coalitions in the mayoral politics of Los Angeles is an oft-cited example of such scholarship. His identification of three pillars of the coalition that brought Los Angeles's first black mayor to power— shared interest, shared ideology, and leadership—offers a significant theoretical insight into cooperative relations. Those scholars who extend these insights to black-Latino contexts also tend to focus on the electoral arena (Henry 1980; Kaufmann 2003b; McClain and Tauber 1998). But just as the uneventful and unintentional coexistence that typifies relations between the two groups is frequently overlooked, so is the fact that most interactions, regardless of character, take place outside the formal political sector among the greater civilian population, not within the narrower more high-profile world of politicians and electoral politics. Although it is certainly true that opinion leaders frame relationships on the ground (see chapter 4, this volume), it is also true that elites respond to grassroots circumstances. It is important to understand how ordinary black and brown people engage with one another and, more specifically, the circumstances under which they cooperate.

Recently, the most prominent popular attention to black-Latino relations has been focused on explosive, often violent conflicts between young people on high school campuses, in gangs, and in prisons. The complex origins and context for these conflicts, including nonracial factors, are often overlooked within sensationalized media coverage. And the trope of conflict of course dominates the discussion. But even as we seek to broaden the frame to consider nonconflictual relations, we do want to explore questions and insights raised by examinations of conflict. Specifically, we are interested in the potential role of generational differences suggested by the high-profile youth-related incidents of conflict mentioned earlier. We know more about how adults relate across group lines than we do about how young people do. Most survey research lacks a concentrated focus on young respondents because samples are generally drawn from voting-age populations. The level of violence associated with these high-profile incidents suggests an urgency to understand the state of black-brown relations among youth. Likewise, though it may sound trite, youth are the future, and their perspectives therefore take on added significance. Some evidence does indicate that black and Latino young people exhibit stronger affinity for one another than their older counterparts (Sanchez 2008), but the racialized fights suggest something else. Surely there are complexities to be understood. This chapter seeks to unpack the dynamic of black-brown relations among young people, querying the circumstances that bring them together to collaborate and work cooperatively .

A first step toward this goal is to explore how the groups feel about one another, the primary assumption being that before groups will actively cooperate, they must have an affinity for one another. Measures of closeness or cohesion both within and between groups differ across studies. Whereas some examine group consciousness measured by perceived levels of discrimination toward and internal commonality with members of the group (Kaufmann 2003b; McClain et al. 2006), others look to measures of pan-ethnicity that collectivize members of different ethnic groups under a larger umbrella identity, in this case Latino or Hispanic (Kaufmann 2003b; Sanchez 2008). Some examine the concept of linked fate, the degree to which individuals see their fate as being tied to the fortunes of the group (Dawson 1994; chapter 2, this volume). Still others use feeling thermometers (Murguia and Forman 2003) or gauge adherence to stereotypical views of group members to measure closeness and affinity (McClain et al. 2006).

Recent research has suggested a connection between intragroup cohesion and intergroup affinity (Kaufmann 2003a; McClain et al. 2006; Sanchez 2008). In other words, the more blacks and Latinos see themselves as being connected to members within their groups, the better they feel about the other group as well. The two groups do vary, however, in the strength of their feelings of closeness to one another: repeated survey results indicate that blacks tend to feel much closer to Latinos than Latinos do to blacks (Mindiola, Niemann, and Rodriguez 2003; McClain et al. 2006). This unevenness seems to strengthen the argument that there is a relationship between intra-group and intergroup connectedness, because African Americans generally have a stronger level of intragroup cohesion than Latinos do (Dawson 1994; Sanchez and Matsuoka 2008).

Although the measures used in these studies are distinct from one another, they share a thrust toward gauging how blacks and Latinos feel about members of their respective groups and about the other group. We gain important understanding of the nuances of how these groups feel about one another from examinations of class, region, and nativity distinctions, but the connection between such feelings and action cannot be assumed. In particular, for our purposes, a con-nection between positive perceptions and actual coalescence cannot be assumed. Just because individuals feel close to members of an-other group does not mean that they will necessarily think that coop-eration between the groups is a good idea, nor does it mean that they feel they are competing. Furthermore, even if they think cooperation is a good idea, such perceptions do not necessarily lead to actual en-gagement. Positive feelings are certainly a basis for considering work-ing together, and such a consideration is an important first step to-ward engaging in coalition behavior, but it is not clear that such feelings are a sufficient predictor of actual coalition behavior. Positive feelings may affect the likelihood of coalitions' forming, but they are not proxies for attitudes about coalition formation, or for actual co-alescence or alliances.

This research bridges the gap between perceptions and actions by examining results from the 2005 University of Chicago Black Youth Project Survey (BYPS) and fieldwork conducted in the Los Angeles area in 2008. The BYPS is a national study that focuses on the atti-tudes of black youth on various social issues, but includes Latino youth in the sample as well. The youths, who ranged in age from fif-teen to twenty-five, were asked to answer a battery of questions con-cerning their understanding of politics, sex, and culture, and how they relate to these concepts. Most important for our purposes, the survey included a number of measures relevant to understandings of black and Latino alliance formation not found in other works. Spe-cifically, the survey emphasizes the importance placed on perceptions and ideas that help shape political and social interactions among young minorities, which we believe is imperative for a more robust understanding of black and Latino relations. Similarly, this is one of the only surveys that includes youth respondents and specifically asks questions related to out-group perceptions and feelings and beliefs about the importance of coalition building.

The Black Youth Project began in 2005 with the intention of getting a more accurate understanding of young black people's perspectives and attitudes on intimacy, political participation, race, sexual orientation, rap music, and religion, among other topics. The sample included close to 1,600 respondents with an oversample of blacks and Latinos: 635 black, 314 Hispanic, 567 white, 18 Asian, and 46 other respondents. The national survey collected data in areas where non-Hispanic blacks and Hispanics made up more than 15 percent of the population. This is one of the only surveys interested in analyzing the opinions and attitudes of young minorities in predominantly urban areas. As this chapter shows, young blacks and Latinos have important insights on multiracial coalitions, insights that have not yet been analyzed by other scholars.

Our analysis of the Black Youth Project Survey uses ordinary least squares (OLS) models and ordered probits to allow for an examination of the correlations and relationships found in the data. To maximize our understanding of coalitional behavior, we complement the results gathered from the survey with data garnered from a number of in-depth interviews conducted with black and Latino youth currently engaged in coalition work. We view these two data sets as being in conversation with one another and our analysis reflects this, ultimately suggesting avenues for furthering the dialog in future research. Before discussing the interviews, it is important to analyze and understand the various statistical results obtained from the survey.

Our reliance on the BYPS focuses on a number of variables related to our central concern with what, if any, connection exists between intragroup consciousness, intergroup affinity, and coalition formation. In addition to using basic demographic data, we analyze variables measuring youth's sense of pride in their racial group, whether they feel their fate is linked with members of their own group, how close they feel to other groups, and whether they support the formation of coalitions among different racial groups.

RACIAL PRIDE AND LINKED FATE

Differences in how black and Latino youth rate their sense of linked fate and racial pride tell us something about the relationship and kin-

Figure 9.1 Respondents with High Levels Linked Fate and Racial Pride

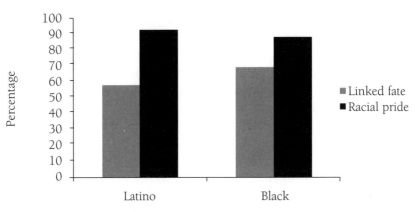

Source: Authors' compilation based on data from the 2005 Black Youth Project Survey (University of Chicago 2005).

ship they feel toward their own group. On both measures, the majority of young black and Latino respondents have a strong affinity for members of their own group. For instance, a large percentage of Latinos, 58 percent, and blacks, 69 percent, agree that they are personally affected by what happens to other Latinos or blacks, as displayed in figure 9.1.[2] These figures contrast sharply with white respondents, of whom only 38 percent link their personal well-being to the status of other whites. These results are consistent with research indicating that African Americans express a high degree of linked fate (Dawson 1994). They also reflect distinctions between African Americans and Latinos in their perceptions of linked fate. Recent scholarship notes that Latino conceptions of linked fate are complicated by the diversity of the population in terms of pan-ethnicity, racial diversity, and immigrant makeup (Sanchez and Masuoka 2008; Jones-Correa and Hernandez 2007). Similarly, as figure 9.1 shows, both Latino and black respondents expressed high levels of racial-ethnic pride, 92 percent and 88 percent respectively.[3]

Linked fate and racial pride are indicators of intragroup affinity and, as the BYPS shows, the majority of both black and Latino respondents appear to have strong ties with their own groups. However, focusing on answers to questions regarding intragroup feelings tells us only part of the story, because we still have no sense of how intragroup affinity will affect out-group affinity or how young black and Latino respondents feel about multiracial coalitions. Out-group affinity can be measured by how individual respondents rate one other using feeling thermometers—measures that ask respondents to assess their closeness to others as points on a thermometer from 0 for distant-coldest, 50 for neutral, and 100 for closest-warmest (Fiorina 1981). Thus our analysis moves to consider how, if at all, racial pride and linked fate affect perspectives and feelings about other racial groups.

FEELING THERMOMETERS

It is unlikely that mere warm or positive feelings for other racial groups can fully determine the extent to which individuals will become a part of a coalition effort. What is important to understand, nonetheless, is how racial pride and linked fate might affect one's perceptions of other groups. Clearly, some level of mutual positive perception between participants must exist to sustain an alliance of various racial groups. To determine individuals' feelings about racial out-groups, responses to various feeling thermometers are used as a measure of affinity.

Figure 9.2 shows how the two groups responded to one another as measured by the feeling thermometer question. For the most part, Latino respondents in the sample tended to have warm feelings toward blacks. Specifically, 55 percent of Latino respondents rated their feelings toward black people between 76 and 100. The BYPS interviewers specifically stated that any rating over 50 indicated favorable or warm feelings toward that group. If we include all respondents who rated their feelings toward blacks as 50 or above, 77 percent of Latino youth would be numbered in the total.

One of the most striking findings in our analysis is an apparent lower affinity of black respondents toward Latinos than vice versa. One-third, 32 percent, of black respondents rated Latinos between 0 and 50. According to survey wording, a rating between 0 and 50 indicated that the respondent felt cool toward or did not care particularly for that group. At the same time, only 23 percent of Latinos rated blacks within the same range. These results contrast with previous work on black and Latino relations that found that blacks tend to have a greater affinity toward Latinos than vice versa (Hochschild and Rogers 2000; Mindiola, Niemann, and Rodriguez 2002; Kaufmann 2003a).

Figure 9.2 Respondents by Level of Feeling Thermometer
            Ratings

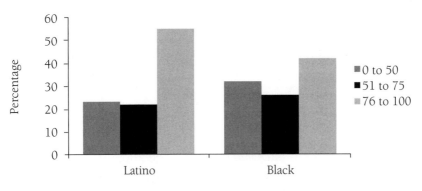

Source: Authors' compilation based on data from the 2005 Black Youth Project Survey (University of Chicago 2005).

We considered three possible explanations for the surprisingly reversed percentages. First, the use of feeling thermometers to correctly gage affinity is widely contested (Fiorina 1981; Green 1988; King et al. 2004). Clearly, there are many limitations to how respondents understand the question and the way respondents decided on a number between 1 and 100. Second, the timing of the survey may offer a contextual explanation for the difference. It is possible that this result is event driven. For example, because the survey was conducted in 2005, we have no way of understanding how current events like immigration policy debates affected African American perceptions of Latinos. Third, and perhaps more interesting for our study, is the possibility of generational differences. As mentioned, work on black and Latino coalition formation has not focused on young blacks and Latinos in urban areas, where discussions of multiracial alliances are more likely to occur. Studies assume that coalition formation among blacks and Latinos begins and ends with adult political actors. If group affinity works in the opposite direction among youth, then a closer look at teen respondents is necessary for a more holistic understanding of race relations in the United States.

Although these findings run counter to conventional understandings of intergroup perceptions, it would be speculative to suggest an explanation without knowing more about the sources of individual evaluations. In other words, although figures 9.1 and 9.2 make clear the percentage of individual respondents who chose to evaluate the other racial groups within the specified categories, we still do not know how and to what extent racial pride and linked fate affect Latinos' affinity toward African Americans and vice versa.

To this end, we constructed a more fully specified feeling thermometer model composed of various social, cultural, and political factors. As well as basic demographic factors such as age, sex, education, and family socioeconomic status (SES), we included social factors such as exposure to other racial groups[4] and attitudes including racial pride, linked fate, positive racial view,[5] personal racism,[6] and feelings about coalitions.[7] This final variable is important to include because it addresses endogeneity concerns. It can be argued that those already in coalitions or who have positive views of multiracial coalitions are the driving force for positive feeling thermometer ratings. By including the variable in the model, we can determine whether, in fact, it is significantly associated with affinity. On the other hand, if acceptance of coalitions is not a driving factor, then we can assume that warm or positive feelings toward other racial groups do not necessarily lead to strong multiracial alliances, as many scholars would have us believe.

Figure 9.3 depicts the linear regression coefficient estimates and associated confidence intervals for blacks' and Latinos' feeling thermometer scores toward the opposite group. The darker and shorter portions of the lines represent a 67 percent confidence interval while the thinner, extended portions of the lines represent a 95 percent confidence interval. Any independent variable that does not intersect with 0 is to be considered significantly associated with the dependent variable.[8] Accordingly, neither racial pride nor linked fate are significantly associated with Latinos' feelings toward blacks. However, the figure does indicate that family SES, exposure, and positive views are marginally associated with Latino ratings of blacks. More specifically, feeling thermometer ratings were positively associated with outgroup exposure for Latinos. Therefore, Latino respondents who had greater exposure to other racial groups also gave African Americans a higher rating. Similarly, as Latino family SES increased, ratings of blacks increased. Finally, the most surprising result came from the variable *Positive View*. The more Latinos believed that other racial groups viewed them in a positive manner, the lower they rated African Americans. Although it is unfortunate to see that acceptance of Latinos by the larger society seems to negatively affect how they rate

Figure 9.3 Predictors of Feeling Thermometer Scores

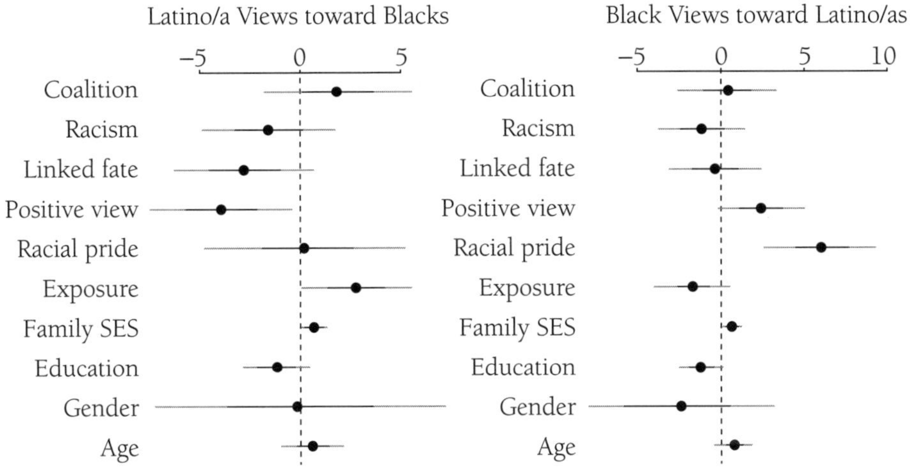

Latino/a Views toward Blacks — Black Views toward Latino/as

Coalition, Racism, Linked fate, Positive view, Racial pride, Exposure, Family SES, Education, Gender, Age

Source: Authors' compilation based on data from the 2005 Black Youth Project Survey (University of Chicago 2005).

blacks, we must keep in mind that we still do not know whether this ultimately has a negative impact on coalition perceptions as well.

The results for the predictors of blacks' evaluations of Latinos include the interesting finding that racial pride appears to have a positive effect on blacks' ratings of Latinos. Specifically, for every unit increase in respondent sense of racial pride, their rating of Latinos increased by 6 points. This increase was significant at the .001 level. In other words, African Americans' sense of racial pride was positively associated with their sense of closeness toward Latinos; therefore, African American respondents were more likely to rate Latinos higher on the feeling thermometer. Other variables with a significant association included *Family SES* and *Positive View*. Again, both of these variables are marginally significant because they barely meet the accepted standard for statistical significance. Finally, *Education* seemed to have the same effect on black respondents that *Positive View* had on Latinos. As education increases, African Americans' affinity toward Latinos decreases. Again we must take into consideration that although some variables did have an effect on affinity, measured through feeling thermometer questions, we have yet to analyze whether they have an impact on coalition efforts.

Ultimately, we are not confident that feeling thermometers are appropriate measures to discuss coalition possibilities. Making conclusions about multiracial alliances by analyzing affinity—in this case measured through feeling thermometers—assumes too much and, as we will see further along in the survey, affinity is not a significant predictor of positive coalition efforts. Although the data suggest that affinity does not influence respondent's beliefs about whom blacks should build coalitions with, if at all, to some degree positive perceptions and feelings are likely to be important to maintain strong and robust coalitions. To the extent that positive feelings are important in maintaining coalitions, it is important to have discussed the variables that positively and negatively affect affinity.

COALITIONS AS STRATEGY

As noted earlier, the focus of this chapter is on understanding how intragroup feelings affect interracial coalition efforts. Various factors in the daily life experiences of many black and Latino youth, of course, inform their reasons for joining or not joining multiracial coalitions. In this chapter, however, we focus on the roles that racial pride and notions of linked fate have on such a decision.

A thorough analysis of the link between racial pride, linked fate, and coalition building is important for at least two reasons. First, understanding how identity functions as a predictor to coalition building among youth is a great pedagogical tool for activists on the ground. Second, as discussed, there is a growing tension in the literature on multiracial coalition building that has as its premise the discussion of a color-blind approach. According to those advocating an identity-blind method, highlighting distinctive cultural identities reifies segregation and actually reduces the willingness by participants to join with other racial groups (Wilson 1999). We hypothesize, however, that a high sense of racial pride and linked fate will increase the likelihood of participants' being willing to coalesce with other racial groups. Support for this hypothesis would cast doubt on the identity-blind argument. In other words, if we find that racial pride and linked fate offer a statistically significant positive association to coalition building, then a case can be made against the logic of identity-blind coalition methods, which, again, suggest that culturally relevant information negatively impacts coalition efforts and should therefore be excluded from the process.

Table 9.1 Assessment of Blacks' Coalition Possibilities, Latino Respondents[a]

	Coalition Possibility	Standard Error	Maximum Difference
Age	−.00	.04	—
Sex	−.07	.20	—
Education	.09*	.05	—
Family SES	−.01	.02	—
Exposure	.02	.08	—
Racial pride	.23*	.14	14%
Positive view	.08	.10	—
Linked fate	.23**	.10	23%
Personal recism	.01	.09	—
Feeling thermometer	.00	.00	—
Sample size	148		
Prob Chi²	0.12		
Pseudo R^2	0.05		

Source: Authors' compilation based on data from the 2005 Black Youth Project Survey (University of Chicago 2005).
[a]Latino respondents were asked: Some people say that blacks would have more political impact if they worked in coalition with other minorities such as Asians or Latinos. Other people say that blacks would have more of a political impact by forming their own political organization. What about you? Do you think that blacks should work with other minorities or form their own organizations?
*$p < .05$; **$p < .01$; ***$p < .001$.

This section begins to discuss the variables that do and do not matter to coalition building specifically. Again, there are limitations to this survey. For one, the coalition question is directed only toward blacks: all respondents are asked whether they believe blacks would do better by forming coalitions with Latinos or with Asians. Latinos are not asked whether it would be better for them to form interracial alliances. Despite this limitation, the data are significant because few surveys have direct coalition questions.

Table 9.1 reports the relationship between a number of independent variables and Latinos' assessment of whether blacks should participate in coalitions. *Linked Fate* had the strongest association with *Coalition Possibilities* among Latino respondents: as a sense of Latino linked fate increased, so did their belief that African Americans would benefit from forming a coalition with Latinos or Asians, or both. This relationship was positively significant at the .01 level, indicating that the association between these two variables did not occur by chance alone. *Racial Pride* and *Education* were only marginally significant, meaning that they missed the .05 significance threshold by a few points. Nonetheless, they should not be completely ignored.

Because ordered probit coefficient estimates are not directly interpretable, we use the software CLARIFY[9] to generate predicted probabilities. Table 9.1 displays the coefficient estimates, from which we calculate predicted probabilities for responses to the dependent variable, *Coalition Possibilities*. Specifically, as shown in the third column, all else being equal, moving from no sense of linked fate to a high sense of linked fate—this is considered the maximum difference—is associated with a 23 percent increase in the probability of Latinos' believing that African Americans should be a part of a multiracial coalition with Latinos or Asians or both. Similarly, moving from no racial pride to the highest degree of racial pride is associated with a 14 percent increase in believing that African Americans should join forces with other racial groups. Again, although the relationship falls slightly short of the statistical significance threshold, there is some indication of the positive direction of the effects of pride and linked fate on coalition beliefs.

Clearly, *Racial Pride* and *Linked Fate* have positive effects on Latinos' belief in the wisdom of forming coalitions. Although the question does not directly ask whether Latinos should join a coalition with African Americans, we can assume that if they believe that African Americans should join coalitions, then it is because they are willing to believe the same about their own racial group joining a coalition with African Americans. Our findings clearly problematize arguments that encourage multiracial coalition efforts to adopt color-blind agendas. As the Latino example demonstrates, having a strong connection with one's own group does not significantly or, more important, negatively affect opinions about coalitions.

Racial Pride and *Linked Fate* are significantly associated with positive coalition views among Latino respondents only, whereas table 9.2 indicates that neither *Racial Pride* nor *Linked Fate* have a significant effect on African Americans' belief in the wisdom of forming a multiracial coalitions. At first glance this may seem to run counter to our argument, but it actually reinforces the finding that color-blind arguments are unfounded. Put differently, the results indicate that because *Racial Pride* and *Linked Fate* do not have an effect on blacks' coalition perceptions, they cannot possibly have a negative effect. By

Table 9.2 Assessment of Blacks' Coalition Possibilities, Black Respondents

	Coalition Possibility	Standard Error	Maximum Difference
Age	−.04	.03	—
Sex	.26*	.14	3%
Education	−.07*	.03	−9%
Family SES	.01	.01	—
Exposure	.02	.06	—
Racial pride	.11	.09	—
Positive view	.07	.06	—
Linked fate	.04	.07	—
Personal racism	.01	.06	—
Feeling thermometer	.00	.00	—
Sample size	309		
Prob Chi²	0.22		
Pseudo R²	0.02		

Source: Authors' compilation based on data from the 2005 Black Youth Project Survey (University of Chicago 2005).
*p < .05; ** p < .01; *** p < .001.

simply looking at the coefficients, one can conclude that linked fate has a positive association to the coalition variable, and whereas *Racial Pride* only has a slight negative association it is not significant. The only two significant variables for African American respondents are *Gender* and *Education*. Moreover, all else being equal, African American women were 3 percent more likely than men to believe that African Americans should be a part of a multiracial coalition. An increase in *Education*, on the other hand, suggests a 9 percent decrease in the probability of choosing to form a coalition when all other independent variables are held constant.

Finally, as tables 9.1 and 9.2 show, the model includes the feeling thermometer as an explanatory variable for coalition beliefs. However, as previously discussed, affinity toward the other racial group does not significantly affect how African Americans or Latino respondents will answer the coalition question. More specifically, although the literature on coalition building assumes that affinity for a particular racial group will determine whether alliances are formed, our findings suggest that there is no such relationship. For instance, of the 268 African American respondents who had the warmest feelings towards Latinos (75 points and above, in the feeling thermometer), 43 percent believed that blacks should form a coalition with Latinos and Asians, 14 percent thought they should be independent, 37 percent believed they should do both and 5 percent thought blacks did not need to do either. Similarly, of the 215 black respondents with the lowest affinity for Latinos (25 points and below), 43 percent still believed that they should form a coalition, 19 percent believed they should work independently, 33 percent answered that they should do both, and 6 percent said neither. How blacks felt about Latinos did not seem to influence their feelings about coalition formation.

Ultimately, African Americans with a greater sense of pride had a greater affinity—measured by the feeling thermometer—toward all other groups. But this affinity did not have a significant relationship to their attitudes about coalition formation. Clearly, these numbers show that affinity is not the driving force for sentiment about coalition building.

More important, what we should take away from the data is that a high sense of racial pride and linked fate does not have a negative impact on opinions about coalitions, regardless of their impact on out-group affinity. Although it is not possible to argue that strong intragroup feelings increase out-group feelings, we can conclude that they do not negatively affect them either. Similarly, *Racial Pride* and *Linked Fate* did not significantly affect the coalition variable, meaning that neither of the two variables can explain why African American individuals would choose to answer that it would be better for African Americans to join a coalition. *Linked Fate* did, however, have a positive and significant impact on Latino respondents. Clearly, survey data suggest that color-blind approaches do not seem to be correct in their assessment that racial pride and consciousness will have a negative impact on coalition efforts. In an attempt to supplement our national survey findings, the next section introduces the voices of students and activist in a functioning black and Latino coalition. Their voices and opinions help fill in the gaps of survey findings in that we see these two methods as being in conversation with each other, allowing one to answer questions that the other cannot.

YOUTH AND COALITIONS—ON THE GROUND

We decided to take the inquiry to the ground for a more open-ended exploration of the possible relationship between identity and coalition formation. In an attempt to move beyond the constraints of hypothetical support of coalitions, we searched for instances where black and Latino youth actively participated in such a coalition. Our goal was to explore attitudes and circumstances that give rise to and sustain such cooperation. This search proved to be a challenge because in fact there are few examples of sustained, organized coalitions. We knew that we would have to look in contexts where blacks and Latinos had ample opportunity to interact. This logically led us to Los Angeles, and to South Los Angeles in particular. The area's long history of multiculturalism and its recent history of conflict between the two groups suggested it as a place to begin. It not only was an opportune site for direct conflict but also offered the opportunity for concrete alliance building. Laura Pulido's (2006) work on the multicultural left and so-called third-world radicalism in Los Angeles suggests that a small number of community organizations are working to bring blacks and Latinos together in Los Angeles. She cites one in particular, the Community Coalition (CoCo), as a strong example (232). Founded in 1990 in response to the devastation of the 1980s crack cocaine crisis, the organization has expanded to address a number of quality-of-life issues in South Los Angeles including the over concentration of liquor stores and other "nuisance" businesses, problems with the foster-care system, and educational inequity. Recognizing that South Los Angeles was demographically a black and brown community, from its inception, the coalition has explicitly sought to engage both groups in membership and leadership of the organization and to promote a relationship between the two communities. CoCo uses what Sylvia Zamora defines in chapter 10 of this volume as an "injustice frame" to coalesce black and Latino residents in South Los Angeles to address quality-of-life issues in their midst. As she describes it, such a frame is "rooted in notions of racial and economic inequality that similarly places both groups at a disadvantage compared with whites." Recognizing that this racialized disadvantage maps onto residential segregation, CoCo uses this frame to collectivize members to push for racial, economic, and place-based equity.

Educational inequity for black and Latino youth in the area was the issue that galvanized formation of CoCo's youth component, South Central Youth Empowered Through Action (SCYEA). With more than fifty members, this group, like CoCo, is explicitly committed to creating black-brown unity. As its mission statement describes, SCYEA is "a group of African American and Latino youth working together to build the next generation of leaders to create positive change in our schools and community."[10] SCYEA operates as an umbrella for what the group calls high school organizing committees (HOCs) on seven area campuses; members have engaged in a number of activities and campaigns, including designing, administering, and analyzing a survey of six thousand local high school students gauging their attitudes about educational conditions, protesting the absence of college-prep classes and counseling on local campuses, and a variety of voter education drives.

The membership and leadership of SCYEA is roughly 50 percent black and 50 percent Latino and our in-depth interviews of fifteen youths, age fourteen to eighteen reflected such a balance as well. The interviews were semi-structured and lasted from one to two hours with the youth volunteering to participate. In addition to the interviews, we observed the youth in meetings and other more public activities to get a sense of their behavior and practices in more natural settings. Adult leaders from CoCo were also interviewed.

Our focus in the interviews was to uncover what if any connection exists between intergroup and intragroup solidarity among black and Latino youth actively working in coalition. We asked a number of the questions taken directly from the BYPS, including those related to group pride, linked fate, group-based feeling thermometers, and the wisdom of coalitions as a strategy for empowerment. Additionally, we asked the youth to offer their perceptions of the role, if any, of intragroup affinity in coalitions. Finally, we asked the youth to assess what it took to initiate and sustain black-Latino coalitions among young people. The results suggest nuanced understandings of some of our results from analysis of the survey and offer fresh insight into the process of black-Latino coalition building and maintenance.

We first turn to the BYPS's measures of intragroup affinity and solidarity. When we asked whether they strongly agreed, agreed, neither agreed nor disagreed, disagreed, or strongly disagreed with the statement, "I am proud of my racial group," we were surprised by the lack of clarity the young people had about what we were asking. It seemed that the majority saw their group as being heterogeneous and had a strong sense of pride in some elements, but not in others. One exchange illustrates the confusion in answering the pride question.

When asked the pride question directly from the survey, the youth inquired, "Is it, 'I'm proud of being Chicana' or 'I'm proud of Chicanos?'" When told that it was in fact *of*, she responded by asking for more clarification, "Um, Is it like, 'Are you proud of Chicanos, are you proud of what they've accomplished?'" When told to interpret the question however she wished, she responded, "I guess I agree. I don't know if I strongly agree because I'm still kind of unclear." Hesitantly, she continued, "I'm proud of what Chicanos do when they claim their identity. I'm proud of what Chicanos have done to create this new culture. I think that's amazing." When asked to explain her initial hesitancy she replied, "Historically, Chicanos a lot of times, what ended up happening is they didn't come back to the community, they kind of went off to college and left the community and I'm not really proud that they've done that you know? Yeah. As a people, I'm proud of what we've done so far" (Maria).[11]

Another student expressed a similarly ambivalent response that still indicates a strong sense of pride: "I strongly agree, but then I'm like the stuff that we're kind of doing now is making me like agree less but for the most part I agree strongly." When asked to say more about what makes her have less pride, she responded, " I'm proud of you know the black Panthers and stuff like that. But now there are gangs" (Jeanetta).

In both of these cases, it is clear the students have a sense of group consciousness and a strong sense of pride in the accomplishments of their group, but they are simultaneously disappointed by members of their group, thus leading to confusion on how to reflect strong pride and disappointment at the same time. Another youth pinpoints a different source of confusion in responding to the question: "Yeah I'm proud to be Hispanic, that's my race, of course I'm going to be like, 'I'm Hispanic' but I'm not gonna be . . . 'Oh Hispanics are better then everyone else' . . . thinking that I'm the best. To me it's just like, you are what you are" (Gisella). Pride does not equal supremacy for her, suggesting that perhaps some answering the question may diminish their statement of pride for fear of appearing supremacist. Her expression of concern over the potential for comparison and competition between blacks and Latinos was echoed in others students' responses when they worried about comparing struggles. One youth observed, "How are you going to tell me that yours was harder than mine. Like some Latinos will say, 'My Mom had to immigrate because things are worse in Mexico than they are here.' But then a black person says, 'Well we've had to struggle all our lives, and my Mother's a crackhead.' And then a Latino person says, 'Well my Dad get's paid one dollar an hour.' And it goes on like that" (Jeanetta).

These responses indicate an identity-based struggle that may be occurring because the youth are engaged in coalition work. They seek to balance their expressions of pride and concern about conditions for their own group with concern for other groups and a need to maintain unity. Such a balancing act relates directly to the debate over how much or how little group consciousness should be emphasized in efforts to foment collaboration across group lines. The youths' responses seem to suggest that pride is perfectly acceptable as long as it is not boastful or competitive.

All of these responses point to complexity that potentially lies beneath the results of the BYPS analysis suggesting that pride was not significantly related to opinions about coalitions. The nuanced understandings of expressions of group affinity expressed by the SCYEA youth may indicate factors that influenced the regression results, diminishing such a relationship. But the fact remains that the majority of survey respondents and all of the youth from SCYEA expressed a sense of pride in their group, and as we will see, both sets of youth also support the formation of coalitions. Therefore pride in and of itself is not a deterrent to coalitions.

In response to the second affinity-solidarity question on whether they saw their fate as being linked to others in their group, the young people were strong and unequivocal in their belief that there was a link. They were asked whether they strongly agreed, agreed, neither agreed nor disagreed, disagreed, or strongly disagreed with the following statement: "I believe that what happens to most people in my racial group in this country affects me." All strongly agreed that there was such a link. Interestingly, those who elaborated pointed to examples of how negative perceptions and stereotypes of their group were often unfairly transferred to them. Several mentioned how it was assumed that they were gang members, or that they were uneducated. But rather than expressing resentment toward members of their group who may in fact exemplify the stereotype, they blamed those who they believed unfairly projected the stereotypical view of their group. As one youth observed, "Yeah it affects me because people go based on generalizations. . . . Say if 60 percent of Mexicans drop out of high school, they expect you to drop out. . . . That's how society sees us" (Juan). Another responded, "I strongly agree. . . . When you see somebody get twenty years to life for stealing a pizza or something like that, you're like dang, they're never gonna see their family. . . . You feel like there's no hope" (Jeanetta).

The youth indicated that they saw their fate as tied to others in their group, including the most marginalized members. Their expressions of anger toward a majority society that generalizes about, stereotypes, and unjustly affects group members' lives and diminishes their sense of hope, seem to confirm that in-group cohesion is reinforced by out-group exclusion. Interestingly, several of the youth indicated that such out-group targeting simultaneously and similarly affected black and brown people and that they distinguished such actions of blacks or Latinos from those presumably coming from the majority society. As one youth observed, "I'm not going to deny that there is conflict between blacks and Latinos. . . . I get those comments . . . like 'dirty Mexican' . . . but I think those little comments matter less than the bigger picture that we're still receiving the short end of the stick, that we're living in poverty, we're getting the worst jobs, the worst food, everything . . . that they discriminate against us" (Maria).

She makes a distinction between little comments and the bigger picture and between we and they. For this young woman and for others in the group there was an assertion of linked fate both with their own group and between blacks and Latinos, even as they recognized the tension between them. This echoes results from other survey research indicating that blacks and Latinos feel a sense of shared fate even as they view one another suspiciously or stereotypically (McClain et al. 2006). The difference here is that these youth, actively engaged in coalition work, recognize but reject the suspicion and the stereotypes. Why they are distinguished in this way becomes an important question.

Our interview questions also included the BYPS measures of intergroup affinity using feeling thermometers. The youth were specifically instructed as follows:

> Now I'd like to get your feelings toward groups of people and individuals. I will use something we call the feeling thermometer and here is how it works: I'll read the name of a group or individual, and I'd like

you to rate that group or person on a scale of 0 to 100. Ratings between 50 degrees and 100 degrees mean that you feel favorable and
warm toward them. Ratings between 0 degrees and 50 degrees mean
that you feel cool or don't care much for that person or group. And a
50 degree rating means you don't feel either warm or cold; you are in
the middle. Don't forget, you are free to pick any number between 0
and 100.

The youth were not asked about their own group, only about others, and the complete list included African Americans, Latinos,
whites, and Asians. All of the black youth expressed strong feelings
of closeness to Latinos and Latino youth expressed equally strong
feelings of closeness to black people. Measures for these two groups
ranged between 80 and 100, obviously suggesting a high degree of
affinity between the two groups. When asked to elaborate on why
they felt so close most answers echoed this: "We basically live together in the same community . . . like a family. We're both treated
the same. We're both looked at the same. You're criminals, cholos or
gangsters living in the ghetto. Like we both live in the same communities. I think both of our races, we have suffered a lot and we basically face racism everyday" (Gisella).

But the youth expressed minimal closeness to whites (between 0
and 50, the majority less than 20) and even less affinity toward
Asians (between 0 and 20, the majority less than 2). Many indicated
their measures were influenced by exposure to groups. As one youth
commented, "I only know two whites, so I guess I give them a 2. If
I knew 100, maybe it would be different" (Maria). Another observed, "I'm sure there are cool white people, I just don't know
them" (Briana). Results from the BYPS do not support these observations: analysis showed a weak link between exposure and the
feeling thermometer measures. This discrepancy is worthy of further exploration and may be suggestive of the need for a further
refinement of both the exposure and feeling thermometer–affinity
variables. Analysis of the BYPS showing a weak link between the
feeling thermometer measures and opinions on coalition strategies
and the surprising inverse of earlier feeling thermometer ratings between blacks and Latinos may yet be explained in part by lack of
exposure. It's difficult to coalesce or want to coalesce if you do not
have the opportunity to do so. Blacks and Latinos in South LA have
it, but those in other cities and regions do not.

Our interviews turned to the BYPS questions related to coalitions as a strategic approach to empowerment. We altered them to move beyond the survey's limited focus on whether blacks should form coalitions, instead asking whether blacks and Latinos should form coalitions, form separate organizations, neither, or both? As we might expect in a coalition setting, none of the youth supported the exclusive formation of separate black or Latino organizations. They were evenly split, however, about whether to do both or to strictly pursue coalition strategies.

Those who thought it best to avoid any separation at all seemed to agree with the following youth's point of view that it was a shame "if you just want to help out your own and not work for everybody . . . if you don't believe it should be equal" (Sophia). Interestingly, those who supported a combined approach were the most senior members of SCYEA. For some, their support for both strategies seemed to reflect recognition of the power of intragroup consciousness in the world beyond SCYEA. As one youth who'd been a member of SCYEA for two years noted,

> There's a value in working with your own, with people that look like you, because those are the people empowering you. We've noticed in our school groups that when you have a teacher sponsoring you that's Latina, you are going to get more Latino youth to come. If it's a black male that's teacher-sponsor of the group, then we're going to get more black males in our group. Its kinda like you're attracted to that because you see someone that looks like you and you're able to find a role model and you're able to listen to that person more because you feel you're on the same level, that you have something in common. And I think that's needed, that's necessary if you're gonna get people to listen to you. . . . But you're not going to be able to do it alone. . . . It starts there but it doesn't stop there. (Maria)

This suggests a pragmatic aspect to combining approaches. Other youth expressed a desire to preserve a space for consideration of issues and opinions that might not be jointly shared. "Sometimes the issues are among the group that you need to sort out first before you talk about mixing it" (Briana). Another student who said she belonged to the black student union at her high school concurred: "Sometimes there needs to be times when you are around your people or your race or whatever because there's going to be some things

said that can't be said with both of the races together. . . . And then
SCYEA is there teaching you that black and brown people can work
together" (Kyra).

In our interviews, black youth were somewhat more supportive of
a combined approach than Latino youth were, which is likely reflec-
tive of higher levels of linked fate found among the black youth in the
BYPS and among black respondents in other surveys. Overall, the
youth who supported a combined approach clearly saw a place for
both intragroup and intergroup strategies, and their participation in
SCYEA is suggestive that the two are not mutually exclusive pursuits.
That the most senior members of SCYEA believe in the combined approach indicates the sustainability of combining active affinity for
members' own racial-ethnic group with participation in collaborative
activities.

Although we cannot be exactly sure whether the respondents to
the BYPS were or were not engaged in black-Latino alliances, because
they were never asked directly about coalition participation, we
might infer most were not, given how rare such formations in fact
are. Thus, it stands to reason that a majority of survey respondents
were speculating about the impact of coalition behavior without having actively participated in it. The youth we interviewed at SCYEA
were actively engaged in coalition work and able to reflect on this as
they responded to the question about political strategies. They know
what it means to engage in such work and this likely enhances their
understanding of its impact.

MAKING COALITIONS WORK

"You start with where you are the same, then you talk about the differences, then you come up with the solutions" (Maria).

Although we replicated many of the questions included in the
BYPS, we took advantage of the opportunity to ask more pointed
questions that moved beyond opinions about whether coalitions
were a good idea to consider how and why they function. Our hope
was to isolate contributing factors and lessons and then generate testable hypotheses that could be explored in future research. In this effort, we were especially focused on gaining perspective on what impact intragroup affinity had on coalition formation and maintenance.
Was attention given to difference, and if so, did it have a negative,
positive, or insignificant impact on the collaborative experience?

When asked whether race, racism, or racial-ethnic differences should be or were in fact discussed in SCYEA, all of the youth agreed that it was important to raise these topics and that this occurred in the organization. As one youth argued, "If you really want to know a lot about someone without like feeling that you're going to offend them, it's better off knowing it so everyone can respect each other. . . . It's better to be aware of what you're doing, what you are and what's going on so you can be right there on the same topic as others. . . . It's better to talk about both similarities and differences 'cause some may agree or disagree, but that's the whole magic about it" (Saul).

Another observed, "If you stay quiet and you don't talk about the differences then you might offend each other" (Victor). There seems to be a practical concern that silencing such discussion may result in offense being taken that could threaten the coalition. Beyond this, there is a belief that understanding the differences can strengthen the collective. A third youth described the importance of raising race as an issue to promote collective behavior: "It [race] has come up and it should come up because we find each other I guess you can say slippin'. Like we had a meeting recently where it was called to our attention that all the Latinos were sitting over here and all the blacks were sitting over here. You know sometimes we do it subconsciously. So yeah, the staff will bring it to our attention and we try to bring it to each other's attention. So yeah, race does play a kind of big role in SCYEA" (Monique).

Collectively the youths' observations run counter to the assumption that focusing on difference derails the coalition process.

As suggested in the last reflection, the staff plays a significant role in guiding the youths' understanding of racial and ethnic difference and identity. As one youth put it, "They [the staff] push us" (Jeanette). This push comes via formal initiatives called "political educations" and through modeling of behavior. One youth described the process this way:

> What we do in SCYEA is we're creating people that are going to be venturing off into the world with a new mentality. . . . We call it the next generation of leaders, right?! . . . This is where the change in mentality is going to happen. We do this through leadership training. We're asking people to question and to learn. To discover new things and don't just take what comes out of the textbook . . . to think critically and be a leader. . . . It's like activist training in a way. . . . Identity

is a big part of that. . . . When you know who you are you are able to lead with consciousness. . . . That's a big leap to take to be able to say "I'm black and I'm proud," "I'm brown and I'm proud." When you do that you're ready for the next step which is to lead others. (Maria)

She went on to identify specific examples of staff-led political education sessions (which she terms *educationals*) that directly invoked racial and ethnic identity: "We do . . . this ethnic studies stuff. We do an educational about the Black Panthers. We do an educational about the Brown Berets. We do an educational about Malcolm X. We do an educational about Corky Gonzalez. So they make sure that it's pretty balanced and that we're not being exclusive" (Maria).

It is clear that racial and ethnic pride and group consciousness are promoted through the invocation of historical examples. But it is significant that the youth emphasize the importance of a balanced approach to presenting such information. This speaks to the concern expressed earlier that competitive recognition of group pride was not conducive to alliance building between blacks and Latinos. The approach seems to involve building intergroup affinity by highlighting comparable, connected sources of intragroup pride.

A number of the youth pointed to particular staff as being role models for their own identity development and their approach to working across racial and ethnic lines.

It's not just the knowledge, it's that someone has come to us to help us personally. Somebody gave us time to reach out to us. Somebody really dedicated, that sits down and gives you the time of day . . . and they connect. . . . I didn't really know how to connect. Like I didn't know my ancestry . . . but stuff that they have taught me . . . or places they've even taken us makes me feel more connected. Like now I kinda know where to get that information. I know about my background and I'm not just blind about it. . . . It helped me understand my own identity . . . and how much we're connected. (Sophia)

The staff they kinda tell us . . . we're going through the same thing and you don't know you might have a lot more in common than you think (Jeanette).

This suggests the impact of leadership on coalition building and echoes one of the key components of Sonenshein's (1993) tripartite formula for coalition building—shared interest, shared ideology, and leadership. Although his theory was drawn from electoral politics and the example of leadership offered by Los Angeles mayor Tom Bradley, the SCYEA experience suggests that it is transferable to a grassroots setting. As Sylvia Zamora indicates in chapter 10 of this volume, leaders use frames to encourage coalition building.

Results from the BYPS indicate strong youth support for coalitions, but moving from support to participation is key. It is also important that the youth in SCYEA were clear in articulating the great challenges that face coalition-building efforts. Many admitted that even though they were dedicated to a black-Latino alliance, outside SCYEA and in some of their classes, their interactions across racial-ethnic lines were more limited. This reinforces the rarity of collaboration, suggests the importance of establishment of an explicit space for such alliance building and the need for a dedicated cadre of leaders pursuing collaboration.

Despite such challenges, the youth in SCYEA expressed a great deal of commitment to collaborative efforts and a tremendous amount of loyalty to and excitement about the organization. Two students comment,

> All the time I brag about it [SCYEA]. 'Cause there's almost like no other organization that does this kind of stuff. 'Cause most other organizations focus on one target, but you can hardly find organizations that target both black and brown youth. And it's kind of hard to do that, you know, 'cause sometimes the stuff you do relates more to one side and not to the other so its kinda hard, you know? (Juan)

> All the things that happen here, they just stick in your head and you can't wait to come back the next time" (Luis).

Others highlight the importance of lifting up such work to counter beliefs that blacks and Latinos can't get along. "I think it's important to put it out there to show that black and brown students can get along and get things accomplished . . . because in the media it shows that there are tensions and that we fight a lot and that we don't get along and that we don't like each other and it's not like that" (Kyra).

It seems important to speculate about whether the members in SCYEA are "average" black and Latino youth or whether they represent a particular type of young people who would pursue collaboration regardless of the strategies employed by the staff and leadership of the organization. Do they come to SCYEA with the inclination to collaborate or is that inclination developed at SCYEA? Our ability to generalize from their experiences seems predicated on the assumption that they do share key characteristics with their peers. It seems that the BYPS results suggest that most youth think coalitions are a good idea—so the key is to figure out what moves them to action. It may be that the SCYEA youth are distinct because they are more willing than their peers to act on their beliefs. Future research should seek to tease out the role played by individuals' leadership proclivity relative to that provided by others.

CONCLUSION

Survey research, including our own, demonstrates that blacks and Latinos have in-group consciousness and intergroup affinity and linked fate. Additionally, our research shows that having a strong sense of pride in and linked fate with one's racial-ethnic group does not damage intergroup affinity or impede development of support for working across group lines. In fact, our findings refute the wisdom of an identity-blind approach. However, the rarity of actual coalitions between the two groups suggests that intergroup affinity, though perhaps necessary, is not a sufficient contributor to coalition behavior. Inquiry must go beyond measuring closeness or openness to the idea of collaboration between the two groups to examine actual coalition behavior, working backward to theorize and conceptualize elements that contribute to its success. Results from the BYPS and interviews from the fieldwork suggest several factors that strongly influence the development and maintenance of black-Latino coalitions among young people, including leadership that explicitly promotes balanced black and Latino group consciousness, open discussion of differences, prioritizing commonly held interests, and space and opportunity for collaboration. Zamora's findings in chapter 10 of this volume about the importance of framing support many of these conclusions that push the discussion of black and Latino relations beyond exploration of feelings and perceptions. Future research might consider translating these strategies into concepts that can be reformulated into survey questions so that more fully specified models can be tested on a broader segment of the population. We might begin by explicitly asking whether individuals have engaged in or know about collaborative behavior, moving beyond opinions about such behavior to measure actual engagement. Respondents might also be asked about their exposure to the other group and to that group's history.

In addition to moving toward a greater understanding of what has an impact on the development and maintenance of black and Latino coalition behavior, we hope this research spawns more interest in the attitudes and actions of black and Latino youth. As one SCYEA member observed, "We [SCYEA] try to see what the youth feel, because sometimes the youth are overlooked. . . . Older folks tend to forget about us and our opinion" (Sophia).

NOTES

1. Although we prefer the terms *black* and *Latino* due to their representativeness, we at times interchange them with *African American* and *Hispanic* respectively when these terms appear in data sets or the work of other scholars. A number of complexities are involved in our decision to use black and Latino as preferred yet distinct terms. These are fluid categories and thus it is of course possible to be both simultaneously. Because we are concerned here with coalitional behavior between individuals who perceive themselves to be working across group lines, we maintain the distinction.

2. Respondents were asked whether they agreed or disagreed or neither agreed nor disagreed with the statement, "I believe that what happens to most [racial group] people in this country affects me."

3. Respondents were asked if they agreed, disagreed or neither agreed nor disagreed with the statement, "I am proud of [black/Hispanic] people."

4. Respondents were asked to determine the portion of people in their school/high school that are/were of the same race as the respondent. Possible answers ranged from All to None.

5. Respondents were asked whether they agreed with the statement, "Other racial groups view [racial group of respondent] in a positive manner."

6. Respondents were asked, "How often were you discriminated against because of your race?"

7. Respondents were asked, "Some people say that blacks would have more political impact if they worked in coalition with other people of color. Other people say that blacks would have more of a political impact by forming their own separate all black political organization. Some say it takes both. What about you? Would you say it is better for them to: work together with other people of color; form their own separate organizations; both; neither; or you don't know?"

8. The fully specified regression table can be found in online appendix

9.A1, available at http://www.russellsage.org/telles_sawyer_online_ap
pendix.pdf.
 9. CLARIFY is a statistical program that allows researchers to convert regression coefficients to predicted probabilities. This in turn allows us to
make interpretations about the coefficients in terms of probability percentages.
10. See the SCYEA website, at http://www.cocosouthla.org/youth/scyeamis-
sion.
11. The names of youths interviewed have been changed to protect their
identity.

REFERENCES

Brown, Michael K., Martin Carnoy, Elliot Currie, Troy Duster, David Op-
penheimer, Marjorie M. Shultz, and David Wellman. 2005. *Whitewashing
Race: The Myth of a Color-Blind Society*. Berkeley: University of California
Press.
Dawson, Michael C. 1994. *Behind the Mule: Race and Class in African-Amer-
ican Politics*. Princeton, N.J.: Princeton University Press.
Falcon, Angelo. 1988. "Black and Latino-a Politics in New York City." In
Latino-as in the Politics System, edited by F. Chris Garcia. Notre Dame,
Ind.: University of Notre Dame Press.
Fiorina, Morris. 1981. *Retrospective Voting in American National Elections*.
New Haven, Conn.: Yale University Press.
Freer, Regina. 1999. *From Conflict to Convergence: Interracial Relations in the
Liquor Store Crisis in South Central Los Angeles*. Ph.D. diss., University of
Michigan, Ann Arbor.
Green, Donald. 1988. "On the Dimensionality of Public Sentiment Towards
Partisan and Ideological Groups." *American Journal of Political Science*
32(3): 758–80.
Guinier, Lani, and Gerald Torres. 2002. *The Miner's Canary: Enlisting Race,
Resisting Power, Transforming Democracy*. Cambridge, Mass.: Harvard
University Press.
Henry, Charles P. 1980. "Black and Latino Politics in New York City." In
Latinos and the Political System, edited by F. Chris Garcia. Notre Dame,
Ind.: University of Notre Dame Press.
Hochschild, Jennifer, and Reuel R. Rogers. 2000. "Race Relations in a Diver-
sifying Nation." In *New Directions: African Americans in a Diversifying Na-
tion*, edited by James S. Jackson. Washington, D.C.: National Policy As-
sociation.
Gay, Claudine. 2006. "Seeing Difference: The Effect of Economic Disparity
on Black Attitudes Toward Latino-as." *American Journal of Political Science* 50(4): 982–97.

Johnson, James H., Jr., Walter C. Farrell Jr., and Chandra Guinn. 1997. "Immigration Reform and the Browning of America: Tensions, Conflicts, and Community Instability." *International Migration Review* 31(4): 1055–96.

Johnson, James H., Jr., and Melvin Oliver. 1989. "Interethnic Minority Conflict in Urban America: The Effects of Economic and Social Dislocations." *Urban Geography* 10(5): 449–63.

Jones-Correa, Michael, and Diana Hernandez. 2007. "Commonalities, Competition and Linked Fate: On Latino-a Immigrants in New and Traditional Receiving Areas." Paper presented at the annual meeting of the American Sociological Association. New York (August 11–14, 2007).

Kamasaki, Charles, and Raul Yzaguirre. 1991. "Black Hispanic Tensions: One Perspective." Paper presented at the annual meeting of the American Political Science Association. Washington, D.C. (August 29–September 1, 1991).

Kaufmann, Karen M. 2003a. "Cracks in the Rainbow: Group Commonality as a Basis for Latino-a and African-American Political Coalitions." *Political Research Quarterly* 56(2): 199–210.

———. 2003b. "Minority Empowerment in Denver, Colorado: How Black and Latino-a Voters Respond to Each Other's Leadership." *Political Science Quarterly* 118(1): 107–25.

King, Gary, Christopher Murray, Joshua A. Salomon, and Ajay Tandon. 2004. "Enhancing the Validity and Cross-Cultural Comparability of Measurement in Survey Research." *American Political Science Review* 98(1): 191–207.

McClain, Paula D. 1993. "The Changing Dynamics of Urban Politics: Black and Hispanic Municipal Employment—Is There Competition?" *Journal of Politics* 55(2): 399–414.

McClain, Paula D., Niambi M. Carter, Victoria M. DeFrancesco Soto, Monique L. Lyle, Jeffrey D. Grynaviski, Shayla C. Nunnally, Thomas J. Scotto, J. Alan Kendrick, Gerald F. Lackey, and Kendra Davenport Cotton. 2006. "Racial Distancing in a Southern City: Latino-a Immigrants' Views of Black Americans." *Journal of Politics* 68(3): 571–84.

McClain, Paula D., and Steven C. Tauber. 1998. "Black and Latino-a Socioeconomic and Political Competition: Has a Decade Made a Difference?" *American Politics Quarterly* 26(2): 237–52.

Mindiola, Tatcho, Jr., Yolanda F. Niemann, and Nestor Rodriguez. 2003. *Black-Brown Relations and Stereotypes*. Austin: University of Texas Press.

Murguia, Edward, and Tyrone Forman. 2003. "Shades of Whiteness: The Mexican American Experience in Relation to Anglos and Blacks." In *Whiteout: The Continuing Significance of Racism*, edited by Woody Doane and Eduardo Bonilla-Silva. New York: Routledge.

Pulido, Laura. 2006. *Black, Brown, Yellow, and Left: Radical Activism in Los Angeles*. Berkeley: University of California Press.

Sanchez, Gilbert R. 2008. "Latino-a Group Consciousness and Perceptions of Commonality with African Americans." *Social Science Quarterly* 89(2): 428–45.

Sanchez, Gabriel, and Natalie Masuoka. 2008. "Brown-Utility Heuristic? The Presence and Contributing Factors to Latino-a Linked Fate." Paper presented at annual meeting of the Western Political Science Association. San Diego, Calif. (March 20–22, 2008).

Sonenshein, Raphael J. 1993. *Politics in Black and White: Race and Power in Los Angeles*. Princeton, N.J.: Princeton University Press.

Ture, Kwame, and Charles Hamilton. 1967. *Black Power: The Politics of Liberation*. New York: Vintage Books.

University of Chicago. 2005. *Black Youth Project Survey, 2005*. Available at: http://www.blackyouthproject.com/survey (accessed May 16, 2011).

Wilson, William Julius. 1999. *The Bridge Over the Racial Divide: Rising Inequality and Coalition Politics*. Berkeley: University of California Press.

CHAPTER 10

Framing Commonality in a Multiracial, Multiethnic Coalition

Sylvia Zamora

M any African Americans and Latinos live under similar socioeconomic conditions in neighborhoods across the country; however, experiencing similar treatment by society at large is not a sufficient condition for creating a sense of commonality or building
sustainable alliances across racial lines. Perceptions of black-Latino
relations are shaped by many factors, including the media, political
elites, and community organizations, each employing varying frames
for interpreting black and Latino relations. Most prominent are media frames, which single out Latino antiblack racism and gang violence as the culprit of black-Latino tension on the one hand, and
African American anti-immigrant sentiments stemming from a perceived sense of threat due to the ever-growing rise in Latino power on
the other. Regions undergoing major demographic shifts may be
more prone to unrest and ethnic collective action when groups are
pitted against one another by political elites seeking their share of
power and resources. Indeed, as Kevin Wallsten and Tatishe Nteta
show in chapter 4 of this volume, ideology shapes the way political
leaders portray black-Latino relations. Whereas liberal political elites
focus attention on the shared circumstances and issues facing both
communities, conservative elites tend to paint a picture of these relations as rife with conflict, competition, and division. Due to such
dominant portrayals of black-Latino relations, and rapid transformation of African American neighborhoods in the face of increased
Latin American immigration, community leaders everywhere are
confronted with the challenge of bridging the black-Latino divide.
The ability of community organizers to reframe the black-Latino
competition discourse is key to developing effective strategies for
building coalitions across racial boundaries.

Although increasing contact and interaction between blacks and

Latinos has historically led to instances of tension and conflict (Vaca 2004; Negrete and Taira 1995), it has also created renewed efforts at coalition building. This chapter examines how organizational leaders at the grassroots level frame perceived commonality across racial-ethnic lines in a region undergoing major demographic changes. Given the concern over potential conflict and competition between native minority and immigrant groups, few studies have been conducted in settings where these two groups interact extensively, and less so in those where cross racial-ethnic coalitional efforts are ongoing. Thus, this chapter, along with chapter 9 in this volume, provides much-needed insight into the actual coalition-building process. Whereas Regina Freer and Claudia Sandoval focus their analysis on the role of racial pride in shaping support for black-Latino coalitions among a critical component, its youth members, this chapter pays attention to how coalition leaders frame commonality between two groups with presumably distinct interests. I present a case study of the Coalition for Social Justice (CSJ), a community-based, nonprofit organization in South Los Angeles that works with African American and Latino community residents to improve their overall socioeconomic conditions. The name of the organization and the names of the residents are fictional. Analysis is drawn primarily from data gathered over six months from June to December of 2006, including participant observations of coalition activities, twenty in-depth interviews with coalition members and leaders, analysis of the organization's literature (newsletters, pamphlets, fliers), and ongoing content analysis of local and national media reporting on black-Latino relations.

Findings from this study demonstrate that grassroots leaders are able to effectively mobilize African Americans and Latinos into coalitions by deploying what William A. Gamson (1992) calls an "injustice frame" rooted in notions of racial and economic inequality that similarly places both groups at a disadvantage compared with whites. Coalition leaders similarly draw on racialized discourse about members' residential location to construct a collective identity as (working-class black and Latino) South LA residents that is directly contrasted with (upper-middle-class, predominantly white) West LA residents. In doing so, grassroots leaders develop a shared minority identity that highlights commonalities between blacks and Latinos and serves as a basis for successful inter-racial-ethnic coalition building. Similarly, as chapter 9 in this volume shows, coalition leaders strategically invoke historical examples to promote racial consciousness and a sense of racial pride in youth members. Both black and Latino youth come not only to appreciate their own identities, but also to find connections and commonalities between both groups' struggles for equality. This chapter illustrates the importance of strategic framing in building interracial alliances, even in the face of more prevalent media discourse that frames these relations as rife with conflict and competition.

FRAMING PROCESSES

Frames are necessary conditions for social action because they help interpret problems and suggest modes of action to remedy the problem (Zald 1996, 265). Frame analysis has provided a conceptual framework to examine social movements, collective action, and collective identity (Benford and Snow 2000; Hunt, Benford, and Snow 1994). Drawing on Erving Goffman's definition that frames denote "schemata of interpretation" that enable individuals "to locate, perceive, identify, and label" occurrences within their life space and the world at large (Goffman [1974, 21], as cited in Benford and Snow 2000, 614), frames function to organize experience and guide action. In other words, individuals make sense of and understand their neighborhood's streets, parks, families, population, and institutions, among other things, through framing narratives (Small 2004). Frames are not static; the verb *frame* is used to imply that "something is being done," and that it is an evolving process (Benford and Snow 2000, 614). Although it is most often movement leaders who "actively engage in the production and maintenance of meaning for constituents, antagonists, and bystanders or observers," people are not passively subject to it (Benford and Snow 2000, 614). Mario Small (2004) suggests that neighborhood framing is a process in which residents have a role in the development of their neighborhood frames while also being affected by them. Overall, framing processes engage in "meaning work"—that is, the struggle over the production of mobilizing and countermobilizing ideas and meanings—and are involved, along with the media, local government, and the state, in the business of meaning construction (Benford and Snow 2000, 613).

Framing is also a mechanism through which organizational leaders attempt to construct collective identities, such as those based on the neighborhood or location where movement participants live or work. Francesca Polletta and James M. Jasper define collective identity as "an individual's cognitive, moral, and emotional connection with a broader community, category, practice, or institution" (2001, 285). It is a perception of a shared status or relation, which may be imagined rather than experienced directly, and it is distinct from personal identities, though it may form part of a personal identity. Frames and collective identities are expressed in cultural materials such as names, narratives, symbols, verbal styles, rituals, clothing, and metaphors (Polletta and Jasper 2001; Zald 1996). For example, in Gerald Suttles's study of Chicago, he found that people's identification with place was powerful enough to overcome ethnic and racial differences and create unity based upon shared residence. He refers to this type of community as the "defended neighborhood," remarking that "members are joined in a common plight whether or not they like it" (1968, 334). The concept of framing collective identities for social action implies that black and Latino coalitions can be mobilized successfully by using cultural materials, such as those associated with people's identification with a place. Examining the effectiveness of the framing strategies deployed in building inter-racial-ethnic coalitions requires first an understanding of the views and perceptions that groups have of one another. In the section that follows, I briefly review African American and Latino views and perceptions of one another as well as key factors that play a significant role in formation of interracial coalitions.

AFRICAN AMERICAN AND LATINO
RACIAL PERCEPTIONS

A common approach to the study of African American and Latino relations has been a focus on African American attitudes and perceptions of Latinos and Latino immigration (Kaufmann 2003; McClain et al. 2006; Mindiola, Niemann, and Rodriguez 2003; Bobo and Hutchings 1996; Johnson and Oliver 1994). Previous studies have found that socioeconomic status and economic incorporation are two important factors shaping blacks' views of Latinos (Gay 2006; Jackson, Gerber, and Cain 1994). African Americans may feel a greater sense of commonality with Latinos, and view them more positively, if they perceive Latinos as a group who shares a similar economic status with blacks (Kaufmann 2003). On the other hand, it has been argued that socioeconomic similarities create labor market

competition and resentment on the part of blacks who feel that Latino immigrants are "taking their jobs away" (Johnson and Oliver
1994, 199; Johnson, Farrell, and Guinn 1997, 405). However, although evidence of competition has been found in specific contexts,
such as the public job sector (Vaca 2004), overall, studies have not
found evidence to show that African Americans hold systematically
negative attitudes toward Latinos or Latino immigration (Oliver and
Wong 2003; Camarillo 2004, 368).

There is no doubt that relative economic status of racial groups is
an important influence on African American attitudes toward out-
groups (Gay 2006). In environments where Latinos are better off economically, blacks are more likely to harbor negative stereotypes of
Latinos and to view their interests as incompatible (Gay 2006). This
is certainly the case in Miami, where Cubans have exerted a considerable amount of power and influence in the city and have consequently
faced tension with African Americans (Grenier and Castro 2001,
150). The effects of Cubans' having more political and economic resources have led to hostile competition between the two groups, and
African American perceptions of Cubans have worsened over time.
African Americans who are trapped in low-quality neighborhoods
tend to feel pessimistic about how race and racism affect their life
chances, which might be related to their negative attitudes and sense
of perceived threat from Latinos (Gay 2006). According to Claudine
Gay, African Americans who live under better socioeconomic conditions tend to have less-negative attitudes (2006). The ethnographic
research presented in chapter 8 of this volume, however, reveals that
upper-middle-class and working-class blacks in Greenville, South
Carolina, hold more-negative attitudes toward Latinos than lower-
middle-class blacks do.

Scholars have shown interest in African American attitudes toward
Latinos and issues like immigration, but little scholarly attention has
been paid to Latino perceptions of African Americans. The few studies that exist do not show promising signs for black-Latino cooperation. Various scholars contend that Latinos hold negative views of
blacks and have shown little interest in a black-Latino alliance (Rodrigues and Segura 2004, 3; Henry 1980, 225; Kaufmann 2003;
McClain et al. 2006; Vaca 2004). Latino immigrants have also been
found to perceive more in common with whites than with blacks
(McClain et al. 2006). Because they do, they may choose to socially

distance themselves from blacks, resulting in further tension. These findings have major implications for the future of black-Latino relations.

Latino views of African Americans are shaped in large part by the racial ideologies that prevail in their country of origin (Johnson, Farrell, and Guinn 1997). Immigrants are said to bring with them the negative perceptions and stereotypes of blacks that emerged from the legacy of Spanish colonial rule, which is based on a racial hierarchy that places whiteness at the top and blackness at the bottom. Also, American media outlets in Latin America have bombarded viewers with negative images of blacks as dangerous criminals, drug addicts, and lazy (Johnson, Farrell, and Guinn 1997). These negative stereotypes, combined with xenophobia toward blacks, may cause Latinos to perceive little in common with African Americans.

The generational status of Latinos may also affect their views. Karen M. Kaufmann's study on perceived commonality between Latinos and African Americans found that second-generation Latinos feel more affinity toward African Americans than their first-generation counterparts (2003). Similarly, Tatcho Mindiola Jr., Yolanda F. Niemann, and Nestor Rodriguez's study in Houston, Texas, found that U.S.-born Latinos had more favorable views of African Americans than foreign-born Latinos (2003). However, U.S.-born Latino perceptions of African Americans were still more negative than African American views of Latinos. Although it appears that Latino views of African Americans may become more favorable with subsequent generations and increased contact, no direct evidence indicates that acculturation or longer duration in the United States causes Latinos to see blacks positively (Kaufmann 2003). A central component of this volume aims to address the question of what direction black and Latino relations are taking as these groups come into increasing contact: Will they have more favorable attitudes toward each other or will growing contact breed contempt?

AFRICAN AMERICAN AND LATINO COALITIONS

The field of interethnic relations is most characterized by the tendency of scholars to focus on conflict, competition, and tension, and to pay less attention to collaboration or accommodation (Camarillo 2004, 368; Hernández-León and Zúñiga 2005, 254). Latinos and African Americans could be natural allies given their politically relevant common characteristics. Both groups have incarceration rates higher and education and income levels lower than the national average (Rodrigues and Segura 2004, 3). Concern over economic conditions, such as poverty and unemployment, is associated with support for coalitions; some scholars therefore suggest that African Americans and Latinos have enough commonality for coalitions to emerge (Rodrigues and Segura 2004, 4; Tedin and Murray 1994; Meier et al. 2004). They also tend to live near each other, so political coalitions would be necessary to fight for public services at the neighborhoods level. Still others have more pessimistic views, such as Nicolás Vaca (2004), who argues that African Americans and Latinos cannot be presumed allies because of the language barriers and competition over jobs and other resources, which have in many cases prevented coalitions from being formed.

Relative group size is a determining factor in coalition prospects. For example, the numerical dominance of Latinos in major cities may contribute to Latino lack of support for black-Latino alliances. If blacks and Latinos are unequal in number, the larger group may not have much of an incentive to cooperate with the smaller (McClain and Karnig 1990; Grenier and Castro 2001). Kaufmann's study on attitudes of blacks and Latinos found that African Americans are more "readily attached to coalitions than Latinos" (2003, 207). If Latinos are able to gain political representation and access to resources without forming coalitions with African Americans, they may show little interest in cooperating in the future. The Latino population is increasing rapidly due to both sustained immigration and natural growth (Clark 1998); thus Latino support for black-Latino coalitions may become less likely as the Latino population grows larger. African Americans may in turn perceive the increasing Latino population as an invasion of their neighborhoods, or as intimidating because of its large size, which can affect their support for a black-Latino coalition.

Last, the outcome of African American and Latino coalitions will vary depending on whether coalitions form at the grassroots level or within the political realm. Albert M. Camarillo's study of Compton, California, for example, shows that while African American and Latino political leaders were engaged in tension and conflict over power, more positive interactions like grassroots organizing between blacks and Latinos were taking place at the neighborhood level (2004, 368). Thus the prospects for coalition formation rest on the ability of black and Latino leadership to work together and frame their interests so as to appeal to both groups, at all levels. This can be achieved by emphasizing the need for collective action in achieving political power, cultural recognition, and social and economic justice (Kaufmann 2003; Sonenshein 1989; Wilson 2000).

CASE STUDY: SOUTH LOS ANGELES' COALITION FOR SOCIAL JUSTICE

Los Angeles, with its large multi-racial-ethnic population, is an excellent location for exploring the changing dynamics of racial-ethnic minority-minority relations. Historically, the South Los Angeles region has been the center of African American cultural and social life in Los Angeles (Tseng 1999, 8). In the last two decades, however, the racial-ethnic composition of South LA changed significantly, from predominantly African American to a Latino majority. During the 1990s, the African American population decreased from 64 percent to 47 percent and the Latino population nearly doubled, from 23 percent to 45 percent. Latinos became the overwhelming majority by 2000, making up 63 percent of South LA's population (Tseng 1999). This trend seems to be continuing.

African American and Latino residents of South Los Angeles experience similar hardships from high rates of poverty, crime, and unemployment, as well as poor quality of education and poor access to health services (Tedin and Murray 1994, 773). Public policy decisions that negatively affect the region are likely to have similarly dire consequences for both racial-ethnic groups. Similarly, improvements in the community in the areas of education, safety and crime, and health will bring major benefits to all residents, regardless of race-ethnicity. These conditions could foster a sense of perceived commonality and linked fate; however, it remains to be seen whether living under similar socioeconomic conditions is a sufficient condition to sustaining alliances across racial boundaries.

The crack epidemic of the 1980s had devastating effects in the South Los Angeles community. As a response, community activists Carol Davis and Lucia Navarro founded the nonprofit Coalition for Social Justice in 1990. CSJ's mission is to mobilize neighborhood residents to create safe neighborhoods, quality schools, and economic development in South LA. Emphasizing the shared socioeconomic status of blacks and Latinos is an explicit agenda of the organization.

METHODOLOGY AND DATA COLLECTION

I first became acquainted with Coalition for Social Justice in the summer of 2006. Throughout the summer, I visited CSJ offices two or three times a week for two to four hours. For six Saturdays, I also participated in two small workshops facilitated by the Popular Education director, "History of the Coalition for Social Justice" and "History of South Los Angeles." During this period, I also observed youth group meetings, called South Central Youth (SCY), once or twice a week for an hour and a half, attended Urban Planning Committee meetings held once a month, and participated in other miscellaneous meetings and events, both open to the public and consisting primarily of staff from CSJ and allied organizations. I also attended special organization events, such as the holiday fundraiser dinner, and volunteered at phone banks and once to translate documents. I took extensive notes of all participant observations in the privacy of my home.

I have also collected organizational literature, including seasonal newsletters, fliers, pamphlets, educational material, and official reports, and I visit their website regularly for updates. Since my initial visit, I have been receiving CSJ's latest newsletters and event fliers by mail, allowing me to follow up on current events and campaigns. In addition, I have gathered numerous news articles from local and national media related to CSJ's campaigns and about African American and Latino relations in Los Angeles more generally.

To recruit subjects for in-depth interviews, I attended community forums organized by one of several committees within the organization. At these meetings, I introduced myself and briefly explained the focus of my study. I interviewed eight African American and eight Latino members, two of whom were previous employees of Coalition for Social Justice. I personally asked five staff members, including the director of Popular Education and three youth organizers, to participate in the study. The staff interviews provided insight into the internal workings of the organization, how the message of black and Latino unity is framed, and how they might address incidents of tension and conflict among members.

The overwhelming majority of respondents in this study either were born in South LA or have lived in the area for at least fifteen years. Many CSJ members have been involved since its inception, and a few others are very new to the organization. All respondents in this study have been CSJ members for five years or more, with the exception of one who joined within the last year. The majority of Latino respondents were born in the United States; two are immigrants; one is undocumented. Responses to interview questions may vary between older and newer members of the coalition, presumably because older members have more experience working in a black and Latino coalition. All interviews lasted anywhere from one to two hours and were conducted in the offices of CSJ, at the respondent's home, or at a local public locale such as a café.

When analyzing data, I first focused on how leaders interpret the everyday neighborhood experience and concerns of CSJ members, and how they frame black and Latino relations. Second, I focused on how leaders draw on comparisons in the racial and economic landscape of West and South LA to organize members around a common South LA resident identity. In addition, I pay attention to mass media portrayals of black and Latino relations to illustrate how dominant discourses on black and Latino relations serve as counterframes that pose a direct challenge to the framing strategies deployed by grassroots leaders.

CSJ is one of few organizations in Los Angeles that specifically organizes its members into an African American and Latino coalition while pursuing its larger goal of social and economic justice. It thus provides unique insight into the complex dynamics of inter-racial-ethnic interactions in a setting where members of each group come together voluntarily. CSJ provides an important case from which lessons may be drawn for developing effective strategies for inter-racial-ethnic coalitions.

(RE)FRAMING EVENTS AS RACIAL AND ECONOMIC INJUSTICE

The two founders of Coalition for Social Justice are strong advocates of black and Latino unity and have laid the foundation for the current strategies used by organizational leaders. Perhaps most revealing about CSJ's great efforts to build black and Latino unity is that both founders, Davis and Navarro, have a history of militant activism in the struggle for third-world solidarity. Davis, a self-identified Chicana, once remarked to me that she is the "brown part" and Navarro, who is African American, the "black part" of the coalition. Although they are no longer part of CSJ staff, their critical analysis of race, class, and coalition politics has heavily informed the framing discourse organizational leaders use today. Perhaps most influential was their involvement in the third-world solidarity movement, in which left-wing radicals, inspired by anticolonial struggles throughout the world, sought to dismantle hegemonic power structures by addressing issues such as North-South relations, race, class, and gender equality, and environmental and health problems through organized action and protest.

Through staff meetings and study groups, often taking place during most of the workday, CSJ leaders convene to read and discuss issues pertinent to their political education, including learning about the history of the area once known as South Central Los Angeles. The staff trainings provide a structural explanation and basis through which leaders can frame the root causes of the current socioeconomic conditions that exist in South Los Angeles. For example, what is known to many as the LA riots is reinterpreted using the more politically charged term *LA uprising of 1992* to signify that people's actions were not random acts of destruction, but rather a reflection of the anger and frustration people have built up over years of societal neglect.

In mobilizing African American and Latino community residents to work together, organizational leaders consistently deploy what is known as an injustice frame, which reinterprets major events and changes in South LA as the effects of a history of socioeconomic inequality and racial injustice. This illustrates how, as Robert D. Benford and David A. Snow have shown, injustice frames are constructed in part as organizational leaders (and members) negotiate and construct a shared understanding of a problematic condition they define as in need of change, attribute who or what is to blame, and urge others to act collectively for change (2000, 615).

Similarly, deindustrialization, a process of social and economic change caused by the reduction or elimination of an industry, had severe economic consequences for inner-city residents of Los Angeles. Between 1970 and 1980, the country witnessed a sharp decline in manufacturing, and many of the largest manufacturing plants in Los Angeles that closed were either in or very close to South LA. Businesses closed down and left, taking with them a stable source of employment, which in turn encouraged white flight and overall urban disinvestment. The process of deindustrialization is central to CSJ's understanding of current distressed conditions in the region. In meetings with members, organizational leaders discuss the transition of South LA from a vibrant, economically successful neighborhood, where many residents held stable jobs with decent wages in the manufacturing sector, to what it is today. For example, elder African American members often recount the days when "good department stores" like Macy's and Woolworth lined the boulevards as a reminder that 99-cent stores, generic brand clothing, and the like have not always been the only available options for retail shopping in South LA. Coalition leaders are thus sure to point out that deindustrialization and economic disinvestment were major structural changes in the economy that had damaging effects on inner cities such as South LA.

Similar to how they reinterpreted the LA uprising, CSJ also reframes one of the most devastating episodes of South LA history: the crack epidemic. In the late 1980s and early 1990s, a relatively high proportion of South LA residents, like those in other distressed urban areas nationally, turned to substance abuse. In attempting to rally members into collective action, CSJ leaders specifically frame the high rates of drug use in South LA as an individual form of self-medication or short-term solution to problems plaguing the neighborhood due to severe economic and racial inequality. At the same time, the period was characterized by heightened police surveillance and arrests of anyone considered gang related, which led to high rates of incarceration and other forms of institutional discrimination. Consequently, CSJ takes a structural approach to explaining one of the region's highest periods of drug use and police abuse of power. Black and Latino people living in South LA, they contend, have faced systematic racism and oppression, leading to desperate conditions from which people sought to escape with what was within their reach: a relatively inexpensive and readily available supply of drugs.

Thus, what Gamson (1992) refers to as the "injustice frame" is used by CSJ leaders to interpret the plight of current black and Latino South LA residents as one caused by factors beyond the control of individuals. Moreover, this frame emphasizes that residents have the agency to change the injustices they face. Injustice frames are a mode of interpretation "generated by those who come to define the actions of an authority as unjust" (Benford and Snow 2000, 615). A key to CSJ's success has been its efforts to pass this particular injustice frame from previous leaders to new ones. As a current CSJ leader explains it, "Carol has moved on to do other things but she made sure to train [staff] in the principles and ideologies that she was guided by and

[to] be able to do the studies and readings that guided her and how she analyzed issues and framed issues . . . [and] now they're in turn passing that on to what they see as the next line of leaders in the organization" (field notes 2006).

Deploying injustice frames is central to the coalition building process because they function as a tool for members to analyze problems from a structural perspective so as not to blame individuals or the "other" racial-ethnic group for the problems plaguing their neighborhood. Most important, the injustice frame allows members to interpret events as similarly unjust to both black and Latino residents of South LA, and to create a sense of perceived commonality based on what Kaufmann (2003) calls a "shared outsider status" as marginalized members of society. Injustice frames focus on conditions that affect blacks and Latinos disproportionately compared with whites, thus making themselves readily available to the creation of cross racial-ethnic collaboration. In the following section, I analyze the deployment of strategic frames in the construction of a common identity within the context of two major organizational campaigns: educational justice and city zoning.

CONSTRUCTING A COMMON IDENTITY

CSJ leaders frame perceived commonality between blacks and Latinos by constructing a collective identity that draws on racialized discourse and residential location. During coalition meetings and campaigns CSJ leaders explicitly compare the working-class, and predominantly black and Latino, South LA to the cleaner, safer, and more economically prosperous white West LA. This creates a sense of we-ness among blacks and Latinos living in South LA. Furthermore, underlying many of the comparisons between West and South LA is a racialized discourse that evokes images of racial and economic discrimination toward blacks and Latinos by the dominant white society. Therefore, in mobilizing coalition members by emphasizing a collective identity as South LA residents versus West LA residents, CSJ activists are also effectively constructing a nonwhite identity behind which blacks and Latinos can rally. This creates a necessary condition for collective action: a sense of common plight centered on a notion of we-ness. Thus, the us-versus-them frame effectively combines injustice and collective identity frames to foster support for a black and Latino coalition. Here, the "us" becomes the bridge between the two groups—once this framing process is under way, solidarity can begin to form.

EDUCATIONAL JUSTICE

CSJ leaders emphasize educational equality as a common interest for blacks and Latinos, and point to the educational injustice that both groups face as a way to create a sense of perceived commonality. Problems confronting youth in South LA schools include overcrowding, unqualified teachers, outdated textbooks, too few academic counselors and college prep courses, and inadequate facilities. The serious lack of resources, funding, and support in local schools has caused many students to perform poorly or drop out, or as they refer to it at CSJ, be "pushed out" of school (field notes 2006). Such devastating conditions set the stage for coalition leaders to stress the hardship and inequality faced by all South LA students, when compared to students in the more affluent West LA schools. Indeed, as chapter 6 in this volume demonstrates, education is the second major issue of concern for both African Africans and Latinos living in Los Angeles.

Youth members of the coalition visit West LA schools to witness and document educational disparities firsthand. On one occasion, students took photographs of bathrooms, cafeterias, football fields, and classrooms in the West LA schools and compared them with those taken in their local high schools. The photos were used in a campaign to secure money from a large bond for South LA schools. The $2.4 million bond was intended to improve Los Angeles Unified School District (LAUSD) schools through beautification projects; however, South LA–area schools were not getting their fair share. As one organization leader explains, "We took pictures of our schools and then saw pictures from schools in the Westside . . . and we saw the big difference, like the bleachers, they had brand new metal seats and . . . in our schools students would get splinters from the [wooden] bleachers. . . . And tiles [were] falling from the ceiling and bathrooms weren't working and it was like this doesn't make any sense, ya'll are gonna have to explain why we ain't getting this money!" (field notes 2006).

Comparing South and West LA schools is a strategy effectively used to highlight the relatively impoverished conditions under which many South LA students receive their education, regardless of whether they are black or Latino. Edward, a Latino high school student, illustrates how coalition youth have learned to reinterpret their views on educational inequality by stating firmly, "This isn't a Latino issue, this isn't a black issue, this is *our* issue. We should be working on this together!" (field notes 2006). Another youth member (race unspecified) is quoted in an organizational brochure affirming, "People always talk about the tensions between African American and Latino youth. But at Coalition for Social Justice, we work together to make our schools more equal, to get college prep classes and to make our community better." News headlines about black and Latino racial wars in LA high schools seem to be the dominant paradigm on black-Latino youth relations. However, coalition leaders aim to bridge the gap by identifying West LA residents as the more privileged Other, thus creating among black and Latino youth a sense of collective identity as students attending South LA–area schools. Most important perhaps, is that the us-versus-them strategy propels coalition members into collective action, which is the most crucial component of a coalition.

Emphasizing the common interests of blacks and Latinos over quality education proved extremely rewarding. The A-G campaign, CSJ's largest and most successful effort to date, centered on gaining access to college preparatory classes for South LA students. This campaign sought to secure the school board's vote for a policy that would mandate all LAUSD high schools to offer all the courses required for college admittance. Previously, schools in South LA underserved their students by failing to provide all the necessary courses (A-G requirements) that would make them eligible for college. Because this was not a district mandate, schools were able to get away with providing only a minimum of the required courses. A school's failure to provide A-G courses was a setback particularly for college-bound students who otherwise could meet college requirements. After six years of campaigning with allied social justice organizations, CSJ secured a victory when the majority of school board officials approved the new policy. In the process, black and Latino parents became involved in demanding better-quality education for their children, and students became empowered by voicing their opinions at school board meetings. The A-G campaign was successful in part because organizers called attention to how underserved South LA schools are compared with those in West LA, and in the process revealed the common struggles faced by black and Latino coalition members.

URBAN PLANNING AND ACCESS TO HEALTHY FOOD

CSJ's earliest campaign addressed the community's concern over the high concentration of liquor stores in South LA. Following the uprising of 1994, when many of the area's liquor stores were looted and burnt down, residents fought to prevent several of them from being rebuilt by lobbying the local city government to refrain from reissuing liquor licenses to the owners. From that successful experience, members formed the Urban Planning Committee (UPC), the main efforts of which involve influencing policymakers on issues pertaining to urban planning and zoning in the neighborhood. UPC members have heavily campaigned to create a safe and healthy living environment by targeting and removing "nuisance businesses," mainly liquor stores, motels, and most recently, fast-food establishments. They also work to attract "responsible" businesses, such as restaurants with a variety of healthy menu items, that will help the local economy and its residents thrive.

An illustration of the explicit contrasts made between South and West LA regarding quality of healthy and fresh eating options is GROW, an earlier campaign led by CSJ members concerned with the low quality of so-called fresh produce and meat offered in a local grocery store. Similar to the educational justice campaign tactics of taking photographs of West and South LA schools, GROW committee members went undercover into their local grocery store to take photos of the rotting meat and vegetables they found on the stands. Karla, a member of GROW, recalls visiting a store from the same grocery chain located in West LA and immediately noticing how "nice everything was . . . the store was well lit and everything was so clean and the vegetables were so fresh!" (field notes 2006). GROW members planned a protest outside the South LA grocery store to bring awareness to the issue and demand that the store manager meet their standards for fresh produce and meat products. The opportunity for CSJ members to venture to West LA and see the disparities for themselves illustrates how the us-versus-them frame, and other strategic frames, can transform members' understandings of a sense of commonality and linked fate with the out-group. The GROW campaign also highlights how frames can be constructed by both members and leaders, and become particularly effective as they derive from members' experiences, rather than imposed on them by organizational leaders.

Most recently, CSJ has become active in a related struggle for equal access to healthy food options. Along with other community allies, CSJ—prompted by the major health disparities between South LA residents and the national population—promoted a moratorium on fast-food restaurants in South LA that made headlines. The Los Angeles Department of Public Health found that 30 percent of adults in South LA are obese, compared with a national rate of 21 percent. To combat this problem, which disproportionately affects African Americans and Latinos, CSJ leaders and members have initiated campaigns to create a more healthy community, mostly aimed at attracting healthier restaurant and grocery store options.

Fast-food outlets predominate in South LA, where, according to city councilwoman Jan Perry, they account for 45 percent of all restaurants in the region. In the summer of 2008, the Los Angeles city council unanimously approved a controversial ordinance that bans fast-food chains from opening in South LA for a year. CSJ was one of the major supporters of this ordinance, which passed into law in August 2008. The food disparity in South LA is emblematic of the decades of racial segregation and economic disinvestment that CSJ is battling against. It is part of a longer history of retailers' either leaving the area or, more recently, refusing to open in a region some may consider unsafe or unprofitable. Some, particularly academics and policymakers, have referred to South LA as a "food desert" for its lack of retail grocery stores.

Organizational leaders at CSJ, however, have termed this disparity "food apartheid" (Mohajer 2008). The intentional use of a politically charged term is meant to show that despite their potential profitability rates, restaurant and store owners refuse to sell their services in South LA, often on the basis of negative stereotypes of black and Latino residents as lazy and unreliable employees and as customers prone to shoplifting. Here, CSJ leaders do not simply call for action to demand fresh food and healthier options, they deploy the injustice frame to interpret it as a race and class issue that has particularly negative health implications to promote a sense of commonality among the African American and Latino residents of South LA. For example, CSJ's executive director was quoted in a newspaper article saying, "Fat is a class issue. . . . Areas that don't have as many people of color and are not poor have a much different diet" (Kingston and Kohler 2008). In addition, many South LA residents are uninsured and have poor access to quality, regular medical care, which only serves to highlight the health disparities between South and West LA residents. Framing the food disparity issue as an injustice against South LA residents because they are poor and minority gives blacks and Latinos common ground: the lack of healthy food options is a major factor in above-average obesity and diabetes for both groups.

As demonstrated, the issue of unequal development throughout Los Angeles is discussed in ways that imply that racial and classist stereotypes about South LA residents discourage developers from establishing potentially profitable businesses ventures in the region. Often, this racial and economic bias on the part of developers is emphasized when contrasting it with the large variety of quality retail and restaurant shops in West LA. For example, Trader Joe's, a grocery store known for its wide range of organic produce and vegetarian-friendly products, has more than ten locations in the West LA region but (according to the store locator feature online) not one in South LA. This stark inequality in access to goods and services has had a large impact on the educational achievements and overall lifestyle options of South LA residents, regardless of race-ethnicity. In this sense, the use of injustice and us-versus-them frames is strategic, in that what one has suffered personally is now shared through an implied "we" (Gamson 1992). It is a strategy that has proved effective for building cross-racial-ethnic alliances aimed at improving their socioeconomic status.

"KEEPING IT REAL": RACIAL-ETHNIC TENSION IN THE COALITION

Although CSJ is a successful model for black-Latino coalition building, achieving this status has certainly not come easy. The impact of immigration has been hard to ignore in places like Los Angeles, particularly in areas with large immigrant communities, such as South LA. Issues of immigration, illegality, and citizenship have been a source of conflict for some African American CSJ members, who fear competition from immigrants for scarce resources, including jobs, schools, social welfare programs, and other valuable commodities or services. The sense of threat is heightened by the economic insecurities that many black residents experience, signaling that what some may perceive as anti-immigrant sentiment may in fact be misplaced frustration over the fear of being displaced.

Jackie, an African American CSJ member, is highly critical of the government and the private sector for causing a shortage of job opportunities for South LA residents. Jackie feels that these institutions leave black and Latino communities to fight over menial, low-paying jobs, for "crumbs." However, Jackie's view is not shared by all African American coalition members. Some feel that by supporting immigration they are supporting the very source of their socioeconomic problems. For example, despite CSJ's endorsement of the historic immigrant rights marches of March 2006, several African American members decided not to support the campaign for immigrant legalization. Patricia, for example, who is an African American member, states that some of her black friends, probably feeling resentful, once said, "A day without immigrants? We need more days like those!" CSJ mobilized a contingent of black and Latino South LA residents who attended the march holding a large banner that read, "South LA Supports Immigrant Rights." Perhaps out of pressure, a few African American members quietly decided to join the marches (though not necessarily for immigration), whereas others decided not to participate. There was also a sense among some African Americans that speaking out against immigration would single them out and create tension within the coalition. Nicky, also an African American member, said that her friends in the coalition "really don't want to be a part of this because [they] don't agree [with] promoting illegal immigrants" and a lot of them "wouldn't want to voice their opinion and weren't holding it against [any person] and were not trying to cause any tempers." Speaking out against an idea or campaign that the coalition supports can be perceived as countering the goals of CSJ and creating conflict. Nicky feels that the organization does not always "keep it real," and at times, to avoid conflict, discourages frank discussion about contentious issues.

Studies focusing on black and Latino coalitions have largely ignored the element of dialogue (or lack thereof) between groups, concentrating instead on other factors that lead to conflict or cooperation. Not dealing head-on with race and immigration among its members can lead to a rift within the coalition. This is also relevant for youth members of the coalition. As Regina Freer and Claudia Sandoval were able to capture in their study, when asked what makes coalitions work, youth members replied, "Talk[ing] about differences," stating that "if you don't talk about differences then you might offend each other" (see chapter 9, this volume). Discussing such differences, however, requires a moderator who can keep the dialogue framed around the larger goal of cross-racial collaboration and social action. For example, respondents in this study revealed that CSJ rarely addresses the common belief that Latinos take jobs from African Americans, even though some African Americans hold that belief. Because many African Americans fear being singled out or accused of being ignorant and causing turmoil within the coalition, they chose to discuss these matters privately with one another. When blacks and Latinos were asked what factors they believe work best in building a black and Latino coalition, the most common response was that the groups need to "come to the table" and be honest with each other about their fears, concerns, and misgivings. Open and honest dialogue between African Americans and Latinos, along with strategic emphasis on the structural and the us-versus-them frame on the part of CSJ leaders and more committed CSJ members is thus critical to resolving conflict and finding feasible solutions together. Further research is needed in this area to identify the best approaches to discussing sensitive or controversial issues among coalition members.

DISCUSSION

African Americans and Latinos in the United States have been described as natural allies in light of their shared "outsider" status (Kaufmann 2003, 202). Their relations, however, have most commonly been framed as rife with conflict and competition (Vaca 2004). In examining the coalition-building process, this chapter rejects the dichotomous conflict-cooperation theory of African American and Latino relations, and instead illustrates the complex dynamics of inter-racial-ethnic relations by showing that coalition members simultaneously work in unison and perceive threat.

Few studies have focused on cases where the groups converge to improve their socioeconomic status. In general, findings in this study support the argument that an organization with strong black and Latino leadership is capable of bridging the racial-ethnic divide to form a sense of community and linked fate. CSJ's case illustrates this point well. Although many studies focus on coalition building in electoral politics (Tedin and Murray 1994; Kaufmann 2003; McClain and Karnig 1990; Jackson, Gerber, and Cain 1994), this study provides insight on framing strategies that work at the grassroots, community level. The Coalition for Social Justice highlights the key role that racially integrated community-based organizations can play in building alliances among a city's distinct racial-ethnic groups (Wilson 2000). CSJ develops a progressive political ideology—one that makes explicit the relationship of African Americans and Latinos as natural allies in the struggle for social justice—to create a sense of commonality. Tensions between the two groups do exist, however. Within the coalition, blacks and Latinos may at times point to each other as the source of larger socioeconomic problems, yet they simultaneously recognize that the only way to improve these conditions is to work together.

As several chapters in this volume illustrate, black-Latino relations are contextual and can vary based on region, nationality, gender, and economic status, among other factors. Economic status is highly important in determining black-Latino relations, particularly blacks' attitudes toward Latinos. Chapter 8 in this volume, for example, shows that middle-class blacks hold more positive attitudes toward Latinos. In environments where Latinos are economically advantaged relative to their black neighbors, blacks were more likely to express negative sentiments toward Latinos (Gay 2006). In this case study, however, black and Latino coalition members hold a similarly disadvantaged social and economic status, at least, coalition leaders frame it as such. Rather than this similarity being framed—as the media so often do—as the cause of competition over scarce resources, coalition leaders have deployed strategic framing to foster a sense of linked fate among poor and working-class blacks and Latinos. This chapter demonstrates an example of black-Latino coalition building that develops when community leaders, particularly in multi-racial-ethnic neighborhoods, prioritize cross-racial collaboration over ethnic-specific mobilization.

CONCLUSION

Although black and Latino relations vary across time and space, the case of South Los Angeles may be applied to most urban scenarios where the arrival of Latinos has significantly changed the racial-ethnic composition of a black neighborhood. This is particularly true when blacks and Latinos are the predominant groups inhabiting the same socially and economically disadvantaged community near a more affluent (and white) community. Along these lines, this study also has implications for the possibilities of coalition building between other racial-ethnic groups, such as working-class Latino and Asian immigrants. Some scholars are skeptical that African American and Latino coalitions are likely to form, and predict that relations between these groups will grow increasingly hostile (Vaca 2004; Meier and Stewart 1991). Given the demographics of these groups, concern about the future of black and Latino relations will likely remain a prominent issue for community leaders and scholars of race and ethnicity and urban politics. Now is the time for black and Latino leaders to begin to seriously explore the benefits to building alliances as a key strategy to empower both groups.

REFERENCES

Benford, Robert D., and David A. Snow. 2000. "Framing Processes and Social Movements: An Overview and Assessment." *Annual Review of Sociology* 26: 611–39.

Bobo, Lawrence D., and Vincent L Hutchings. 1996. "Perceptions of Racial Group Competition: Extending Blumer's Theory of Group Position to a Multiracial Social Context." *American Sociological Review* 61(6): 951–72.

Camarillo, Albert M. 2004. "Black and Brown in Compton: Demographic Change, Suburban Decline, and Intergroup Relations in a South Central Los Angeles Community, 1950–2000." In *Not Just Black and White: Historical and Contemporary Perspectives on Immigration, Race, and Ethnicity in the United States*, edited by Nancy Foner and George M. Fredrickson. New York: Russell Sage Foundation.

Clark, W. A. V. 1998. *The California Cauldron: Immigration and the Fortunes of Local Communities*. New York: Guilford Press.

Gamson, William A. 1992. *Talking Politics*. New York: Cambridge University Press.

Gay, Claudine. 2006. "Seeing Difference: The Effect of Economic Disparity on Black Attitudes Toward Latinos." *American Journal of Political Science* 50(4): 982–97.

Grenier, Guillermo, and Max Castro. 2001. "Blacks and Cubans in Miami: The Negative Consequences of the Cuban Enclave on Ethnic Relations." In *Governing American Cities: Inter-Ethnic Coalitions, Competition, and Conflict*, edited by Michael Jones-Correa. New York: Russell Sage Foundation.

Henry, Charles P. 1980. "Black-Chicano Coalitions: Possibilities and Problems." *Western Journal of Black Studies* 4(4): 202–32.

Hernández-León, Rubén, and Victor Zúñiga. 2005. "Appalachia Meets Aztlán: Mexican Immigration and Intergroup Relations in Dalton, Georgia."
In *New Destinations: Mexican Immigration in the United States*, edited by
Rubén Hernández-León and Victor Zúñiga. New York: Russell Sage Foundation.

Hunt, Scott, Robert D. Benford, and David A. Snow. 1994. "Identity Fields:
Framing Processes and the Social Construction of Movement Identities."
In *New Social Movements: From Ideology to Identity*, edited by Enrique
Larana, Jank Johnston, and Joseph R. Gusfield. Philadelphia, Pa.: Temple
University Press.

Jackson, Byran O., Elisabeth R. Gerber, and Bruce E Cain. 1994. "Coalitional Prospects in a Multi-Racial Society: African American Attitudes
Toward Other Minority Groups." *Political Research Quarterly* 47(2): 277–
94.

Johnson, James H., Jr., Walter C. Farrell Jr., and Chandra Guinn. 1997. "Immigration Reform and the Browning of America: Tensions, Conflicts, and
Community Instability in Metropolitan Los Angeles." *International Migration Review* 31(4): 1055–95.

Johnson, James H., Jr., and Melvin Oliver. 1994. "Interethnic Minority Conflict in Urban America: The Effect of Economic and Social Dislocations."
In *Race and Ethnic Conflict*, edited by F. L. Pincus and H. J. Ehrlich. Boulder, Colo.: Westview Press.

Kaufmann, Karen M. 2003. "Cracks in the Rainbow: Group Commonality as
a Basis for Latino and African-American Political Coalitions." *Political Research Quarterly* 56(2): 199–210.

Kingston, Anne, and Nicholas Kohler. 2008. "L.A.'s Fast-Food Drive-By."
Macleans.ca. Available at: http://www.macleans.ca/science/health/article
.jsp?content=20080813_34253_34253 (accessed June 19, 2009).

McClain, Paula D., Niambi M. Carter, Victoria M. DeFrancesco Soto, Mo-
nique L. Lyle, Jeffrey D. Grynaviski, Shayla C. Nunnally, Thomas J. Scotto,
J. Alan Kendrick, Gerald F. Lackey, and Kendra Davenport Cotton. 2006.
"Racial Distancing in a Southern City: Latino Immigrants' Views of Black
Americans." *Journal of Politics* 68(3): 571–84.

McClain, Paula D., and Albert K. Karnig. 1990. "Black and Hispanic Socioeconomic and Political Competition." *American Political Science Review*
84(2): 535–45.

Meier, Kenneth J., Paula D. McClain, J. L. Polinard, and Robert D. Wrinkle.
2004. "Divided or Together? Conflict and Cooperation Between African
Americans and Latinos." *Political Research Quarterly* 57(3): 399–409.

Meier, Kenneth J., and Joseph Stewart Jr. 1991. "Cooperation and Conflict
in Multiracial School Districts." *Journal of Politics* 53(4): 1123–33.

Mindiola, Tatcho, Jr., Yolanda F. Niemann, and Nestor Rodriguez. 2003.
Black-Brown Relations and Stereotypes. Austin: University of Texas Press.

Mohajer, Shaya Tayefe. 2008. "Urban Areas Struggle to Find Grocers, Fresh

Food." MSNBC.com. Available at: http://www.msnbc.com/id/28300393/ (accessed May 23, 2009).

Negrete, Edward, and Susan Shimizu Taira. 1995. "Blacks and Latinos: Understanding and Resolving Racial Conflict." *California Association of Human Relations Organizations* newsletter, 1995.

Oliver, Eric J., and Janelle Wong. 2003. "Intergroup Prejudice in Multiethnic Settings." *American Journal of Political Science* 47(4): 567–82.

Polletta, Francesca, and James M. Jasper. 2001. "Collective Identity and Social Movements." *Annual Review of Sociology* 27: 283–305.

Rodrigues, Helena Alves, and Gary M. Segura. 2004. "A Place at the Lunch Counter: Latinos, African-Americans, and the Dynamics of American Race Politics." Presented at the conference "Latino Politics: The State of the Discipline." Texas A&M University (April 30–May 1, 2004).

Small, Mario Luis. 2004. *Villa Victoria: The Transformation of Social Capital in a Boston Barrio.* Chicago: University of Chicago Press.

Sonenshein, Raphael J. 1989. "The Dynamics of Biracial Coalitions: Crossover Politics in Los Angeles." *Western Political Quarterly* 42(2): 333–53.

Suttles, Gerald D. 1968. *The Social Order of the Slum: Ethnicity and Territory in the Inner City.* Chicago: University of Chicago Press.

Tedin, Kent L., and Richard W. Murray. 1994. "Support for Biracial Political Coalitions Among Blacks and Hispanics." *Social Science Quarterly* 75(4): 772–89.

Tseng, Thomas. 1999. "Common Paths: Connecting Metropolitan Growth to Inner City Opportunities in South Los Angeles." Paper published by the Institute for Public Policy, Pepperdine University, May 1999.

Vaca, Nicolás C. 2004. *The Presumed Alliance: The Unspoken Conflict Between Latinos and Blacks and What It Means for America.* New York: HarperCollins.

Wilson, William Julius. 2000. "Rising Inequality and the Case for Coalition Politics." *Annals of the American Academy* 568(March): 76–99.

Zald, Mayer N. 1996. "Culture, Ideology, and Strategic Framing." In *Comparative Perspectives on Social Movements: Political Opportunities, Mobilizing Structures, and Cultural Framings*, edited by Doug McAdam, John D. McCarthy, and Mayer N. Zald. Cambridge: Cambridge University Press.

PART VI

Interaction in
Street Culture

CHAPTER 11

Ethnic Succession and Ethnic Conflict

James Diego Vigil

In recent years observers have noted the possibility of a widespread black and brown conflict in Los Angeles's inner-city gang neighborhoods.[1] Generally, these commentators claim that the basis for the hostility and antagonism stems from race and racism, that aggressive and violent acts and actions are sparked by the skin color that differentiates one group from the other. Print and television accounts mostly underscore the race card even though other factors might be at work. For example, any specific episode might easily stem from youthful exuberance, perceived neighborhood boundary violations, drug turf contentions, a personal vendetta, a case of mistaken identity, and any number of other reasons as well as any combination.

Research indicates that neither statistical evidence nor personal insights and observations of informed residents supports the notion that racism is the principal source of brown and black violent conflict in inner-city Los Angeles.[2] Instead, it suggests that the friction that exists between African Americans and Latinos is mostly a street-based phenomenon that is more episodic than endemic, largely sporadic rather than group structured. Further, even the interethnic incidents that occur are minor in comparison with the majority of gang conflicts. This tendency to blame the group, the gang, is part of a recent law enforcement and media development to seek fault in the aggregate rather than in the individual. A recent antigang sweep in Varrio Hawaiian Gardens, the biggest gang takedown in American history, focused on the drugs and guns in the area but could not resist mention of the "usual suspect" of racism against blacks.[3]

Quantitative data are especially relevant to this assessment, and when qualitative evidence is added to the equation it becomes clear that race and racism as a source of conflict is relatively insignificant in respect to other factors, such as cultural and historical differences (Macias 2008; Alvarez 2008), police relations (Escobar 1999), drug networks,[4] and demographic factors.[5] One incontrovertible fact underscores this position: nine in ten black-Latino homicide victims in Los Angeles were killed by someone from their racial or ethnic group.[6] When the ethnographic evidence is amassed, the reasons become clearer.

WHAT DOES THE EVIDENCE SAY?

In certain instances race does dominate the explanation authorities offer. However, a recent study commissioned by the Los Angeles Police Department (LAPD) cites several particularly significant facts. John Hipp, George Tita, and Lindsay Boggess conducted a study of LAPD data gathered from 2000 to 2006 and found that black offenders were nearly eight times more likely to kill another black person than to kill a Latino (2007). Similarly, Latinos were nearly twice as likely to kill another Latino.[7] The homicide report gathered by the *Los Angeles Times* discovered similar trends: of the 236 homicide cases from 2006 in the four most violent LAPD precincts, just twenty-two involved individuals who crossed racial lines.[8] Thus, 90 percent of the suspects and victims were of the same race. Although gang rivalries in these precincts are long-standing, the conflicts that do occur are along gang lines, and territorial claims, rather than a "race" thing.[9]

Former chief Ed Bratton of the LAPD, concurring with these reviews, has said that the problem is overblown by the media, which created a straw man to cover other anxieties, such as poverty, immigration, and changing demographics. He pointed out that the department's south bureau has had only one victim of such interracial violence, and this in an area where African American and Latino American gangs overlap most extensively. In 2007, Los Angeles County figures show 562 homicides, 90 percent of which involved individuals killed by members of their own ethnic-racial group.[10]

Gregory Rodriquez, a regular *Los Angeles Times* opinion contributor, suggests that much of the discussion on interracial violence is sensationalized out of proportion to the actual events and trends.[11] Ironically, Rodriquez could have cited as an example a *Los Angeles Times* report that same year characterizing the interaction between blacks and Latinos as more like "ethnic cleansing."[12] Citing the Hipp, Tita, and Boggess report, Rodriquez emphasizes that Anglo Americans are suffering from "Anglo race fatigue." Tired of and exasperated by being the racist culprit for everything that ails blacks, Anglos are looking for company and point to Latinos as co-racists; "It's not just us," some apologists say.

EVIDENCE POINTS TO DEMOGRAPHICS NOT RACE

What eventually emerges as a better explanation for the number and tone of ethnic hostilities and conflicts is not ethnic animosity or hostility but the resounding ethnic succession that stems from destabilizing demographic changes and transformation in neighborhoods where blacks and Latinos are in close proximity. For more than a hundred years in Los Angeles, black and brown residents in such neighborhoods coexisted with a deference and respect toward one another that marked their general attitude and interactions. The African American population of Los Angeles peaked in the 1980s, when newcomers of Latino immigrants from Mexico and Central America were arriving in large numbers daily. Since then, Latinos have increased both in number and as a proportion of the total population, and whites and blacks have moved out of many neighborhoods as Latinos have moved in, including South Central Los Angeles. South Central LA has historically been populated mostly by blacks and Mexicans, largely because of restrictive racial covenants and other discriminatory practices in place until the 1960s.

In 1970, the African American and Latino populations made up 17 and 18 percent of the city population, respectively. That roughly even balance changed dramatically in the following three decades, however, as the Latino population grew in number more than threefold and the black population diminished slightly (see table 11.1). In relative terms, blacks ended up only 11 percent of the city's population in 2000, and the Latino population had grown to nearly half (47 percent) of all Angelenos. That change has been especially apparent in South Central Los Angeles, where, until 1980, the large majority of the population was black but, by 2000, Latinos had become nearly half of the area's population.

EARLIER ERA

In 1940s South Central Los Angeles, for instance, the music, dress styles, and socializing among youth from each group reflected the fact that they were second-generation offspring of migrants from the

Table 11.1 Population in Los Angeles City, 1970 to 2000

Census Year	1970	1980	1990	2000
African American	486,674 (17%)	504,674 (17%)	454,289 (13%)	401,986 (11%)
Latino	519,842 (18%)	816,331 (28%)	1,401,063 (40%)	1,728,138 (47%)
Total population	2,811,801	2,966,850	3,485,398	3,364,820

Source: Author's compilation based on U.S. Census Bureau (2000).

Old South, on the one hand, and rural Mexico, on the other, and were becoming acculturated together to life in California. Since that time, Mexicans have been strongly influenced by the urban lifestyle struck by blacks, and swing and jazz have been joined by rhythm and blues, Motown, and hip hop (Macias 2008; Alvarez 2008; McWilliams 1949). One can safely assert that the diffusion of this music and culture was the precursor of the broader, deeper spread that is occurring now through globalization. In countless urban areas across the world, music and clothing style mimic what has happened and is happening in the large cities of the United States.

The rise of street gangs in black and Latino communities also shows many similarities. In each community, for example, population growth was rapid in the wake of migrations from rural and small-town areas of Mexico and the southern U.S. states. The new arrivals experienced marked discrimination in housing, employment, and even schooling. Although sizeable majorities in each migrant community coped with these obstacles to build productive lives, some succeeding well beyond that, a significant minority fell sharply behind. The stresses and strains from crowded living conditions, inadequate schooling, unemployment, limited social and recreational outlets, and poverty—what I have called elsewhere multiple marginality (Vigil 2002, 2007)—created households from which children, especially males, would seek refuge in the streets. There they encountered peers from similar households to form street gangs in a process I term street socialization (Vigil 1988, 1996).

In light of these developments, the question to answer is whether Mexicans or any other group can admire and emulate another ethnic group even as they dislike the group for racial-ethnic reasons. Without delving into the social psychological implications of a love-hate relationship, research, as noted, historically shows that the general attitude between blacks and Mexicans has been one of accommodation, a coexistence that reflected many background similarities: recent migration, second-generation acculturation, poverty and segregation, and limited access to dominant institutions. Mutual accommodation varied from a live-and-let-live mutual avoidance to mutual curiosity about and cooperation with one another.

Witness, for example, the reports and other observations made during the Zoot Suit episode of 1943 where blacks and browns struck a more collective stance against racism and police mistreatment (McWilliams 1949; Escobar 1999). During the infamous Zoot Suit riots of June 1943 whites staged at least five nights of terror, attacking Mexican "zoot suiters," beating them and ripping off their clothing as the police followed, arresting the victims (Vigil 2002).

Other racial flare-ups occurred in the city in the early 1940s, such as the incident when white students at Fremont High School threatened their African American schoolmates in 1941, burning them in effigy and displaying posters declaring, "We want no niggers at this school." Similar incidents were the catalyst for the first African American street gangs in Los Angeles, which emerged as a defensive response to white violence in the schools and streets during the late 1940s. Chicano gangs had begun forming even earlier in East Los Angeles. Racial gang wars erupted, for instance, at Manual Arts High in 1946, at Canoga Park High in 1947, and at John Adams Junior High in 1949 (Davis 1992). "Possibly as a result of their origin in these school integration–transition battles," Mike Davis suggests, "black gangs until the 1970s tended to be predominantly defined by school-based turfs rather than by the microscopically drawn neighborhood territorialities of Chicano gangs" (1992, 293). Furthermore, early South Central gangs—which had names such as the Businessmen, Slausons, Gladiators, Farmers, Parks, Outlaws, Watts, Boot Hill, Rebel Rousers, Roman Twenties, and so on—served also as the architects of social space in new and usually hostile settings. As tens of thousands of 1940s and 1950s black immigrants crammed into the overcrowded, absentee-landlord neighborhoods of the ghetto's Eastside, low-rider gangs offered easy urban socialization for poor young newcomers from rural Texas, Louisiana, and Mississippi (Davis 1992, 293).

Emergent gangs in Los Angeles from that era, such as Florencia and the Slausons, coexisted on the streets but rarely confronted one another. Bird, a leader of the Slausons, pointed out to me in an interview three decades later that "blacks and Chicanos got along in a very relaxed and respectful manner back then." A deeply rooted modus vivendi kept them together in the same neighborhood but apart from each other when it came to gang rivalry and conflict. This has changed in recent years, but for reasons other than race.

CHANGES OVER THE DECADES

By the late 1990s, Mexican immigration was growing immensely and was joined by that of Central Americans, especially Salvadorans. In South Los Angeles, as noted, major demographic changes were under way as Latinos began to move into black city neighborhoods and replace African American residents, almost overnight, just as blacks had once overtaken mostly white communities in the 1950s and 1960s. One long-term Mexican resident who lived in the same house during the 1950s experienced these dramatic ethnic shifts, and claimed that racial relations improved with the arrival of more blacks as "Mexicans and blacks sensed that they were both discriminated against" (field notes).

Over a fifteen-year period, from 1981 to 1995, when I commuted from my home in Whittier to the University of Southern California where I worked, I frequently drove surface streets along the same route every day to avoid freeway traffic. This took me through the Exposition Park area at the southern end of downtown, which abuts South Central Los Angeles. Making mental notes along the way, I would observe the number of people on the streets, what they were doing, and what ethnic group they belonged to. During those fifteen years, the color of the people went from black to brown, a decided ethnic switch that left relatively few blacks in an area of mostly Mexicans.

A similar shift was occurring in many areas of South Central Los Angeles, as well as elsewhere throughout the county. One example full of complexities is enough for this ethnic succession. Fremont High School is located just south of the Florencia-Slauson neighborhood, and its student population in the early 1950s was a mix of blacks, browns, and whites. As a white student remarked years later, "Fremont had a mix of racial groups but we were all proud of being from South Central LA, and there was a whole lot of give and take and, of course, the music standard for all was rhythm and blues" (field notes). A good example of this is Bobby Rose, who was both white and the substitute singer for Don Julian and the Meadowlarks, an early rhythm and blues group. A feeder school near Fremont, McKinley Elementary, however, was primarily staffed by white personnel. By the late 1960s, the student body had become overwhelmingly black. Local black parents began to clamor and push for changes, such as a curriculum that included mention of black contributions to history and teachers and other personnel of African American descent. These protestations, of course, came in the midst of the civil rights era. In time, the changes were instituted and students and teachers shared more or less the same ethnic background. In 1997, as director of a University of California–Los Angeles (UCLA) program where I then worked, I sent student researchers to McKinley; the student population was almost entirely of Mexican descent, and many were even first-generation immigrants. The black principal of the school said that he had been working for several years on changes that would "benefit the needs and problems of the largely poor, black children of the neighborhood. . . . But now with more Mexican children coming in every day," he added, "I now have to think about culture and language as barriers to learning."

Such ethnic succession transformations often led to repercussive upheaval. Not only were school personnel, as in the white-to-black phase, bombarded by demands and requests that reflected the needs of the largely newcomer student body, the demographic change transpired as the school curriculum and mission continued to undergo educational changes based on a primarily black student body. One of the black parents complained, "We have been working for years trying to do something for our kids and the new Mexican parents are copying us. Will there be anything left if we share with Johnny-Come-Latelys?" Teachers, like their earlier white counterparts, felt beleaguered, betrayed, and bewildered, and behaved testily, especially when activist Mexican parents became confrontational. Four or five Mexican mothers came in to see the school counselor, who was black, and angrily demanded that more bilingual teachers be hired in the next year. According to the counselor, one of the mothers yelled, "You only think of your group and not ours, and you should try to make room for us, too." The counselor subsequently told me that she took this as a personal affront, because she had worked harder than anyone else on campus to accommodate the newcomers, and as a counselor had always stuck to a motto of helping all children, not simply one group or another.

What happened at this school was a microcosm of the changes in South Central Los Angeles generally. An initiative known as the Ten Schools had been launched several years before—McKinley Elementary was one of the ten—with the aim of specifically addressing the needs of low-achieving black children and the methods and goals had to be altered right in the midst of the learning program. As noted, the ethnic makeup of the neighborhood was being transformed, as were the institutions that served the population. In addition, Mexican American politicians were beginning to challenge the entrenched black elected leaders, and the city council began to reflect the shift in population. Local hospitals, police department practices, and other public institutions found that they could not make the changes fast enough to please either the long-term black residents or the Latino newcomers. The next chapter in this volume contends that the black-brown relations of youth in gangs showing distance and deference indicate avoidance rather than accommodation. This apparent decline in mutual cooperation reflects the fact that the two populations are so different today, not least with respect to the competition over street drug–trafficking networks. Avoidance, in short, is actually a survival mechanism for street gangs in both communities: The less contact and conflict, the better for business.

HOW GANGS CHANGED

Related to all these on-the-ground transitions is the issue of the changing nature of street gangs. No one can deny that from the 1950s to 2010 the gangs have become more lethal. Gang members use and abuse drugs and alcohol more regularly and intensively today. This mindset adds to the deep-seated locura (that is, wild craziness stemming from many early childhood traumas) that triggers violent acts, many of which are random shootings.

For a short but significant time, during the 1960s, the use and abuse of drugs was somewhat tempered by the civil rights movement, for both blacks and Chicanos. Many gang youths at this time were involved with "the generational awakening of black power," and did not, therefore, play an entirely negative role in the community. During one protest at a local whites-only drive-in restaurant, for instance, it was the timely arrival of the Slausons gang that saved the protestors from an attack by whites. In this way, gangs such as the Slausons and the Gladiators, from the 54th Street area, "became a crucial social base for the rise of the local Black Liberation movement" (Davis 1992, 297). Following the Watts riots of August 1965, furthermore, there was a period of three to four years when rival gang hostilities were put aside to some degree, and African American youth instead immersed themselves in the black power revolution. Even later, on the heels of another disturbance, the 1992 King incident, black street leaders strove to preach peace among the Crips and Bloods. Similarly, Chicano youth energies were drawn to the militant Brown Berets and a string of boycotts and protests aimed to change schools, police relations, and other areas (Vigil 2002). Gang membership fell during this time. If anything, black and brown militants attempted to coordinate their efforts to bring about constructive changes for both communities. For example, the Community Alert Patrol, begun by black militants and adopted by Chicano activists, aimed to monitor police patrol cars by closely following in vehicles driven by blacks and Chicanos to ensure that the laws were properly administered.

Economic forces were behind the rise of drug trafficking, in a ghetto version of an opportunity structure (Vigil 2002, 2007). During the 1980s, for example, 40 percent of African American children lived below or barely above the poverty line (Davis 1992). In addition, politically motivated attacks on programs instituted during the War on Poverty led to an end to most of them, leaving the inner-city African American and Latino youth with nowhere to turn. Indeed, with the dismantling of the NYC (Neighborhood Youth Corps) and the termination of the Comprehensive Employment and Training Act (CETA), as well as the ending of Job Corps, this retreat from the inner city had obvious ill effects only slightly offset by the Clinton administration's reintroduction of programs such as AmeriCorps. In any event, for gang members virtually no job alternatives to choose from remain. As one social worker noted, "You could pull 80 percent of gang members, seventeen years old or younger, out of gangs, if you had jobs, job training and social alternatives" (Davis 1992, 307).

In the context of major changes in the last decade, impoverished neighborhoods, especially street populations like gangs, have increasingly turned to the informal and illicit economy. Ways of making money and spending it have changed dramatically. What once were penny ante drug sales have evolved into drug-trafficking enterprises, what were bad check signings have grown into identity theft and credit card fraud, and other street-level criminal practices like "taxing" have been introduced as new money-making ventures. These deviant activities have led to another level of conflict and violence among street gangs, and added to the mayhem and aura of aggression found in the streets.

To magnify matters, in the last fifteen years or so, prison gang rhetoric and influences have been spilling over onto the streets. Eme—the Mexican Mafia prison gang founded in the 1950s—initially focused on drug sales and other illicit activities, but after the release of the movie *American Me* in 1992, and the unraveling of the Eme leadership on the death of its founder Joe Morgan, upstart leaders competed for the Eme mantle. To take advantage of the jockeying and confusion, some associates of the old leadership decided to expand the drug sales network to include the many street-gang drug enterprises, and concocted an interesting plan to effect this end. The organization launched a thinly veiled effort aimed at all Mexican street gangs (Rafael 2007).

According to gang members I interviewed (Vigil 2007), Eme had forbidden all of them from conducting drive-bys because innocent people were being hit by stray bullets. Such random episodes brought unnecessary attention and intervention from law enforcement; furthermore, it interfered with the drug-trafficking business. It was common for Eme leaders to set up meetings in different barrios (that is, neighborhood gangs) of the greater Los Angeles area, with two or three Mafia members showing up to hector a hundred or two hundred gang members into following their instructions. If any barrio or gang members did not obey this dictum, then Eme would put a "green light" on them, that is, make them fair game for anyone to shoot and kill.

Ostensively, this intrusion appeared to border on an enlightened pro-social intervention, but that it was a ruse soon became clear. Eme used this controlling initiative to begin taxing gangs that had cultivated a lucrative drug-sales business, expecting either a portion of the monies earned or an expensive automatic pistol as payment. One Cuatro Flats veterano (4th Streets Flats veteran) described how "two guys from Eme would show up every week in a green Lexus and visit the gang members. They came to pick up a new automatic handgun that was a tax for the week's drug profits charged against the whole gang. Every week they would do the same thing, and all the gang members were sure to pool the money to buy the gun. Prison guys forced their way on the street kids" (field notes).

By that time, black gangs had developed their own street drug-trafficking practices and networks, and it was these illicit entrepreneur activities that brought black and brown gangs together for the first time in a contentious venue. As early as twenty years ago, the black Rolling Eighties and Latino 18th Street gangs were locked in this type of drug turf battle. Thus, the streets themselves became a place of economic enterprises and activities and a context for competition and rivalry among all street gangs. All of this was new to the gang subculture once known primarily as deviants that were gang-bangers; slanging (a dialect variation of slinging, that is, dealing drugs) was added to gangbanging. Moreover, a new street-gang enterprise, known as taxing, emerged. Sometimes taxing was aimed at other drug traffickers who had less street "juice" (power) because they had either weaker manpower or less fire power behind them. However, the taxing enterprise also expanded to plunder Popsicle and corn-on-the-cob venders, who were usually undocumented workers, pushing their small carts through harsh neighborhoods.

THE OAKWOOD INCIDENT

Even with the demographic shifts and worsening street-gang practices, however, the black-brown issue remained relatively calm and contained to certain areas and particular subgroups. As several incidents erupted and threatened to get out of hand, calmer spirits and heads quieted the affairs. One such was the Oakwood neighborhood case in the 1990s. In this area of the Venice beachfront, in the process of being gentrified mostly by whites, Oakwood had long experienced the juxtaposition of blacks and Latinos in one location, with very little negative, much less racially based, interaction. As noted earlier, the area was seeing all the demographic and other changes under way in other locations, combining developers set on gentrifying a "barrio by the bay," high immigration rates of Mexicans to join well-established barrios from an earlier era, political tensions between old versus newer residents, and generally a community in flux (see figure 11.1).

As the drug trade increased in significance to fill the voids left by a

Figure 11.1 Map of Los Angeles Neighborhoods

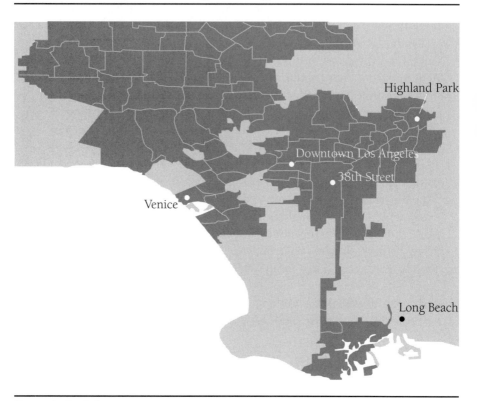

Source: Author's figure.

weak economy, black and Latino traffickers began to compete over enterprise drug zones, particularly customers among the well-established more affluent residents as well as the yuppies integral to the gentrification. This brought together Venice 13 (Mexican) and Shoreline Crips (black) gang members in Oakwood over lucrative drug turf issues, which led to a spate of shootings and killings that lasted for several years, ending only in 1994 after a truce was negotiated (Unemoto 2006). Significantly, this long-running event and its end are living testimony to what causes volatile and negative attitudes and interactions between black and Latino street populations and, more important, to how interventions can bring matters under control. The neighborhood has remained quiet since then even though the Venice 13 and Shoreline Crips still roam the streets.

ETHNOGRAPHIC RESEARCH

Among the barrios I have recently investigated, two others provide particular insights in what they tell us about race and ethnicity as an issue: the Avenues and 38th Street (see figure 11.1). The Avenues in Highland Park is a classic gang from the 1950s in a neighborhood of whites and Mexicans that borders the northern stretch of the Pasadena Freeway and takes its name from the numbered avenues in the area. I investigated a case of a Chicano gang member shooting and killing two adult black men, according to media reports, for no apparent reason other than that they were black. The reports asserted that the violence was racially charged and stemmed from prison gang orders to gang members of the Avenues barrio. I visited the barrio on several occasions and talked with neighborhood residents either in their homes or on the streets. The questions I asked always led to whether a green light had been given to local gangs to kill any black person in the area. One older, former gang member observed that "there are hardly any blacks in the area, never have been, and I don't see any big movement of them here now. The neighborhood here is the Avenues and they only have pedo [conflict] with Chicano gangs. I don't know what they [media and police] are talking about. Maybe it is one or two persons that don't like negros [pronounced as in Spanish], but the rest of us just don't care" (field notes).

Most of my other informal exchanges provided no evidence that such a street command was in place, or ever existed in the first place. Visits to public institutions, schools, park employees, antigang programs, and political representatives' offices in which more formal interviews were conducted provided the same answer. It turned out that federal authorities were prosecuting a case based on the incident in federal court and were using hate crime laws to prosecute the defendant. After winning the case, and within a year from the time of the trial, the authorities stated that the Avenues gang was not promoting the killing of blacks in the neighborhood. Newspapers duly followed with reportage of authorities' new and reversed position. Had I not conducted research in this area, I would have had only the media reports to rely on.[13]

The 38th Street gang is even older than the Avenues, and is a classic barrio of the 1930s, immortalized in the Sleepy Lagoon case of 1942 and featured in the *Zoot Suit* play and movie. Since its inception as a barrio, it has coexisted in a black-brown, run-down residential area near the industrial town of Vernon. Nearby Jefferson High School had a nearly 95 percent black student body in the 1950s, but Mexican students have always been there as well. Today, the student composition is predominantly Mexican. The primary rival gang for 38th Street gang members was Florencia, to the south, not any of the black gangs in the immediate vicinity.

In my visits there in 2006, I was able to observe and interview residents and students and record their responses on the state of black-brown relations. As in the Avenues case, their expert views were in the affirmative that no such ethnic cleansing activities were common in the area, that conflicts and animosities were defined more by personal disagreements that had gotten out of hand. One household, in fact, a Mexican family, raved about an older black woman who was better off but made herself available to help with any problem that arose for them. This was particularly so when the family faced obstacles the American authorities presented; the woman was a champion for the poor and underserved. When I talked with her, she was simple and direct and based what she said on fact rather than emotion: "These people [the family] here have had to go through a lot in the last year. Their son was arrested and they were not informed why. When they discovered that it was because he had waved a gun at another kid, they tried to explain to the authorities that the son was on medication and sometimes was not in control of his emotions and irrational. Did you think they listened to them? No! They just kept him in jail and still haven't considered their plea." The family made sure I knew that it was the woman who had visited and pushed the police to answer the questions the family had. She took on their battle as if it were her own.

CONCLUSION

Today, despite the tendency of the media and other public alarmists to frame a racist explanation for the continuing drama of two poor ethnic groups struggling to survive in the same space, confronting similar economic pressures and dealing with the pull of street socialization for youth, it is demography that speaks to the issue. Such rapid and uneven neighborhood and community changes have shaken human networks and patterns in ways such that repercussions are still being felt in heretofore unheard-of areas; schools and law enforcement immediately come to mind.

In large part, the problems in Los Angeles can be traced to global-ization and neo-liberal policies and programs that have brought about major upheavals in Mexico and Central America. Uprooting hundreds of thousands of peasants and displacing small town and urban workers has released a large labor pool that is seeking survival primarily in the United States. Human migration in this era has sur-passed anything we know of before it, and—to reiterate—the arrival of so many people, one wave cascading on another, makes adaptation and integration in the host country difficult indeed. Thus a volatile situation is generated, new groups jockeying for position with earlier groups, intensifying marginalization, which deepens both competi-tion and conflict. Even spontaneous, marginal innovations, such as gangs, have suffered ripple effects of major proportions under welfare reform, cutbacks of safety nets, a zero school tolerance on gangs, and shrinking job training and opportunities for youth.

Although street gangs are involved in the story's plot, their role is more flash than substance. My research points to other factors in the equation of why conflict arises in the first place. First, prison culture has spilled over onto the streets to pressure some gangs and gang members into doing their will, but with uneven results. De-cades of animosity and violence among ethnic groups in California prisons have been exacerbated by cutbacks in education and reha-bilitation programs, more punitive laws and practices, drops in health services, and overcrowding due to the state's economy. Orig-inally, the prison was a place to send problems, but now problems have found their way out. Racism is just another factor that moti-vates incarcerated inmates as they fight for space and resources, and because so many gang youth eventually find themselves in deten-tion facilities, it makes sense that prison regulars provide what amounts to a pre-prison training program. That this racist stance has an expected practical outcome, control of drug networks, makes for a rather logical outcome (Vigil 2010).

Some of the bigger and stronger gangs, like 18th Street, have been able to ignore the pressure from Eme and other prison elements and to occasionally weave a modus vivendi with black gangs who are also in business.[14] Prison orders to green light blacks are not fail-safe, given that many gang members know nothing about it and those who might know simply ignore it if doing so is to their benefit. Neverthe-less, this prison-to-street spillage must at least be recognized as a factor in the initiation and increase of violent black-brown incidents.

A second factor in the equation of why conflict even arises, the nature of the street-gang subculture, has transitioned into something quite different from what it used to be. What once was neighborhood youth hanging around together, in the 1940s for Chicanos and the 1950s for blacks, has evolved into deadly violent episodes that strike fear into the hearts of city residents (Vigil 2010). Largely ignored by city authorities at the onset, gangs have matured into deeply rooted and decidedly deviant street groups. Crime and criminal activities gradually became woven into the gang subculture and especially when, as noted, drug trafficking and its attendant machinations were introduced. Competition over turf as space is one thing, but over illicit funds and resources is another. The temptations of the streets have become suffused with other motives and the locura orientation of gang members has taken on a new challenge, pecuniary interests.

Additionally, in previous decades, both black and brown populations were newcomers. Second-generation children, responding also to economic and social program cutbacks and the pressures of marginalization, were forced into a street socialization mode. Today, the area is overwhelmingly second-generation Mexican American, and blacks are third- or fourth-generation Angelinos. Since the mid-twentieth century, matters have changed and the populations of impoverished areas have been particularly hard hit. Globalization, and its attendant forceful and unpredictable human migratory upheavals, is a major contributor to this pressure-cooker effect. Jostling for a semblance of space in an already overcrowded neighborhood causes friction and conflict generally, and today, for the reasons noted, the problem has worsened.

NOTES

1. Joe Mozingo, "4 Los Angeles Latino Gang Members Convicted of Anti-Black Conspiracy," *Los Angeles Times*, August 2, 2006, A3; Scott Glover and Richard Winton, "Dozens Arrested in Crackdown on Latino Gang Accused of Targeting Blacks," *Los Angeles Times*, May 22, 2009, A1; Thomas Watkins and Christina Hoag, "Thorny Issue of Racism in Los Angeles Gang Crime Resurfaces," *Los Angeles Times*, May 22, 2009, A23; Tanya Hernandez, "Roots of Latino-Black Anger," *Los Angeles Times*, January 7, 2007. In the 1960s, as the Chicano movement emerged, comparisons with the continuing African American civil rights movement led to the coining of *brown* and *black* for the two pro-

test groups. This usage solidified with the rise of the Brown Berets, who explicitly strived to unify the protest movements. Although younger scholars are less apt to use these terms, they are historically rooted and I continue to find them useful.

2. Hipp, Tita, and Boggess 2007; Vigil 2007; Gregory Rodriquez, "L.A.'s 'Race War' That Isn't," *Los Angeles Times*, October 1, 2007, A13.
3. Watkins and Hoag, "Thorny Issue of Racism'; Glover and Winton, "Dozens Arrested in Crackdown."
4. Will Beall, "Street gang Realpolitik; Black and Latino Gangsters Aren't at War with Each Other, They're Business Partners," *Los Angeles Times*, March 27, 2007, M1.
5. Rodriquez, "L.A.'s 'Race War.'"
6. Joel Rubin and David Helfand, "Gang Killings in L.A. Plunge 27 Percent," *Los Angeles Times*, January 11, 2008, B3.
7. Jill Leovy, "Study Finds No Racial Crime Wave: In L.A., Black-on-Black and Latino-on-Latino Crime Is a Much Bigger Problem than Intergroup Violence, The Statistics Suggest," *Los Angeles Times*, September 22, 2007, B4.
8. Leovy, "Study Finds No Racial Crime Wave."
9. Leovy, "Study Finds No Racial Crime Wave."
10. Leovy, "Study Finds No Racial Crime Wave."
11. Rodriquez, "L.A.'s 'Race War.'"
12. Hernandez, "Roots of Latino-Black Anger."
13. Sam Quinones, "Racial Conflict at Center of L.A. Gang Trial," *Los Angeles Times*, July 14, 2006, A1; Mozingo, "Los Angeles Gang Members Convicted."
14. Beall, "Street Gang Realpolitik."

REFERENCES

Alvarez, Luis. 2008. *The Power of the Zoot: Youth Culture and Resistance during World War II*. Berkeley: University of California Press.
Davis, Mike. 1992. *City of Quartz*. London: Verso Press.
Escobar, Edward. 1999. *Race, Police, and the Making of a Political Identity: Mexican Americans and the Los Angeles Police Department, 1900–1945*. Berkeley: University of California Press.
Hipp, John, George Tita, and Lindsay Boggess. 2007. *Measuring Intra- and Inter-Group Violent Crime for African Americans and Latinos in South Bureau, Los Angeles*. Irvine: University of California.
Macias, Anthony. 2008. *"Mexican American Mojo": Popular Music, Dance, and Urban Culture in Los Angeles, 1935–1968*. Durham, N.C.: Duke University Press.

McWilliams, Carey. 1949. *North from Mexico*. Boston, Mass.: Little, Brown.

Rafael, Tony. 2007. *The Mexican Mafia*. New York: Encounter Books.

Unemoto, Karen. 2006. *The Truce: Lessons from an L.A. Gang War*. Ithaca, N.Y.: Cornell University Press.

U.S. Census Bureau. 2000. *Census 2000*. Available at: http://www.census.gov/main/www/cen2000.html (accessed July 19, 2011).

Vigil, James D. 1988. *Barrio Gangs: Street Life and Identity in Southern California*. Austin: University of Texas Press.

———. 1996. "Street Baptism: Chicano Gang Initiation." *Human Organization* 55(2): 149–53.

———. 2002. *A Rainbow of Gangs: Street Cultures in the Mega-City*. Austin: University of Texas Press.

———. 2007. *The Projects: Gang and Non-Gang Families in East Los Angeles*. Austin: University of Texas Press.

———. 2010. *Gang Redux: A Balanced Anti-Gang Strategy*. Prospect Heights, Ill.: Waveland Press.

CHAPTER 12

Conflict, Cooperation, and Avoidance

Cid Martinez and Victor M. Rios

This study compares black-Latino gang relations in two California cities that have seen a similar demographic transformation in the past twenty years: Latino immigrants settling in traditionally black neighborhoods. Our thesis is that avoidance is the dominant outcome in black-Latino social relations in marginalized urban communities. We examine two other processes, conflict and cooperation, and find that despite the almost exclusive focus of the media and researchers on conflict or cooperation when examining African American and Latino relations, these outcomes are rare in everyday life among the youths we studied. Gangs are ideal case studies because their members frequent the streets more often than many other groups in the neighborhoods we studied. The more often residents inhabit the streets, the more likely they are to come into contact with other racial groups. This study emphasizes the importance of taking the role of neighborhood dynamics in shaping interracial dynamics seriously. In particular, we show how poor, urban, multiracial neighborhoods structure interracial relations through informal neighborhood practices, which are not reducible to ecological change factors, such as an increase in the Latino population.

Our findings are consistent with previous research suggesting that interracial violence between Latinos and African Americans is uncommon. Moreover, our work sketches a portrait of the conditions under which the two groups conflict, and more important, how they avoid conflict with one another. If interracial conflict is rare, other types of relationships emerge between Latinos and African Americans. Our work thus complements Diego Vigil's (see chapter 11, this volume) by providing a more comprehensive perspective on the various types of relationships that exist in poor, multiracial, urban neighborhoods.

The larger goal of this study is to highlight the reality of new-millennium urban marginality that many urban scholars have neglected to study—its African American and Latino demographics and unique social relations.[1] Youth gangs provide key insights to this question because their members constantly navigate the streets on which much African American and Latino contact takes place. Gang members have a more consistent presence on the streets than any other group we encountered. Gangs have also been emphasized in the recent national media focus on racial violence in African American communities.

In recent years, interracial violence between African Americans and Latinos has become a growing concern for politicians, law enforcement, and the public. The common perception is that, as urban neighborhoods in areas such as Los Angeles and East Oakland become increasingly multiracial, racial violence follows. This view is especially common in areas such as South Los Angeles (South LA) and East Oakland, where Latinos have gradually become the majority population in traditionally black neighborhoods.

In this chapter, we demonstrate how neighborhood processes shape interethnic relations between Latino and African American gangs. In contrast to media's portrayal, we argue that the dominant outcome in black-Latino relations, among even the most marginalized groups, is avoidance, and that conflict and cooperation are uncommon. We demonstrate how relations between African American and Latino gang members are predicated on four key factors: territorial affiliation, control of the illicit underground economy and neighborhood, gang affiliation, and race. Often it is the presence of a combination of these factors that leads to interracial cooperation, avoidance, or conflict.

This study demonstrates how the heterogeneous character of urban life shapes interethnic relations between Latinos and African Americans. More important, it illustrates how interethnic relations are negotiated between Latino and African American gangs in the ghetto. Previous studies of urban street life have focused exclusively on the experience of African Americans and their marginal position relative to whites. In this respect, this chapter's findings add a new dimension to understanding how race operates in multiracial settings.

Conflict between African Americans and Latinos has made headlines in the media, as well as in scholarly and political commentary in recent years. One recent example is the gang violence taking place in Los Angeles, California. This conflict received national attention when Cheryl Green, a fourteen-year-old African American girl, was murdered by Latino gang members. Mass media and politicians portrayed blacks and Latinos as vicious archenemies. In 2006, in response to the growing Latino population in many inner cities, *Newsweek* questioned, "Can the venerable black-Latino coalition survive the surge in Hispanic power?" (Cose 2006). In 2007, *Newsweek* described Latino and black gang conflict as racial cleansing (Murr 2007).

Extreme cases of hate crimes and interracial violence have occurred in recent years as Latinos have moved into traditionally African American neighborhoods, but our extensive observations and interviews in two dynamic black-Latino neighborhoods indicate that interracial conflict is in fact the least common outcome between gangs. However, contrary to the other extreme in the debate, that African Americans and Latinos are in harmony with one another and in constant coalition-building mode, we find that collaboration is also a rare outcome among gang members in the inner city. The most common social relational strategy is instead avoidance. Avoidance, as we conceive it, is the process by which residents acknowledge one another's presence, the codes that govern the social organization of the community, and the give and take—the practice of compromise—involved in maintaining nonviolent social relations in a dangerous environment.

UNDERSTANDING INTERRACIAL GANG RELATIONS

Three dominant views have been used to explain interracial relations. These explanations can be reduced to three general categories: social disorganization theory, ethnic competition theory, and routine activities theory. Social disorganization theory emphasizes the breakdown of social controls as a source of interracial violence (Shaw and McKay 1942; Kornhauser 1978). Ecological and structural changes—such as increased immigration, poverty, and heterogeneity—are believed to undermine social controls, making it difficult for residents to reach consensus about common goals and laws, thereby causing a breakdown, leading in turn to violence among various groups. This perspective fails to consider how informal social controls may arise in the place of formal ones to regulate behavior. It also assumes that structural changes undermine social controls in a seemingly natural process, which ignores the choices of individuals, groups, and institutions.

A second explanation focuses on interethnic competition as a source of conflict. Competition for scarce resources heightens group boundaries and identities, which causes ethnic groups to align their interests (Lyons 2007; Olzak 1990). Although this view is useful, most of this literature has focused on black victimization by whites. This theory partially explains the conflict between Latino and African American gangs, but ignores how social norms can mediate disputes and disagreements.

A third view focuses on routine activities as a source of interracial interaction. Peter Blau's *Inequality and Heterogeneity* details how social structure and social integration shape the likelihood of intergroup contact (1977). The frequency of intergroup association and contact is determined by opportunities to do so. This theory has been used by scholars to explain how interracial crime occurs when individuals of different groups have the opportunity to come into contact with one another (Messner and South 1992). Thus, individuals with similar patterns of activities are more likely to come into contact, providing an opportunity for crime and interracial violence to occur. This theory provides a promising framework to examine interracial relations between Latino and African American gangs.

These studies provide important insights, but they fail to explain the interracial relations between Latino and African Americans we found in the field. First, they focus for the most part on black and white interracial violence. Second, most of them do not directly focus on relations between people who regularly frequent the streets and therefore come into contact with one another. More important, these theories fail to recognize the centrality of shared notions of giving and taking, the interracial codes of conduct developed in locales where space is scarce and conflict is a constant threat.

In contrast to the outlined studies, a fourth and more recent perspective considers the role of neighborhood type in shaping interracial relations. Martín Sánchez-Jankowski develops a conceptual framework that explains how poor urban neighborhoods are transformed by the influx of immigrant newcomers, and how, over time, they transition into stable areas (2008). He argues that areas that undergo ethnic transformation are likely to become contested neighborhoods, characterized by hostility between groups and territorial separation. Underlying this neighborhood type are ethnic differences. Over time, these neighborhoods transition into what Sánchez-Jankowski refers to as fragmented neighborhoods. Social divisions are based on length of residence in these neighborhoods, origin of birth, citizenship, employment status, occupation, and gender. Sánchez-Jankowski's framework advances beyond the theories outlined earlier by highlighting the role of neighborhood dynamics in providing a context of interaction that shapes relations among residents. It helps us take into account interracial dynamics between Latinos and African Americans in specific settings.

In contrast, we show that conflict is not always a dominant outcome in areas that have undergone ethnic change. We demonstrate that neighborhoods that have done so do not necessarily have an evolutionary trajectory—from conflict (contested) to cooperation (fragmented)—but instead, we argue, multiracial urban marginal neighborhoods operate under a matrix of forms of social interaction that occur simultaneously. In this case, conflict, cooperation, and avoidance are all at play in social relations, but avoidance dominates.

Building on these insights, we sketch an alternative neighborhood typology that moves beyond ecological factors, such as immigration and ethnic change, and emphasizes the informal norms and practices that regulate interracial relations between Latinos and African Americans. We develop a new concept of multiracial neighborhood type that can explain the conditions under which cooperation, conflict, and avoidance occur in the new urban metropolis. Our cases and our conception of multiracial neighborhood life suggest that interracial gang relations are informally and collectively defined by shared notions of giving and taking of street life in East Oakland and South LA. Relations among residents are not simply reducible to chance or individual inclination, but are structured in an unwritten consensus that regulates the conduct of residents. Gang members, who frequent the streets more than other residents, are an ideal type through which to understand these social relations (see Keller 1968, 36).[2]

DATA AND METHODS

Data from this study come from two distinct ethnographies conducted in East Oakland and South Los Angeles between 2003 and 2004. Our primary method in both field sites was participant observation. After collecting observations, our goal was to examine commonalities across cases. We focused on the dominant themes and frames used by respondents in South LA and East Oakland. Similarly, we focused our analyses on the anomalies used by gang members in these settings.

Our goal was to uncover the meanings of interethnic relations held by black and Latino gang members within their specific cultural contexts. Taking on a comparative approach allowed us to bolster our concepts and test our preliminary theories in specific neighborhoods. As such, we used a case-based logic that uncovered the why and how of black-Latino gang relations. This logic relied on analytical induction, through which we sought to uncover the uniqueness of our cases, compare commonalities, and develop a hypothesis that would apply to the specific cases we examined (Burrawoy 1991; Yin 2002; for a more recent and compelling discussion of this approach, see Small 2008). This method offers several benefits. First, case studies, though neither random nor representative, provide rich, detailed data that allow us to explore the how and why of interracial relations among Latino and African American gang members. We suggest that understanding this process provide for a breadth and depth of analysis often lacking in analysis based on surveys with random samples. Indeed, we suggest that the ethnographic process provides a scientific insight missing from random samples. Second, the rich ethnographic data drawn for this study provide a context for uncovering the meaning of interactions of groups and individuals.

Before beginning the project, we met regularly to develop interview questions and our research and observation approach. We then conducted participant observation and in-depth interviews for one year in both South Los Angeles (Martinez) and East Oakland (Rios). During this period, we corresponded by telephone and email to compare findings. After individually analyzing our data, we reported our main findings to each other. We then selected common themes in both cases and reanalyzed our data. This allowed us to uncover common processes in two similar communities three hundred miles apart.

GANG RELATIONS

During our study, journalists and law enforcement officials had been predicting a race war in South LA and East Oakland among Latinos and African Americans. The belief was that as the Latino population increased, its gang presence would simultaneously rise. As Miles Corwin, a beat reporter covering South LA homicide for the *Los Angeles Times* during the 1990s, explained in a 2003 interview, "Law enforcement has long anticipated a race war between both groups since the early 1990s and it just has not happened." In East Oakland, high schools hired youth counselors who focused on preventing race riots—that is, fights between African American and Latino gangs. Although intraracial gang fights were more common, schools had been pressured by media coverage of the handful of incidents that did occur to invest resources in preventing black-Latino violence from taking place.

The criminologist George Tita and colleagues John Hipp and Lyndsay Boggess reviewed nearly five hundred homicides committed from 1999 to 2004 in one violent South LA police district and found that almost all were black-on-black or Latino-on-Latino (Hipp, Tita, and Boggess 2009). Their findings suggest that interethnic violence in South LA is rare. Police data in East Oakland show that intraracial violence makes up the majority of victimization cases. Our fieldwork also revealed that black-Latino violence was rare. Observations and interviews demonstrated that conflict was a last-resort option for many residents, even those young people who based part of their identities on crime and violence.

Based on our fieldwork in South LA and East Oakland, three types of common relationships between Latino and African American gangs were identified. In this section, we chronicle the prevalence of each relationship, and provide background and foreground factors that influence the outcomes of each type. Relationships can be characterized as follows: conflict was rare, cooperation occurred occasionally, and avoidance was common.

AVOIDANCE

The most prevalent and common type of relationship between Latino and African American gangs was avoidance. An interview with an LAPD (Los Angeles Police Department) Gang Task Force member of the 77th Division—notorious for its high concentrations of violent gangs in the LA area—highlights the relationship between the two.

> Aron: Latinos and African Americans stay mostly separated in the 77th [district] of South LA. Every once in a while you will have a problem here or there, but they mostly stay to their own. Shootings tend to be black-on-black or Hispanic-on-Hispanic, mostly black-on-black though.

Martinez: So would you say that they avoid each other out of respect?

Aron: I wouldn't even say they have respect for each other. They
just leave each other alone. Occasionally, you may get both groups
battling over territory. They have had a handful of shootings over on
Florence where it is black-on-Hispanics; the Rolling 60s against Flor-
encias, for probably dope reasons.

Officer Aron's comments are telling because they highlight the lack
of interethnic homicides between African American and Latino gang
members. In a place with disproportionate amounts of violence, victimization is sporadic and rare between groups.

An interview with Captain Diaz and a member from the LAPD's
Gang Task Force of the Southeast Division, which covers the Watts
section of Los Angeles, adds insight into the phenomenon of black-
on-black and Latino-on-Latino violence. The perspective provided
by the Southeast Division is consistent with the account provided by
the 77th Division. Insights from individuals in the Southeast Division are important because the area the division encompasses often
alternates with the 77th Division for the distinction of having the
largest number of homicides in the city of Los Angeles.

Lieutenant Leiker of the Southeast Division Gang Task Force states
that most homicides and gang-related shootings occur between African Americans and not between Latinos and African Americans. Both
Leiker and Diaz agree that Latino gangs mostly deal with and interact
with other Latino gangs, whether they are friends or enemies. The
same holds true for African American gangs.

Gang-related activities, such as drug sales, often take place between gangs and customers of the same race. Leiker said during the
interview, "There are quite a number of Latino gangs in the Watts
area who engage in drug trafficking. They mostly deal with members
of their own ethnic group. This is also true for African Americans."

Intraethnic homicide among African American gangs results from
members' trying to profit personally from drug sales. Often, pursuing
individual profits means turning against members of one's gang, who
more often than not are of the same race. As Leiker explains, "Gang
members would turn on one of their own gang brothers if they could
make money."

In East Oakland, black and Latino gangs keep social distance from
each other. Regular observations of a street corner that two gangs,

one African American and one Latino, controlled were insightful. Like a department store with different sections of goods, the street corner catered to different tastes, which tastes were observed to vary by ethnicity. For example, each group controlled specific drug sells based on race. Drug addicts who had acquired a taste for heroin or cocaine, often Latino, approached the Latino gang members. Latinos sold the heroin and cocaine; blacks specialized in crack cocaine and ecstasy. Both groups distributed crystal meth because of its recent popularity. Methamphetamine was consumed by drug addicts of all races and sold by dealers of all races. Black and Latino dealers gave each other change, informed each other about police, and warded off each other's rivals. The two groups lived, spent leisure time, and hustled next door to each other, but often maintained a social distance. Blacks stood in front of the liquor store located one building over from the street corner; Latinos sat on the steps of the apartment building on the corner, approximately eighty feet away. Chuco, a seventeen-year-old gang member, describes his relationship with African Americans on this corner, where he grew up:

> One of the guys I looked up to the most was a black dude named Drew. He and his homies were some of the downest and realest people I ever came across. They had their morals and looked out for everybody. If you starved, we all starved. If you triumphed, we all made it. You know? But it was also very limited. By the time I grew up and started to hang around the [Latino] gang I had to choose. We weren't fighting with blacks, but we also weren't supposed to hang together. . . . So, I just say, "what's up" to them, and keep walking. We back each other up when we need to. But mostly we leave each other alone.

Resources for cooperating were available to young people when they needed support or backup. However, when dealing with matters of day-to-day life, such as selecting friendships, finding peer networks, and establishing intimate relationships, each racial group defaulted to the informal rules established in the neighborhood. In this case, the rules demanded that each group maintain a social distance from the other. Clear boundaries could protect each group from confusion and from "throwing off" the give and take of the social order. Young people reminded one another about the boundary they were all supposed to respect. This process allowed avoidance to remain a dominant outcome in black and Latino relations. Avoidance prevented interracial conflict from arising and allowed young people to feel safe, as long as they followed the informal social order.

In South LA, both groups also specialized in different types of drug sales. Members from the Southeast Police Division also highlighted the different types of drug sales that Latinos and African Americans tended to distribute in the community. African American gangs commonly sold crack cocaine and marijuana, and Latino gangs tended to distribute crystal meth and marijuana. Historically, most homicides in South LA and East Oakland had been majority black-on-black, but the number of Latino-on-Latino murders was growing. Although South LA and East Oakland had large numbers of Latinos and African Americans living side by side, social interaction and economic exchange continued to be bounded and limited to members of the same race. Because gangs engaged in underground activities with members of their own ethnic group, they were more likely to turn on these compatriots if the opportunity for profit through drug sales presented itself.

According to LAPD officials, another reason that Latino gangs in South LA avoided conflict with African Americans was the distinct types of illicit income-generating strategies each group pursued. Most often, Latino gangs have pursued activities that did not compete directly with African American gangs in South LA. According to officials from the Southeast Division, Latino gangs conducted illegal activity outside Watts, in other parts of Los Angeles. This was especially true if the Latino gangs were involved in robbery, auto theft, or other crime motivated by economic incentives. As Lieutenant Leiker explained, "There isn't a lot of material stuff to rip off because people are poor in Watts." Thus Latino gangs pursued activities outside the area, which did not compete directly with African American gang activity.

In East Oakland, African American and Latino gangs found unique ways to avoid conflict, despite vying for control of the same territory. Dante, an eighteen-year-old African American gang member from the Murder Tres gang,[3] explains the order:

> Rios: So, how is it that there can be two gangs, one black, one brown, on the same corner?
> Dante: The black dudes claim Murder Tres and the Mexican dudes claim E-One-Seven [the East 17th gang]. They handle their business and we handle our business.

Rios: Do you guys ever get together to, you know, handle business together?

Dante: If mothafucka's from another 'hood try to smash, we scrape them.

Rios: Black, brown?

Dante: Don't matter. Race don't matter when you got to handle business. We handle it. We smash. We got they back if they need it.

WHEN AFRICAN AMERICANS AND LATINOS WORK TOGETHER

Although the most common relationship between African American and Latino gangs is avoidance, in many instances they worked cooperatively with one another. In this section, we flesh out the conditions under which both Latino and African American gangs were able to do so. This relationship was noticeably less common than avoidance. However, when gang members felt that their neighborhood was disrespected, when economic opportunities were threatened by outsiders, or when gang members reflected on the common struggles and experiences growing up in the same community, they cooperated.

An interview with members of the Gang Taskforce of the Southeast Division of the LAPD highlights the way in which the groups were able to maintain interethnic relations.

Martinez: How would you describe relations between Latino and African American gangs?

Leiker: They mostly avoid each other. They occasionally work together, nine out of ten times when we follow the drug connection back to the source there are Hispanic gangs involved. Think about it like this. Imagine you have a warehouse full of drugs and your distributors are African American. Why would you want to go after people that are helping you make money? It doesn't make sense from a financial standpoint for both groups to kill each other, because they both stand to make money working together.

Throughout the interview, Leiker explained that the drug connection offered by Latinos is one of the key reasons the groups are able to work cooperatively. In essence, the Latino drug connection acts as a basis for the establishment of positive relations between groups.

According to Leiker, the changing structure of gangs, now motivated by profits versus neighborhood and race relations, has created the conditions where previous barriers and boundaries have been broken down. Throughout the interview, Leiker expressed the idea that boundaries of gang affiliation, race, neighborhood, and the like have gradually eroded in the face of potential for profit. Thus, the motive for financial gain has the opposite double effect of both breaking down and strengthening relations between groups.

The story provided by Gang Taskforce members of LAPD were corroborated in interviews conducted with youth involved in gang activity in South LA. African American and Latino respondents, male and female, consistently identified the same factors that led to cooperative relations between groups. An interview with Mafioso, a sixteen-year-old Latino male from South LA, illustrates a key factor in building cooperative relations between Latino and African Americans: "Black and Latino gangs get along when they make money together. Over where I live two gangs that are Latino and African American grew up with each other and they share their turf. When they are sharing the hood, they make money. When other people come into the hood, they have to pay taxes."

Mafioso's comments illustrate that when African American and Latino gangs collectively agree to share neighborhood territory, positive relations can be formed. The comments from F, an eighteen-year-old African American from South LA, captures the common sentiment expressed by African Americans: "For the most part, relations between African Americans and Latinos are not good. There is always that one Hispanic who has a good connection. That can be the basis of a good relationship."

In East Oakland, collaboration appeared when the neighborhood was perceived to be threatened. If rival gang members, new drug dealers, or police crackdowns entered the picture, African Americans and Latinos communicated, making plans and executing joint ventures together. For example, one day Rios shadowed Peanut, a sixteen-year-old black gang member from Oak Park. Rios asked Peanut to give him a walk-through of Peanut's regular routine. The two walked past the street corner into an alley behind the building that the Latino gang, East Side Locos, controlled. Peanut often stashed the marijuana he sold in this area. The Latino gang knew about Peanut's stash but never tampered with it. Peanut believed that this was the best place to stash his drugs. According to him, "The ese's protect my shit" (*ese* being a street term for "homeboy"). As we walked into the alley, we heard gunshots. We ducked. When we came out to see what had happened, the Latino gang members yelled out, "It was them bustas from the North Side!" Another Latino gang, the North Side Locos, had committed a drive-by shooting in an attempt to scare or hurt the East Side Locos. Peanut was disappointed, not so much because they had tried to hurt his neighbors, the East Side Locos, but because they had violated his turf: "Why they gotta' come out here and fuck with our shit?" An attack on the East Side Locos, by default, was an attack on Peanut and the other black youths who hung out at the alley. "You let me know what you need and I'll get it for you, B.G.," he told one of the Latino gang members. I later heard that Peanut and his crew got together with B.G. and his crew. They all drove to North Side's neighborhood and retaliated.

Interviews with youth in gangs who displayed a pattern of interethnic cooperation provided further insight into the factors that led to their ability to work positively. As argued earlier, most important was the ability for both groups to pursue profits in the illicit economy through drug sales and to defend the neighborhood they mutually occupied. Shared collective use of and control of public space acted as an impetus to forge positive relations, which contributed to the groups' working positively together in the underground economy and in everyday life.

Latino and African American respondents in many of the interviews said that the ability to control neighborhoods was one of the key goals of gangs. In this respect, gangs did not simply seek to maximize profits, but also to regulate and control all types of illicit activities beyond drug sales, such as gun sales, prostitution, stolen merchandise dealing, and even street vending. This included regulating who was allowed to enter a neighborhood. For this reason, many residents often said they felt limited as to where they could go in South LA and East Oakland because of their neighborhood gang affiliation.[4]

When control of designated territory was collective, cooperation between Latino and African American gangs emerged. In numerous interviews, Latinos and African American respondents alluded to the idea of "sharing the hood" to denote sharing territory to pursue illicit activities that generated revenue for gang members. One important consequence of sharing territory was the ability of both gangs to operate in the same geographic area.

An interview with K, an African American male in his early twenties, who grew up and spent most of his life in the Jordan Downs Housing Project, illustrates the nature of gang relations in this setting.

> K: Gangs in the Jordan Downs Project have a common enemy, and you know who I am talking about [referring to a rival gang in a neighboring housing project]. Gang members bring heat home.
>
> Martinez: I have heard that having a common enemy is what allows Latinos and African American gangs to unite together. Is that right?
>
> K: Having a common enemy doesn't explain everything. Living together is what brings people together. Look, if you live in Jordan Downs, black and brown in Jordan Downs are going to be in the Grape Street gangs. Both groups working together, that's just the way it's going to be. The projects are an experiment that put both of us here, and now we are trying to work all this shit out. There is East Grape Street and South Grape Street and they have it divided up. Blacks have control of South Grape and Latinos who live outside public housing have control of East Grape Street, and they merged together to make one.

K's insight is similar to that expressed in the interview about the conditions that allowed 18th Street and Hoover Street gangs to work together. K also brings to light another factor, that living in the same geographical space gives rise to relationships that transcend racial differences.

Sharing the hood can also apply to cooperation in everyday life that does not include illicit activity. Play, recreation, shelter, and using the street as a zone for protection are all at play when it comes to collaboration among African American and Latino youth. For example, many of the youth in the East Oakland case came from broken homes. Many did not return home because their parents were missing, they were homeless, they had been kicked out, or they were on the run from law enforcement. Even at eleven on a Monday night, one could find a dozen or so African American and Latino teenagers scattered across the block of International Avenue under study. Some sold drugs, but others were there simply to pass the time. African American and Latino gang members helped each other out when they saw that someone from the neighborhood needed back-up.

Another form of collaboration takes place when gang members develop a sense of common struggle and become politicized. Community organizations play a key role in this process. Former gang members who have become politicized often work for gang outreach programs aimed at preventing violence and incarceration. These individuals have a keen sense of the larger structures at play in creating marginality in their communities. Big Ram, a former notorious Latino gang member from East Oakland, who at the time of the interview worked as a gang prevention counselor, explained his theory:

> Big Ram: In our culture in America, American means white supremacy, and it marginalizes and makes others inferior, but in racist white culture they have their own supremacy, they got the KKK. So you got the brown and black folks who are made to think they are stupid.
>
> Rios: Now, in terms of when you are changing your life around . . . helping young people out, what have you learned about not just the good things, but also the bad things, about black and brown relationships?
>
> Big Ram: I had never heard of Malcolm X, but Malcolm X went through a lot just like us. He went from hustling on the streets to religion, and he got betrayed, you know, but he advocated for equality and education, so he is one of my role models. He is a role model for Raza [Latinos] too.

While shadowing Big Ram during his gang outreach work, Rios noticed Big Ram's charismatic ability to politicize young gang members. Although few abandoned the gang, most became convinced by the racial harmony discourse that Big Ram passed on. Many of them attributed their negative experiences to structures of inequality. In doing so, they realized the common struggle that African Americans and Latinos experienced. This in turn led some of the older, more mature members to maintain the peace, to reinforce the informal rules that called for respecting each other's space, and to demand that the youngsters understand the give-and-take process.

In sum, three key factors seem to promote cooperative relationships between Latino and African American gangs. First is the possibility of generating profits for both groups through the illicit economy, though generating profits presupposes control of territories to engage in illicit activities. Second is control of neighborhood territory and a mutual agreement to share a given area in underground economic activity and in the hustle of everyday life. Finally, growing up and living in the same place can also foster social ties that promote interethnic cooperation among gangs. This can also lead to a politicization that allows gang members to see African American and Latino struggles as a common ground to build collaboration or, at the very least, as a common ground to allow avoidance.

BLACK AND LATINO GANG CONFLICT

Although conflict between black and Latino gangs was not common, it did occur occasionally. In this section, we argue that race can be a significant factor—under a given set of circumstances—in creating conflict between both groups. Race alone, however, is not enough to create interethnic conflict. Instead, a confluence of factors creates the conditions in which interethnic conflict can emerge. In addition to race, we suggest that three other key factors affect interethnic relations: competition for control of territory, interrupting someone's ability to hustle, and the ability to generate income and revenue for individual gang members.

During our fieldwork in East Oakland and South LA in 2003 and 2004, two major wars erupted between Latino and African American gangs in South LA, and five major school race riots occurred in East Oakland. The first war in South LA was between the Black P-Stones, an African American gang, and the 18th Street gang, a predominantly Latino group, in Baldwin Village.

To learn about the LA conflict, Martinez did a ride-along with Officer Maria Marquez of the LAPD's 77th Division. They toured Baldwin Village, also known as the Jungle. Officer Marquez explained that the area, in the past, had been controlled by the Black P-Stones, which had a long history in the Crenshaw area of South LA. The gang, according to Marquez, was responsible for regulating drug sales in the Baldwin Village area, and for other types of illicit activities, such as gun sales.

During the ride-along and interview, when asked why 18th Street and the Black P-Stones were fighting, Marquez explained that the feud was serious, and that the Black P-Stones and 18th Street groups were each responsible for murdering members of the opposing gang. The war, in Marquez's view, was about who would control drug sales in the Jungle and its surrounding area. According to Marquez, the 18th Street gang was very aggressive in the battle, often initiating incidents and killing members of the Black P-Stones. This was uncommon in South LA, because most Latino gangs were not that aggressive. Marquez elaborated, "I think their mentality is now that they have numbers [referring to the increasing Latino residents and potential customers]. They feel they should control the area."

Unlike relations between African American and Latino gangs in other parts of South LA, there was no avoidance in Baldwin Village. The 18th Street gang refused to adopt the informal rules of avoidance, and instead choose to preemptively attack the P-Stones. Eighteenth Street believed that they had control of the territory, and that give and take was not an option. The increasing number of 18th Street members demanding more territory and economic opportunity, combined with the gang's unwillingness to compromise, led to conflict. Race became a mechanism by which 18th Street determined how the illicit economy and the territory would be divided.

Many of the same themes Marquez touched on were echoed by youth who lived in the area where the Black P-Stones and 18th Street operated. An interview with Early 8K, a seventeen-year-old African American female, provides further insight.

> Early 8K: There really weren't any Latino gangs in the area until 1998. Eighteenth Street came out real big; they started messing with black gangs. They have a reputation for killing innocent people. Both gangs are constantly testing each other.
>
> Martinez: Would you say it's more of a territory issue or a race issue that is the source of the conflict?
>
> Early 8K: I would say that both race and territory are the issue. It seems like it's more of a race issue. Black gangs have been in the area longer, this makes it racial because they see another group coming in and taking over. Things tend to become racial and most of the time there is conflict.

The comments from Munchie, an eighteen-year-old Latino male, provide a similar perspective: "There is a battle between 18th Street and the Black P-Stones. Your enemies are based on territory. But some Latinos don't like African Americans, so they don't get along. So, it's about the hood and race, but I would still say it's more of a territory issue. [Here it is hood and race]."

Based on the interviews with Marquez, Early 8K, and Munchie, we suggest that it is likely that several key factors contribute to the violence between African American and Latino gangs. First, the interviews highlight the role of maintaining control of a given area as a significant factor that underpins violence between these two groups.

Second, having control of the area is important, because this determines who regulates illicit activities in the area, which has a direct bearing on the ability of gangs to generate profits. Finally, the comments of Munchie and 8K show that racial differences can play a role in dividing gangs and can act as a basis for conflict.

Another example of interethnic confrontation in 2003 and 2004 South LA occurred between Florencia, a large Latino gang originally from Southeast LA, and Hoover Crips, an African American gang. In casual conversations, youth from the research site school expressed the idea that Florencia was a racist group. The insights from La Chola, an eighteen-year-old Latino who lived in the area of conflict and was an active member of the Florencia gang, captures the essence of the conflict between the groups in question: "Florencia does not like Hoover Crips. A lot of people say that it's because Florencia is a racist gang. They don't like blacks. But it's not just that; it's territory too. Territory is more important than race. Business control of the area is at stake."

Many African American youth who lived in the area where the gang operated echoed the racist view. They did, however, also express the idea that control of territory was an important factor in undermining relations between the two groups.

Interviews with youth, African American and Latino, who were directly involved with both gangs illustrate that the same factors were perceived to shape interethnic relations. Both examples of interethnic conflict between Latino and African American gangs were shaped by the confluence of the same factors, namely, race, territory, the hustle, and the drive to control illicit activity in a designated area. Although conflict between African American and Latino gangs was encountered in each of our studies, the most common process operating to maintain order in each neighborhood was avoidance. Young people set up an intricate system of codes, rules, and values that functioned to prevent interracial violence.

CONCLUSION

In the two multiracial neighborhoods we examined, avoidance was the dominant outcome in Latino and African American gang relations. Gang members consistently shaped their social interactions to accommodate a balance that allowed for a give-and-take process. When conditions were ideal, gang members cooperated; on the rare occasions that avoidance failed, conflict broke out. Gang members shared geographic space with an understanding that organized daily routines had to be protected. Rather than representing social disorder, the gangs in our study served to maintain an interracial order where interactions were based on avoidance. Although the media and law enforcement continue to reinforce the view that interethnic violence is a reality and inevitable, the evidence from this study indicates that in fact avoidance is more common.

Diego Vigil argues in chapter 11 of this volume that ethnic conflict is rare, but that when it does occur it is a result of ethnic succession. In contrast, we argue that avoidance is the dominant outcome between Latinos and African Americans. Furthermore, when interracial conflict does occur, it is a result of the inability of neighborhood gangs to develop informal norms regarding the regulation of territory, which then becomes a proxy for racial tension. Several factors make our findings complementary to Vigil's work. First, like Vigil, we agree that interracial conflict is rare. Second, we also believe that when conflict does arise it is often motivated by factors such as competition. This conclusion raises the question of what black-Latino relations look like when conflict is not the dominant outcome. Our work begins to answer this question. We highlight the conditions under which alternatives to conflict emerge, namely, avoidance and cooperation.

Jeanette Covington has noted that interracial violence is the dominant form of violence among all racial groups because of close social proximity (1995). We find that although African Americans and Latinos live physically near one another, avoidance has prevented much violence.

NOTES

1. Building on Mario Luis Small's work (2009) we abandon the strong use of the term *ghetto*, where it is defined as an institution with a set of recurring patterns and processes, and instead focus on urban marginality and multiracial neighborhood type to describe the ghettoes we study.
2. There is a parallel between the way in which relations between neighbors are structured and those who are involved in gangs.
3. Gang names have been changed to protect subjects.
4. The idea that gangs have moved beyond drug distribution has recently been documented (Venkatesh 2006). Sudhir Venkatesh argues that in Chicago's public housing, gangs began to move beyond the confines of crack distribution and to gradually regulate illicit activities in their surrounding locale. His analysis provides a fresh insight into the contemporary role of African American gangs and their relationship to the environ-

ments in which they operate. In many respects, gangs in South LA and East Oakland seek to regulate neighborhood affairs just as Venkatesh documented. Unlike Chicago, however, South LA and East Oakland neighborhoods are predominantly multiracial, where Latino and African American gangs exist side by side and often compete for control of territory.

REFERENCES

Blau, Peter M. 1977. *Inequality and Heterogeneity: A Primitive Theory of Social Structure.* New York: The Free Press.

Burrawoy, Michael. 1991. *Ethnography Unbound: Power and Resistance in the Modern Metropolis.* Berkeley: University of California Press.

Cose, Ellis. 2006. "Black Versus Brown. Can the Venerable Black-Latino Coalition Survive the Surge in Hispanic Power?" *Newsweek*, July 3, 2006.

Convington, Jeanette. 1995. "Racial Classification in Criminology: The Reproduction of Racialized Crime." *Sociological Forum* 10(4): 547–68.

Hipp, John, George Tita, and Lyndsay Boggess. 2009. "Inter- and Intra-Group Violence: Is Violent Crime an Expression of Group Conflict or Social Disorganization?" *Criminology* 47(2): 321–564.

Keller, Suzanne. 1968. *The Urban Neighborhood: A Sociological Perspective.* New York: Random House.

Kornhauser, Ruth. 1978. *Social Sources of Delinquency.* Chicago: University of Chicago Press.

Lyons, Christopher J. 2007. "Community (Dis)Organization and Racially Motivated Crime." *American Journal of Sociology* 113(3): 815–63.

Messner, S. F., and S. J. South. 1992. "Interracial Homicide: A Macrostructural Opportunity Perspective." *Sociological Forum* 7(3): 517–36.

Murr, Andrew. 2007. "Racial 'Cleansing' in L.A." *Newsweek*, October 24, 2004.

Olzak, Susan. 1990. "The Political Context of Competition: Lynching and Urban Racial Violence, 1882–1914." *Social Forces.* 69(2): 395–421.

Sánchez-Jankowski, Martín. 2008. *Cracks in the Pavement: Social Change and Resilience in Poor Neighborhoods.* Berkeley: University of California Press.

Shaw, Clifford R., and Henry D. McKay. 1942. *Juvenile Delinquency in Urban Areas.* Chicago: University of Chicago Press.

Small, Mario L. 2009. "How Many Cases Do I Need? On Science and the Logic of Case Selection in Field-Based Research." *Ethnography* 10(1): 5–38.

Venkatesh, Sudhir Al. 2006. *Off the Books: The Underground Economy of the Urban Poor.* Cambridge, Mass.: Harvard University Press.

Yin, R. 2002. *Case Study Research.* Thousand Oaks, Calif.: Sage Publications.

Index

Boldface numbers refer to figures and tables.